LANDLORD AND TENANT LAW

THE RESIDENTIAL SECTOR

LANDLORD AND TENANT LAW
THE RESIDENTIAL SECTOR

Úna Cassidy
BCL, BARRISTER-AT-LAW

Jennifer Ring
LLB, SOLICITOR

ROUND HALL  THOMSON REUTERS

Published in 2010 by
Thomson Reuters (Professional) Ireland Limited
(Registered in Ireland, Company No. 80867.
Registered Office and address for service:
43 Fitzwilliam Place, Dublin 2)
trading as Round Hall

Typeset by
Carrigboy Typesetting Services

Printed in England
by MPG Books, Bodmin, Cornwall

ISBN 978–1–85800–502–7

A catalogue record for this book
is available from the British Library

To our Parents
– and –
In memory of our wonderful friend and colleague Emer Casey

FOREWORD

The development of the law which regulates the relationship of landlord and tenant and their respective rights and obligations reflects the development of politics and society in Ireland from the middle of the 19th century. The fundamental precept which still governs the relationship of landlord and tenant—that it is based on contract and not on tenure—dates from the Landlord and Tenant Law (Amendment) Act (Ireland) 1860, which is commonly referred to as Deasy's Act.

In the late 19th century, at the height of the land war, the new liberal government under Gladstone procured the enactment of the Land Law (Ireland) Act 1881, which provided for the "three Fs": fair rent, fixity of tenure and freedom of sale, and provisions to safeguard tenants who paid a fair rent from unjust eviction and to compensate those who vacated holdings for improvements made. It established the Land Commission. Over the following century, through the implementation of the statutory functions of the Land Commission, agrarian land became almost universally owner occupied rather than tenant occupied.

In the residential sector, the precursor of the Rent Restrictions Act, which was enacted after the end of the First World War, also had the objective of meeting the prevailing social needs in relation to the regulated residential sector by ensuring that rents were affordable and that the tenants had security of occupation. Those objectives were reflected almost half a century later in the Rent Restrictions Act 1960, the long title of which declared it to be an Act "to make provision for restricting the increase of rent and the recovery of possession of premises in certain cases ...". However worthy the objectives, by 1980 the result was that landlords of controlled dwellings were in receipt of only a small proportion of the passing market rent and the capital value of their interest in the premises was grossly deflated. It is hardly surprising that in *Blake v The Attorney General* [1982] I.R. 117 the Supreme Court held that provisions of the 1960 Act, by restricting the property rights of one group of citizens for the benefit of another group, without compensation and without regard to the financial capacity or the financial needs of either group, and without limitation on the period of restriction and by giving no opportunity for review and by allowing no modification of their operation, constituted an unjust attack on the property rights of landlords of controlled dwellings and were contrary to the provisions of Art.40.3.2 of the Constitution.

The first attempt by the Oireachtas to put matters right in relation to the controlled residential sector failed at the first hurdle, in that, on a reference under Art.26 of the Constitution, the Supreme Court held that the Housing (Private Rented Dwellings) Bill 1981 was repugnant to the Constitution. That led to the Housing (Private Rented Dwellings) Acts 1982 and 1983, which, as the authors point out, still apply to dwellings which were previously controlled under the rent restrictions legislation.

The most recent development in the regulation of the private rented residential sector has been the enactment of the Residential Tenancies Act 2004, which is the main focus of this text.

When I was called to the Bar in 1971, landlord and tenant legislation, in particular, in the frequently amended Rent Restrictions Acts, was perceived as being extremely technical and complicated. I think it is true to say that briefs in that area were relegated to perceived nerds. It was technical and complicated in reality. I spent many hours trying to grasp the intricacies of the legislation of the 1960s, the 1970s and the 1980s, both as a practitioner and as the first Chairman of the Rent Tribunal, which was established in 1983. However, those endeavours paled into insignificance when, in 2007, I had to get to grips with the intricacies of the 2004 Act. I would have been very grateful then for the analysis and guidance which this text provides.

From the perspective of a practitioner, this book is invaluable for a number of reasons. It explains the various elements of the dispute resolution process of which the Private Residential Tenancies Board (PRTB), established under the 2004 Act, has seisin. Moreover, in outlining and analysing the substantive provisions of the 2004 Act, the authors refer to decisions of the tenancy tribunal of the PRTB, and of the District and Circuit Courts in the limited areas in which those courts have jurisdiction. In general, this text contains a comprehensive exposition and analysis of very difficult legislation and makes accessible the sources which the practitioner needs to be aware of to properly advise his or her client.

The timing of the publication of this text is opportune. The 2004 Act has been in operation for just over five years. It has been subject to amendment recently in the Housing (Miscellaneous Provisions) Act 2009. In particular, s.100 of the 2009 Act now provides that definition of "tenancy" does not include a tenancy, the term of which is more than 35 years, although that amendment does not affect any matter referred to the PRTB for resolution before the coming into operation of s.100. The importance of that amendment has been underlined by the recent decision of the High Court (Budd J.) (reported in the *Irish Times* on April 24, 2010) in which the decision of Judge Linnane in the Circuit Court in *S. & L. Management Ltd v Mallon & PRTB* in May 2009, cited by the authors, was upheld. The amendment was necessary to remove, inter alia, disputes in relation to service charges payable by owners holding under long leases of apartments in apartment complexes from the jurisdiction of the PRTB. While the jurisprudence on the 2004 Act is developing, and it is reasonable to predict that further legislative amendments may be introduced in the not too distant future, the scheme provided for in the 2004 Act has been in force for a sufficient period to demonstrate how it is operating in practice. This the authors do ably.

I have no doubt that this text will become the standard work on landlord and tenant law in the residential sector, which, at this point in time, needs the type of treatment it is given by the authors. It will be of immense benefit to students and practitioners alike. It is to be hoped that it will be kept up to date in later editions, as the 2004 Act is amended and as the jurisprudence develops.

MARY LAFFOY,
High Court, May 11, 2010

PREFACE

The Residential Tenancies Act 2004 (the "RTA 2004") brought welcome reform to landlord and tenant law but also posed new challenges for practitioners, letting agents, landlords and tenants within the private rented sector. The RTA 2004 introduced, amongst other things, the new concept of a "Part 4 Tenancy", provided new rules for terminating tenancies and provided a mechanism for setting "market rent". It also established the Private Residential Tenancies Board to replace the role of the courts in relation to the majority of tenancy disputes. Although the RTA 2004 introduced significant changes to landlord and tenant law in the private rented sector, pre-existing legislation continues to have application in certain instances. The general consensus among practitioners is that the RTA 2004 is complex and difficult to apply in practice.

We are fortunate to have advised and represented both landlords and tenants, as well as the Private Residential Tenancies Board. Whilst it has been exciting advising on a new area of law, it has also been a challenge in light of the limited jurisprudence on, and academic consideration of, the subject. In July 2007, after giving a seminar in Cork, we debated whether the RTA 2004 was in fact as complex as it was perceived to be or whether, as a new piece of legislation, it simply required analysis and interpretation to become an uncontroversial part of day to day practice. The result of that debate was this book.

The aim of this text is to simplify the complexities of the RTA 2004. In practice, dealing with the issues that arise in the context of the landlord and tenant relationship, such as the termination of tenancies, requires extensive cross-referencing between the individual sections of the RTA 2004. We have analysed those issues and attempted to provide guidance on the interaction between the provisions of the RTA 2004. This book also aims to capture, as part of that analysis, other legislation and legal principles that apply to the private rented sector.

There have been several people who have assisted and supported us in writing this text and we acknowledge their contributions with gratitude.

We would like to thank Ms Justice Laffoy who has very kindly written the foreword. We would also like to thank Brian Buggy for his guidance at the outset and encouragement to write this book. We are extremely grateful to our many colleagues who generously gave their time and provided comments on the chapters of our draft text—Deirdre Bignell, Anne Cassidy, Emilie Fary, Paul Finnegan BL, Mary Gordon BL, Rachel McCrossan BL, Michael McGrath BL, Emma Murphy, Brian Ormond, Peggy O'Rourke BL, Scott Smalley, Lisa Smyth, Deborah Weekes and Hilda Wrixon.

Úna would like to thank her friends and family, in particular her parents, Hugh and Phil, for their support and encouragement in writing this book. Úna would also like to thank her co-author and friend Jennifer, whose idea it was to undertake the challenge of writing this book. Her good humour, attention to detail and commitment to this project made it a pleasure to work alongside her.

Jennifer would like to thank her parents Veronica and William and her sister Deirdre for their constant and always reliable support and kind-heartedness. Jennifer also thanks the many friends who have provided endless encouragement when writing this book, in particular that provided by Joanna Fellows. Jennifer acknowledges those who have guided her career in the litigious areas of landlord and tenant law, Hilary Prentice and Lisa Broderick. Jennifer also wishes to thank her co-author, colleague and friend Úna, for her patience, relentless hard work, enthusiasm and humour in writing this book.

We are also extremely grateful to all at Thomson Reuters who were involved in this project. In particular we would like to thank Frieda Donohue, commissioning editor, for her enthusiasm in taking on this project and our editor, Kristiina Kojamo, for her patience and hard work in editing this text. We would also like to thank Maura Smyth for her assistance in marketing the book.

This text is aimed at assisting practitioners, letting agents and students of landlord and tenant law. It is hoped that it will also serve as a useful reference tool for landlords and tenants. As there is no legal text on the RTA 2004 to date, we hope that our work goes at least in part towards filling that gap.

We have stated the law from materials available to us as of April 30, 2010. The views expressed are our own. The authors accept no liability for any errors or omissions in the text.

Úna Cassidy and Jennifer Ring
Dublin/Melbourne
May 19, 2010

CONTENTS

TABLE OF CASES

IRELAND TENANCY TRIBUNAL DECISIONS

ENGLAND

NORTHERN IRELAND

EUROPEAN COURT OF HUMAN RIGHTS

TABLE OF LEGISLATION

IRISH CONSTITUTION

IRISH LEGISLATION

STATUTES

STATUTORY INSTRUMENTS

NEW ZEALAND LEGISLATION

AUSTRALIAN LEGISLATION

INTERNATIONAL TREATIES

CHAPTER 1

INTRODUCTION

1. OVERVIEW

1–01 Since the introduction of the Residential Tenancies Act 2004 (the "RTA 2004"), the law concerning the residential landlord and tenant relationship in the private sector has substantially changed. The RTA 2004 was aimed at clarifying and simplifying this complex area of law and striking a balance between the rights and duties of both the landlord and tenant. Its principal changes included the introduction of a measure of security of tenure for tenants, specified minimum obligations applying to landlords and tenants, rent to be determined by the concept of market rent and the termination of tenancies to be assessed by set notice periods linked to the duration of a tenancy. Arguably, the most significant change introduced by the RTA 2004 is that the jurisdiction to deal with disputes between landlords and tenants is now vested in the Private Residential Tenancies Board (the "PRTB"). Since the enactment of the RTA 2004, the courts play a limited role in the determination of residential landlord and tenant disputes. The PRTB is also charged with operating a system of tenancy registration and developing policy on landlord and tenant issues.

1–02 An important aspect of the RTA 2004 is that it contains an anti-avoidance provision—it is not possible to contract out of it by including an opt-out clause in a written tenancy agreement.[1] Of note, however, is that while the RTA 2004 substantially amends landlord and tenant law in the residential sector, it does not consolidate legislation governing residential tenancies and to a considerable degree regard must still be had to other legislation for a full picture of the law relating to residential lettings. Notable areas which are not covered by the RTA 2004 are the provision of rent books and minimum standards. The Housing (Rent Books) Regulations 1993, as amended by the Housing (Rent Books) Regulations 2004 (the "Rent Book Regulations"), still governs a landlord's obligation to provide rent books to a tenant. The Housing (Miscellaneous Provisions) Act 1992 (as amended) (the "1992 Act") and the regulations made under s.18 of that Act still govern the area of minimum standards of a dwelling which a landlord must adhere to.[2]

---

[1] Section 3 of the RTA 2004 provides that it applies to "every dwelling, the subject of a tenancy" including a tenancy created before the passing of the RTA 2004.

[2] Section 12 of the RTA 2004 provides that a landlord must carry out to the structure of the dwelling all such repairs as are, from time to time, necessary and ensure that the structure

2. BACKGROUND

1–03 A Working Group on Security of Tenure (the "Working Group") was established in November 1994 by the then Minister for Justice, Equality and Law Reform to examine and report on the position of security of tenure in the private rented sector, with particular reference to any amendments which may be desirable to the Landlord and Tenant (Amendment) Act 1980 (the "1980 Act"). The Working Group reported to the Minister for Justice, Equality and Law Reform in 1996.[3] It found that in practice many landlords terminated tenancies when approaching 20 years in order to circumvent the effect of Pt II of the 1980 Act, which entitled tenants to a further 35-year tenancy under the long occupation user provisions.[4] The Working Group concluded that although Pt II of the 1980 Act was intended to provide tenants with greater security of tenure, the operation of that Part had proved quite different, having in fact the opposite effect and working instead in favour of the landlord. In addition, in relation to tenancies generally, a landlord could terminate a tenancy without giving a reason to the tenant, as long as the requisite amount of notice was given, which invariably was the 28 days minimum notice required by the 1992 Act.[5] The only remedy available to some tenants whose tenancy was terminated, was to seek compensation for improvements and disturbance.[6]

As one of the range of measures in response to the Working Group's report titled "The Housing Market: An Economic Review and Assessment", the Government announced on March 9, 1999 its decision to establish a commission to examine issues relating to security of tenure in the private rented sector. The commission would take into account the report of the Working Group but would examine the issue of security of tenure on a much broader basis, including the complex legal and constitutional issues inherent in the landlord and tenant relationship. The Commission on the Private Rented Sector (the "Commission") was launched on July 22, 1999 by Mr Robert Molloy TD, Minister for Housing and Urban Renewal. It was originally envisaged that it would primarily address

---

complies with any standards for houses for the time being prescribed under s.18 of the 1992 Act. The Housing (Standards for Rented Houses) Regulations 1993 (S.I. No. 147 of 1993) and the Housing (Standards for Rented Houses) Regulations 2008 (S.I. No. 534 of 2008) (as amended) have been enacted under s.18. See paras 5–07 to 5–10. Other legislation which must be referred to get to a full view of the legislative provisions concerning the landlord and tenant relationship are the Landlord and Tenant Law Amendment Act (Ireland) 1860 ("Deasy's Act"); Landlord and Tenant (Amendment) Act 1980; Fire Services Act 1981 (as amended); Equal Status Act 2000 (as amended); Environmental Protection Agency Act 1992 (as amended) concerning noise pollution and the European Communities (Unfair Terms in Consumer Contracts) Regulations 1995 (S.I. No. 27 of 1995) (as amended).

3   The group presented its report in July 1996 and it was published by the Minister for Justice, Equality and Law Reform in February 1999.

4   See Ch.7.

5   1992 Act, s.17.

6   1980 Act, ss.45–63. For further detail of the law prior to the introduction of the RTA 2004, see Wylie, *Landlord and Tenant Law*, 2nd edn (Dublin: Butterworths, 1998).

the controversial issue of security of tenure. However, it was finally decided that security of tenure could not be dealt with in isolation and other issues such as supply and quality of accommodation, investment return and market considerations and constraints to the development of the sector needed to be addressed also.[7]

1–04 Many of the recommendations of the Commission are incorporated into the RTA 2004. The Terms of Reference of the Commission focused on three specific areas. The Commission was required to examine the working of the landlord and tenant relationship and to make recommendations as it considered were proper, equitable and feasible with a view to improving security of tenure of tenants in the occupation of their dwellings. Secondly, the Commission was required to make recommendations on ways to maintain a fair and reasonable balance between the respective rights and obligations of landlords and existing and future tenants and thirdly, to make recommendations on how to increase investment in and the supply of residential accommodation for renting including the removal of any identified constraints to the development of the sector.[8]

1–05 A major difficulty experienced by the Commission in researching the residential sector was the dearth of information available on the size, composition and characteristics of the private rented sector in Ireland.[9] The Commission, nevertheless, identified the main concerns of both the landlord and the tenant. Tenants were primarily concerned with security of tenure, reasonable rent and rent reviews, equality of access to rented accommodation, incentives to encourage increased supply of "secure, affordable, quality private rented housing",[10] a cost-effective rapid dispute resolution framework, information and advice services, higher mimiumum standards in legislation and the development of professional management company practices within the sector.[11] The issues identified by landlords were mainly fiscal and regulatory in nature. Landlords were concerned with taxation of rental income, with bringing the tax treatment of rental income from residential property in line with other businesses, stamp duties, capital gains tax roll over relief, refurbishment expenditure, deductions to be allowed in respect of personal pension plans on the basis of rental profits, capital acquisitions tax to be extended to the letting of properties and deductibility of interest on borrowings for investment in rented property. Within the context of the regulatory framework, landlords were concerned with antisocial behaviour, tenant obligations, dispute resolution, registration of tenancies and tenure to be linked to the length of the lease.[12] The Commission in its report

---

[7] Report of the Commission on the Private Rented Residential Sector, July 2000 ("Report of the Commission"), "Introduction", p.1.
[8] Report of the Commission, "Introduction", p.1.
[9] Report of the Commission, para.2.1.1.
[10] Report of the Commission, para.2.6.2.
[11] Report of the Commission, para.2.6.2.
[12] Report of the Commission, para.2.6.3.

commented that while no one can be forced to become a landlord, this was not the same for tenants who were in the more vulnerable position and could be forced into a situation beyond their control having no other choice.[13]

1–06 The Commission identified two types of tenancies in the residential sector—unfurnished dwellings were formerly rent controlled by the provisions of the Rent Restrictions Act 1960 (the "Rent Restrictions Act"), until Pts II and IV of that legislation were held to be unconstitutional.[14] The Housing (Private Rented Dwellings) Act 1982, as amended by the Housing (Private Rented Dwellings) (Amendment) Act 1983, currently applies to dwellings which were previously controlled under the Rent Restrictions Act. However, as dwellings subject to the provisions of that legislation had to be built before May 7, 1941, this is a declining segment of the private rented sector.[15] The RTA 2004 explicitly excludes from its provisions the formerly rent controlled sector.[16]

1–07 The practice of letting furnished accommodation was a mechanism used by landlords to avoid rent control. The legislation governing this sector prior to the introduction of the RTA 2004, were the various Landlord and Tenant Acts 1860–1980 and the 1992 Act. However, notwithstanding these legislative provisions, the regulation of the landlord and tenant relationship was limited and in effect, its full extent was that landlords had to provide rent books, comply with minimum standards in rented accommodation and register tenancies with the local authority. The Commission in its Report noted that there was poor compliance in practice with the standards and regulations that did exist and that limited action was taken by local authorities who were responsible for the enforcement of these provisions.[17] It was further noted that although landlords were required to comply with minimum standards set out in the 1992 Act, this was counteracted by the fact that tenants did not have security of tenure and were reluctant to complain about the standard of their rented accommodation in fear that the landlord would terminate their tenancy or increase the rent.[18]

1–08 The Commission gave specific consideration to the lack of security of tenure in the private rented sector. A landlord did not have to give a reason for terminating a tenancy, unless he or she was required to do so by the lease agreement. A fixed-term tenancy would automatically terminate on the last day

---

[13] Report of the Commission, para.2.12.
[14] *Blake & Others v Attorney General* [1982] I.R. 117; *Madigan v Attorney General* [1986] I.L.R.M. 136. The Rent Restrictions Act 1960 had been amended by the Rent Restrictions (Amendment) Act 1967 and the Landlord and Tenant (Amendment) Act 1971.
[15] Report of the Commission, para.2.4.2.
[16] See s.3(2)(b) of the RTA 2004.
[17] Report of the Commission, para.4.8.4.
[18] Report of the Commission, para.4.8.4.2.

of the agreed term and a periodic tenancy had to be terminated by serving a notice to quit, which had to be in writing giving at least 28 days' notice.[19] Where a tenant refused to vacate the dwelling, the most common relief sought was ejectment for overholding.[20] Where a tenant failed to pay rent, ejectment for non-payment of rent was the appropriate statutory remedy.[21] Forfeiture was also a remedy available to a landlord where the tenant was in breach of a covenant or condition of the tenancy.[22] The Commission noted that recourse to the courts was costly and did not suit the needs of many tenancy situations, where it considered a speedy, effective and less costly dispute resolution system was more appropriate. As the setting of rent was unregulated, rent could be increased at the end of any week or month (for example) in the case of a periodic tenancy, unless there were specific provisions contained in a lease agreement which prevented such an increase. With limited regulation, the parties were bound by the terms and conditions agreed between them, which were invariably oral in nature in the residential sector.[23]

1–09 The Commission identified other areas it considered were not working satisfactorily in the private rented sector. The quality of accommodation was not acceptable and there were also issues in relation to supply of rented properties and affordability for low income tenants. However, although the Commission identified the need to deal with and address these issues, it was conscious of achieving an equitable and fair regulation of the private rented sector without acting as a deterrent to investors.[24] The Commission's overall vision for the private rented sector was a:

> "vibrant, thriving, well-managed and diverse sector which satisfactorily meets a range of housing needs, provides an adequate supply of secure, affordable, good quality accommodation and operates within a regulatory framework which protects the interests of tenants and landlords".[25]

3. BALANCING RIGHTS OF THE LANDLORD AND TENANT

A. Bunreacht na hÉireann

1–10 It is often argued that the private property rights protected by the Constitution are obstacles to providing security of tenure and controlling rents.

---

[19] 1992 Act, s.16.
[20] Deasy's Act, s.72.
[21] Deasy's Act, s.52.
[22] Where a forfeiture is effected, a landlord is entitled to enter the dwelling and recover possession provided entry can be gained peacefully.
[23] Report of the Commission, Chs 5 and 8.
[24] Report of the Commission, Chs 5 and 8.
[25] Report of the Commission, para.8.1.1.3

In this regard, the Commission in its Report considered the Supreme Court decision in *Blake & Others v Attorney General*,[26] which was a challenge to the validity of the Rent Restrictions Acts 1960 and 1967. That legislation restricted the level of rents landlords could require of tenants in possession of dwellings to which the legislation applied and also restricted the recovery of possession of those dwellings.[27] The effect of the controls on rent was that rents were essentially restricted by reference to the rents payable on June 8, 1966, resulting in a high disproportion with market rents. The Supreme Court held that an arbitrary legislative scheme providing for security of tenure and rent control in certain cases, without making provision for compensation for landlords amounted to an unjust attack on the property rights of the plaintiff. O'Higgins C.J. stated:

> "[The] absence of any power to review such rents, irrespective of changes in conditions, is in itself a circumstance of inherent injustice which cannot be ignored ... the provisions of Part II ... restrict the property rights of one group of citizens for the benefit of another group. This is done, without compensation and without regard to the financial capacity or the financial needs of either group, in legislation which provides no limitation on the period of restriction, gives no opportunity for review and allows no modification of the operation of the restriction. It is, therefore, both unfair and arbitrary."[28]

In relation to restrictions imposed on recovery of possession of dwellings, which were contained in Pt IV of the Rent Restrictions Act 1960, it was held that it was not necessarily invalid but as Pt IV was an integral part of an arbitrary and unfair scheme, it must also fall.[29]

1–11 In *Blake & Others v Attorney General*, the Supreme Court did not suggest that rent control was per se invalid but that rent control is valid provided a reasonable balance is struck between affected interests. In *Madigan v Attorney General*,[30] the Supreme Court emphasised that an interference with property

---

[26] [1982] I.R. 117.

[27] See paras 3–29 to 3–31, which considers the dwellings to which the Rent Restrictions Act applied.

[28] [1982] I.R. 117 at 139–140.

[29] The legislature responded by introducing the Housing (Private Rented Dwellings) Bill 1981, which was referred by the President to the Supreme Court under Art.26 of the Constitution (*In the matter of Article 26 of the Constitution and in the matter of the Housing (Private Rented Dwellings) Bill, 1981* [1983] I.R. 181). The Supreme Court held that the provisions contained in the legislation were different but still constituted an unjust attack on property rights: "In such circumstances, to impose different but no less unjust deprivations upon landlords cannot but be unjust having regard to the provisions of the Constitution", per O'Higgins C.J. [1983] I.R. 181 at 191. Ultimately, the Housing (Private Rented Dwellings) Act 1982 was enacted and currently applies (as amended by the Housing (Private Rented Dwellings) (Amendment) Act 1983) to dwellings which were previously controlled under the Rent Restrictions Acts 1960 and 1967.

[30] [1986] I.L.R.M 136.

rights was not an unjust attack if it was in accordance with social justice and inspired by the exigencies of the common good. The Commission was of the view that although the scheme controlling rent and security of tenure within the context of the Rent Restrictions Acts 1960 and 1967 was deemed unconstitutional, contrary to the property rights protected by Art.40.3.2° of the Constitution, there was room to control rents to some degree and provide a level of security of tenure without violating those rights, once a balance was struck. The Commission in its Report also had regard to the Supreme Court decision in *Dreher v Irish Land Commission*[31] that focused on the requirements of the "common good" which the Commission considered would be necessary to have cognisance of when considering the development of the housing market and facilitating a greater level of regulation of the landlord and tenant relationship.[32] The Commission also referred to the opinion of the Constitution Review Group, which concluded that property rights could be interfered with as long as the interference is not arbitrary and provided that the legislature has due regard to the principles of proportionality.[33]

B. European Convention on Human Rights

1–12 In assessing what is proportionate in the restriction of property rights, the developing jurisprudence of the European Court of Human Rights (the "ECtHR") provides helpful guidance. The European Convention on Human Rights (the "Convention") was incorporated into Irish law by the European Convention on Human Rights Act 2003 (the "ECHR Act"). Article 8 and art.1 of the First Protocol of the Convention are the most relevant articles when considering property rights.

Article 8 of the Convention guarantees everyone "the right to respect for his private and family life, his home and his correspondence".[34] Article 8 creates a right to respect for a person's home and limits the extent in which that right can be interfered with. Article 1, Protocol I provides as follows:

> Every natural or legal person is entitled to the peaceful enjoyment of his possessions. No one shall be deprived of his possessions except in the public interest and subject to the conditions provided for by law and by the general principles of international law.
>
> The preceding provisions, shall not, however, in any way impair the right of a State to enforce such law as it deems necessary to control the use of

---

[31] [1984] I.L.R.M. 94.

[32] Report of the Commission, para.4.3.6.

[33] "Report of the Constitution Review Group", 1996, p.360.

[34] See *Connors v United Kingdom* (2004) 40 EHRR 189, where it was held by the ECtHR that the procedural safeguards are of crucial importance in assessing the proportionality of the interference. An interference with art.8 will be considered "necessary in a democratic society" for a legitimate aim if it answers a "pressing social need" and in particular it if is proportionate to the legitimate aim pursued. See also *McCann v United Kingdom* (2008) 47 EHRR 913.

property in accordance with the general interest or to secure the payment of taxes or other contributions or penalties.

1–13 The jurisprudence of the ECtHR demonstrates that interference with rights protected by the Convention is authorised where it is in accordance with law, is necessary in a democratic society and is proportionate to the aim sought. In *Spadea and Scalabrino v Italy*,[35] interference with the privacy of the home was found to be justified on the grounds of legitimate social and economic policies. In the decision of *Hutten-Czapska v Poland*,[36] the decision of the Grand Chamber of the ECtHR held that the restrictive system of rent control, which set a ceiling on rent levels so low that landlords were left in a position where they could not recoup their maintenance costs, let alone make any profit, was held to be in contravention of art.1 of the First Protocol of the Convention. It held that the rent-control system scheme in Poland originated in the continued shortage of dwellings, the low supply of flats for rent and the high costs of acquiring a flat. It was thus implemented to secure the social protection of tenants especially tenants in a poor financial situation. The ECtHR accepted that in the social and economic circumstances of the case, the legislation in question had a legitimate aim in the general interest. Nevertheless, it held the legislation placed a disproportionate and excessive burden on the landlord, which could not be justified. In addition, the ECtHR held that the violation of the applicant's rights was not exclusively linked to the levels of rent chargeable but rather consisted in the combined effect of the system's defective provisions on the setting of rent and various restrictions on the landlord's rights in respect of termination of leases. The statutory financial burdens imposed on the landlord and the absence of any legal ways and means making it possible for them, either to offset or mitigate the losses incurred in connection with the maintenance of property or to have the necessary repairs subsidised by the State in justified cases, were deemed to be an unlawful interference with the right to property.[37]

1–14 Even before the ECHR Act was enacted, the Irish courts had cause to consider the implications of the Convention on property rights. *In the matter of Article 26 of the Constitution and in the matter of Part V of the Planning and Development Bill, 1999*,[38] in upholding the constitutionality of the social and affordable housing provisions set out in Pt V of the Bill, the Supreme Court considered the interaction of the Convention with property rights. Keane C.J. restated the test of compliance as stated by Costello J. in *Heaney v Ireland*[39] where State provisions seek to interfere with a protected right:

---

[35] (1995) 21 EHRR 482.

[36] No. 35014/97, ECtHR 2006-VIII (19.6.06).

[37] The applicant was awarded €30,000 in non-pecuniary damage and €22,500 in respect of costs and expenses.

[38] [2000] 2 I.R. 321.

[39] [1994] 3 I.R. 593.

"The objective of the impugned provision must be of sufficient importance to warrant overriding a constitutionally protected right. It must relate to concerns pressing and substantial in a free and democratic society. The means chosen must pass a proportionality test. They must –
(a) be rationally connected to the objective and not be arbitrary, unfair or based on irrational considerations;
(b) impair the right as little as possible; and
(c) be such that their effects on rights are proportional to the objective."[40]

Therefore, in regulating property rented in the residential sector, a balance must be struck between the property rights of the landlord under art.1 of the First Protocol to the Convention and the right to privacy in the family home as guaranteed under art.8 of the Convention.

1–15 Article 14 of the Convention has also been considered relevant in assessing property rights. Article 14 provides:

The enjoyment of the rights and freedoms set forth in this Convention shall be secured without discrimination on any ground such as sex, race, colour, language, religion, political or other opinion, national or social origin, association with a national minority, property, birth or other status.

In *Larkos v Cyprus*,[41] the ECtHR held that the domestic law of Cyprus, which deprived state tenants of the security of tenure provisions that private tenants could avail of, was unjustifiable having regard to art.14 of the Convention, which guarantees equal enjoyment of rights. The ECtHR held that there was no reasonable and objective justification for not extending these protections to state tenants also. One could argue that a similar situation possibly arises in the context of the RTA 2004, which only applies to the private residential sector and not to social or state housing. Tenants of dwellings provided by the State can therefore not avail of the extended security of tenure provisions and notice periods for termination of tenancies provided for by the RTA 2004.

1–16 The Commission did not consider in any great detail the jurisprudence of the ECtHR. It did conclude, however, that there was no existing constitutional or legal impediment to recommending a system of rent control provided that such a system was framed within the context of the common good and was fair and not oppressive paying due regard to the rights and interests of both parties.[42]

---

[40] [2000] 2 I.R. 321 at 349.
[41] (1999) 30 EHRR 597.
[42] Report of the Commission, para.5.3.6.

4. THE COMMISSION'S RECOMMENDATIONS

1–17 The Commission recommended that there should be provision for speedy resolution of disputes between landlords and tenants. Recourse to the courts was considered to be too lengthy a process, which on occasion deterred tenants from taking legal action but also was used by other tenants to avoid eviction and continue in occupation of a dwelling without paying rent. On this basis, they recommended the establishment of a body which would govern disputes between landlords and tenants in a speedy, informal and confidential manner. This statutory board, now known as the PRTB, would deal with dispute resolution and have other functions such as operating a tenancy registration system.

The Commission also recommended the introduction of new security of tenure rules. If a tenant was in occupation of a dwelling for a period of six months and neither party terminated the tenancy during that period, the tenant would be entitled to a further three-and-a-half-year tenancy. Termination of the tenancy within that four-year period would be limited to specific grounds such as the landlord wishing to sell the property, live in the property him or herself or where the tenant breached his or her obligations under the tenancy. It further recommended that rent reviews could not take place more regularly than once a year and that rent was to be assessed on the basis of market rent.

5. THE RESIDENTIAL TENANCIES ACT 2004

1–18 The Residential Tenancies Bill 2003 was introduced into Dáil Éireann on May 25, 2003 and proposed major reform of the law governing landlord-tenant relations in the private rented sector. It aimed to achieve an appropriate balance of rights and duties between landlords and tenants, to ensure that both parties were on a level playing field. The Bill included many of the recommendations contained in the Commission's Report and in introducing the Bill to the Seanad at the Second Stage, the Minister of State at the Department of the Environment, Heritage and Local Government, Noel Ahern TD stated that, "The reforms it will bring to the private rented sector remain true to the report of the commission on the private residential sector."[43] He further stated:

> "The Bill provides for a modern, efficient, user-friendly and largely litigation-free legal framework for the private rented sector. Key provisions relate to improved security of tenure, restriction of rent to market level, clarification of obligations of tenants and landlords, and the establishment of a private residential tenancies board to operate a State-subsidised statutory dispute resolution service, a new tenancy registration system and to undertake a number of other key functions and reform of certain legal provisions that have been problematic. It is a progressive measure that will benefit both landlords

---

[43] Minister Ahern, TD, Seanad Éireann, Vol.177, Col.722, July 2, 2004, second stage.

and tenants and will help to promote the development of the private rented sector and underpin an enhanced role for it in meeting housing needs in the future."[44]

1–19 The long title of the RTA 2004 sets out the purpose and objective of the legislation, which is:

> to provide –
> (a) in accordance with the exigencies of the common good, for a measure of security of tenure for tenants of certain dwellings,
> (b) for amendments of the law of landlord and tenant in relation to the basic rights and obligations of each of the parties to tenancies of certain dwellings,
> (c) with the aim of allowing disputes between such parties to be resolved cheaply and speedily, for the establishment of a body to be known as the Private Residential Tenancies Board and the conferral on it of powers and functions of a limited nature in relation to the resolution of such disputes,
> (d) for the registration of tenancies of certain dwellings, and
> (e) for related matters.

1–20 The RTA 2004 contains 202 sections divided into nine Parts. Part 1 sets out the scope and application of the legislation. The RTA 2004 applies to "every dwelling", the subject of a tenancy (both written and oral), including a tenancy created before the passing of the RTA 2004.[45] It does not apply to residential licences. It also excludes certain dwellings from its application including social[46] or owner occupied[47] housing, the rent controlled sector,[48] long occupation equity tenancies,[49] business[50] or holiday lettings,[51] a dwelling where the tenant is entitled to acquire the fee simple,[52] a dwelling occupied under a shared ownership lease[53] and a dwelling where the landlord's spouse, parent or child resides and no written tenancy agreement has been entered into by any person resident in the dwelling.[54] The RTA 2004 no longer applies to tenancies with a term that is longer than 35 years.[55]

---

[44]   Minister Ahern, TD, Seanad Éireann, Vol.177, Cols 722–723, July 2, 2004, second stage.
[45]   RTA 2004, s.3(1).
[46]   RTA 2004, s.3(2)(c).
[47]   RTA 2004, s.3(2)(g).
[48]   RTA 2004, s.3(2)(b).
[49]   RTA 2004, s.3(2)(i).
[50]   RTA 2004, s.3(2)(a).
[51]   RTA 2004, s.3(2)(f).
[52]   RTA 2004, s.3(2)(d).
[53]   RTA 2004, s.3(2)(e). The Housing (Miscellaneous Provisions) Act 2009 makes provision for the replacement of the shared ownership lease scheme. See para.3–50.
[54]   RTA 2004, s.3(2)(h).
[55]   Housing (Miscellaneous Provisions) Act 2009, s.100; see also the decision of Linnane J. in *S&L Management Limited v Mallon and PRTB*, unreported, Circuit Court, April 3, 2009; unreported, High Court, Budd J., April 23, 2010. For a detailed consideration of the application of the RTA 2004, see Ch.3.

1–21 Part 2 of the RTA 2004 deals with the minimum tenancy obligations applying to landlords and tenants, regardless of whether there is a written tenancy agreement or not. Some of the obligations of a landlord and tenant provided for in Pt 2 would previously have been contained in a written tenancy agreement, such as a landlord's obligation to repay the deposit and carry out repairs and the tenant's obligation to pay rent on time.[56] With the passing of the RTA 2004, the provisions contained in Pt 2 impose minimum requirements in respect of the duties of landlords and tenants and whether written tenancy agreements have regard to such obligations is irrelevant. These obligations are implied into every tenancy agreement falling within the remit of the RTA 2004. In addition, it is not possible to contract out of the obligations imposed on landlords and tenants by the RTA 2004, although the parties are free to agree on additional terms which are more favourable for the tenant.[57] An interesting inclusion to the obligations of landlords is that imposed by s.15 of the RTA 2004, which provides that a landlord owes a duty to certain third parties to enforce the obligations of tenants. Failure to do so will entitle a third party affected by a tenant's behaviour to refer a dispute to the PRTB against the landlord for his or her failure to enforce the particular obligation of the tenant concerned.[58] Another, notable obligation imposed on a landlord is not to penalise a tenant in certain specified circumstances—for example where a tenant refers a dispute to the PRTB, makes a complaint to An Garda Síochána or to the local authority in relation to his or her occupation of the dwelling.[59]

1–22 As referred to at para.1–02 above, the 1992 Act, the Rent Book Regulations and the RTA 2004 must be considered together, particularly for the purposes of ascertaining a landlord's obligations. Section 12(1) of the RTA 2004, states that the obligations of landlords imposed by that section, are "in addition to the obligations arising by or under any other enactment". Included in the obligations imposed by s.12 is an explicit requirement to maintain the structure and the interior of the dwelling. A landlord is in breach of his or her obligations under the RTA 2004, if he or she fails to adhere to the minimum standards set down in the 1992 Act, including any regulations enacted under s.18.[60] A landlord will also be in breach of his or her obligations if he or she fails to provide a rent book under the Rent Book Regulations, which remain in force post enactment of the RTA 2004. Failure to record payments of rent in the rent book or alternatively to provide receipts is an offence pursuant to s.34 of the 1992 Act. However,

---

[56] RTA 2004, ss.12 and 16 respectively.

[57] RTA 2004, s.18. See Chs 4 and 5 for a detailed consideration of these provisions.

[58] For detailed consideration of s.15, see paras 5–49 to 5–55 and paras 9–17 to 9–24.

[59] RTA 2004, s.14. For a more detailed consideration of s.14 of the RTA 2004, see paras 5–47 to 5–48.

[60] Standards under s.18 of the 1992 Act are contained in the Housing (Standards for Rented Houses) Regulations 1993 (S.I. No. 147 of 1993), as amended by the Housing (Standards for Rented Houses) Regulations 2008 (S.I. No. 534 of 2008) and the Housing (Standards for Rented Houses)(Amendment) Regulations 2009 (S.I. No. 462 of 2009). See the review undertaken by the Department of the Environment, Heritage and Local Government, "Action on Private Rented Accommodation Standards" (September 2006).

s.201 of the RTA 2004 has increased the penalties for such offences. Enforcement of the Rent Book Regulations and the regulations imposing minimum standards for rented houses, remains the responsibility of local authorities.

1–23 A tenant's obligations under the RTA 2004 include paying rent on time, allowing the landlord entry to carry out repairs and not to assign or sub-let the dwelling without the landlord's consent.[61] A tenant also has a responsibility to remedy any disrepair other than normal wear and tear attributable to the tenant's acts or omissions. A tenant is also prohibited from engaging in antisocial behaviour. In addition, he or she must not act in a way which would cause the landlord to be in breach of his or her obligations under any enactment, in particular s.18 of the 1992 Act.[62]

1–24 Part 3 of the RTA 2004 provides for rent and rent reviews. Rent is to be no more than the open market rate and rent reviews are not to take place more frequently than on a yearly basis, unless there is a substantial change in the nature of the rented dwelling. However, it is open to parties to agree to rent which is below the market rent.[63]

1–25 Part 4 of the RTA 2004, guarantees security of tenure based on four-year cycles as recommended by the Commission. Once a tenant has been in occupation of a dwelling for six months and the tenancy has not been terminated, the tenant is entitled to a further three-and-a-half-year tenancy.[64] The first cycle is called a Part 4 tenancy and each subsequent cycle is called a further Part 4 tenancy. A tenant is free to terminate a Part 4 tenancy at any time without giving a reason, as long as the requisite notice period is given. Landlords on the other hand can only terminate a Part 4 tenancy if one of the grounds specified in s.34 of the RTA 2004 exist. Those grounds are failure by the tenant to comply with the obligations of the tenancy, the dwelling being no longer suited to the accommodation needs of the occupying household, the landlord intending to enter into a contract to sell the dwelling within three months, the landlord requiring the dwelling for his or her own occupation or that of a family member, the landlord intending to refurbish substantially the dwelling such that vacant possession would be required and the landlord intending to change the use of the dwelling. If a landlord requires the dwelling for his or her occupation or that of a family member, changes the use of the dwelling or carries out substantial refurbishment and the dwelling subsequently becomes available for re-letting, a tenant who keeps the landlord updated with his or her contact details must be offered the opportunity to re-occupy the dwelling.[65]

---

[61]   RTA 2004, s.16.
[62]   For a detailed consideration of the obligations of tenants, see Ch.4.
[63]   For a detailed consideration of Pt 3 of the RTA 2004, see Ch.6.
[64]   RTA 2004, s.28.
[65]   For a detailed consideration of Pt 4, see Ch.7 and also Ch.8 for relevant provisions relating to the terminaton of Part 4 tenancies.

1–26 Part 5 of the RTA 2004 is complimentary to Pt 4 and sets down the procedures which must be followed if a tenancy is to be terminated. Notice periods are linked to the length of the tenancy. A landlord or tenant wishing to terminate a tenancy must serve a "notice of termination".[66] No longer is it possible for a landlord to terminate a tenancy by serving a notice to quit or by allowing a tenancy to come to its natural end, as previously existed in the case of fixed term tenancies.[67] Failure to comply strictly with the required form of a notice for termination or failure to give the appropriate notice period, invalidates any attempt to terminate a tenancy and the person to whom the notice is addressed has no duty to comply with it. The old remedies available where a tenant did not vacate a dwelling on foot of a notice to quit, including ejectment, forfeiture and re-entry, are no longer available.[68] Instead, a landlord must refer a dispute to the PRTB under Pt 6 of the RTA 2004.[69]

1–27 Part 6 of the RTA 2004 introduces a dispute resolution process for disputes concerning residential tenancies of private rented dwellings. Any dispute between a landlord and tenant falling within the ambit of the RTA 2004 must be dealt with by the PRTB. The dispute resolution process consists of two stages. Stage one is mediation or adjudication and is a confidential process. If mediation is unsuccessful or there is an appeal of an adjudicator's determination by either party, the matter will be referred to a tenancy tribunal, whose hearings are to be conducted in public. The terms of a determination of a tenancy tribunal can be affected on a point of law to the High Court. If there is no appeal or if an appeal is unsuccessful, the PRTB will make a "determination order" in terms of the decision of the tenancy tribunal. The PRTB will also issue a determination order of any decision made by an adjudicator (if not appealed) or of any agreement reached at mediation. Determination orders are binding on the parties concerned. A determination order can be enforced in the Circuit Court and it is an offence for a person to fail to comply with one or more terms of a determination order.[70]

1–28 Part 7 of the RTA 2004 sets out the procedures for registration of a tenancy. Section 10(2) of the RTA 2004 revokes the Housing (Registration of Rented Houses) Regulations 1996, which required landlords to register tenancies with local authorities. The new registration system under Pt 7 requires landlords to

---

[66] The requirements of a notice of termination are set out in s.62 of the RTA 2004.

[67] Minister Ahern TD was of the view that, "[i]n the future, except where a fixed term tenancy expires, termination must always be by a formal notice, regardless of who is terminating or what is the reason". Seanad Éireann, Vol.177, Col.726, July 2, 2004, second stage. This would appear to be at odds with ss.58, 59 and Pt 4 of the RTA 2004 and indeed the judgment of Laffoy J. in *Canty v Private Residential Tenancies Board* [2007] IEHC 243 where it was held that a tenancy could only be terminated by serving a notice of termination.

[68] RTA 2004, s.59. See also *McGovern v O'Ceallacháin* (TR07/DR154/2006, March 23, 2006).

[69] For a detailed consideration of Pt 5, see Ch.8.

[70] For a detailed consideration of Pt 6, see Ch.9.

register all tenancies of a dwelling with the PRTB. The registration scheme under the RTA 2004 is more onerous than before, necessitating landlords to provide greater details relating to the tenancy. Failure to register a tenancy, which comes within the remit of the RTA 2004, is an offence. In addition, failure to register excludes a landlord from availing of the dispute resolution procedures under Pt 6, although non-registration does not prevent a tenant referring a matter to the PRTB.[71]

1–29 Part 8 of the RTA 2004 establishes the PRTB which has responsibility for dispute resolution, registration of tenancies, the provision of policy advice, the review of the operation of the RTA 2004 and the carrying out of research regarding the private rented residential sector.[72]

1–30 Part 9 of the RTA 2004 is the "Miscellaneous" section of the legislation. It deals with many important areas not to be overlooked. First, it provides for the abolition of the entitlement to apply for a long occupation equity lease under the 1980 Act,[73] within five years of the coming into force of the RTA 2004, namely September 1, 2009. The RTA 2004 provided a renunciation option during that five-year period, so that a tenant entitled to apply for a long occupation equity lease could, if he or she so elected, benefit from the provisions of the RTA 2004. This was of particular relevance where the termination of the tenancy was imminent.[74] Part 9 also allows for the PRTB to apply for injunctive relief to the Circuit Court, in aid of the dispute resolution process under Pt 6. This is an important provision to assist the PRTB in dealing with the more serious of disputes, such as those involving antisocial behaviour or illegal evictions.[75] Section 193 confirms that a number of statutory provisions no longer apply to dwellings to which the RTA 2004 applies, namely s.42 of Deasy's Act, s.14 of the Conveyancing Act 1881, ss.2, 3 and 4 of the Conveyancing and Law of Property Act 1892, ss.66, 67 and 68 of the 1980 Act and s.16 of the 1992 Act.

1–31 The Schedule to the RTA 2004 deals with sub-tenancies and contains a number of important provisions in relation to those tenancy arrangements. The Schedule sets down important provisions concerning a sub-tenant's Part 4 tenancy rights and establishes how those Part 4 tenancy rights interact with the Part 4 tenancy's rights of the head-tenant. The Schedule also provides that head-landlords and sub-tenants owe certain obligations to each other.[76]

---

[71] Part 7 is considered in detail at Ch.10.

[72] Part 8 is considered in detail at Ch.11.

[73] 1980 Act, s.13(1)(b).

[74] One of the findings of the working group recorded in the Report of the Commission was that many landlords would terminate a tenancy just before a tenant was eligible to apply for a tenancy under the long occupation user provisions of the 1980 Act. See the Report of the Commission, para.1.4.4.2.

[75] See also paras 9–111 to 9–117.

[76] See Ch.4 on Tenant Obligations, Ch.5 on Landlord Obligations, Ch.7 on Security of Tenure and Ch.8 on Termination of Tenancies.

1–32 The RTA 2004 was commenced on a phased basis. The Residential Tenancies Act 2004 (Commencement) Order 2004[77] set September 1, 2004 as being the commencement date for Pt 1, Pt 4, Pt 5 (with the exception of s.71 and s.72), Pt 7, Pt 8 (with the exception of s.159(1)), Pt 9 (with the exception of s.182, s.189, s.190, s.193(a) and (d) and s.195(4) and (5)) and the Schedule to the RTA 2004. The establishment date for the PRTB under Pt 8 of RTA 2004 was also September 1, 2004 pursuant to the Residential Tenancies Act 2004 (Establishment Day) Order 2004.[78] The outstanding provisions of the RTA 2004 were commenced on December 6, 2004 by the Residential Tenancies Act 2004 (Commencement) (No. 2) Order 2004,[79] namely Pt 2, Pt 3, s.71, s.72, Pt 6, Pt 8, s.159(1), s.182, s.189, s.190, s.193(a) and (d) and s.195(4) and (5).

1–33 The RTA 2004 overhauled the legal and regulatory framework, which existed before its introduction. It is now the principal legislation governing residential tenancies in the private rented sector and therefore, primary focus in this text will be on the provisions of that Act. However, as stated above, the RTA 2004 does not consolidate the law relating to the private rented sector and other legislation and rules must be considered to provide a complete overview of the legal framework applicable. In addition, there are certain residential tenancies excluded from the remit of the RTA 2004 by s.3(2). The old rules that existed prior to the enactment of the RTA 2004 will still apply to those tenancies and therefore the law governing those areas must be considered for those tenancies which do not fall within the jurisdiction of the RTA 2004.

The RTA 2004 has been described by Laffoy J. in *Canty v Private Residential Tenancies Board*[80] as "an extremely complex piece of legislation".[81] In particular Laffoy J. referred to the provisions in Pt 4 of the RTA 2004 as being "very technical and confusing".[82] This text considers each Part of the RTA 2004 and endeavours in so far as possible to deal with its provisions in a clear and concise manner. Where relevant, reference will be made to other statutory provisions so that a complete overview of the statutory framework relating to landlord and tenant law in the private sector can be provided.

---

77 S.I. No. 505 of 2004.
78 S.I. No. 525 of 2004.
79 S.I. No. 750 of 2004.
80 [2007] IEHC 243.
81 [2007] IEHC 243, at p.11.
82 [2007] IEHC 243, at p.23.

CHAPTER 2

THE LANDLORD AND TENANT RELATIONSHIP

1. IMPORTANCE OF ESTABLISHING A LANDLORD AND TENANT RELATIONSHIP

2–01 This chapter explores the different tests which have been developed by the courts in assessing whether a landlord and tenant relationship exists. Although much of the judicial consideration to date on the landlord and tenant relationship arises in the context of commercial tenancies, the same general principles apply in the residential context.

2–02 For a landlord and tenant relationship to come into being, certain criteria need to be established. Failure to satisfy these criteria will mean that the relationship is some other type of relationship, which will not attract any of the legislative and common law rules concerning landlords and tenants. Indeed, the Residential Tenancies Act 2004 (the "RTA 2004") makes it explicit that it only applies to tenancies[1] and all other relationships fall outside of its remit.[2] Examples of other relationships, which do not fall within the category of a landlord and tenant relationship are the various types of licence agreements.[3]

2–03 If the tenancy is a tenancy to which the RTA 2004 applies, both the landlord and tenant can avail of the rights set out in that legislation. Therefore, from a practical perspective, both the landlord and tenant can refer a dispute to the Private Residential Tenancies Board (the "PRTB"),[4] they can avail of the

---

[1] A tenancy is defined for the purposes of the RTA 2004, as including "a periodic tenancy and a tenancy for a fixed term, whether oral or in writing or implied, and where the context so admits, includes a sub-tenancy and a tenancy or sub-tenancy that has been terminated" (RTA 2004, s.5). See para.3–18.

[2] Section 3(1) of the RTA 2004. A tenancy will, however, also fall outside the jurisdiction of the RTA 2004 if the dwelling is one excluded from its scope by s.3(2). The application of s.3(2) of the RTA 2004 is considered in detail in Ch.3.

[3] Although certain rights are given to licensees under the RTA 2004. See paras 2–22 to 2–27. A licence is a permission given by an owner of an interest in land to another person to enter his or her land, which entry would otherwise be a trespass: *Thomas v Sorrell* (1823) Vaugh 330, 124 ER 1098. See Lyall, A., *Land Law in Ireland*, 2nd edn (Dublin: Roundhall Sweet & Maxwell, 2000) at Ch.18. Other arrangements which may be regarded as licences, although not strictly so-called, include a caretaker's agreement, persons sharing a house under a "rent a room" scheme or in "digs", agreements with lodgers and guests and where the person occupying accommodation does not have exclusive possession.

[4] A landlord cannot refer a matter to the PRTB if the tenancy is not registered. In contrast, a

rules on termination of tenancies contained in Pt 5 and a tenant can benefit from the security of tenure provisions contained in Pt 4. For residential tenancies falling outside the ambit of the RTA 2004, the statutory provisions which existed before its enactment still apply. In that instance, the landlord can avail of remedies such as ejectment for non-payment of rent or breach of the tenant's other obligations,[5] while the tenant can avail of the statutory rights such as compensation for disturbance and compensation for improvements.[6] Again, all of these rights and remedies apply only where a relationship of landlord and tenant exists, in the absence of which they will have no application.

2–04 A further important aspect to the landlord and tenant relationship is that it creates a property interest in land. This interest can be transferred by subletting or assignment, subject to the terms of the tenancy agreement or any applicable statutory provisions.[7] A tenant is also entitled to exclusive possession of the dwelling for the period of the tenancy, which he or she can assert not only against third parties but also against the landlord.[8] In contrast, a licence arrangement generally only creates personal rights, which cannot be assigned or passed on to someone else. This means that a licensee cannot transfer their interest and third parties who purchase the licensor's interest, take it free of the licence and are not bound by it.[9] In addition, a licensee has no right to exclusive possession.

2–05 It is difficult to assess what exactly is required to establish that a tenancy relationship is in existence and this has been the subject of much litigation.[10] The courts have endorsed certain principles, which set out the elements of a landlord and tenant relationship. However, although the existence of these elements are indicative of the relationship of landlord and tenant, they merely

---

tenant can refer a matter to the PRTB even if the tenancy is not registered. See Ch.9 on Dispute Resolution.

[5] Section 52 of the Landlord and Tenant Law (Amendment) Act (Ireland) 1860.

[6] See paras 7–51 to 7–52.

[7] If the RTA 2004 applies to the dwelling, s.16(k) requires that the tenant obtains the landlord's consent before a tenant can sublet or assign his or her interest. See paras 4–23 to 4–24. See para.1.18 of the Law Reform Commission's paper on General Law of Landlord and Tenant (LRC CP28-2003), whereby the Commission's preliminary conclusion was that Irish law should retain the notion that all tenancies confer an estate or interest in the land in the tenant and that legislation should make clear that the absence of this prevents the relationship of landlord and tenant from arising.

[8] Section 16(c) and 16(e) of the RTA 2004 require the tenant to allow the landlord or any person or persons acting on the landlord's behalf to have access to the dwelling for the purposes of inspecting the dwelling at a time convenient to the tenant and for the purposes of carrying out repairs. See para.4–10.

[9] *Winter Garden Theatre London Ltd v Millennium Productions* [1948] A.C. 173; *Ashburn Anstalt v Arnold* [1989] Ch. 1; *Gale v First National Building Society* [1985] I.R. 609.

[10] See Wylie, *Irish Landlord and Tenant Law*, 2nd edn (Dublin: Butterworths, 1998), Ch.2 for further discussion.

act as indicators in determining whether a tenancy exists and failure to satisfy all of these elements does not necessarily mean that there is no landlord and tenant relationship. Suffice to say that regard is taken of certain factors which suggest the existence of a landlord and tenant relationship, whilst no one factor will be determinative. These different factors are considered individually below.

2. ELEMENTS OF THE LANDLORD AND TENANT RELATIONSHIP

A. Deasy's Act

2–06 The basis of the landlord and tenant relationship was fundamentally changed by the Landlord and Tenant Law (Amendment) Act (Ireland) 1860, commonly known as Deasy's Act, which defined the landlord and tenant relationship at s.3 as follows:

> The relation of landlord and tenant shall be deemed to be founded on the express or implied contract of the parties and not upon tenure of service, and a reversion shall not be necessary to such relation, which shall be deemed to subsist in all cases in which there shall be an agreement by one party to hold land from or under another in consideration of any rent.

Few Irish decisions have referred to s.3 of Deasy's Act in assessing whether a landlord and tenant relationship is in existence and it is doubtful whether it has been of much aid to judges in this regard.[11] Section 3 does not mention any positive indicia of a tenancy (other than rent)[12] but that said, it would seem that its purpose was not really to define the landlord and tenant relationship but to effect a change in the nature of the relationship from one based on service to a contractual one.[13] The fact that the section refers to the relationship based on an "express or implied" contract suggests that it is the intention of the parties that is important, whether this is contained in a written or oral contract or can be implied by the parties' conduct.

B. Construction of the Agreement

2–07 The starting point in assessing whether a landlord and tenant relationship exists or not is the agreement itself. The construction of an agreement can

---

[11] *Irish Shell & BP Ltd v Costello Limited* [1981] I.L.R.M. 66. Also see, Wylie, *Landlord and Tenant Law*, 2nd edn (Dublin: Butterworths, 1998), Ch.2 for further discussion of the section and the Law Reform Commission's *Consultation Paper on General Law of Landlord and Tenant* (LRC CP28-2003).

[12] Rent is considered in the context of s.3 of Deasy's Act and generally in assessing the existence of a landlord and tenant relationship at paras 2–20 to 2–21.

[13] See Wylie, *Landlord and Tenant Law*, 2nd edn (Dublin: Butterworths, 1998), para.2.10.

indicate whether the parties intended a landlord and tenant relationship to come into existence. In *Irish Shell & BP Ltd v Costello Ltd*,[14] Griffin J. stated:

> "One must look at the transaction as a whole and at any indications that one finds in the terms of the contract between the two parties to find whether in fact it is intended to create a relationship of landlord and tenant or that of licensor and licensee."[15]

If the tenancy is a written agreement, regard should be had to the terms of the agreement. The terms of an agreement will shed light on what the parties agreed and whether there was an intention to enter into a landlord and tenant relationship. If the tenancy is not a written agreement, the terms of the agreement can be determined by the terms as expressed orally between the parties or terms which can be implied by the nature of the conduct between them.[16] However, it is important to note that a court will not deem the terms set down in an agreement as always reflecting the true nature of the relationship of the parties and will go behind any label that the parties put on the agreement or the terms of the agreement which do not in fact reflect the reality of the situation.

C. Intention of the Parties

2–08 In assessing what type of relationship has been created, the court in construing the agreement will try and ascertain the true intention of the parties. The case of *Gatien Motor Co. Ltd v Continental Oil Co. of Ireland Ltd*[17] is a good illustration of how the court goes about this exercise. In that case, the landlord refused to agree to a renewal of the tenant's three-year lease, unless the tenant left the premises on the expiration of the three years for one week, to then resume occupation after the premises was vacant for that one-week period. The reason for insisting on this arrangement was to prevent the tenant acquiring statutory rights to a new tenancy. The tenant, however, refused to give up possession.[18] It was finally agreed that the tenant could stay on in the property on condition that for one week, when the three-year lease came to an end, he would occupy the premises as a caretaker and not as a tenant and a new lease agreement could be entered into after the expiration of that week. When the lease expired the tenant claimed a statutory right to a new tenancy.

The Circuit Court held that the tenant occupied the premises under a tenancy when the caretaker's agreement was signed by the parties. Ultimately, the

---

¹⁴ [1981] I.L.R.M. 66.
¹⁵ [1981] I.L.R.M. 66 at 70. Approved in *Governor of the National Maternity Hospital v McGouran* [1994] 1 I.L.R.M. 521.
¹⁶ *Bellew v Bellew* [1982] I.R. 447.
¹⁷ [1979] I.R. 406.
¹⁸ This case related to a business tenancy and the tenant refused to vacate as he was of the view that the goodwill of his business would be damaged.

Supreme Court held that the agreement between the parties during that one-week period did not amount to a tenancy agreement, stating there was no basis to depart from the express terms of the written caretaker's agreement. The Supreme Court emphasised a clause in the agreement which stated that the person in possession occupied as a caretaker. In addition it was stated that no rent was payable by the occupier during the caretaker's week. It is clear in that case that the Supreme Court was not prepared to go behind the express terms of the agreement. The parties had set out the terms of the agreement in writing and those terms were considered to be clear evidence as to what the parties intended.

2–09 In an earlier decision of *David Allen & Sons, Billposting, Ltd v King*,[19] the court limited itself to the express terms of the agreement to ascertain the intention of the parties. In the agreement the parties were described as licensor and licensee. The agreement gave permission to the licensee to place advertisements by the side of a cinema in Dublin. The licensor subsequently granted a lease to a third party but it did not contain the clause which allowed for placing advertisements along the side of the cinema wall. The licensee sued for breach of the licence agreement. It was held that no tenancy had been created and that all that was in being was a licence agreement.[20] This decision was upheld in the Irish Court of Appeal and was further upheld on appeal to the House of Lords.[21] The House of Lords limited itself solely to the words of the agreement which the parties had entered into. Lord Buckmaster L.C. stated:

> "I attach some considerable importance to this phrase; it is the description in the body of the document of what the parties intended that the document should be, and it is stated in plain language that the description of the document is that of a licence. It is not a letting or a tenancy or anything of the kind, but a licence."[22]

The High Court in *Governors of the National Maternity Hospital v McGouran*[23] adopted a similar approach. In that case, in May 1986, the Secretary Manager of the plaintiff hospital approached the defendant and inquired if she would be interested in running a shop in the hospital premises, which the defendant agreed to. During negotiations between the parties reference was made to the "lease" or "tenancy", however, the agreement which was drawn up and signed by both parties stated that "the provisions of this agreement are intended to constitute a licence only. Possession of the premises shall be retained for the hospital subject to the rights granted by and to the provisions of this agreement and nothing in

---

[19] [1915] 2 I.R. 213.

[20] Madden J. held that, "it is in plain terms a licence, and I am at a loss to conceive why we should exercise our ingenuity for the purpose of giving to it a different character or effect, whether by way of demise, restrictive covenant, or grant of an incorporeal hereditament", at p.246.

[21] *King v Allen & Sons, Billposting* [1916] 2 A.C. 54.

[22] [1916] 2 A.C. 54 at 59.

[23] [1994] 1 I.L.R.M. 521.

this agreement is intended to confer any tenancy on the licensee".[24] Morris J. in the High Court stated that nothing could be clearer from the express terms in the agreement signed by both parties. He also emphasised that the defendant was "a business like person and I am satisfied that she got legal advice in relation to this matter."[25]

2–10 In *Irish Shell & BP Ltd v Costello Ltd (No. 2)*,[26] the Supreme Court had cause to further consider the nature of the relationship of the parties. In that case it was required to consider the situation where the agreement between the parties had expired and when negotiating a further agreement during a period of four months, the defendant continued on in occupation and continued to make payments to the plaintiff for the same amount as the monthly hire charge set out in the original agreement. The plaintiff referred to these payments as "licence fees". On failing to come to any agreement, the plaintiff demanded occupation of the premises. The issue to be determined by the Supreme Court was whether the defendant's occupation during that four-month period amounted to a tenancy or not.

This case demonstrates how difficult it is to conclude whether an agreement amounts to a landlord and tenant agreement, with the Supreme Court divided on the issue and the judges being unable to reach a consensus as to the nature of the agreement during the four-month period.[27] O'Higgins C.J. was of the view that the parties' relationship during that period was one of landlord and tenant but that the tenant was only a tenant at will. He stated:

> "The defendants' continued occupation was the same as that of the previous six months under the expired agreement, and the payments which they made were similar. The reason that they so continued in occupation was the fact that negotiations for a new agreement were proceeding. If the defendants held under a tenancy during the previous six months, it is difficult to accept that their continued occupation, with the plaintiffs' concurrence, changed in character from that of a tenancy into a mere licence as the plaintiffs now contend. In my view, the defendants continued in occupation of the premises in a landlord and tenant relationship, but their tenancy was then merely a tenancy at will … While tenancies at will are not inferred as frequently now as formerly was the case, I believe that they should readily be inferred where there is continued exclusive possession during such a transition period, as appears to have existed in this case."[28]

On the other hand, Henchy J. was of the view that upon termination of the agreement, the defendants continued in occupation as licensees until the demand

---

[24] [1994] 1 I.L.R.M. 521 at 527.
[25] [1994] 1 I.L.R.M. 521 at 525.
[26] [1984] I.R. 511.
[27] The majority held that once the agreement was terminated the defendant continued on in occupation as a trespasser.
[28] [1984] I.R. 511 at 514; O'Higgins C.J. also considered *Heslop v Burns* [1974] 3 All E.R. 406.

of possession was made by the plaintiffs, whereupon the defendants became trespassers. He stated as follows:

> "I am satisfied that a tenancy is not to be inferred. It is true that this Court construed the "licence" of the 14th February 1974, as a tenancy (or a lease as defined by Deasy's Act) but it expressed no opinion on the relationship between the parties when that agreement expired on the 30th June 1974. Notwithstanding that the defendants paid and the plaintiffs accepted, the monthly sum of £111.20 for four months after the expiration of the agreement of 1974, such sums were expressly accepted by the plaintiffs as 'licence fees'. The terms of the written agreement of 1974 (which were the main reason why this Court held that the agreement created the relationship of landlord and tenant) were no longer in operation. I construe the four payments made by the defendants as being part of a tentative and interim arrangement while the parties were negotiating a new agreement."[29]

Henchy J. further stated that there was no objective test which could be applied to a situation and the essential test was establishing the intention of the parties:

> "In all cases it is a question of what the parties intended, and it is not permissible to apply an objective test which would impute to the parties an intention which they never had. It is open to either party to give evidence of the true circumstances of the payments. Thus, if it were shown that such payments as were made by the former tenant were merely provisional payments and had been made in the expectation that a new tenancy would be expressly granted, the payments would not be treated as supporting the presumption of a new tenancy; to treat them as supporting that presumption would be to impute to the parties an agreement which in fact they had never reached."[30]

McCarthy J. dissenting was of the view that the tenancy continued after the agreement expired, and that the defendants were occupying the premises under a periodic tenancy from month to month, and as no notice to quit was served purporting to terminate the tenancy, the defendants were entitled to stay on in possession.[31]

D. Going behind the Terms of the Express Agreement

2–11 Notwithstanding the authorities considered at paras 2–08 to 2–10 above, if the court is of the view that a written agreement does not reflect the true intentions of the parties, the court will look behind its terms and/or the label the parties put on it. *Kenny Homes & Co. Ltd v Leonard*[32] and *Smith v CIE*[33] serve

---

[29]   [1984] I.R. 511 at 517.
[30]   [1984] I.R. 511 at 517–518.
[31]   [1984] I.R. 511 at 523.
[32]   Unreported, High Court, December 11, 1997; unreported, Supreme Court, June 18, 1998.
[33]   Unreported, High Court, October 9, 2002; [2002] IEHC 103.

to illustrate that this can be a difficult exercise. In both cases, the leases concerned commercial agreements, drafted in very similar terms. In *Kenny Homes*, Costello P. in the High Court was of the view that the terms of the agreement could not have been clearer, indicating that the parties did not intend to create a tenancy agreement. This judgment was upheld in the Supreme Court with Lynch J. describing the agreement as being "crystal clear". However, in *Smith*, Peart J. was of the view that a tenancy had been intended by the parties, despite the similarity in the terms of the agreement with that in *Kenny Homes*.

2–12 The Supreme Court went behind the terms of the parties' agreement in the case of *Irish Shell & BP Ltd v Costello Ltd*.[34] In that case, the original agreement entered into on February 14, 1974, stated that the agreement was a licence agreement, while also including a clause stating that nothing in the agreement should be deemed to confer on the hirer the right to exclusive possession or to create the relationship of landlord and tenant. On expiry of the licence agreement, it was replaced with a new agreement, which did not include a similar clause. The Supreme Court held that although the agreement was called a licence agreement, the court would go behind the label which the parties had put on their relationship and held that a tenancy agreement did exist. Griffin J. stated that:

> "Although a document may be described as a licence it does not necessarily follow that merely on that account, it is to be regarded as amounting only to a licence in law."[35]

2–13 In the case of *Whipp v Mackey*,[36] the Supreme Court was willing to look behind the terms of an agreement, where the parties were described as "landlord" and "tenant". It was held that the agreement was more akin to a licence agreement than a tenancy agreement and that neither the application of the term rent to the annual payments or the description of the grantee as the tenant, would be sufficient to determine the character of the document as a tenancy agreement rather than a licence agreement.[37] Similarly, in the case of *Ó'Siodhacháin v O'Mahony*,[38] Kearns J. in the High Court in referring to the decision of *Gatien Motor Co. Ltd v Continental Oil Co. of Ireland Ltd*[39] stated that:

> "in just the same way as the description of a tenancy arrangement as a licence cannot convert a lease into a licence, the converse seems to me to be equally true, namely, that the description under the name of a lease, a licence or

---

[34] [1981] I.L.R.M. 66.
[35] [1981] I.L.R.M. 66 at 70.
[36] [1927] I.R. 406.
[37] Per Kennedy C.J., at 382.
[38] [2002] 4 I.R. 147.
[39] [1979] I.R. 406.

caretaker's agreement cannot operate to convert a permissive occupant into a tenant where all the usual characteristics of a leasing agreement are absent. In the instant case, there is no mention in the first contract of even a single covenant such as would characterise a lease".[40]

2–14 *Gatien Motor Co. Ltd v Continental Oil Co. of Ireland Ltd*[41] demonstrates that the bargaining position of the parties is a factor that may be considered in determining whether the court should go behind the terms of the agreement. Griffin J. stated:

> "The parties negotiated at arms length, both were fully advised legally, and the caretaker's agreement which was signed by [the tenant] expressed the intention of the parties and was entered into at the behest of the solicitors for the tenant."[42]

2–15 The Law Reform Commission[43] has described this aspect of the landlord and tenant relationship, considered at paras 2–11 to 2–14 above, as the most controversial being a subjective requirement which "has gone too far and has resulted in considerable uncertainty in the law and practice".[44]

E. Exclusive Possession

2–16 The right to exclusive possession is an essential characteristic of a tenancy. However, whilst a tenancy cannot exist unless the tenant lives in the dwelling with the benefit of exclusive possession, the fact that there is exclusive possession is not necessarily conclusive that the relationship is one of landlord and tenant. Other types of relationships may also include exclusive possession but this will not elevate the relationship to one of a tenancy.[45] In *Smith v CIE*,[46] Peart J. stated that, "[f]or a tenancy to exist, there is no doubt that exclusive possession of the premises is a pre-requisite … the fact that there is exclusive possession does not preclude the agreement from being a licence."[47]

In determining whether the relationship between two parties is that of landlord and tenant, the Irish courts have attached much weight to the existence of "exclusive possession", although as alluded to above, will not regard it as conclusive. Kenny J. in the Supreme Court decision of *Gatien Motor Co. Ltd v Continental Oil Co. of Ireland Ltd*[48] stated the following:

---

[40] [2002] 4 I.R. 147 at 156.
[41] [1979] I.R. 406.
[42] [1979] I.R. 406 at 415.
[43] *General Law of Landlord and Tenant*, 2003 (LRC CP28–2003).
[44] *General Law of Landlord and Tenant*, 2003 (LRC CP28–2003), para.1–27.
[45] Wylie, *Landlord and Tenant Law*, 2nd edn (Dublin: Butterworths, 1998), para.2.35.
[46] Unreported, High Court, October 9, 2002; [2002] IEHC 103.
[47] Unreported, High Court, October 9, 2002, at p.22.
[48] [1979] I.R. 406.

"When determining whether a person in possession of land is to be regarded as a tenant or as being in some other category, exclusive possession by the person in possession is undoubtedly a most important consideration but it is not decisive. The existence of the relationship of landlord and tenant or some other relationship is determined by the law on a consideration of many factors and not by the label which the parties put on it."[49]

Applying those principles to the case before it, the Supreme Court held that although the occupant had possession which could be described as exclusive, he was still a caretaker and not a tenant. Wylie is of the view that "the rule now may be stated that, if the 'grantee' of the land in question does not have exclusive possession of it, he is clearly not a tenant. If he does have such possession, he may be a tenant but this is not necessarily the case".[50]

2–17 The concept of exclusive possession is an elusive one and a distinction can be made between sole occupation rights and exclusive possession.[51] Persons staying in hotels, guesthouses and hostels will have sole occupation of the room they are staying in but will not have exclusive possession of it. In addition, a person who rents a room from an owner-occupier[52] will generally be deemed to be a licensee, as the owner retains control or continues to exercise dominion over the demised premises.[53]

2–18 Where exclusive possession exists, the tenant will be in control of the premises and the landlord will not have a general right to enter the premises whenever he or she so chooses.[54] In *Governors of the National Maternity Hospital v McGouran*,[55] the defendant argued that she had exclusive occupation of the shop as she was the sole key holder. Morris J. found that this was the full extent of her possession and that the reality of the situation was that the hospital "exercised a dominion over the premises" and the running of it.[56] In reaching this conclusion he looked at the following factors—the hospital required that Mrs McGouran provide a price list for the patrons, they fitted safety catches to the windows to prevent patients from having an accident, they supplemented

---

[49] [1979] I.R. 406 at 420.
[50] Wylie, *Irish Land Law*, 3rd edn (Dublin: Butterworths, 1997), p.904.
[51] See Wylie, *Landlord and Tenant Law*, 2nd edn (Dublin: Butterworths, 1998), para.2.36.
[52] In such a scenario the owner may be availing of the rent a room relief pursuant to s.32 of the Finance Act 2001.
[53] See Ryall, "Lease or Licence? The Contemporary Significance of the Distinction" (2001) 6(3) C.P.L.J. 56.
[54] Where the RTA 2004 applies, a landlord is entitled to reasonable access to the dwelling for the purposes of carrying out an inspection at a time convenient to the tenant and for the purposes of carrying out repairs. See s.16(c) and (e) of the RTA 2004.
[55] [1994] 1 I.L.R.M. 521.
[56] [1994] 1 I.L.R.M. 521 at 528.

fans to the smoke extractor unit and regulated the hours of opening so as not to clash with the hospital canteen.

In *Kenny Homes & Co. Ltd v Leonard*[57] it was also held that the fact that the occupant was the only person in possession of keys to the demised premises, did not necessarily mean that the occupation was exclusive. In that case Costello P. focused on the fact that the licensors had "contractual rights over the site which they could enforce at any time"[58] and held that at most what the occupiers had was a licence. Again this case demonstrates that even if an occupant has sole occupation of a dwelling, it does not necessarily mean that their possession is exclusive. If the owner retains control or dominion over the premises, then the possession will not be exclusive.[59]

2–19 A landlord is obliged by s.12 of the RTA 2004 to give a tenant "peaceful and exclusive occupation" of the dwelling.[60] Therefore, although one of the indicators of a landlord and tenant relationship is that the tenant has exclusive possession of the dwelling, the absence of exclusive possession at a particular time could in fact be a breach of the tenancy agreement, without actually undermining the existence of the landlord and tenant relationship itself.

F. Rent

2–20 As noted at para.2–06 above, s.3 of Deasy's Act provides that an agreement must be made "in consideration of any rent", if it is to amount to a tenancy. Section 1 of Deasy's Act defines rent as "any sum or return in the nature of rent, payable or given by way of compensation for the holding of any lands". However, even if rent is provided for, it will not necessarily mean that a landlord and tenant relationship exists—it is one factor that must be considered in the exercise of determining the nature of relationship.[61] There has been much controversy as to whether rent is necessary for a landlord and tenant relationship to come into being.[62] This was considered in the case of *Irish Shell & BP Ltd v Costello Ltd*,[63] where the issue to be determined by the Supreme Court was whether a licence agreement under which a petrol station was operated constituted a tenancy. The agreement required the hirer to pay hiring fees for use of petrol tanks and pumps, machinery and other items. It was argued that these

---

[57] Unreported, High Court, December 11, 1997; followed in the Supreme Court, unreported, June 18, 1998.
[58] Unreported, High Court, December 11, 1997 at p.16.
[59] See also English decisions on this issue: *Street v Mountford* [1985] A.C. 809; *SG Securities Ltd v Vaughan* [1988] 2 All E.R. 173; *Antoniades v Villiers and Anor* [1988] 3 All E.R. 1058.
[60] RTA 2004, s.12(1)(a).
[61] See *Whipp v Mackey* [1927] I.R. 406 where rent was provided for in the agreement but the Supreme Court held that it was in fact a license agreement.
[62] See Wylie, paras 2–37 to 2–38; *General Law of Landlord and Tenant* (LRC CP28–2003) at 1.21.
[63] [1981] I.L.R.M. 66.

fees did not amount to rent within the meaning of s.3 of Deasy's Act. The Supreme Court held that these fees were in substance rent within the meaning of Deasy's Act and thus created the relationship of landlord and tenant. More recently in *Ó'Siodhacháin v O'Mahony*,[64] Kearns J. held that the relationship under consideration in that case did not amount to a relationship of landlord and tenant as the lease failed to specify any rent.

2–21 The Law Reform Commission provisionally recommended that it should be made clear by statute that the universal rule is that a tenancy does not exist unless the occupier of the land in question is obliged to pay rent or some other form of consideration in return for the right to occupy.[65] Under the RTA 2004, for a dwelling to fall within its jurisdiction, it must be let for rent or valuable consideration.[66]

3. LICENSEES UNDER THE RTA 2004

2–22 In the private rented sector, where the relationship is not one of landlord and tenant, it is often the case that a person's right to occupy a dwelling exists in the nature of a licence. Licenses are ordinarily said to exist where

    (a) a person is staying in a hotel, guesthouse or hostel;
    (b) a person is sharing a house or apartment with its owner under the "rent-a-room"[67] scheme or "in digs";
    (c) a person occupying accommodation under a formal licence arrangement, where the owner is not resident, where the occupants are not entitled to its exclusive use and the owner has continuing access to the accommodation; and
    (d) where a person is staying in rented accommodation at the invitation of the tenant.

2–23 The RTA 2004 does not apply to licensees except in the limited circumstances discussed at paras 2–25 to 2–27 below. For the RTA 2004 to apply to a licensee, there must always be at least one tenant in the premises. In that instance, the licensee is not present in the premises with the permission of the landlord but with the permission of the tenant.[68] In this regard tenants are under a statutory obligation to inform the landlord of the identity of all persons who are residing in the premises, although the consent of the landlord is not first required in respect of a licensee's occupation, unless required by the terms of a

---

[64] [2002] 4 I.R. 147 at 156.
[65] *General Law of Landlord and Tenant* (LRC CP28–2003), para.1.23.
[66] RTA 2004, s.4(1).
[67] Finance Act 2001, s.32.
[68] Licences must not be confused with sub-lettings or an assignment.

tenancy agreement.[69] Therefore, the landlord has no right to object to the licensee residing in the premises as he or she would in the context of a prospective tenant.

2–24 Where a licensee occupies a dwelling he or she is not bound by the terms of the tenancy agreement. It is the tenant who must perform all duties under the tenancy agreement and it is the tenant who obtains rights by reason of the tenancy. In addition, a tenant is responsible for all of the acts and omissions of their licensees. For example, if the licensee engages in antisocial behaviour that may be a ground on which the landlord may be permitted to terminate the tenancy agreement. It is important therefore for a tenant taking in a licensee that the agreement between them will ensure that the tenant will be in a position to meet his or her obligations under the tenancy agreement.

2–25 Section 50(7) of the RTA 2004 gives a licensee a right to request the landlord of a dwelling to allow him or her become a tenant of the dwelling. A licensee has this right only where he or she is in lawful occupation of the dwelling[70] and the tenancy has the status of a Part 4 tenancy.[71] Under s.50(8), the landlord may not unreasonably refuse to accede to such a request. If the request is acceded to, the landlord's acceptance must be in writing and must acknowledge that the person has become a tenant of the landlord.[72] The terms of the agreement will be the same terms as the Part 4 tenancy or as appropriately modified.[73] The benefit of a Part 4 tenancy will not apply until the former licensee has completed six months of continuous occupation, which is calculated counting time in continuous occupation as a licensee or as a licensee and tenant.[74]

2–26 As discussed in the preceding paragraph, under s.50(8) of the RTA 2004, a landlord cannot unreasonably refuse to accede to a licensee's request to become a tenant of a tenancy. There is no guidance given in the RTA 2004, as to what will be deemed an unreasonable withholding of consent. However, if for example, a landlord wishes to move into the dwelling or wishes to carry out refurbishment or renovations, refusal of consent in those circumstances would not be deemed unreasonable.[75] Further, if for example the reason for the

---

[69] RTA 2004, s.16(n).

[70] As referred to at para.2–23, s.16(n) of the RTA 2004 requires a tenant to notify the landlord in writing of the identity of all persons ordinarily residing in the dwelling. Accordingly, it is arguable that if the tenant failed to inform the landlord of the persons residing in the premises that would make the licensee's occupation unlawful.

[71] RTA 2004, s.50(7). A Part 4 tenancy arises after a tenant has resided in a dwelling for six months. The effect of a Part 4 tenancy is to give the tenant security of tenure for a further period of 3½ years. Part 4 tenancies, their meaning and effect are considered in detail in Ch.7.

[72] RTA 2004, s.50(8)(a).

[73] RTA 2004, s.50(8)(b)(i).

[74] RTA 2004, s.50(5).The requirement is that there is six months continuous occupation. It does not matter that the person may have been a licensee during part or all of this period.

[75] Section 34 of the RTA 2004 permits the termination of a Part 4 tenancy on these grounds.

landlord's refusal of consent is because the licensee has been engaging in anti-social behaviour, it seems that such a refusal would be reasonable in those circumstances.

2–27 A licensee has locus standi to refer a dispute to the PRTB for dispute resolution services, where the landlord has refused consent to the licensee becoming a tenant of the tenancy.[76] This is the only circumstance where a licensee can refer a dispute to the PRTB. The PRTB does not have jurisdiction to deal with any other disputes referred by licensees. Therefore, if for example, a tenant has failed to pay a deposit back to a licensee, the PRTB has no jurisdiction to deal with that dispute. However, if a licensee is of the view that he or she is actually a tenant, that person may refer that matter to the PRTB, who can determine whether the relationship is in fact a landlord and tenant relationship or merely a licensee relationship. If it is the latter, the PRTB will have no jurisdiction to consider the matter further.

4. PRTB CASES

2–28 There have been very few cases before the PRTB, where the issue in dispute relates to whether the relationship between the parties amounts to a landlord and tenant relationship. In the tenancy tribunal decision of *Leonard v McHugh & Anor*[77] the landlord submitted that the PRTB had no jurisdiction to deal with the dispute as the tenants did not have exclusive possession of the dwelling and because the dwelling was her principal private residence.[78] In support of this argument, she stated that some of her possessions were in one of the bedrooms of the dwelling, that she had resided in the property with the exception of six months, that she had many friends over to the dwelling, hosted a birthday party there and had all her bank statements and tax documents posted to the dwelling. The tenants argued that there was no evidence of the landlord's possessions in the dwelling, that all the rooms were empty, that all the utility bills were put in the tenants' names and that the landlord or her friends never stayed in the dwelling. The tenancy tribunal concluded that on the balance of probabilities, the tenants had sole occupancy of the dwelling.[79]

In the case of *PRTB v Coilog*,[80] the landlord was prosecuted by the PRTB pursuant to s.126 of the RTA 2004, for his failure to comply with the terms of a determination order of the PRTB. The matter was dealt with by way of adjudication hearing before the PRTB and subsequently on appeal by a tenancy

---

[76]   RTA 2004, s.76(4). See also para.9–16.
[77]   TR44/DR476/2007, June 29, 2007.
[78]   RTA 2004, s.3(2)(g).
[79]   Consequently, the tenants were able to claim damages for the unlawful termination of the tenancy and were each awarded the sum of €5,000 by way of compensation.
[80]   TR41/DR832/2006, September 18, 2006.

tribunal. The landlord did not raise the issue of whether the relationship was one of landlord and tenant until he was served with a summons for the purposes of the section 126 prosecution. During the hearing of the prosecution he claimed that there was no landlord and tenant relationship in existence, as the tenant was never considered by him to be a tenant and that he did not pay a security deposit. Both the District Court and the Circuit Court on appeal were satisfied that the relationship between the parties did amount to one of landlord and tenant and convicted him of an offence pursuant to s.126 of the RTA 2004.[81]

---

[81] On conviction the landlord was fined €2,000, with three months to pay, and 10 days in default. He was also ordered to pay compensation to one of the tenants in the sum of €6,158, with one month to pay and 10 days in default. The PRTB was awarded its costs in both the District Court and the Circuit Court. (District Court hearing, January 7, 2008. Circuit Court hearing, July 3, 2008.)

Chapter 3

THE APPLICATION OF THE RESIDENTIAL
TENANCIES ACT 2004

1. Background

3–01 The Commission on the Private Rented Residential Sector (the "Commission") was launched in July 1999 by the Minister for Housing and Urban Renewal,[1] to consider what was described by many as a much awaited reform of the residential sector.[2] The Commission was charged with the task of examining the working of the landlord and tenant relationship in respect of residential tenancies in the private sector and with making such recommendations, including changes to the law, as the Commission considered proper, equitable and feasible.[3] As enacted, the Residential Tenancies Act 2004 (the "RTA 2004") mirrors to a considerable degree the recommendations made by the Commission.[4] Its work, therefore, was an important factor in shaping the framework for the application of the RTA 2004 and the jurisdiction of the Private Residential Tenancies Board (the "PRTB").

3–02 The RTA 2004 applies to every dwelling the subject of a residential tenancy.[5] The RTA 2004 provides a measure of security of tenure for tenants and specifies minimum obligations applying to landlords and tenants. It also contains provisions relating to rent setting and reviews and procedures for the termination of tenancies, including fixed notice periods linked to the duration of a tenancy. In particular, however, one of the main consequences of the enactment of the RTA 2004 was the establishment of the PRTB.[6] For the first time in the residential sector in Ireland, a body was charged with responsibility for the operation of the landlord and tenant regime generally, as opposed to certain discrete aspects of it. The PRTB was given the function of operating a

---

[1] *Report of the Commission on the Private Rented Residential Sector*, July 2000 (the "Report of the Commission"), "Introduction", p.1. See also para.1–03.
[2] See for example Seanad Éireann, Vol.177, Col.723, July 2, 2004, second stage.
[3] Report of the Commission, "Introduction", p.1.
[4] The Commission's recommendations are contained in the Report of the Commission, at paras 8.3–8.10.
[5] There are limited exceptions to the application of the RTA 2004. These are provided for at s.3(2) and 3(3) of the RTA 2004. Note that s.3(3) of the RTA 2004 was inserted by s.100(2)(b) of the Housing (Miscellaneous Provisions) Act 2009.
[6] "Private Residential Tenancies Board, Annual Report, 1/9/2004–31/12/2005", p.2.

system of tenancy registration and providing information and policy advice. The PRTB was empowered to prosecute landlords and tenants who breached various aspects of the landlord and tenant code provided for under the RTA 2004. Most importantly, however, the PRTB was given jurisdiction (taking over from the courts) to operate a dispute resolution service, so that disputes arising between landlords and tenants could be resolved "cheaply and speedily".[7] All of this was in contrast to the situation that existed previously, where bodies such as local authorities were given jurisdiction over certain aspects only of the private rented sector, such as the registration of residential tenancies and the enforcement of rent book and housing standards regulations. Any dispute arising between a landlord and a tenant was a matter that could only be resolved before the courts.[8]

3–03 This chapter explores the application of the RTA 2004, considering the type of dwellings which are explicitly excluded from its scope, in addition to the meaning given to a number of key terms which bear on the application of the legislation, such as "landlord", "tenant" and "dwelling". The jurisdiction of the PRTB is considered in the context of its dispute resolution functions in Ch.9.

2. APPLICATION OF THE RTA 2004

3–04 The RTA 2004 applies to every dwelling the subject of a residential tenancy.[9] There are limited exceptions to this which are dealt with at paras 3–21 to 3–62.[10] The RTA 2004 has no application in circumstances where two parties agree (either orally or in writing) that they will enter into a tenancy arrangement. An actual tenancy must be or have been in existence for a matter to come within the jurisdiction of the RTA 2004.[11]

As the RTA 2004 applies to tenancies only, it excludes from the jurisdiction of the PRTB, a number of disputes relating to residential accommodation that

---

[7] The Long Title to the RTA 2004.

[8] The complex nature of the RTA 2004 has, however, been the subject of judicial comment. Laffoy J. in *Canty v Private Residential Tenancies Board*, described the RTA 2004 as "an extremely complex piece of legislation" ([2007] IEHC 243; unreported, High Court, Laffoy J. August 8, 2007, at p.11).

[9] Section 3(1) of the RTA 2004 provides that "[s]ubject to subsection (2), this Act applies to every dwelling, the subject of a tenancy (including a tenancy created before the passing of this Act)." The RTA 2004, therefore, applies even to a tenancy of a dwelling created before its enactment. Given the definition of a tenancy includes a tenancy that has terminated, the effect of s.3(1) is that even a tenancy that was terminated prior to September 2004, comes within the scope of the RTA 2004. In practice, however, this is of limited relevance (and is even more so with the passing of time), in particular given that the new obligations imposed by the RTA 2004 on landlords and tenants are not retrospective. In addition, there are time limits imposed for the referral of particular disputes to the PRTB under Pt 6 of the RTA 2004. See paras 9–45 to 9–53.

[10] These exceptions are the subject of s.3(2) and s.3(3) of the RTA 2004.

[11] RTA 2004, s.3(1). See also the definition of "contract of tenancy" at s.4(1) of the RTA 2004, which provides that a contract of tenancy "does not include an agreement to create a tenancy".

arise in the private rented sector. Most frequently these disputes concern the payment of booking deposits or monies paid in advance to secure accommodation before a tenancy comes into being. A common example of such a dispute is set out in the following scenario:

Example

"*X*" views a dwelling for rent that is owned by "*Y*". *X* indicates to *Y* that he is interested in renting the dwelling. *Y* informs *X* that she will rent the dwelling to *X*, provided he pays the sum of €250 upfront, as part payment of a €500 deposit and returns within three days with the remainder of the deposit and one month's rent. Two days later *X* returns with the remainder of the deposit and one month's rent, to find that *Y* has let the dwelling to another individual, who is now in occupation of the dwelling. *Y* refuses to refund *X* the part payment of the deposit of €250 which he paid to her.

The scenario involving *X* and *Y* is not a case which falls within the jurisdiction of the RTA 2004, as no tenancy can be said to have come into existence. The arrangement between *X* and *Y* is in effect no more than an agreement to enter into a tenancy. The consequence is that the aggrieved party *X* cannot avail of the dispute resolution procedure provided for under Pt 6 of the RTA 2004 and accordingly, cannot refer a dispute to the PRTB for the purposes of seeking to recover the payment of €250 made by him. As was the case prior to the coming into force of the RTA 2004, the remedy available to *X* is to pursue *Y* through the courts. For this reason, the Small Claims Court continues to deal with disputes relating to the payment of monies to secure residential accommodation, in circumstances where no tenancy has come into existence.[12]

3. INTERPRETATION

3–05 Sections 4 and 5 are the interpretation provisions of the RTA 2004 and provide for the definition of a number of key terms. Of particular relevance for the purposes of dealing with the application of the RTA 2004, is the definition of (a) "dwelling", (b) "landlord", (c) "tenant", (d) "tenancy", (e) "contract of tenancy", (f) "lease" and (g) "tenancy agreement". Each of these definitions is considered in turn below.

---

[12] Disputes relating to deposits paid for a holiday letting or a dwelling where the landlord resides, are other examples of similar type disputes that fall outside the jurisdiction of the PRTB and may still therefore be referred to the Small Claims Court. The procedure for referring a dispute to the Small Claims Court is provided for under the District Court Rules 1997 (S.I. No. 93 of 1997) and the District Court (Small Claims Procedure) Rules 1999 (S.I. No. 191 of 1999). The monetary jurisdiction of the Small Claims Court is €2,000.

A. Dwelling

(i) Definition

3–06 A dwelling is defined at s.4(1) of the RTA 2004 as follows:

> "dwelling" means, subject to subsection (2), a property let for rent or valuable consideration as a self-contained residential unit and includes any building or part of a building used as a dwelling and any out office, yard, garden or other land appurtenant to it or usually enjoyed with it and, where the context so admits, includes a property available for letting[13] but excludes a structure that is not permanently attached to the ground and a vessel and a vehicle (whether mobile or not).

In essence, a dwelling for the purposes of the RTA 2004 is a property let for rent or valuable consideration, as a self-contained residential unit and is a structure that is permanently attached to the ground. These characteristics of a dwelling as defined by the RTA 2004 are considered separately below.

(ii) Rent

3–07 In Ireland, the payment of rent or a sum equivalent to rent has been a necessary component for the existence of a tenancy.[14] Section 1 of the Landlord and Tenant Law Amendment Act (Ireland) 1860 ("Deasy's Act") defines rent as including "any sum or return in the nature of rent, payable or given by way of compensation for the holding of any lands". There is no requirement in Deasy's Act that rent be in the form of money.[15] Under the RTA 2004, a dwelling must be let for "rent or valuable consideration" for it to fall within its jurisdiction. Accordingly, where an individual occupies a dwelling, without paying rent or otherwise compensating the owner with valuable consideration for a right of possession, the dwelling concerned will not be one to which the RTA 2004 applies.

3–08 What is sufficient to constitute rent is not always clear.[16] In *Irish Shell & BP Ltd v Costello Ltd*,[17] the Supreme Court was divided as to whether rent was payable on the facts of the case before it, which involved a commercial agreement between the owner and occupier of a petrol station. Griffin J. stated "the periodic payments made by the defendants were in fact rent, although

---

[13] As noted at para.3–04, a tenancy of a dwelling must be or have been in existence for the application of the RTA 2004 to arise. Accordingly, although the definition of a dwelling includes a property "available for letting", the RTA 2004 will nevertheless have no application, unless a tenancy is or was in existence.

[14] Section 3 of Deasy's Act provides that, "[t]he relation of landlord and tenant ... shall be deemed to subsist in all cases in which there shall be an agreement by one party to hold land from another in consideration of any rent."

[15] See also Wylie, *Landlord and Tenant Law*, 2nd edn (Dublin: Butterworths, 1998), para.10.04.

[16] See Ch.2 that considers rent in the context of the landlord and tenant relationship.

[17] [1981] I.L.R.M. 66.

cloaked under the guise or under the label of payment for hire of the equipment".[18] While this reflected the decision of the majority of the Supreme Court, Kenny J. dissented on this point and was of the view that there was nothing in the nature of rent payable.

What constitutes rent or valuable consideration for the purposes of the RTA 2004, is a matter that is yet to be considered in any great detail in the PRTB's tenancy tribunal decisions. A promise by a tenant to paint the outside walls of a dwelling once a year at his or her own expense, would arguably satisfy the requirement of "valuable consideration". It will, however, be a question to be determined in each case having regard to all the circumstances and with consideration to whether all the other elements of a tenancy relationship exist.[19] In *Kelly v Warnham*[20] the appellant was the landlord of a property that had been occupied by the respondent's sister.[21] The landlord argued that no tenancy of a dwelling within the meaning of the RTA 2004 arose by reason, amongst other matters, that the respondent's sister had not paid rent but merely contributed to the utility bills and the running costs of the dwelling. The landlord maintained that the respondent's sister had initially paid the sum of IR£20 per week and later €30 and that she sometimes paid no rent,[22] such as when she was between jobs. The landlord also stated that he regarded the respondent's sister as a friend and not a tenant. The tenancy tribunal in its findings stated (without elaborating further) that it did not accept the landlord's claim that the payments made by the respondent's sister were "contributions" and not rent.

3–09 When considering if an amount of rent or valuable consideration is payable, it is not necessary to consider whether the agreement between the parties is adequate. In other words, there is no requirement under the RTA 2004 that the rent or valuable consideration reflects the true value of the agreement between the parties, which would generally be the market rental value of the property.[23] This is demonstrated in *Kelly v Warnham*[24] where weekly (or often less frequent) payments of IR£20 and €30, satisfied the requirement of "rent or

---

[18]   [1981] I.L.R.M. 66 at 71. Also see Wylie, *Landlord and Tenant Law*, 2nd edn (Dublin: Butterworths, 1998), para.2.37.

[19]   See Ch.2 on the Landlord and Tenant Relationship.

[20]   TR147/DR20/2007, June 4, 2008.

[21]   The respondent's sister was the former tenant of the dwelling the subject of the dispute. The respondent's sister had died during the course of the tenancy. The respondent referred a dispute to the PRTB seeking the return of her sister's belongings. The respondent claimed that she had locus standi to refer the dispute in the capacity as her sister's personal representative. See also para.3–10 that considers this case further.

[22]   The tenancy tribunal report refers to the payment of "rent" in summarising the landlord's arguments, although it is clear from the report as a whole that the landlord's contention was that no rent was paid by the respondent's sister but merely that she contributed to the utility bills and the running costs of the dwelling.

[23]   Note, however, that s.19(1) of the RTA 2004, prohibits the setting of rent at an amount that is greater than the "market rent" for the tenancy at that time. See para.6–04.

[24]   TR147/DR20/2007, June 4, 2008.

valuable consideration" to bring the dwelling concerned within the scope of the RTA 2004.

(iii) Self-contained residential unit

3–10 A dwelling must comprise a self-contained residential unit for it to fall within the jurisdiction of the RTA 2004. "[S]elf-contained residential unit" is defined in the RTA 2004 as "includ[ing] the form of accommodation commonly known as "bedsit" accommodation".[25]

In *Kelly v Warnham*[26] the landlord had agreed with the respondent's sister that she might occupy a granny flat, which was attached to his family dwelling house, pending the completion of an apartment that the landlord was constructing for her. As considered above, the landlord argued that the dispute did not come within the jurisdiction of the PRTB on the basis that no tenancy of a dwelling existed for the purposes of the RTA 2004. In the submissions made by the landlord to the tenancy tribunal, he outlined that planning permission for the construction of the granny flat required that it not be let out but that it be for family occupation only. The tenancy tribunal rejected the landlord's contentions that no tenancy of a dwelling existed for the purposes of the RTA 2004. In its findings the tenancy tribunal stated that it was satisfied the apartment constituted a "dwelling" within the meaning of s.4 of the RTA 2004, as it was a property let for rent as a self-contained residential unit, with its own separate entrance and with no direct access from the adjoining dwelling, which was the landlord's family home. It further found the "fact that services such as heating and electricity were provided from the adjoining dwelling, and not separately metered or billed to the tenant, did not take the dwelling outside the definition in Section 4".[27]

In *Mutoola and Ors v Butt*[28] the downstairs of a rented house was used for the purposes of a mosque. The rest of the house was used by the applicants, who each maintained that they were tenants to whom the RTA 2004 applied. There were four bedrooms upstairs in the house (which the applicants occupied)[29] and a kitchen downstairs. Evidence was given on behalf of the applicants that the people who attended the mosque used the bathroom and the kitchen but only with the applicants' permission. The applicants submitted to the tenancy tribunal that the residential component of the premises was self-contained, which the tenants occupied as tenants in common, while having a tenancy in their own particular rooms. The respondent, who was the landlord of the house, maintained that the intention was that it was to be let as one unit for the benefit of an Islamic Centre.[30]

---

[25] RTA 2004, s.4(1).

[26] TR147/DR20/2007, June 4, 2008.

[27] Tenancy tribunal report, p.7.

[28] TR113/DR1203/2007, November 21, 2007.

[29] The occupant of the fourth room did not join as a party to the application made to the PRTB for dispute resolution services.

[30] The landlord of the premises was the respondent to the application for dispute resolution

The tenancy tribunal concluded that it was not satisfied that the premises occupied by the applicants was a "dwelling" as defined in s.4(1) of the RTA 2004. In its report it recorded that there was evidence to support the view that the occupation of the rooms was an integral part of the activities of the Islamic Centre. It gave the example that one room was occupied by one of the applicants rent free in his capacity as Imam to the Islamic community. The tenancy tribunal also had regard to what it called the intimate nature of the relationship between the parties. It considered that this was persuasive; in particular, the fact that one of the applicants was the company director of the Islamic Centre and was extensively involved with its running. The tenancy tribunal found insufficient evidence to support the contention that the residential portion of the premises constituted a separate dwelling as required by the RTA 2004.

3–11 The Rent Restrictions Act 1960 excluded from its application "a dwelling which is a separate and self-contained flat forming part of any buildings which, after the commencement of this Act, were reconstructed by way of conversion into two or more separate and self-contained flats".[31] While the Rent Restrictions Act 1960 has been repealed, it is interesting to consider the judicial interpretation of "separate and self-contained flat" for the purposes of that legislation,[32] when considering the meaning of "self-contained residential unit" as defined in the RTA 2004.

In *Broadhead v Knox*[33] a landlord let the two top floors of a house and the lavatory on the middle floor to one tenant, while letting the floor below the lavatory to another tenant. The issue before the Circuit Court was whether the upper levels were a "separate and self-contained flat" for the purposes of the Rent Restrictions Act 1960. It was argued that the upper flat was not separate and self-contained, on the basis that there was no physical division or barrier between the upper and lower sections of the house let separately. In addition, the tenant of the lower flat could see up the stairs to the door of the lavatory. It was held that the upper flat was a separate and self-contained flat.[34]

In *Elkinson v Cassidy*[35] the defendant was a tenant under a tenancy agreement of a flat in a house. There was no toilet in the flat but the tenancy agreement allowed the tenant to use a toilet in another part of the house or one in the yard of the house. In considering whether the flat was a dwelling which was excluded

---

services made to the PRTB. The immediate tenant of the premises was the Islamic Centre. The applicants who submitted the application for dispute resolution services to the PRTB, claimed that their interest in the dwelling was in the nature of a sub-tenancy, with the Islamic Centre being the head-tenant.

[31] Rent Restrictions Act 1960, s.3(2)(g).
[32] See also Wylie, *Landlord and Tenant Law*, 2nd edn (Dublin: Butterworths, 1998), at para.29.18, which also considers the meaning of "separate and self-contained flat" in the context of the Rent Restrictions Act 1960.
[33] [1975] 109 I.L.T.R. 116.
[34] [1975] 109 I.L.T.R. 116.
[35] [1976] 110 I.L.T.R. 27.

from the provisions of the Rent Restrictions Act 1960, the Circuit Court held that a dwelling without its own toilet was not a self-contained flat. In context of the RTA 2004 however, it seems unlikely that such an authority could be upheld, given s.4(1) of the RTA 2004 defines "self-contained residential unit" as including "the form of accommodation commonly known as "bedsit" accommodation".[36] In this regard, bed-sit accommodation in the private rented sector, generally involves the use of shared bathroom or toilet facilities.

(iv) Permanently attached

3–12 A dwelling as defined under the RTA 2004, excludes a structure that is not permanently attached to the ground and a vessel and a vehicle regardless of whether it is mobile or not.[37] Accordingly, a mobile home or a caravan that is let for residential purposes will not come within the jurisdiction of the RTA 2004. In certain cases, however, it may be arguable that a mobile home is permanently affixed to the ground by reason, for example, of concrete encasing and particular plumbing features. This is an issue that is yet to be considered in the PRTB's tenancy tribunal decisions.

(v) Excluded from the s.4(1) definition of a dwelling

3–13 The meaning of a "dwelling" for the purposes of the RTA 2004, is complicated by the fact that the definition of a dwelling at s.4(1) (as considered in the preceding paragraphs), does not apply to certain specific references to a dwelling in the RTA 2004. These references are listed at s.4(3) and in those instances the following definition of a dwelling at s.4(2) of the RTA 2004 applies instead:

> The definition of "dwelling" in subsection (1) shall not apply in relation to the construction of references to "dwelling" to which this subsection applies; each such reference shall be construed as a reference to any building or part of a building used as a dwelling (whether or not a dwelling let for rent or valuable consideration) and any out office, yard garden or other land appurtenant to it or usually enjoyed with it.

In essence a "dwelling" as defined at s.4(2) (the "second definition"), is simply a reference to a residential dwelling that may or may not be one to which the RTA 2004 applies. In practice, the second definition of a dwelling will generally be a reference to a third party dwelling in the vicinity of or in the same property or apartment complex, as the dwelling (the subject of a tenancy) that falls within the jurisdiction of the RTA 2004. The instances where the second definition of a

---

[36] RTA 2004, s.4(1).

[37] Note in contrast the definition of "dwelling" at s.2 of the Family Home Protection Act 1976. Section 2 defines "dwelling" (in the context of the family home) as meaning "(a) any building, or (b) any structure, vehicle or vessel (whether mobile or not) …".

dwelling is used are limited, as it applies only in the context of ss.12(1)(h), 17(1)(c), 25(2), 136(h), 187(1) and 188(1) of the RTA 2004.[38] Each of those sections make reference to both a dwelling as defined in s.4(1) and to the second definition of a dwelling at s.4(2). As the interpretation of a dwelling at ss.12(1)(h), 17(1)(c), 25(2), 136(h), 187(1) and 188(1) requires much cross-referencing, these provisions have been transcribed in the table below, with the references to a "dwelling" or "dwellings" underlined where the *second definition* applies:

RTA 2004

Section 12(1)(h): Obligations of landlords	(h) If the dwelling is one of a number of <u>dwellings</u> comprising an apartment complex – (i) [the landlord shall] forward to the management company, if any, of the complex any complaint notified in writing by the tenant to him or her …[39]
Section 17(1)(c): "Behave in a way that is anti-social"	"behave in a way that is anti-social" means – (c) engage, persistently, in behaviour that prevents or interferes with the peaceful occupation – (i) by any other person residing in the dwelling concerned, of that dwelling, (ii) by any person residing in any other <u>dwelling</u> contained in the property containing the dwelling concerned, of that other <u>dwelling</u>, or (iii) by any person residing in a <u>dwelling</u> ("<u>neighbourhood dwelling</u>") in the vicinity of the dwelling or the property containing the dwelling concerned, of that <u>neighbourhood dwelling</u>.[40]
Section 25: Non-application of Part 4	(1) This Part does not apply to a tenancy of a dwelling where the conditions specified in subsection (2) are satisfied if the landlord of the dwelling opts, in accordance with subsection (3), for this Part not to apply to it. (2) Those conditions are – (a) the dwelling concerned is one of <u>2 dwellings</u>[41] within a building,

---

[38] RTA 2004, 4(3).
[39] RTA 2004, s.4(3)(a).
[40] RTA 2004, s.4(3)(b).
[41] Note that the second definition of a dwelling only applies to whichever of the dwellings is occupied by the landlord.

        (b) that building, as originally constructed, comprised a single <u>dwelling</u>, and

        (c) the landlord resides in the other <u>dwelling</u>.[42]

Section 136(h): Particulars to be specified in a registration application	(h) if the dwelling is one of a number of <u>dwellings</u> comprising an apartment complex, the name of the management company (if any) of the complex and the registered number and registered office of that company,[43]
Section 187(1): Duty of management companies in relation to certain complaints	(1) This section applies where a tenant of a dwelling which is one of a number of <u>dwellings</u> comprising an apartment complex makes a complaint of the kind referred to in section 12(1)(h) to the landlord of the dwelling and that complaint (the "relevant complaint") is forwarded to the management company of the complex (the "relevant company").[44]
Section 188(1): Provision of information in relation to service charges by management companies	(1) A tenant of a dwelling which is one of a number of <u>dwellings</u> comprising an apartment complex may request the management company (if any) of the complex ("the company") to furnish to him or her particulars in writing of the service charges made by the company in respect of the dwelling in a specified period and how those charges have been calculated.[45]

B. Landlord

(i) Definition

3–14 A "landlord" is defined for the purposes of the RTA 2004, as a person who is entitled to receive rent paid by the tenant of a dwelling. A landlord is also defined as a person who used to be entitled to receive the rent paid by a tenant but no longer is because the tenancy has been terminated.[46]

---

[42] RTA 2004, s.4(3)(c) and (d).

[43] RTA 2004, s.4(3)(e).

[44] RTA 2004, s.4(3)(e).

[45] RTA 2004, s.4(3)(e).

[46] RTA 2004, s.5(1). The definition of a "landlord" to include a person "who has ceased to be so entitled [to receive the rent paid] by reason of the termination of the tenancy" is important as it ensures that the PRTB is not prohibited from dealing with a dispute and making a determination against or in favour of a landlord because the tenancy concerned has terminated. The same applies in the context of the definition of a "tenant", which also includes a person who has ceased to be a tenant by reason of the termination of the tenancy. Further, the definition of a "tenancy" includes a tenancy that has terminated.

(ii) Agents

3–15 An agent or any other person who is entitled (or was entitled) to receive rent on behalf of a landlord, is explicitly excluded from the definition of a landlord under the RTA 2004.[47] In fact, the RTA 2004 has no application to, and consequently, imposes no obligations on letting agents operating within the residential sector. Accordingly, where a letting agent has caused a landlord to be in breach of his or her tenancy obligations or obstructs the PRTB in carrying out its functions,[48] there is no sanction for the agent under the RTA 2004. That said the PRTB has been successful in dealing with uncooperative agents, in the context of applications that it has made to the Circuit Court pursuant to s.189 of the RTA 2004.[49] In the *Private Residential Tenancies Board v Sancta Maria Properties Limited T/A Citi Properties*[50] the PRTB made an application to the Circuit Court for interim relief pursuant to s.189. It sought and was granted an order requiring the respondent (agent of the landlord) to furnish the name and address of the landlord to the PRTB's solicitors.[51]

C. Tenant

(i) Definition

3–16 A "tenant" is defined for the purposes of the RTA 2004 as a person who is entitled to the occupation of a dwelling under a tenancy. The definition of a tenant also includes a former tenant of a dwelling, being a person who has

---

[47] RTA 2004, s.5(1). Section 5(1) defines "landlord" as a person for the time being entitled to receive "otherwise than as agent for another person" the rent paid in respect of a dwelling.

[48] For instance by refusing to provide the PRTB with up-to-date contact details for a landlord.

[49] Section 189 of the RTA 2004 provides that on the request of a person who has referred a dispute to the PRTB, it may make an application for interim or interlocutory relief to the Circuit Court in aid of the Part 6 dispute resolution procedure.

[50] Unreported, Circuit Court, ex tempore, Linnane J., October 27, 2006.

[51] The Commission considered the role and regulation of letting agents in the private rented sector. The Report of the Commission identified how an auctioneer's licence is required to auction goods, including real property and a house agent's licence is required for buying, selling or renting houses for remuneration. It was noted, however, how accommodation agencies are not required to be registered or bonded and that no licence is required to simply provide information on property available for letting. The Commission concluded that letting agencies should be required to have a licence to operate and recommended that legislation be introduced in this area (Report of the Commission, paras 2.10 and 8.10). In July 2004, the Minister for Justice, Equality and Law Reform commissioned the Auctioneering/Estate Agency Review Group (the "Review Group") to examine the licensing and regulatory requirements for property services providers, including auctioneers, estate agents, letting agents and property management agents. The Government, on foot of the Review Group's report, established the Property Services Regulatory Authority (PSRA). The Property Services (Regulation) Bill 2009, which provides for the establishment of the PSRA on a statutory basis, was published on May 11, 2009. The principal role of the PSRA will be to control and supervise providers of property services (auctioneers, estate agents, letting agents and property management agents) and to improve standards in the provision of those services. At the time of publication, the Bill was at the second stage before Seanad Éireann.

ceased to be entitled to occupation by reason of the termination of his or her tenancy.[52]

(ii) Licensees

3–17 Licensees and tenants are treated separately under the RTA 2004. Licensees do not enjoy the rights afforded to tenants and with one limited exception, do not come within the jurisdiction of the RTA 2004. This exception arises in the context of s.50(7) of the RTA 2004, which gives a licensee[53] of a tenant, the right to request the landlord of the dwelling to allow him or her to become a tenant.[54]

D. Tenancy

3–18 A "tenancy" is defined for the purposes of the RTA 2004 as including a periodic tenancy and a tenancy for a fixed term, whether oral or in writing or implied. The definition of a tenancy also includes a sub-tenancy, as well as a tenancy and a sub-tenancy that has been terminated.[55]

E. Contract of Tenancy, Lease and Tenancy Agreement

3–19 "Contract of Tenancy" for the purposes of the RTA 2004 is defined as "not includ[ing] an agreement to create a tenancy".[56] The type of issues and disputes which fall outside the scope of the RTA 2004, by reason of the fact that agreements to create a tenancy do not come within its jurisdiction, are considered at para.3–04.

"Lease" is separately defined under the RTA 2004 as meaning "an instrument in writing, whether or not under seal, containing a contract of tenancy in respect of a dwelling".[57] "Tenancy agreement" is defined as "includ[ing] an oral tenancy agreement".[58]

3–20 If a tenancy agreement is entered into by way of deed[59] it must be executed by both the landlord and the tenant. Section 4 of Deasy's Act provides

---

[52] RTA 2004, s.5(1). See also fn.46 at para.3–14 above.

[53] A licensee for the purposes of s.50(7) of the RTA 2004, is a person who is lawfully in occupation of the dwelling concerned as a licensee of the tenant during the subsistence of a Part 4 tenancy.

[54] The landlord may not unreasonably refuse to accede to this request and if the landlord does refuse, the licensee may refer a complaint to the PRTB for resolution pursuant to s.76(4) of the RTA 2004. See paras 2–25 to 2–27 and 9–16.

[55] RTA 2004, s.5(1). See also fn.46 at para.3–14 above.

[56] RTA 2004, s.4(1).

[57] RTA 2004, s.5(1).

[58] RTA 2004, s.4(1).

[59] A deed is an agreement executed under seal.

that a written agreement not involving a deed must be signed by the landlord but there is no requirement that it be signed by the tenant. The result is that if the landlord does not sign the agreement he or she will not be bound by its terms even if the tenant has signed it. On the other hand, if the tenant does not sign the agreement the tenant will be estopped from denying that he or she has become a tenant on those terms, where he or she has acted on the basis that such an agreement exists.[60]

Where a contract of tenancy, lease and tenancy agreement are in writing, the RTA 2004 is silent as to whether it must be signed by the landlord and/or the tenant. In *Rouse v Harrington*[61] the tenancy tribunal in its findings said it was satisfied that an agreement in writing is not required to be signed by the tenant.

4. Exclusion of Certain Dwellings

3–21 Section 3(1) provides that the RTA 2004 applies to every dwelling the subject of a tenancy. This section is subject to s.3(2), which excludes 10 categories of dwellings from the jurisdiction of the RTA 2004. Each of these categories is considered in turn below.

A. Business Premises

3–22 A dwelling which is used wholly or partly for the purposes of carrying on a business does not come within the jurisdiction of the RTA 2004. Section 3(2)(a) of the RTA 2004 provides:

> a dwelling that is used wholly or partly for the purpose of carrying on a business, such that the occupier could, after the tenancy has lasted 5 years, make an application under section 13(1)(a) of the Landlord and Tenant (Amendment) Act 1980 in respect of it

Notably there is no requirement that the tenancy has in fact lasted five years or that the tenant has actually made an application under s.13(1)(a) of the Landlord and Tenant (Amendment) Act 1980 (the "1980 Act"). The dwelling will be excluded from the application of the RTA 2004 if the tenant "could", after the tenancy has lasted five years, make such an application.

(i) The 1980 Act

3–23 Under Pt II of the 1980 Act a tenant is entitled to a new tenancy of up to 20 years, if the tenant can establish a right to what is known as a "business

---

[60] Wylie, *Landlord and Tenant Law*, 2nd edn (Dublin: Butterworths, 1998), paras 5.35–5.36.
[61] TR05/DR32/2008, May 15, 2008.

equity". Section 13(1)(a) of the 1980 Act sets out the requirements for a business equity. To establish a business equity a tenant must prove that he or she (or his or her predecessor in title) has been in continuous occupation of a tenement[62] for five years[63] and that the tenement has been bona fide used wholly or partly for the purposes of carrying on a business.[64] "Business" is broadly defined under the 1980 Act and includes any trade, profession or business, whether or not it is carried on for gain or reward and any activity for providing cultural, charitable, educational, social or sporting services.[65]

3–24 The High Court considered the application of s.13(1)(a) of the 1980 Act in the matter of *Plant and Anor v Oakes and Anor.*[66] In that case the applicants claimed that they were entitled to a new lease by reason of the business equity provision at s.13(1)(a) of the 1980 Act. The applicants lived in a house leased from the respondent, which they used as their family home. The house was set back approximately 500 yards from a main road. At the road frontage was a garage where the first applicant carried on a business. There was a small office annexed to the garage but it was never used as such. All the secretarial and book-keeping work was said to have been carried out by the second-named applicant in the dining room of the family home, where a typewriter and filing cabinets were kept. O'Hanlon J observed that the dining room was not used exclusively for office work.

On the evidence before him, O'Hanlon J. held that the house was being used partly for the purposes of carrying on the garage business and as a necessary adjunct to the operations carried out in the garage proper. In his judgment, he also gave consideration to the meaning attributed to the phrase "bona fide used" in s.13(1)(a) of the 1980 Act. He said that these words were "probably intended to exclude a claim based on purported business user which was not genuine but was merely embarked upon as a subterfuge for the purpose of building up a 'business equity' as a basis for a claim to a new lease under the 1980 Act".[67] This "bona fide" requirement may be an important consideration in certain cases falling for determination before the PRTB, if the tenant attempts to exclude the application of the RTA 2004 by claiming an entitlement to a business equity. In the High Court decision of *O'Byrne v M50 Motors Ltd,*[68] it was held by

---

62 "Tenement" is defined at s.5 of the 1980 Act. See para.7–44.
63 Section 13(1)(a) of the 1980 Act was amended by s.3 of the Landlord and Tenant (Amendment) Act 1994, resulting in the required period of occupation changing from three to five years.
64 Section 13(1)(a) (as amended) provides that Pt II of the 1980 Act will apply to a tenement at any time if "the tenement was, during the whole of the period of [five] years ending at that time, continuously in the occupation of the person who was the tenant immediately before that time or of his predecessors in title and bona fide used wholly or partly for the purpose of carrying on a business".
65 1980 Act, s.3.
66 [1991] 1 I.R. 185. See also Wylie, *Landlord and Tenant Law,* 2nd edn (Dublin: Butterworths, 1998), paras 30.13–30.14.
67 [1991] 1 I.R. 185 at 187.
68 [2002] 4 I.R. 161.

O'Caoimh J. that where a tenant has knowingly breached an express term of a tenancy agreement prohibiting the use of a premises for the purposes of carrying on a business, any resulting business user cannot be said to be a bona fide user within the meaning of the 1980 Act.

3–25 Another relevant issue in considering an occupier's right to claim a business equity, is whether a failure to apply for change of user under the Local Government (Planning and Development) Acts should defeat a claim to a new tenancy. In *Terry v Stokes*[69] it was held such a failure should not defeat a claim to a new tenancy.

(ii) Application of the business exception

3–26 In *Mulvany v Grant*[70] the tenancy tribunal gave consideration to the application of s.3(2)(a) of the RTA 2004. In that case three different properties on the one site were rented to the tenant. The properties consisted of a house in which the tenant and his family lived, an annex to the house and a warehouse where the tenant carried out a business. The tenant claimed that the three properties on the one site were rented to him at different times with separate agreements. The landlord on the other hand claimed that all three properties "came as a package", to be covered by one lease, which the tenant had refused to sign. The tenancy tribunal found that three separate leases existed but only two came within the PRTB's jurisdiction, namely the lease of the house and the lease of the annex to the house. The tenancy tribunal determined that the warehouse was a business letting and therefore the RTA 2004 did not apply.

3–27 The requirement under the RTA 2004 that a dwelling must be a "self-contained" residential unit to fall within its jurisdiction, means that a unit used for residential purposes within a building can be treated separately from any part of the building that may be used to carry on a business. For instance, where a building operates as a business premises on the lower level and serves as a residential dwelling on the upper level, a tenancy of the upper unit will fall within the jurisdiction of the RTA 2004, provided the upper level is a self-contained residential unit. Where there is no sharing of common facilities between the two levels and both units have separate entrances, it is clear that the unit on the upper level will constitute a "self-contained residential unit" for the purposes of the RTA 2004. The situation will be less clear, however, where the residential unit can be accessed through the business premises only, where there is common use of certain facilities such as the toilet or kitchen facilities or where the residential units form an integral part of the business being operated. In *Mutoola and Ors v Butt*[71] the downstairs of the rented building was used for the

---

[69]　[1993] 1 I.R. 204.
[70]　TR08/DR210/2007, March 5, 2007.
[71]　TR113/DR1203/2007, November 21, 2007.

purposes of a mosque, while the bedrooms upstairs in the dwelling were used as sleeping accommodation by the applicants, who said that the bathroom and the kitchen were only used by the people who attended the mosque with their permission. In its report, the tenancy tribunal stated that the RTA 2004 requires that to fall within its remit, the premises must be a "dwelling" as set out in s.4(1) of the RTA 2004 and must be self-contained. The tenancy tribunal stated that it was not satisfied that the premises occupied by the applicants could be so defined.[72]

3–28 With advances in technology it is becoming increasingly common that people carry on businesses from their homes.[73] This raises interesting questions in relation to the scope of s.3(2)(a) of the RTA 2004. Its application is yet to be explored fully in the determinations of the PRTB's tenancy tribunals. The following factors will be relevant:

- "business" is defined broadly for the purposes of the 1980 Act and includes any trade, profession or business, whether or not it is carried on for gain or reward and any activity for providing cultural, charitable, educational, social or sporting services[74];
- s.13(1)(a) of the 1980 Act does not require that the premises be used wholly for the purposes of carrying out a business with partial business use being sufficient;
- s.3(2)(a) of the RTA 2004 does not require the occupier to have established the right to a business equity but rather that he or she "could" after the tenancy has lasted five years, make an application under s. 13(1)(a) of the 1980 Act[75];
- a claim to a new tenancy under s.13(1)(a) of the 1980 Act will not be defeated by the tenant's failure to apply for "change of user" permission under the Local Government (Planning and Development) Acts.[76]

---

[72] The tenancy tribunal report refers to an application that was also pending before Linnane J. of the Circuit Court for relief on the basis of "business user". The tenancy tribunal report records that the evidence presented to it suggested that Linnane J. had not determined the matter and considered that the PRTB had jurisdiction over the portion of the dwelling being used for residential purposes.

[73] In *Ironside v Allen* (TR62/DR1045/2008, November 18, 2008), the tenant of a residential dwelling had conducted a photographic business over the internet from a room he had set up as an office in the dwelling. In evidence, the landlord said that he had formed the view early in the tenancy that the tenant was carrying on a business in the premises and he was very unhappy about that. He rejected the tenant's contention that planning permission was not required for this change of use and he was very uncomfortable about any implications there might be in relation to this matter. The tenancy tribunal did not raise any concern in relation to its jurisdiction to deal with the dispute before it, by reason of the fact that the dwelling was being used in part for the purpose of carrying on a business.

[74] 1980 Act, s.3.

[75] See para.3–22.

[76] See para.3–25.

In contrast:

- the entitlement to a new tenancy on the basis of business equity, applies only where the premises is used "bona fide" for the purposes of carrying on a business[77];
- a "dwelling" for the purposes of the RTA 2004, is a property let for rent or valuable consideration as "a self-contained residential unit"[78];
- s.16(m) of the RTA 2004 imposes an obligation on a tenant not to use the dwelling for any purpose other than as a "dwelling" without the written consent of the landlord, which the landlord has a discretion to withhold.

B. Rent Controlled Dwellings

(i) Part II of the Housing (Private Rented Dwellings) Act 1982

3–29 The RTA 2004 does not apply to a dwelling to which Pt II of the Housing (Private Rented Dwellings) Act 1982 (the "1982 Act") applies.[79] Part II of the 1982 Act applies to dwellings[80] which were formerly controlled under the Rent Restrictions Acts 1960 and 1967 (the "Rent Restrictions Acts"). The Rent Restrictions Acts placed statutory restrictions on rents payable by tenants of controlled dwellings. It was held that parts of the Rent Restrictions Act 1960 amounted to an unconstitutional interference with the property rights of landlords.[81] The 1982 Act repealed the Rent Restriction Acts.[82] It provided instead for a scheme of security of tenure, the fixing of rent and other terms of tenancies, in respect of dwellings which would have been controlled under the Rent Restrictions Acts.[83]

3–30 To determine, therefore, whether a dwelling is one to which Pt II of the 1982 Act applies, regard must be had to whether the dwelling was a controlled dwelling under the Rent Restrictions Acts when the 1982 Act came into operation.[84]

---

[77] 1980 Act, s.13(1)(a). See para.3–24.

[78] RTA 2004, s.4(1).

[79] RTA 2004, s.3(2)(b).

[80] Section 2(1) of the 1982 Act defines a dwelling as meaning "a house let as a separate dwelling, or a part so let, of any house, whether or not the tenant shares with any other persons any portion thereof or any accommodation, amenity or facility in connection therewith". However, in considering whether the dwelling is one to which Pt II of the 1982 Act applies, it is necessary to determine whether it was a controlled dwelling under the Rent Restrictions Acts 1960 and 1967 when the 1982 Act came into operation. This is considered below.

[81] See *Madigan v Attorney General* [1986] I.L.R.M. 136; *Blake v Attorney General* [1982] I.R. 117.

[82] 1982 Act, s.6. This section also repealed s.10 and s.11 of the Landlord and Tenant (Amendment) Act 1971.

[83] The 1982 Act came into operation on July 26, 1982 (S.I. No. 216 of 1982 – Housing (Private Rented Dwellings) Act, 1982 (Commencement) Order 1982).

[84] Excluded from the application of the 1982 Act, however, are dwellings held at its commencement under a contract of tenancy for greater than from year to year (1982 Act, s.8(1)). See also s.8(3) of the 1982 Act which sets out the circumstances where Pt II of the 1982 Act ceases to apply to a dwelling, namely where (a) the tenant's entitlement to retain possession of the

Section 3(1) of the Rent Restrictions Act 1960 provided that it applied to every dwelling, except the type of dwellings explicitly excluded by s.3(2).[85] Accordingly, a dwelling will not be controlled and Pt II of the 1982 Act will have no application, if on July 25, 1982, it fell within any of the categories of dwelling described in s.3(2) of the Rent Restrictions Act 1960. These categories of dwelling are set out at para.3–31 below. As a general guide however, a dwelling can only be a controlled dwelling if it was built before 1941 and had a rateable valuation below those valuations set out at para.3–31. Another good rule of thumb is that if the dwelling was let unfurnished and the rent remained the same over a number of years prior to the enactment of the 1982 Act, it is likely to be a controlled dwelling.[86] Controlled dwellings now make up an increasingly smaller part of the private rented sector.[87] The type of dwellings which are controlled under the Rent Restrictions Acts are considered in greater detail in other texts.[88]

3–31 A dwelling will not be controlled and Pt II of the 1982 Act will have no application, if on July 25, 1982, it fell within any of the following categories:

(a) A dwelling with a rateable valuation exceeding any of the following limits:

A: For dwellings situate in the county borough of Dublin or borough of Dún Laoghaire:

Rateable Valuation	Type of Dwelling
IR£30	A separate and self contained flat
IR£40	A house
IR£60	All other dwellings

B: For dwellings situate in all other areas:

Rateable Valuation	Type of Dwelling
IR£20	A separate and self contained flat
IR£30	A house
IR£40	All other dwellings[89]

---

dwelling ceases, (b) the tenant assigns or sub-lets the dwelling, (c) the landlord recovers possession of the dwelling.

[85] Section 3(2) of the Rent Restrictions Act 1960, was amended by s.2 of the Rent Restrictions (Amendment) Act 1967.

[86] "A Brief Guide to the Rent Tribunal", Department of the Environment, published July 1993.

[87] See for example, "Rent Tribunal, Annual Report & Accounts 2007" (PRN A8/1451), p.6.

[88] For a further and more detailed consideration of controlled dwellings, see Coghlan, *The Law of Rent Restriction in the Republic of Ireland*, 3rd edn (Dublin: Incorporated Council of Law Reporting, 1979) and Wylie, *Landlord and Tenant Law*, 2nd edn (Dublin: Butterworths, 1998), Ch.29.

[89] Rent Restrictions Act 1960, s.3(2)(a), as amended by s.2(1) of the Rent Restrictions (Amendment) Act 1967. Note that s.3(4) of the Rent Restrictions Act 1960 (as amended by

    (b) A dwelling erected after May 7, 1941 or which was in the course of being erected on that day[90];

    (c) A dwelling let under the Labourers Acts 1883 to 1958 or the Housing of the Working Classes Acts 1890 to 1958[91];

    (d) A dwelling where the rent paid includes payments for furniture or services such as heat, hot water, fuel and electricity. This exception to the application of the Rent Restrictions Acts does not apply (and accordingly a dwelling will be controlled) where the part of rent attributable to the dwelling alone equals or exceeds three quarters of the total amount of rent payable[92];

    (e) A house occupied by the owner at the commencement of the Rent Restrictions Act 1960 or becomes occupied by the owner after this time[93];

    (f) A house in the possession[94] of the landlord at the commencement of the Rent Restrictions Act 1960 or thereafter comes into possession[95];

    (g) A dwelling which is a separate and self-contained flat which forms part of any buildings, which after the commencement of the Rent Restrictions Act 1960, were reconstructed by way of conversion into two or more separate and self-contained flats. Any separate and self contained flat in possession of the landlord on June 8, 1966 or after this time and not being a flat forming part of any such converted building, is also excluded from the application of the Rent Restrictions Acts[96];

---

s.2(1) of the Rent Restrictions (Amendment) Act 1967), provides that if the rateable valuation of a controlled dwelling is increased and as a result comes to exceed the valuation applicable in s.3(2)(a) as set out above, the dwelling will remain controlled unless the landlord comes into possession of the dwelling. In the present context this means that a dwelling that was controlled, will still be controlled for the purposes of the 1982 Act, even if at the time of the commencement of the 1982 Act, the rateable valuations exceeded the limits set out at para.3–31 above.

90 Rent Restrictions Act 1960, s.3(2)(b).

91 Rent Restrictions Act 1960, s.3(2)(c).

92 Rent Restrictions Act 1960, s.3(2)(d).

93 Rent Restrictions Act 1960, s.3(2)(e). See also, the definition of an owner at s.3(6) of the Rent Restrictions Act 1960, which provided that an "owner" was to be interpreted as including a person who held an interest in the house under a lease of more than 21 years. Section 2(6) of the Rent Restrictions Act 1967 amended this position to provide for the application of the Rent Restrictions Acts to a person occupying a house for the purposes of his or her own residence under a lease of more than 21 years. However, once the person holding the house under such a lease ceased to occupy the house, the Rent Restrictions Acts would no longer have application and the house would no longer be controlled.

94 Section 3(7) of the Rent Restrictions Act 1960 (as amended by s.2(5) of the Rent Restrictions (Amendment) Act 1967), provides that "possession" means actual possession, and a landlord shall not be deemed to have come into possession by reason only of a change of tenancy made with his consent.

95 Rent Restrictions Act 1960, s.3(2)(f) as amended by s.2(2) of the Rent Restrictions (Amendment) Act 1967. Note that if the landlord came into possession of the house prior to June 8, 1966, for this exception to the Rent Restrictions Acts to apply, it was necessary that the rateable valuation of the house exceeded IR£30 if the house was situate in the county borough of Dublin or the borough of Dún Laoghaire and IR£25 in all other cases.

96 Rent Restrictions Act 1960, s.3(2)(g) as amended by s.2(3) of the Rent Restrictions (Amendment) Act 1967.

(h) A dwelling let with land other than the site of the dwelling, if the rateable valuation of that land exceeds the lesser of either (i) half the rateable valuation of the site including the building(s) on it or (ii) IR£10 in the case of a dwelling situate in the county borough of Dublin or the borough of Dún Laoghaire or IR£5 in any other case[97];

(i) A dwelling with a rateable valuation exceeding IR£10 being a house where after the commencement of the Rent Restrictions (Amendment) Act 1967, the tenant is a bachelor or spinster over 21 years of age but under 65.[98]

If a dwelling falls within any of the categories described above, Pt II of the 1982 Act will not apply and a residential tenancy of that dwelling will fall within the jurisdiction of the RTA 2004. This is subject, of course, to any other limitations on the application of the RTA 2004 that may apply.

(ii) Right of possession of formerly controlled dwellings[99]

3–32 The tenants of formerly controlled dwellings have the right to remain in the dwelling for life.[100] Any spouse living in the dwelling at the time of the tenant's death may stay there for life also.[101] Any member of the family who resided there at the time of the death of the tenant[102] was entitled to remain in the dwelling until July 26, 2002[103] or for a period of five years after the death of the tenant[104] (whichever is the later).[105] Those successor tenants could apply for a new tenancy in accordance with s.13 of the 1980 Act before September 1, 2009.[106] Otherwise, those tenancies would fall within the jurisdiction of the RTA 2004.

3–33 In *Kenny v O'Farrell and Anor*,[107] the tenant to the dispute before the PRTB was the son of a woman who had resided in a controlled dwelling. She

---

97   Rent Restrictions Act 1960, s.3(2)(h).
98   Rent Restrictions Act 1960, 3(2)(i), as inserted by s.2(4) of the Rent Restrictions (Amendment) Act 1967.
99   1982 Act, s.9. Note that the right to remain in possession of a controlled dwelling as provided for by s.9, is subject to the landlord's right to recover possession under s.16 of the 1982 Act. Both ss.9 and 16 do not apply to a dwelling let to a person in connection with his continuance in office, appointment or employment or to a dwelling let bona fide for the temporary convenience or to meet a temporary necessity of the landlord and tenant (1982 Act, s.8(2)).
100   1982 Act, s.9(1).
101   1982 Act, s.9(2).
102   "[D]eath of the tenant" in this context includes the death of a spouse who had become entitled to remain in possession of the dwelling for life under s.9(2) of the 1982 Act.
103   1982 Act, s.9(3). See the definition of "relevant period" at s.9(7) of the 1982 Act. The 1982 Act commenced on July 26, 1982. See also fn.83 at para.3–29 above.
104   1982 Act, s.9(6).
105   Where that family member died, another family member was entitled to remain in possession until July 26, 2002 (1982 Act, s.9(4)).
106   RTA 2004, s.192.
107   TR25/DR562/2006, August 10, 2006.

died on July 19, 2000. The tenancy tribunal found that as she had died before July 26, 2002 and was succeeded to the tenancy by her son, the 1982 Act continued to apply to the dwelling until the fifth anniversary of her death.[108] In these circumstances, the tenancy tribunal was satisfied that the 1982 Act ceased to apply to the dwelling on July 20, 2005, as did its exclusion from the scope of the RTA 2004 by virtue of s.3(2)(b). Furthermore, the tenancy tribunal found that as no notice of intention to claim relief was served under the 1980 Act, and accordingly no application made for a new tenancy pursuant to its provisions, the possible exclusion of the PRTB's jurisdiction by reason of s.3(2)(i) of the RTA 2004[109] could also not apply.

(iii) Rent Tribunal and PRTB

3–34 Under the 1982 Act where the landlord and tenant could not agree the terms of the tenancy of the dwelling to which the 1982 Act applied, the landlord or tenant was entitled to make an application to the District Court to fix the terms of the tenancy.[110] The Housing (Private Rented Dwellings) (Amendment) Act 1983 established the Rent Tribunal to take over from the District Court in determining the terms of tenancies of dwellings falling within the scope of the 1982 Act. Since October 2009, the PRTB has assumed the functions of the Rent Tribunal. Notwithstanding this, a dwelling to which Pt II of the 1982 Act applies still falls outside the jurisdiction of the RTA 2004.

C. Public Authorities and Approved Bodies

3–35 The RTA 2004 does not apply to dwellings let by, or to, a public authority.[111] The general effect of this exception is to exclude from the jurisdiction of the RTA 2004 social housing, State accommodation provided for the elderly and the disabled, and accommodation leased directly to students by educational institutions. "Public authority" is defined for the purposes of the RTA 2004 as follows:

> (a) a Minister of the Government or a body under the aegis of a Minister of the Government[112];
> (b) the Commissioners of Public Works[113];

---

[108] By virtue of s.9(6) of the 1982 Act.
[109] Section 3(2)(i) provides that the RTA 2004 has no application to a dwelling which is the subject of a tenancy granted under Pt II of the 1980 Act or which is the subject of an application made under s.21 of the 1980 Act and the court has yet to make a determination in the matter. See paras 3–56 to 3–61.
[110] 1982 Act, ss.11 and 12. Section 12 was amended by s.9 of the Housing (Private Rented Dwellings) (Amendment) Act 1983.
[111] RTA 2004, s.3(2)(c)(i).
[112] RTA 2004, s.4(1)(a).
[113] RTA 2004, s.4(1)(b).

    (c) a local authority[114];

    (d) the Health Service Executive ("HSE")[115];

    (e) a voluntary body standing approved of by the Minister for Health and Children or by the HSE for the purpose of providing accommodation for the elderly or persons with a mental handicap or psychiatric disorder[116];

    (f) a recognised educational institution, namely, any university, technical or secondary college, or other institution approved by the Minister for Education and Science for the purpose of providing an approved course of study[117];

    (g) the Shannon Free Airport Development Company.[118]

3–36 Consideration of the type of dwellings which fall outside the application of the RTA 2004, by reason of the fact that they are let either by or to a public authority, is best demonstrated by reference to the type of scenarios that most commonly arise. A number of practical examples are set out below:

Scenario 1

A local authority[119] leases a dwelling from a landlord in the private rented sector. The local authority then sub-lets the dwelling to a family who qualify for social housing.

The tenancy arrangement between the landlord and the local authority falls outside the jurisdiction of the RTA 2004, being a letting *to* a public authority. The RTA 2004 also has no application to the letting between the local authority and the family, as it is a letting *by* a public authority.

Scenario 2

A dwelling is let by a landlord in the private rented sector, directly to an individual who receives a supplementary welfare allowance ("SWA") rent supplement.

This tenancy arrangement comes within the jurisdiction of the RTA 2004, as the tenancy arrangement has been entered into between the landlord and tenant, neither of whom are a public authority for the purposes of the RTA 2004. The fact that the tenant receives a SWA rent supplement is of no

---

114 RTA 2004, s.4(1)(c). "Local Authority" is defined separately at s.4(1) of the RTA 2004 as meaning "a local authority for the purposes of the Local Government Act 2001".

115 RTA 2004, s.4(1)(d) and (e). The Health Act 2004 transferred the functions of specified pre-existing health boards and authorities to the HSE. References to those specified bodies in any legislation passed before January 1, 2005, are to be read as references to the HSE (Health Act 2004, s.66).

116 RTA 2004, s.4(1)(f).

117 RTA 2004, s.4(1)(g).

118 RTA 2004, s.4(1)(h).

119 It can be presumed that the local authorities referred to in scenarios 1–3, are each a "public authority" by reason of s.4(1)(c) of the RTA 2004.

relevance, notwithstanding the rent supplement may be paid directly to the landlord by the public authority charged with operating the scheme.[120] The contract of tenancy is one between the landlord and the tenant.

Scenario 3

Accommodation is let under the Rental Accommodation Scheme (RAS).[121] The local authority enters into a contractual arrangement with the owner of a dwelling to make the dwelling available for rent for an agreed medium-to-long-term period. The local authority then nominates a RAS recipient to the accommodation who signs a residential tenancy agreement with the landlord. The local authority is a party to this agreement as the guarantor of the rent. The RAS recipient and the local authority will be parties to a separate agreement whereby the local authority agrees that it will make rental payments to the landlord on the recipient's behalf. The local authority pays the full rent to the owner on behalf of the RAS recipient.

The contractual arrangement between the owner of the dwelling and the local authority, and the tenant and local authority, both fall outside the jurisdiction of the RTA 2004, as no tenancy arises in either scenario. A tenancy does arise, however, between the landlord and the RAS recipient, and it is this arrangement to which the RTA 2004 applies. The fact that the local authority guarantees the rent and pays it directly to the landlord does not bring the tenancy of the dwelling concerned outside the jurisdiction of the RTA 2004.

Scenario 4

A dwelling owned by a university[122] is let by it directly to students.

The tenancy in this scenario falls outside the jurisdiction of the RTA 2004, as the dwelling concerned is let *by* a public authority.

Scenario 5

A dwelling is let by a landlord in the private rented sector to a university. The dwelling is then sub-let by that university to students.

The tenancy between the landlord and the university falls outside the jurisdiction of the RTA 2004 being a dwelling let *to* a public authority. The tenancy between the university and the students also falls outside the jurisdiction of the RTA 2004, as it is a dwelling let *by* a public authority.

---

[120] Section 4(1) of the RTA 2004 defines a dwelling as "a property let for rent or valuable consideration as a self-contained residential unit". There is no requirement that the tenant of the dwelling actually pays the rent to the landlord. The requirement is that rent or valuable consideration is payable.

[121] See *www.environ.ie*.

[122] It can be presumed that the universities referred to in scenarios 4–6, are each a "public authority" by reason of s.4(1)(g) of the RTA 2004.

Scenario 6

A university operates a service whereby it sources accommodation for students. Landlords in the private rented sector can register with that university if they have a dwelling available to let to students. Once the university has matched students with suitable accommodation, a lease agreement is then entered into between the landlord of the dwelling and the students.

No letting by or to a public authority arises in this scenario. A tenancy agreement is neither entered into between the landlord and the university nor the students and the university. However, any tenancy agreement entered into between landlord and students will constitute a tenancy of a dwelling to which the RTA 2004 applies.

D. Accommodation of Voluntary Bodies and the Co-operative Sector

3–37 The RTA 2004 does not apply to a dwelling let by or to a body standing approved for the purposes of s.6 of the Housing (Miscellaneous Provisions) Act 1992 (the "1992 Act") and which is occupied by a household assessed under s.20 of the Housing (Miscellaneous Provisions) Act 2009 (the "Housing Act 2009") as being qualified for social housing support.[123] In practice, the dwellings which fall outside the RTA 2004 as a result of this exception principally comprise accommodation leased by or to the voluntary and co-operative sector and which is provided to persons deemed eligible for social housing support by a Housing Authority.[124]

3–38 Information in relation to bodies approved for the purposes of s.6 of the 1992 Act can be obtained from the Department of the Environment, Heritage and Local Government.[125] The RTA 2004 will have no application to a dwelling let by or to one of these bodies, where the lessee has been assessed as qualifying for social housing support under s.20 of the Housing Act 2009. Section 20 of the Housing Act 2009 deals with assessments carried out by housing authorities of a household's eligibility and need for social housing support[126] where the household has made an application to it for support. For the purposes of s.20 a

---

[123] RTA 2004, s.3(2)(c)(ii), as amended by s.100(2)(a) of the Housing Act 2009.

[124] On November 4, 2009, Michael Finneran TD, Minister for Housing Local Services, announced the preliminary results of a review of the RTA 2004. Amongst the main issues it considered needed to be addressed in amending legislation was the inclusion within the remit of the RTA 2004, of those segments of the voluntary and co-operative housing sector that most closely parallel the current remit of the RTA 2004 (i.e. standard social housing). See Press Release, "Minister Michael Finneran announces significant changes to Private Residential Tenancies Board (PRTB) legislation", November 4, 2009, *www.prtb.ie.*

[125] *www.environ.ie.* The Simon Community is an example of a body approved for the purposes of s.6 of the 1992 Act.

[126] Section 2(1) of the Housing Act 2009 provides that "social housing support" is to be read in accordance with s.19. Section 19(2)(b) provides that social housing support may include dwellings provided by an approved body.

"household" is to be read as including "a reference to 2 or more persons who, in the opinion of the housing authority concerned, have a reasonable requirement to live together".[127] The Minister for the Environment, Heritage and Local Government may make regulations relating to social housing support. The Minister is empowered to do so by s.20, and any regulations made can prescribe the means by which the eligibility of households for social housing support is to be decided, and the form such social housing support shall take. Regard should be had to any regulations made under s.20 to determine whether a person has been assessed as qualifying for social housing support.

E. Ground Rents

3–39 The RTA 2004 does not apply to a dwelling where the occupier is entitled to acquire the fee simple of the dwelling under Pt II of the Landlord and Tenant (Ground Rents) (No.2) Act 1978 (the "1978 Act").[128] This right to acquire the fee simple in land was initially introduced by the Landlord and Tenant (Ground Rents) Act 1967 (the "1967 Act").[129] It was part of a series of legislative reforms to address the inequitable situation faced by tenants of leases known as building and proprietary leases,[130] who had no security of tenure or right to compensation for improvements or disturbance on the termination of their lease.[131] The term "ground rent" is not defined but is intended to refer to rent paid by a tenant where the tenant built the buildings on the land and the amount of the rent reserved reflects this.[132]

3–40 The 1967 Act was amended significantly by the 1978 Act. Sections 9–15 of the 1978 Act deal with the circumstances where a right to purchase the fee simple under Pt II arise. Each of these provisions is considered briefly below. If a lessee of a dwelling satisfies these provisions and qualifies to purchase the fee simple of it, the RTA 2004 will have no application to that dwelling.

---

[127] Housing Act 2009, s.20(1).
[128] RTA 2004, s.3(1)(d). Section 8 of the 1978 Act provides that a person to whom Pt II applies shall, subject to the provisions of that Part, have the right as incident to his existing interest in land, to enlarge that interest into a fee simple and for that purpose to acquire by purchase the fee simple in the land and any intermediate interests in it. Part II of the 1978 Act is amended by the 1980 Act and the Landlord and Tenant (Amendment) Act 1984.
[129] 1967 Act, s.3. Section 3 (except for s.3(5)) was repealed by s.7 of the 1978 Act.
[130] A building lease was essentially a lease granted to a person who erected, or agreed to erect, buildings on the land. A proprietary lease was a sub-lease of a building lease. See Wylie, *Landlord and Tenant Law*, 2nd edn (Dublin: Butterworths, 1998), paras 31.02–31.03.
[131] See Brennan, *Ground Rents, A Practioner's Guide* (Dublin: Thomson Round Hall, 2005) for a more detailed consideration of the background to the ground rents legislation.
[132] Brennan, *Landlord and Tenant Law*, 4th edn (Dublin: Law Society of Ireland, 2007), Ch.11, p.170.

(i) Sections 9 and 10 of the 1978 Act

3–41 A lessee will be entitled to enlarge his or her interest in land to a fee simple, where all of the conditions in s.9 and one of the conditions in s.10 of the 1978 Act are satisfied.[133] The conditions that must be satisfied in s.9 are that:

(a) there are permanent buildings on the land and the portion of the land not covered by those buildings is subsidiary and ancillary to them[134];

(b) the permanent buildings are not an improvement within the meaning of s.9(2)[135]; and

(c) the permanent buildings were not erected in contravention of a covenant in the lease.[136]

3–42 Once all these conditions in s.9 have been satisfied, one of the following conditions contained in s.10 must also be satisfied before the lessee will qualify to purchase the fee simple interest in the land:

(a) the permanent buildings were erected by the person who was entitled (at the time the buildings were being erected) to the lessee's interest under the lease or were erected in accordance with an agreement for the grant of a lease upon the erection of the permanent buildings[137];

(b) the term of the lease is not less than 50 years and the yearly rent or the greatest rent reserved[138] is less than the amount of the rateable valuation of the property at the date of service of a notice of intention to acquire the

---

[133] The right to acquire the fee simple under Pt II of the 1978 through compliance with ss.9 and 10 is subject to the restrictions imposed by s.16 which are dealt with at para.3–46. Section 30(2)(a) of the 1980 Act provides that a person who satisfies the conditions in s.9 of the 1978 Act (which includes one of the alternate conditions in s.10) is entitled to a reversionary lease of the land. Section 30(2)(b) of the 1980 Act extends the application of s.9(1) and (2), ss.10–12 and s.14 of the 1978 Act to reversionary leases. Reversionary leases are considered briefly at para.3–48 but otherwise fall outside the scope of this chapter. See Wylie, *Landlord and Tenant Law*, 2nd edn (Dublin: Butterworths, 1998), Ch.29, for consideration of reversionary leases.

[134] 1978 Act, s.9(1)(a). See also s.14 of the 1978 Act which deals with a situation where the portion of land which is not covered by the permanent buildings is not wholly subsidiary and ancillary to those buildings. Section 14 is considered in further detail at para.3–44.

[135] 1978, s.9(1)(b). Section 9(2) of the 1978 Act provides that "improvement" in relation to buildings in s.9(1)(b) means any addition to or alteration of the buildings and includes any structure which is ancillary or subsidiary to those buildings but which does not include any alteration or reconstruction of the buildings so that they lose their original identity.

[136] 1978 Act, s.9(1)(c). See also s.9(3)–(5) of the 1978 Act relevant to the erection of permanent buildings. Section 9(5) of the 1978 Act provides that the arbitrator may declare a person to be a person to whom Pt II of the 1978 Act applies, notwithstanding that the buildings were, in whole or in part, erected in contravention of a covenant, if he or she is of opinion that it would be unreasonable to order otherwise.

[137] 1978 Act, s.10, condition 1.

[138] See s.11 of the 1978 Act that applies in calculating the greatest rent reserved for the purposes of s.10 of the 1978 Act.

fee simple or the date of an application to the Registrar of Titles for the vesting of the fee simple in the lessee. For this condition to apply the permanent buildings on the land demised by the lease must not have been erected by the lessor or any superior lessor or any of their predecessors in title[139];

(c) the lease was granted by a lessor to the nominee of a builder to whom the land was originally demised for the purposes of erecting buildings on it. The buildings must have been erected in accordance with an agreement between the lessor and the builder, that the builder having contracted to sell the buildings, would surrender his or her lease in consideration of the lessor granting new leases to the builder's nominees[140];

(d) the lease was granted by a lessor to the nominee of a builder. This grant was made in accordance with an agreement between the lessor and the builder that the lessor would grant leases to the Builder's nominees once buildings were erected on the land[141];

(e) the lease was granted, either at the time or subsequent to the expiration or surrender of a previous lease, at a rent less than the rateable valuation of the property at the date of the grant of the lease or to the person entitled to the lessee's interest under the previous lease. The application of this condition is subject to the requirement that the previous lease would have been a lease to which Part II of the 1978 Act would have applied had the 1978 Act then been in force[142];

(f) the lease is a reversionary lease granted under the Landlord and Tenant Act 1931, the Landlord and Tenant (Reversionary Leases) Act 1958 or the 1980 Act[143]; or

(g) the lease is of a term that is not less than 50 years[144] and was made partly in consideration of the payment of money (other than rent) by the lessee to the lessor at or immediately before the grant of the lease and/or was made partly in consideration of the expenditure (otherwise than on decoration) of a sum of money by the lessee on the premises. The sum paid or expended or the total of those sums must not have been less than fifteen times the yearly amount of the rent or the greatest rent reserved by the lease, whichever is less.[145]

---

[139] 1978 Act, s.10, condition 2, as amended by s.30(2)(c) of the 1980 Act.

[140] 1978 Act, s.10, condition 3.

[141] 1978 Act, s.10, condition 4. This is similar to condition 3 of s.10 of the 1978 Act. However, the difference is that for the purposes of condition 4, no lease is first entered into between the builder and the lessor.

[142] In other words the lessee of the previous lease would have been entitled to acquire the fee simple under Pt II of the 1978 Act, had it been in force during the term of the lease. 1978 Act, s.10, condition 5, as amended by s.71 of the 1980 Act.

[143] 1978 Act, s.10, condition 6, as amended by s.30(2)(c) of the 1980 Act.

[144] Section 12 of the 1978 Act extends condition 7 to leases of less than 50 years, if the lease was granted in consideration of an undertaking by the lessee to carry out specified works and certain other conditions are met. Section 72 of the 1980 Act extends condition 7 of s.10 and s.12 of the 1978 Act to certain sub-leases with terms of less than 50 years.

[145] 1978 Act, s.10, condition 7. See s.11 of the 1978 Act that applies in calculating the greatest rent reserved for the purposes of s.10 of the 1978 Act.

3–43 If a lessee complies with all of the conditions in s.9 and at least one of the conditions in s.10 of the 1978 Act as set out above, the dwelling, the subject of the lease, will fall outside the jurisdiction of the RTA 2004.[146] In addition, the RTA 2004 will have no application where the occupier is entitled to acquire the fee simple under s.14 or s.15 of the 1978 Act.[147] Sections 14 and 15 extend the right to acquire the fee simple to persons who would otherwise be excluded from the application of Pt II of the 1978 Act by reason of the fact that the "subsidiary and ancillary" requirement in s.9(1)(a) had not been complied with or because they are yearly tenants.

(ii) Subsidiary and ancillary requirement—built on leases

3–44 Section 14 applies where a person holds land under a lease which would entitle him or her to acquire the fee simple under Pt II of the 1978 Act but for the fact that the portion of the land which is not covered by the permanent buildings is not wholly subsidiary and ancillary to those buildings.[148] In these circumstances there will be deemed to be two leases. The first lease, termed the "built-on lease" comprising the portion of the land covered by permanent buildings, together with so much of the land as is subsidiary and ancillary to those buildings.[149] The second lease will be termed the "vacant lease" comprising the residue of the land.[150] The built-on lease is a lease to which Pt II of the 1978 Act applies, entitling the lessee to acquire the fee simple of it, provided all of the other conditions in s.9 and one of the conditions in s.10 are satisfied.[151] If these conditions are met the RTA 2004 will have no application.[152]

(iii) Yearly tenants

3–45 Section 15(1) of the 1978 Act gives yearly tenants the right to acquire the fee simple in land if the following conditions are satisfied:

> (a) the land is covered wholly or partly by permanent buildings and any land not so covered is subsidiary and ancillary to those buildings[153];

---

[146] This right is subject to the restrictions imposed on the right to acquire the fee simple by s.16 of the 1978 Act, which are dealt with at para.3–46.

[147] Section 13 of the 1978 Act also makes provision for a lessee under an expired lease to acquire the fee simple of land under Pt II. However, s.13 is no longer of relevance as it only gave a lessee of an expired lease the right to acquire the fee simple in land, within 12 months from the commencement of the 1978 Act.

[148] 1978 Act, s.9(1)(a), see para.3–41.

[149] 1978 Act, 14(2)(a).

[150] 1978 Act, 14(2)(b).

[151] 1978 Act, 14(4).

[152] A lessee's right to acquire the fee simple under s.14 (as amended by s.30(2)(b) of the 1980 Act) is subject to the restrictions imposed by s.16 of the 1978 Act. See para.3–46.

[153] 1978 Act, s.15(1)(a). Section 15(2)–(5) provides for the application of Pt II of the 1978 Act, where the land would be land to which s.15(1) would apply but for the fact that the portion of

(b) the land is held under a yearly tenancy arising under contract or by operation of law or by inference on the expiration of a lease or under a statutory tenancy implied by holding over property on the expiration of a lease which reserves a yearly rent[154];

(c) the land has been continuously held under any one of the tenancies referred to at (b) above (including any expired lease) by the person or his or her predecessors in title for a period of not less than twenty-five years prior to the date of service by the person of a notice of intention to acquire the fee simple[155];

(d) the yearly rent is less than the rateable valuation of the property at the date of service of a notice of intention to acquire the fee simple or an application to the Registrar of Titles for the vesting of the fee simple or in the alternative it is proved that the permanent buildings were erected by the tenant or a predecessor in title[156];

(e) the permanent buildings were not erected by the immediate lessor or any superior lessor or any of their predecessors in title[157];

(f) the contract of tenancy is not a temporary convenience letting[158]; and

(g) the contract of tenancy is not a letting made for or dependent on the person continuing in any office, employment or appointment.[159]

The RTA 2004 will have no application to a tenancy of a dwelling where the conditions in s.15 of the 1978 Act are satisfied and the lessee is therefore entitled to acquire the fee simple.[160]

(iv) Restrictions on the right to acquire the fee simple

3–46 There are restrictions on the right to acquire the fee simple under Pt II of the 1978 Act, which are set out in s.16. If any of these restrictions apply, a tenant will not be entitled to acquire the fee simple and the tenancy of the dwelling will fall instead within the jurisdiction of the RTA 2004.[161] Section 16 provides that a person shall not be entitled to acquire the fee simple in any of the following circumstances:

---

the land which is not covered by the permanent buildings is not wholly subsidiary and ancillary to those buildings. See para.3–44 in relation to s.14 of the 1978 Act which provides for the application of Pt II of the 1978 Act in similar terms as under s.15(2)–(5).

[154] 1978 Act, s.15(1)(b).
[155] 1978 Act, s.15(1)(c).
[156] 1978 Act, s.15(1)(d) as amended by s.9 of the Landlord and Tenant (Amendment) Act 1984.
[157] 1978 Act, s.15(1)(e).
[158] 1978 Act, s.15(1)(f).
[159] 1978 Act, s.15(1)(g).
[160] A lessee's right to acquire the fee simple under s.15 is subject to the restrictions imposed by s.16 of the 1978 Act. See para.3–46 below.
[161] Subject to any other jurisdictional limitations on the application of the RTA 2004 that may apply.

(a) where a person has been declared not entitled to a reversionary lease[162];

(b) in the case of a lease of land used for the purposes of a business or includes a building containing four or more self-contained flats and the lease contains provision for a rent review within 26 years from its commencement.[163] However, a rent review provision will not operate to exclude the right to acquire a fee simple under Pt II of the 1978 Act, if it permits the rent to be altered once only and (i) within five years from the commencement of the lease, or (ii) on the erection of buildings, or (iii) on the breach of a covenant in the lease[164];

(c) in the case of a business lease granted before March 1, 1967, where the lease restricts the lessee to carrying on a business on the land that deals in whole or in part with commodities produced or supplied by the lessor[165];

(d) where the lease contains a covenant requiring the lessee to erect building(s) on the land or to carry out development on the land and if (and so long as) the lessee has not substantially complied with this covenant[166];

(e) the lease has been granted by the Commissioners of Irish Lights or a lease made by a harbour authority[167] and the Minister for Transport is satisfied and certifies that such acquisition would not be in the public interest[168]; or

(f) in the case of a sub-lease of land granted by a lessee who is not a person to whom Pt II of the 1978 Act applies[169] (i) on or after February 27, 2006 or (ii) before that date, unless before that date a notice of intention to acquire the fee simple in the land was served by the sub-lessee in accordance with s.4 of the 1967 Act or an application was made by the sub-lessee to the Registrar of Titles under Pt III of the 1978 Act.[170]

(v) Prohibition on the creation of ground rents

3–47 The Landlord and Tenant (Ground Rents) Act 1978 was enacted for the purposes of preventing the creation of new leases reserving ground rents on

---

[162] 1978 Act, s.16(1).

[163] 1978 Act, s.16(2)(a). See also s.8 of the Landlord and Tenant (Amendment) Act 1984, which provides that a right to acquire the fee simple under Pt II of the 1978 Act existing at the commencement of the Landlord and Tenant (Amendment) Act 1984 shall, notwithstanding s.16(2)(a) of the 1978 Act, not be excluded by reason only of any provision in a reversionary lease granted after that commencement for a review of the rent reserved by the lease.

[164] See Wylie, *Landlord and Tenant Law*, 2nd edn (Dublin: Butterworths, 1998), para.31.37.

[165] 1978 Act, s.16(2)(b).

[166] 1978 Act, s.16(2)(c).

[167] Within the meaning of the Harbours Act 1946.

[168] 1978 Act, s.16(2)(d) and (e), as amended by s.70 of the 1980 Act.

[169] Note this exception does not apply if, at the date on which the sub-lease is granted, the sole reason why the lessee is not a person to whom Pt II of the 1978 Act applies is that a covenant by the lessee to erect permanent buildings on the land has not been substantially complied with and after that date the covenant is substantially complied with by the lessee (1978 Act, s.16(3) as inserted by s.76(1)(c) of the Registration of Deeds and Title Act 2006).

[170] 1978 Act, s.16(2)(f) as inserted by s.76(1)(b) of the Registration of Deeds and Title Act 2006.

dwellings.[171] Section 2(1) provides that a lease of land made after May 16, 1978 shall be void if the lessee would have the right to enlarge his or her interest into a fee simple and the permanent buildings are constructed for use wholly or principally as a dwelling.

There still remains a number of leases within the Republic of Ireland where the occupiers have the entitlement to acquire the fee simple in the lands under Pt II of the 1978 Act. In the matter of *Shirley & Ors v O'Gorman & Ors*[172] the plaintiffs challenged the constitutionality of the ground rents legislation. This challenge was unsuccessful in the High Court before Peart J.[173]

Further and detailed consideration of the ground rents legislation and the application of Pt II of the 1978 Act falls outside the scope of this text. Both are considered in further detail in other publications.[174]

(vi) Reversionary leases

3–48 Part III of the 1980 Act applies to reversionary leases.[175] A person is entitled to a reversionary lease under the 1980 Act if they comply with the conditions in s.9 and one of the conditions in s.10 of the 1978 Act as outlined at paras 3–41 to 3–42 above.[176] Where a lessee claims a reversionary lease and the parties cannot agree on its terms, they will be fixed by the Circuit Court.

The RTA 2004 is silent as to its application in the context of reversionary leases granted under Pt III of the 1980 Act. Accordingly the RTA 2004 will apply to such leases except in so far as they have been granted for a term of greater than 35 years.[177] As the term of a reversionary lease granted by a court must not be for less than a period of 99 years, reversionary leases will generally fall outside the scope of the RTA 2004.[178] Reversionary leases rarely arise in practice anymore. One reason is that where the right to obtain a reversionary lease arises, the tenant will also be entitled to acquire the fee simple under Pt II of the 1978 Act, an option preferred by most tenants.

---

[171] See the long title to the Landlord and Tenant (Ground Rents) Act 1978.

[172] [2006] IEHC 27; unreported, High Court, January 31, 2006.

[173] At the time of publication the judgment of Peart J. had been appealed to the Supreme Court.

[174] See for example, Brennan, *Ground Rents, A Practioner's Guide* (Dublin: Thomson Round Hall, 2005).

[175] 1980 Act, s.11 repealed the Landlord and Tenant (Reversionary Leases) Act 1958 and it was replaced by Pt III of the 1980 Act.

[176] These are the same conditions that must be complied with to acquire the fee simple under Pt II of the 1978 Act. If these conditions are satisfied, even though a lessee may ultimately elect to apply for a reversionary lease over-exercising their right to acquire a fee simple (rare in practice), the dwelling concerned will fall outside the jurisdiction of the RTA 2004 by reason of s.3(2)(d). In these circumstances, the exclusion of the application of the RTA 2004 will be until such time as a reversionary lease is granted and provided, once granted, its term is for a period of less than 35 years.

[177] The RTA 2004 has no application to leases with a term of more than 35 years. See para.3–62 below.

[178] 1980 Act, s.34(2).

F. Shared Ownership Leases

3–49 The RTA 2004 does not apply to a dwelling occupied under a shared ownership lease.[179] A shared ownership lease is a lease granted for a term of more than 20 years but less that 100 years, on payment to the lessor of a sum of money being not less than 25 per cent and not more than 75 per cent of the market value of the house. It must also provide for the right of the lessee to purchase the interest of the lessor in the demised house at a consideration determined in accordance with the provisions of the lease.[180]

Shared ownership leases were introduced by s.2 of the 1992 Act as a measure of social housing policy.[181] Their purpose was to facilitate home ownership for those who could not afford to purchase a dwelling in one go, even by way of mortgage.[182] Shared ownership leases allowed a person to buy an interest in a house to begin with, increasing their percentage of ownership until they owned the entire interest. Anyone was entitled to grant a shared ownership lease but in practice they were created by housing authorities only. The granting of shared ownership leases by housing authorities were subject to s.3 of the 1992 Act and the Housing (Sale of Houses) Regulations 1995.[183]

3–50 Section 7 of the Housing Act 2009 repealed s.2 and s.3 of the 1992 Act. Shared ownership leases are to be replaced by affordable dwelling purchase arrangements provided for in Pt 5 of the Housing Act 2009.[184] At the time of publication Pt 5 had not been commenced. Sections 2 and 3 of the 1992 Act and any Regulations made under that Act will continue to apply to shared ownership leases until Pt 5 is commenced.[185] On the coming into operation of Pt 5, a housing authority shall notify in writing each household who has applied for shared ownership leases under s.3 of the 1992 Act that it considers their application to be an application to purchase an open market dwelling under an affordable dwelling purchase arrangement provided by Pt 5 of the Housing Act 2009. Any such household is required to notify the housing authority in writing within three months of the date of such notification where the household does not wish to proceed with the application concerned on that basis.[186]

---

[179] RTA 2004, 3(2)(e).

[180] 1992 Act, s.2.

[181] See Programme for Economic and Social Progress (1991, Prl 7829, Stationary Office, Government Publications, Department of An Taoiseach) and A Plan for Social Housing (Department of the Environment, Heritage and Local Government, February 1991).

[182] See Wylie, *Landlord and Tenant Law*, 2nd edn (Dublin: Butterworths, 1998), para.4.51.

[183] S.I. No. 188 of 1995.

[184] Under Pt 5 the purchase transaction will be largely unchanged from the affordable purchaser's perspective. However, instead of units being sold at a discounted price, with the value of the discount being subject to a reducing clawback, the State will take an equity stake in affordable units sold. The purchaser will have the option of either buying out the remaining equity in steps or at the end of a fixed period.

[185] Housing Act 2009, s.96(5).

[186] Housing Act 2009, s.96(4).

G. Holiday Homes

3–51 A dwelling that is let to a person whose "entitlement to occupation is for the purpose of a holiday only" does not come within the jurisdiction of the RTA 2004.[187] Accordingly, in determining whether this exception applies, it is the person's "entitlement to occupation" that must be considered. For instance, although a dwelling may have been built for the purposes of serving as a holiday home (for example, a dwelling within a holiday village), if it is let to an individual as their principal place of residence, a tenancy of that dwelling will fall within the jurisdiction of the RTA 2004.[188]

Although a dwelling may have been initially let to a person for the purposes of a holiday, it is also possible that a person's entitlement to occupation could change during the period in which they occupy the dwelling. For instance, a dwelling could be let to a person for the purposes of a three-month holiday, but at the expiration of the three-month period, the person remains in occupation, having decided to relocate permanently to the area in which the holiday home is situate. If the landlord consents to that person remaining in occupation for a further period that is no longer connected with their occupation for the purposes of a holiday, that person's entitlement to occupation will have changed and the dwelling will be one to which the RTA 2004 applies. The person's entitlement to occupation will not be so clear, however, where he or she remains in possession on the expiration of the original three-month holiday letting but the terms of his or her continuing occupation are not clarified with the landlord. In these circumstances, consideration of all the facts, including the nature of any letting agreement and the actions of the landlord and tenant,[189] would be required before a determination as to the person's entitlement to occupation could reasonably be made. Where a landlord does not consent to a person remaining in occupation for a purpose other than a holiday or where the tenant of a holiday letting overholds, it seems that such a dwelling would fall outside the scope of the RTA 2004, as the person's *entitlement* to occupation (for the purposes of a holiday) has not changed.

---

[187] RTA 2004, s.3(2)(f).

[188] In *Devlin v MacDermot-Roe* (TR30/DR511/2007, April 26, 2007), a dispute was referred to the PRTB relating to a dwelling known as Seafield Cottage No. 3. Although it was not specifically addressed in the tenancy tribunal report, it is implicit from the facts and evidence given that the dwelling concerned was a type of dwelling which may also have been suitable to serve as, or have been built for, the purposes of a holiday home. In *Devlin v MacDermot-Roe* the jurisdiction of the PRTB was not, however, called into question on the basis of s.3(2)(f) of the RTA 2004.

[189] For instance, whether the actions of the landlord or tenant were consistent with the existence of a holiday letting or on the other hand, a residential tenancy arrangement.

H. Landlord's Residence

3–52 The RTA 2004 has no application to a dwelling within which the landlord also resides.[190] Accordingly, in circumstances of an owner-occupied dwelling where the owner rents one of the bedrooms to a third party, that dwelling will not come within the jurisdiction of the RTA 2004. This situation should be distinguished, however, from circumstances where a property is divided into a number of self-contained residential units, each of which constitutes a "dwelling" within the meaning of s.4(1) of the RTA 2004, for example where a property owned by "X" is divided into three separate bedsits. If X resides in one of those bedsits and rents the other two bedsits to two tenants Y and Z, the bedsits leased to Y and Z will come within the jurisdiction of the RTA 2004. X does not reside in either of those latter two bedsits, but in a separate self-contained residential unit. For the purposes of the RTA 2004, each of the three bedsits (occupied by X, Y and Z respectively) are dwellings within the same property, as opposed to the property comprising a dwelling within which the landlord also resides.

3–53 In *Leonard v McHugh and Anor*[191] the landlord claimed that she was residing in the dwelling, the subject of the dispute, and this was her principal place of residence. She said that she had been continuously resident in the dwelling since she had returned from a trip to Australia and that in her absence her father had rented a room to the respondent tenants to help pay the mortgage. The landlord gave evidence that some of her possessions were in one of the bedrooms in the dwelling and relied on affidavits submitted to support her contention that many friends had been to stay with her at the dwelling and had also been present at her birthday party which was held there. The landlord also said that she had bank statements and tax documents posted to her at the dwelling. One of the tenants gave evidence that when he viewed the house it was unoccupied and that there was no evidence whatsoever of the landlord having any of her personal possessions in the dwelling. All the rooms were empty except for beds and cupboards. He gave further evidence that all of the utility bills were placed in the tenants' names and that he had organised for NTL and a telephone. Witnesses gave evidence on behalf of the tenants that there was no evidence that anyone other than the tenants were occupying the dwelling. In its report the tenancy tribunal alluded to the conflicting evidence of the parties but concluded on the balance of probabilities that the tenants had sole occupancy of the dwelling. Accordingly, the tenancy of the dwelling fell within the jurisdiction of the PRTB and the tenancy tribunal proceeded to make a determination in the matter.

---

[190] RTA 2004, s.3(2)(g).
[191] TR44/DR476/2007, June 29, 2007.

I. Occupation by Spouse, Parent or Child of Landlord

3–54 The RTA 2004 does not apply to a dwelling within which the spouse, parent or child of the landlord resides, *provided* no lease or tenancy agreement in writing has been entered into by *any* person resident in the dwelling.[192] Accordingly, where a dwelling is occupied by a spouse, parent or child of the landlord, the RTA 2004 will only apply to a tenancy of that dwelling where there is a written lease or tenancy agreement between the landlord and any party residing in the dwelling.

In practice therefore, a landlord can ensure that he will not owe any obligations to persons residing in a dwelling which is also occupied by his or her spouse, parent or child, by not entering into a written lease or tenancy agreement with anyone resident in the dwelling. If on the other hand the landlord enters into such a lease or tenancy agreement with any of the occupants,[193] the RTA 2004 will apply to the tenancy of the dwelling. In those circumstances, all the occupants (including the landlord's spouse, parent or child) will be entitled to the protections afforded by the RTA 2004 and they too will owe obligations to the landlord.[194]

3–55 In the matter of *Rouse v Harrington*[195] the landlord submitted that the dwelling was not subject to the provisions of the RTA 2004, as the landlord had at all times one or other of his sons in occupation of the dwelling and had at no time entered into anything other than oral agreements with the other tenants. The tenancy tribunal found, however, that the documents submitted by the landlord to the PRTB had the required elements of a tenancy agreement.[196] The tenancy tribunal did not specify in its report which of the documents submitted by the landlord had the required elements of an agreement. However, amongst the documents that the landlord did submit to the PRTB and to which the tenancy tribunal did have regard was a document dated September 16, 2007, which stated: "Having a long association with Connaught Avenue [>50 years] I would be respectful of the needs of both residents and students to co-exist in harmony. This is reflected in our tenancy agreement with both our sons and other students [see enclosed documentation]".[197] The tenancy tribunal also had regard to a letter dated June 14 constituting an offer of accommodation for the academic year at a rent of €90 per week, together with rent in advance and a deposit. This letter was signed by the landlord and his wife.[198] In addition a rent book was submitted

---

[192] RTA 2004, s.3(2)(h).

[193] Including the spouse, parent or child of the landlord.

[194] Section 3(2)(h) provides that the RTA 2004 does not apply to "a dwelling within which the spouse, parent or child of the landlord resides and no lease or tenancy agreement in writing has been entered into by *any person* resident in the dwelling" (emphasis added).

[195] TR05/DR32/2008, May 15, 2008.

[196] In its report the tenancy tribunal also stated that it was satisfied that a tenancy agreement in writing is not required to be signed by the tenant.

[197] Tenancy tribunal report, p.3.

[198] Before the tenancy tribunal the landlord accepted that he could not be sure that he had not issued this letter to any tenant of the dwelling.

into evidence and the landlord accepted that he had issued this to the tenants. The rent book set out "special conditions of rental" and stated that it was to be signed by the landlord and the tenant to indicate acceptance.[199] The tenancy tribunal found that on the evidence presented and on the balance of probabilities, it was satisfied that the provisions of s.3(2)(h) of the RTA 2004 did not apply in this instance.

J. Business, Long Occupation and Improvements Equity Leases

(i) Overview

3–56 The RTA 2004 does not apply to a dwelling the subject of a tenancy granted under Pt II of the 1980 Act or which is the subject of an application made under s.21 of the 1980 Act and the court has yet to make its determination in the matter.[200] The RTA 2004 also does not apply to a lease that was granted under Pt III of the Landlord and Tenant Act 1931 (the "1931 Act").

Part II of the 1980 Act affords tenants the right to apply for a new tenancy on the termination of his or her previous tenancy if they can establish a business equity, long occupation equity or an improvements equity.[201] The terms of the new tenancy are those agreed between the landlord and tenant or where no agreement can be reached, as determined by the court on application to it.[202] Section 20(1) of the 1980 Act provides that to maintain a claim for a new tenancy under Pt II of the 1980 Act the tenant must, within the times limited by s.20(2), serve a notice of intention to claim relief on the landlord. Section 21 provides that a person who serves a notice of intention to claim relief may, at any time not less than one month thereafter, apply to the court to determine his or her right to relief and if he or she is found entitled to a new tenancy, to fix its terms. If the tenant does not make an application to court within three months after service of the notice of intention to claim relief, the landlord may make such an application.

(ii) New tenancies under the 1980 Act

3–57 The circumstances in which a business equity arises are considered at para.3–23. Where a tenant is in a position to establish a business equity he or she will be entitled to apply for a new tenancy with a term of up to 20 years.

A long occupation equity arises where the dwelling concerned was occupied by the tenant or his or her predecessor in title for a continuous period of 20

---

[199] Tenancy tribunal report, p.4. The tenancy tribunal report does not specify whether the rent book was in fact signed.

[200] RTA 2004, s.3(1)(i).

[201] 1980 Act, s.13(1). See also paras 7–43 to 7–52, which consider the right to a new tenancy and other reliefs under the 1980 Act.

[202] See s.18 of the 1980 Act, which applies where the court finds the tenant is entitled to a new tenancy.

years.[203] A long occupation equity entitles a tenant to a new tenancy for a term of up to 35 years.[204] The right to a new tenancy on the basis of a long occupation equity is considered in further detail in Ch.7.[205]

An improvements equity arises where improvements are made to the dwelling and the tenant would, if Pt II of the 1980 Act did not apply, be entitled to compensation for those improvements under Pt IV of the 1980 Act, provided that not less than one-half of the letting value of the dwelling at that time was attributable to those improvements.[206] An improvements equity also entitles a tenant to a new tenancy for a term of up to 35 years.[207] The grant of a new tenancy on the basis of an improvements equity has rarely occurred in practice given the amount of investment required on improvements for the right to arise.[208] The right to a new tenancy on the basis of an improvements equity is also considered in Ch.7.[209]

3–58 From September 1, 2009, a tenant's right to a new tenancy on the basis of a long occupation equity and an improvements equity under Pt II of the 1980 Act has been abolished for all dwellings which fall within the jurisdiction of the RTA 2004. There is one exception to this, and that is where the tenant, prior to September 1, 2009, served a notice of intention to claim relief in accordance with s.20 of the 1980 Act.[210]

(iii) The 1931 Act

3–59 The 1980 Act repealed the 1931 Act.[211] The 1931 Act had also made provision for the grant of a new tenancy on the basis of business use, long occupation and improvements carried out. Where the court fixed the terms of the new tenancy under the 1931 Act, it had jurisdiction to grant a tenancy for a period of up to 99 years, with a minimum term of 21 years.[212] As the general practice of the courts was to grant a lease for a term of 21 years,[213] there will be few leases in existence now that were granted under the 1931 Act. Where such leases do arise, the RTA 2004 will have no application.

---

[203] 1980 Act, s.13(1)(b).
[204] 1980 Act, s.23(2), as amended by s.5 of the Landlord and Tenant (Amendment) Act 1994.
[205] See paras 7–43 to 7–50.
[206] 1980 Act, s.13(1)(c).
[207] 1980 Act, s.23(2), as amended by s.5 of the Landlord and Tenant (Amendment) Act 1994.
[208] Wylie, *Landlord and Tenant Law*, 2nd edn (Dublin: Butterworths, 1998), para.30.17.
[209] See paras 7–43 to 7–50.
[210] RTA 2004, s.192. See also paras 7–49 to 7–50. For all dwellings which fall outside the jurisdiction of the RTA 2004, Pt II of the 1980 Act will still apply.
[211] 1980 Act, s.11.
[212] 1931 Act, s.29(c).
[213] See Landlord and Tenant Commission, "Report on Occupational Tenancies under the Landlord and Tenant Act 1931" (Pr No 9685), para.251; Mr Andrews, TD, Seanad Éireann, Vol.91, Col.459, March 7, 1979, second stage; Wylie, *Landlord and Tenant Law*, 2nd edn (Dublin: Butterworths, 1998), para.30.54.

(iv) Cases before the PRTB

3–60 In *Toffoli v Bolger*[214] submissions were made to the tenancy tribunal in relation to the tenant's position under the 1980 Act. The tenant had initiated the process to claim a tenancy under the 1980 Act by serving a notice of intention to claim relief. At the tenancy tribunal hearing, the chairperson indicated that the tenancy tribunal would not deal with the 1980 Act as it did not have jurisdiction to do so, except for the requirement to establish under s.3 of the RTA 2004 whether or not the dwelling fell within its jurisdiction.

However, in the matter of *O'Sullivan v Clarke*[215] the tenancy tribunal adopted as its determination a settlement agreed between the parties, which included the following terms:

> "The parties hereby agree that if the landlord's son ... does not commence occupying the premises, on or before 31 August 2009, and continue to do so for a year thereafter:–
> (a) ...
> (b) The tenant shall, for all purposes, including the Landlord and Tenant Amendment Act, 1980 (the '1980 Act') be deemed to have been in continuous occupation of Unit 1 during the period that he was in occupation of Unit 4;
> (c) The tenant shall be entitled to rely on the notice to claim relief under the 1980 Act served on 24 October 2008;
> (d) The Landlord will not object to or otherwise take issue with the tenant's entitlement to the new lease under the 1980 Act, on the grounds of the tenant's non-occupation of Unit 1 or any other grounds whatsoever".[216]

It appears from the tenancy tribunal report that at the time of making its determination, a tenancy had not been granted under Pt II of the 1980 Act, nor an application made to the court under s.21 of the 1980 Act, and accordingly the PRTB had jurisdiction to deal with the case. The determination order that was ultimately issued by the PRTB[217] also incorporated the terms of the settlement set out above. In the event of there having being non-compliance with the terms of the determination order dealing with the 1980 Act, it seems enforcement by the PRTB would be problematic, in particular if, in accordance with s.21 of the 1980 Act, the tenant had applied to the court to determine his right to a new tenancy.

3–61 In *Kenny v O'Farrell and Anor*[218] the tenancy tribunal found that the tenant was entitled to a new tenancy under the provisions of the 1980 Act. However, no notice of intention to claim relief under s.20 of the 1980 Act had

---

[214] TR104/DR948/2007, September 5, 2007.
[215] TR82/DR399/2008, February 25, 2009.
[216] Tenancy tribunal report, p.3.
[217] Determination Order, April 1, 2009.
[218] TR25/DR562/2006, August 10, 2006.

been served by the tenant on the landlord and no application made for relief to the court under s.21. Accordingly, the tenancy tribunal found that the possible exclusion of the dwelling concerned from the scope of the RTA 2004 by virtue of s.3(2)(i) could not apply in that case.

5. EXCLUSION OF LONG LEASES

3–62 The RTA 2004 has no application to a tenancy of dwelling with a term of more than 35 years. Section 3(3) of the RTA 2004[219] provides as follows:

> Notwithstanding the definition of "tenancy" in section 5(1), in this section a reference to a tenancy does not include a tenancy the term of which is more than 35 years.

This exception to the application of the RTA 2004 was inserted by s.100(2)(b) of the Housing Act 2009. Prior to this amendment, in *S&L Management Limited v Mallon and Private Residential Tenancies Board*, Linnane J. in the Circuit Court[220] held that the RTA 2004 applied to long leases as they were not explicitly excluded from its provisions. *S&L Management Limited* related to a claim brought by the plaintiff management company for outstanding service charges allegedly owed by the defendant lessee. It was argued by the lessee that although he held the apartment under a 500-year lease, the relationship between the management company and himself was one of landlord and tenant. Therefore any dispute arising, including in relation to service charges, fell within the jurisdiction of the RTA 2004 and could no longer be determined by the courts.[221] The PRTB, a notice party, argued that long leases, where the lessee pays substantial consideration for a residential lease (€200,000 in that case), were never intended by the legislature to come within the remit of the RTA 2004. Linnane J. held, however, that the lease came within the jurisdiction of the PRTB and accordingly that the Circuit Court had no jurisdiction to deal with the matter. Linnane J. stated:

> "In my view it is clear from section 3(1) of the 2004 Act that all dwellings are included by the provisions of that Act save those expressly excluded as set out and specified in Section 3(2), that this is a dwelling to which the Act applies and the Court is precluded from dealing with the dispute. The Defendant argues that the PRTB is the proper forum and I accept the argument so advanced."[222]

---

[219] As inserted by the Housing Act 2009, s.100(2)(b).
[220] Unreported, Circuit Court, Linnane J., April 3, 2009.
[221] See s.182 of the RTA 2004.
[222] Unreported, Circuit Court, Linnane J., April 3, 2009, at p.4. The High Court upheld the decision of Linnane J. in judicial review proceedings taken by the PRTB; unreported, High Court, Budd J., April 23, 2010.

CHAPTER 4

TENANT OBLIGATIONS

1. INTRODUCTION

4–01 Before the introduction of the Residential Tenancies Act (the "RTA 2004"), the obligations of a tenant who rented a dwelling for residential use depended very much on the terms of a tenancy agreement, and unless an obligation was expressly provided for, obligations imposed by statute or at common law were limited. The principal statutes dealing with tenant obligations were the Landlord and Tenant Law Amendment Act (Ireland) 1860 ("Deasy's Act"), the Landlord and Tenant (Amendment) Act 1980 (the "1980 Act") and the Housing (Miscellaneous Provisions) Act 1992 (the "1992 Act").

Since the enactment of the RTA 2004, additional obligations of a tenant have been introduced through s.16. It is not possible for a landlord or tenant to opt out of the provisions of s.16.[1] These are minimum standards which must be complied with. It is also not possible for a landlord to impose more onerous obligations on a tenant in a tenancy agreement, except and in so far as those additional obligations are consistent with the RTA 2004. This does not, however, preclude parties from agreeing on more favourable terms for the tenant.[2]

4–02 As the RTA 2004 does not consolidate all statutory provisions governing residential tenancies, the statutory obligations imposed on a tenant under the RTA 2004 are in addition to the obligations arising by or under any other enactment.[3] Accordingly, in determining the obligations of a tenant in any particular circumstance, it may be necessary to have regard to a number of legislative provisions.

2. DUTY TO PAY RENT

A. Prior to the Enactment of the RTA 2004

4–03 Invariably, the obligation to pay rent is set down in the terms of the tenancy or lease agreement, together with terms setting out the amount of rent

---

[1] RTA 2004, s.18(1).
[2] RTA 2004, s.18(2) and (3).
[3] RTA 2004, s.16.

payable and the date on which it is to be paid. Prior to the enactment of the RTA 2004, s.42 of Deasy's Act implied a provision into a tenancy that a tenant is required to pay "when due, the rent reserved".[4] Therefore, if a tenant failed to pay rent he or she would be in breach of the tenancy agreement, regardless of whether it contained a provision specifically imposing an obligation on the tenant to pay rent. A landlord had (and still has) a common law right to sue for the rent due.[5] An action for rent could be brought in the District Court, Circuit Court or High Court depending on the amount of the arrears. The landlord could also bring proceedings for ejectment or forfeiture for non-payment of rent where a year's rent was in arrears. Section 42 of Deasy's Act no longer applies to tenancies falling within the jurisdiction of the RTA 2004.[6] However, s.42 and the reliefs available for its breach still apply to tenancies falling outside the remit of the RTA 2004.[7]

B. The RTA 2004

4–04 A tenant has an obligation to pay the rent agreed between the parties on the date when it falls due and also to pay any charges or taxes contained in a lease or tenancy agreement. The obligation of a tenant to pay rent is imposed by s.16(a) of the RTA 2004, which requires a tenant to[8]:

(a) pay to the landlord or his or her authorised agent (or any other person where required to do so by any enactment) –
   (i) the rent provided for under the tenancy concerned on the date it falls due for payment, and
   (ii) where the lease or tenancy agreement provides that any charges or taxes are payable by the tenant, pay those charges or taxes in accordance with the lease or tenancy agreement (unless provision to that effect in the lease or tenancy agreement is unlawful or contravenes any other enactment).

---

[4] Section 1 of Deasy's Act defines "rent" as including "any sum or return in the nature of rent, payable or given by way of compensation for the holding of any lands". See para.3–07.

[5] This right was confirmed in s.45 of Deasy's Act: "Every person entitled to any rent in arrear, whether in his own right or in right of his see, dignity, benefice, or corporation, or in right of his wife, or as executor or administrator of any party deceased, under any lease or other contract of tenancy, whether of freehold or for years or both, and whether the estate or interest in such lease or contact shall be continuing or not, shall be entitled to recover such arrear from the tenant of such lands at the time of the accruing of the said rent, or his executors or administrators, by an action …".

[6] RTA 2004, s.193(a).

[7] See Ch.8 on Termination of Tenancies.

[8] RTA 2004, s.16. Rent is not defined in the RTA 2004. However, a dwelling is defined at s.4(1) as "a property let for rent or valuable consideration as a self-contained residential unit". The meaning of "rent or valuable consideration" is considered at paras 3–07 to 3–09.

4–05 A tenant is required to pay rent even if the landlord is in breach of his or her obligations under the RTA 2004. In the matter of *Brown v Monthe*,[9] the tenancy tribunal made it very clear that a tenant's obligation to pay rent continued even if the landlord had failed in his or her obligation to effect repairs to the property. A tenant is also obliged to continue to pay rent pending the determination of a dispute between the landlord and the tenant referred to the PRTB. The only exception to this is where the landlord and tenant agree to the payment of rent being suspended pending the PRTB's determination.[10]

4–06 A large volume of disputes referred by landlords to the Private Residential Tenancies Board (the "PRTB") for resolution concern a tenant's failure to pay rent.[11] As the only method available to a landlord to terminate a tenancy under the RTA 2004 is by serving a notice of termination, it is not possible to issue proceedings for ejectment or forfeiture for non-payment of rent as previously existed under the old statutory regime.[12] Therefore to terminate a tenancy because the tenant has failed to pay rent, a 14-day warning letter must be served stating the amount of rent in arrears and giving the tenant 14 days to pay that sum. If 14 days elapse and the tenant has failed to pay the rent arrears, the landlord may then serve a notice of termination, giving the tenant just 28 days' notice of the termination of the tenancy.[13] On the expiry of the 28-day period, if the tenant fails to pay outstanding rent arrears or fails to vacate the dwelling, a landlord can refer a dispute to the PRTB for dispute resolution services.[14]

4–07 In dealing with disputes relating to rent arrears that are referred to the PRTB for resolution, the approach of the tenancy tribunal has been to ascertain whether the landlord has furnished the tenant with a rent book to keep a record of the rent paid. If the landlord has not kept a rent book, the onus will be on the landlord to establish through other evidence that rent is due.[15] If the landlord cannot prove that rent is due, a landlord's claim for his or her arrears will be

---

9   TR25/DR147/2007, March 4, 2007.
10 RTA 2004, s.86(1)(a) and s.86(2)(a). See para.9–106.
11 "Private Residential Tenancies Board, Annual Report & Accounts 2008" records that dispute cases, either solely or partially involving tenants' rent arrears, represented the largest category of cases submitted to the PRTB by landlords in 2008 (p.30). See *Brady v Sherlock* (TR12/DR143/2007, March 14, 2007); *Brady v Whelan* (TR13/DR121/2007, March 22, 2007); *Early v Chinaka*, (TR15/2007/DR1235/2006, April 4, 2007); *Brown v Monthe* (TR25/DR147/2007, March 4, 2007); *Callely v Cooney* (TR110/DR1226/2007, November 16, 2007); *Kelly v Bruton* (DR540/2005, determination order, November 15, 2006); *Brady v Macharia* (DR29/2005, determination order, November 15, 2006); *Clarke v Kirwan* (DR533/2006, determination order, February 14, 2007); *Neary v Kavanagh* (DR470/2005, determination order dated June 30, 2006).
12 These reliefs are still available for tenancies falling outside the provisions of the RTA 2004. See Ch.8 on Termination of Tenancies.
13 RTA 2004, s.67(2) and (3). There are additional requirements if the tenancy is a Part 4 tenancy (see para.8–34).
14 See Ch.8 on Termination of Tenancies and Ch.9 on Dispute Resolution.
15 See *O'Connor v Ryan and Anor* (TR30/DR1228/2008, November 18, 2008), where the tenancy tribunal accepted the sworn evidence of the landlord as to the amount of rent.

unsuccessful.[16] In *O'Brien v Connolly*[17] the landlord did not provide a rent book and the tenancy tribunal held that in the absence of a rent book, the onus is on the landlord to establish that rent is due.

C. Charges and Other Taxes

4–08 When drawing up a lease or tenancy agreement, care should be taken to ensure that responsibility for payment of various outgoings, charges and taxes relating to the dwelling is clearly allocated as between the landlord and tenant. Charges relating to the supply and use of services such as water, gas and electricity are generally payable by the consumer to whom the service is supplied and the tenant would therefore be responsible for them. It does arise occasionally, however, that the parties agree that the landlord will pay for all of the charges and the rent will be inclusive of all or some of the charges payable. In *Walsh v Quinn*,[18] the landlord claimed that he was entitled to be paid for waste disposal charges. The tenancy tribunal decided that as there was no express provision for the payment of waste disposal charges in the letting agreement, the landlord had failed to show any basis on which the tenant should be obliged to make the payment. In *Joyce v Fortune*,[19] the tenant was directed to pay the landlord the sum of €818.47, in respect of outstanding electricity charges.[20]

3. Tenant must Ensure Landlord not in Breach of Statutory Obligations

4–09 A tenant must ensure that no act or omission by the tenant results in the landlord breaching his or her statutory obligations in relation to the tenancy or the dwelling, in particular, the landlord's obligations under regulations made under s.18 of the 1992 Act.[21]

4. Access to the Dwelling

4–10 A tenant is obliged to allow the landlord, or any person or persons acting on the landlord's behalf, access to the dwelling at reasonable intervals for the

---

[16] See *Amarat and Anor v Loughnane* (TR83/DR532/2007) November 30, 2007 where the landlord had no evidence that rent was unpaid for a period of up to four months and his claim was refused.

[17] TR38/DR1055/2008, October 16, 2008.

[18] TR14/DR365/2007, Determination Order dated March 26, 2007.

[19] DR417/2005, March 15, 2006.

[20] See *Early v Chinaka* (TR15/2007/DR1235/2006) April 4, 2007, where one of the issues for determination was whether service of the heating system was the responsibility of the landlord or the tenant.

[21] RTA 2004, s.16(b).

purposes of inspecting the dwelling. That obligation is subject to agreement being reached in advance between the landlord and tenant in relation to the date and time for the inspection.[22]

A tenant is also obliged to allow the landlord, or any person or persons acting on the landlord's behalf, reasonable access to the dwelling for the purposes of allowing any works to be carried out which are the responsibility of the landlord.[23] The obligation to allow the landlord access for the purposes of carrying out such works is not subject to an agreement being reached in advance between the landlord and tenant in relation to a date and time for the works to be carried out. That said, where the landlord wishes to carry out works on or to the dwelling, it is necessary to first acquire the consent of the tenant before entering the dwelling.[24]

If the tenant refuses to allow the landlord access to the dwelling either to inspect the dwelling or carry out necessary works or repairs, the only course of action open to the landlord is to refer the matter to the PRTB for dispute resolution services. In the matter of *Callely v Cooney*[25] the tenancy tribunal stated that the landlord's apparently unilateral decision to allow workmen to enter into the home of a tenant without the tenant's prior knowledge and consent was unacceptable.

5. Must Notify Landlord of any Defect in the Dwelling

4–11 It was settled law before the introduction of the RTA 2004 that where a landlord was expressly responsible for repairs, he did not incur liability unless he knew, or perhaps ought to have known, of the repairs required.[26] To this extent, the tenant was under an obligation to draw to the landlord's attention to any repairs which are required in the dwelling.[27]

The RTA 2004 specifically imposes an obligation on tenants to notify the landlord, or his or her authorised agent, of any defect that arises in the dwelling that needs to be repaired. This obligation, contained at s.16(d) of the RTA 2004, enables the landlord to comply with his or her statutory obligations in relation to the dwelling or the tenancy. In *Kelly and Anor v O'Loughlin*[28] the tenant was found to be in breach of s.16(d) by failing to report a leak in a timely manner.

---

[22] RTA 2004, s.16(c).
[23] RTA 2004, s.16(e).
[24] A landlord is obliged to allow the tenant to enjoy peaceful and exclusive occupation of the dwelling (RTA 2004, s.12(1)(a)). See also para.5–05
[25] TR110/DR1226/2007, November 16, 2007.
[26] For example where the landlord has knowledge of repairs required through a third party.
[27] See Wylie, *Landlord and Tenant Law*, 2nd edn (Dublin: Butterworths, 1998), para.15.16.
[28] TR72/DR605/2008, November 3, 2008.

6. REPAIRS

A. Dwellings outside the Jurisdiction of the RTA 2004

4–12 Section 42 of Deasy's Act places an obligation on a tenant to "keep the premises in good and substantial repair and condition" and "to give peaceable possession of the demised premises, in good and substantial repair and condition on the determination of the lease". Section 42 does not apply to an oral tenancy and must give way to an express provision on repairs or maintenance in the lease or tenancy agreement. Section 42 does not apply to a dwelling which falls within the remit of the RTA 2004 and therefore its application is limited to those dwellings which fall outside its jurisdiction.[29] There is also provision under s.23 of the 1980 Act where the Circuit Court may require an applicant for a new tenancy to carry out repairs to the tenement in question.[30]

4–13 Parties are free to impose a repair obligation on a tenant in a lease agreement if the tenancy falls outside the provisions of the RTA 2004.[31] The wording of such an obligation in a lease or tenancy agreement has been considered in many decisions at common law. It has been held that using the concept "repairs" can be used to impose an obligation to cure defects in the dwelling and "improvements" to provide for an obligation to add to the demised premises. A distinction has been drawn between "to repair" and "to keep in repair". The former requires action to effect any necessary repairs. The latter relates to a warranty that the premises will not fall into a state of disrepair and if it does, a breach of covenant arises immediately.[32] Very onerous repair obligations were imposed on tenants and it has been held on a number of occasions that, "if genuine repair involves, as it often does, inevitable improvement, that does not enable the covenantor to say he will not do the repair. He is often obliged in this way to give back a better house than the one he got".[33] In the case of *Groome v Fodhla Printing Co. Ltd*,[34] which involved a major work taking down and rebuilding half a wall and just over half the roof of a building, the Supreme Court held that this came within the remit of the repair covenant.

---

[29] RTA 2004, s.193(a).

[30] Note, however, that from September 1, 2009, a tenant's right to a new tenancy on the basis of a long occupation equity and an improvements equity under Pt II of the 1980 Act has been abolished (RTA 2004, s.192). See also paras 3–58 and 7–53.

[31] Subject to any repair obligations of the landlord which may apply pursuant to s.18 of the 1992 Act (as amended). See Ch.5.

[32] See *Whelan v Madigan* [1978] I.L.R.M. 136; *Earl v Meath & Cuthbert* (1876) IR 10 CL 395; *Groome v Fodhla Printing Co. Ltd* [1943] I.R. 380; *McEvoy v O'Donnell* [1946] Ir. Jur. Rep. 38.

[33] *Groome v Fodhla Printing Co. Ltd* [1943] I.R. 380, at 414–415.

[34] *Groome v Fodhla Printing Co. Ltd* [1943] I.R. 380.

B. RTA 2004

(i) Duty of tenants

4–14 Under the RTA 2004, there is no obligation on the tenant to carry out repairs or to maintain the dwelling.[35] However, a tenant has a duty not do any act "that would cause a deterioration in the condition the dwelling was in at the commencement of the tenancy."[36] Normal wear and tear is excepted. The test, therefore, to be applied in determining whether the tenant has breached his or her obligations, is whether the deterioration in the condition of the dwelling is over and above that of normal wear and tear. The following factors are relevant:

   (a) the time that has elapsed from the commencement of the tenancy;
   (b) the extent of occupation of the dwelling the landlord must have reasonably foreseen would occur since the commencement of the tenancy; and
   (c) any other relevant matters.[37]

If the tenant does cause damage to the dwelling above normal wear and tear, the tenant will be in breach of his or her tenancy obligations and must then:

   (a) take such steps as the landlord may "reasonably" require to be taken for the purpose of restoring the dwelling to the condition it was at the commencement of the tenancy; or
   (b) to pay any costs incurred by the landlord in taking such steps "as are reasonable" to restore the dwelling to the condition it was at the commencement of the tenancy.[38]

(ii) Normal wear and tear

4–15 In practice, it can be difficult to assess what damage has been caused by normal wear and tear and what damage is above that.

A landlord cannot expect the dwelling to be in a similar condition as it was at the commencement of the tenancy. In *Ugwunnaya v Kane*[39] the tenancy tribunal appeared to accept that in assessing whether a tenant is in breach of his or her obligation not to cause a deterioration in the condition of the dwelling above normal wear and tear, a landlord cannot expect the dwelling to be in a condition which would allow it to be immediately re-let and if repairs are required, which would have been normal for the length of the tenancy, the landlord will not be able to claim for these.

---

[35] See para.4–18 which considers whether repair obligations can be imposed on tenants.
[36] RTA 2004, s.16(f).
[37] RTA 2004, s.16(f)(i)–(iii).
[38] RTA 2004, s.16(g).
[39] TR27/DR788/2008, October 7, 2008.

In *Hanley v Foy and Anor*,[40] the tenancy tribunal had regard to the length of the tenancy in assessing whether damage was as a result of normal wear and tear:

> "It must be expected that there would be considerable wear and tear to the dwelling over such a period and further, there is an obligation on the landlord under Sec.12(1)(b) of the Act to ensure that necessary repairs and replacements are made to maintain it in the condition in which it was at the commencement of the tenancy."[41]

In the tenancy tribunal decision of *Mooney v Miller*,[42] the tenant had been residing in the dwelling for a period of almost 10 years. The tenancy tribunal's determination that the landlord return the tenant's deposit suggests that it accepted evidence given during the hearing that one would expect "a considerable amount of wear and tear after such a lengthy tenancy".[43]

In *O'Neill v EL Fridah and Anor*,[44] the matter which arose for determination was whether the landlord could recover losses incurred as a result of damage to the property. The landlord sought compensation for damage to the garage door, glass repairs and waste disposal. However, he also claimed for painting and decoration, replacement of locks for the patio door, damage to the shower and replacement of carpet. The tenancy tribunal found that the costs incurred by the landlord for damage to the shower and the replacement of locks on the patio doors "would fall into the category of normal wear and tear and cannot be allowed for".[45] The tenancy tribunal did, however, determine that the landlord was entitled to compensation for the damage to the garage door, waste disposal and glass repairs. It stated in relation to the damage caused to the garage door, which the tenants contended they were not responsible for, that the:

> "Tenants were under an obligation to take good care of the property and equipment and not to do or allow any one else to do any damage to them … The Tribunal was not in a position to make a finding as to who damaged the garage door, but clearly this was the responsibility of the Respondent Tenants while the tenancy subsisted under Clause 2.8 of the Tenancy Agreement and Section 16(f) of the Act, and they should have repaired the damage and/or notified the landlord or his agent of the damage as required by Sec 16(d) of the Act."[46]

---

[40] TR59/DR1254/2008, November 25, 2008.
[41] Tenancy tribunal report, pp.8 and 9. The tenant had been in occupation of the dwelling for almost five years.
[42] TR70/DR585/2008, November 18, 2008.
[43] Tenancy tribunal report, p.4.
[44] TR41/DR333/2007, June 29, 2007.
[45] Tenancy tribunal report, p.6. As no receipts were provided for painting, decoration or replacement of carpet, these costs were also not allowed.
[46] Tenancy tribunal report, p.7.

In *Early v Chinaka*,[47] the tenancy tribunal allowed €418.70 out of an amount claimed of €618.70 for contract cleaning as a figure commensurate to deterioration in the condition of the dwelling caused above that of normal wear and tear.

C. Costs Incurred by the Landlord

4–16 Where a landlord seeks compensation for damage caused to the premises, which is considered to be over and above that of normal wear and tear, he or she must be in a position to prove the costs incurred in repairing the dwelling. There have been many cases where an adjudicator or a tenancy tribunal has refused to allow for certain alleged costs incurred by a landlord where those losses are not vouched.

In *Callely v Cooney*,[48] the landlord claimed €5,500 in respect of damage and refurbishment, but as no evidence was provided to the tenancy tribunal of the costs of the damage or the value of the furniture, the tenancy tribunal would only allow the sum of €500 for damage to the premises. In *Early v Chinaka*,[49] in relation to a claim for compensation for damage caused to furniture, the tenancy tribunal refused to make an award to the landlord, as no evidence had been produced of the condition of the furniture at the start of the tenancy. A similar finding was made in the tenancy tribunal decision of *Scanlon v O'Toole*,[50] where the landlord was unsuccessful in seeking compensation for cleaning and remedial works required to be carried out to the dwelling. Although the landlord submitted receipts for the cleaning and remedial work to the tenancy tribunal, the landlord had no evidence showing the condition of the property before or after the tenancy in question. Consequently, the tenancy tribunal did not accept the receipts constituted grounds for an entitlement to retain the security deposit.

D. Additional Obligations

4–17 Parties can agree to additional tenancy obligations than those provided by the RTA 2004 but any additional obligations imposed on a tenant must be consistent with its provisions. In these circumstances, it is possible to impose additional obligations on a tenant such as, for example, an obligation to maintain the garden. In *Walsh v Quinn*,[51] the landlord claimed that the tenant was in breach of the tenancy agreement by failing to maintain the garden. The tenancy tribunal made a finding that as the tenant was not provided with appropriate equipment to keep the garden in good repair, the landlord could not claim that

---

[47] TR15/2007/DR1235/2006, April 4, 2007.
[48] TR110/DR1226/2007, November 16, 2007.
[49] TR15/2007/DR1235/2006, April 4, 2007.
[50] TR58/DR376/2008, November 21, 2008.
[51] TR14/DR365/2007, March 26, 2007.

there was breach of the tenancy agreement. There may be other types of additional obligations that may be imposed on a tenant that are consistent with the RTA 2004. In *McCarney and Anor v Walsh and Anor*,[52] the tenancy tribunal decided that, contrary to any clause in the lease agreement, the "Disposal of rubbish is the responsibility of the tenant in line with waste management practices and on the principle that the polluter pays."[53] The landlord was entitled to deduct an amount from the security deposit to cover the costs of cleaning and disposing of rubbish.

4–18 The RTA 2004 imposes obligations on landlords to repair the interior and exterior of a dwelling.[54] These obligations cannot be contracted out of.[55] As a result, it seems that an obligation to repair the interior or exterior of a dwelling is not an additional obligation consistent with the RTA 2004 that may be imposed on a tenant. However, although repair obligations may not be imposed on a tenant, as discussed above, a tenant is obliged not to cause deterioration to the dwelling beyond normal wear and tear. The question therefore arises as to whether there is a positive duty on a tenant to maintain the dwelling? In *O'Neill v EL Fridah and Anor*,[56] the tenancy tribunal was of the view that a tenant was also under an obligation to take good care of the property and equipment and not to do, or allow anyone else to do, any damage to them. In *Anderson v Flood and Anor*,[57] the letting agreement signed by the parties required the tenant to keep the interior of the premises in good and tenantable repair, order and condition. The tenancy tribunal upheld this covenant but found that there was no evidence that the tenant had breached it.

E. Obligations owed by the Sub-tenant

4–19 A sub-tenant of a Part 4 tenancy also owes obligations to the head-landlord (as if he or she were the head-tenant) pursuant to s.16(f) and (g) of the RTA 2004. These obligations are owed to the head-landlord for as long as the sub-tenancy continues in being.[58] The sub-tenant's obligations are:

> (a) not to cause a deterioration to the condition of the dwelling, over and above normal wear and tear, and

---

52   TR43/DR416/2007, July 18, 2007. The tenancy tribunal in this case also found the tenants were in breach of the letting agreement by failing to keep the garden in order.

53   Tenancy tribunal report. Note the obligation imposed on landlords by s.100(3) of the Housing (Miscellaneous Provisions) Act 2009, to provide receptacles suitable for the storage of rubbish outside the dwelling. See para.5–21.

54   RTA 2004, s.12(1)(b).

55   RTA 2004, s.18.

56   TR41/DR333/2007, June 29, 2007.

57   TR56/DR379/2008, December 12, 2008.

58   RTA 2004, para.4(2) of the Schedule. None of the other obligations in s.16 of the RTA 2004 are owed by the sub-tenant to the head-landlord of a Part 4 tenancy.

(b) if the tenant does cause a deterioration to the condition of the dwelling above normal wear and tear, to carry out such steps as the head-landlord may reasonably require to restore the dwelling to the condition it was in at the commencement of the tenancy or to pay the costs of doing so.[59]

7. ANTISOCIAL BEHAVIOUR AND THIRD PARTIES

4–20 A tenant must not "behave within the dwelling, or in the vicinity of it, in a way that is antisocial or allow other occupiers of, or visitors to, the dwelling to behave within it, or in the vicinity of it, in such a way".[60] Antisocial behaviour has been defined at s.17 as follows:

(a) engage in behaviour that constitutes the commission of an offence, which is reasonably likely to affect directly the well-being or welfare of others;
(b) engage in behaviour that causes or could cause fear, danger, injury, damage or loss to any person living, working or otherwise lawfully in the rented dwelling concerned or its vicinity, including engaging in violence, intimidation, coercion, harassment or obstruction of, or threats to, any person; or
(c) engage, persistently in behaviour that prevents or interferes with the peaceful occupation of a dwelling:
   (i) by any other person residing in the rented dwelling concerned,
   (ii) by any person residing in any other dwelling in the property containing the rented dwelling concerned, or
   (iii) by any person residing in a neighbouring dwelling in the vicinity of the rented dwelling concerned.

In *O'Riordan and Anor v Harrington*,[61] the tenancy tribunal said that:

"the clear intention of the Oireachtas, in adopting the definition of anti-social behaviour, concerned itself with acts, or persistent acts, that verged on the criminal, if indeed they were not actually criminal, that caused fear, injury, intimidation or threat to the occupants of a neighbouring dwelling."[62]

4–21 Therefore, a tenant has an obligation not to engage in antisocial behaviour but must also ensure that any visitors to the rented dwelling do not engage in antisocial behaviour. If a tenant is engaging in antisocial behaviour, as described within s.17(1)(a) and (b), the landlord may terminate the tenancy and need only give seven days' notice to the tenant to vacate.[63] From tenancy tribunal's

---

[59] See Ch.5 on Landlord Obligations.
[60] RTA 2004, s.16(h).
[61] TR45/DR546/2007, June 18, 2007.
[62] Tenancy tribunal report, p.9.
[63] See para.8–76 on Termination of Tenancies.

determinations, it appears that there is a high burden of proof imposed on the person alleging antisocial behaviour. In many situations, the PRTB has determined that the tenant has engaged in certain behaviour that may be in breach of his or her tenancy obligations but that the behaviour did not reach the threshold of antisocial as defined in s.17(1)(a) and (b) of the RTA 2004. In those circumstances, termination of a tenancy giving seven days' notice will be invalid. In *Sweeney v O'Reilly*,[64] the tenancy tribunal stated that it was:

> "fully aware that losing one's home at notice as short as 7 days is a particularly serious life event and would require a heavy burden of proof to be justified".[65]

The tenancy tribunal was satisfied in that instance that the tenant had behaved in a way that was antisocial within the meaning of s.17(1) of the RTA 2004, as he threatened the landlord in a manner that caused sufficient fear to justify the service of a notice of termination giving seven days' notice. In *Travers v Smyth and Anor*,[66] the behaviour of the tenants was considered antisocial within the meaning of s.17(1)(b) of the RTA 2004 where the tenants had engaged in a violent domestic fight. The PRTB made a determination order which required the tenants to vacate the property and to pay the landlord €7,500[67] for breaching their obligation not to engage in antisocial behaviour.

In contrast, in *Byrne and Anor v Reddington and Anor*[68] the tenancy tribunal concluded that although there was improper behaviour, including loud domestic arguments, the tenant had not behaved in an antisocial manner. As the landlord had sought to terminate the tenancy on the basis of antisocial behaviour, the termination was therefore invalid. In *Egan v Rushe*,[69] a third party complaint was made against a landlord for alleged antisocial behaviour by his tenants. The tenancy tribunal determined that the noise from the rented house had clearly caused some annoyance to the neighbours but the tenants had not engaged in antisocial behaviour within the meaning of the RTA 2004.

7. INSURANCE

4–22 A tenant must not act, or allow other occupiers of or visitors to the dwelling to act, in a way which would invalidate the insurance policy for the dwelling.[70] If any act of the tenant or occupier or a visitor to the premises results

---

[64] TR37/2007/DR995&1148/2006, April 18, 2007.
[65] Tenancy tribunal report, p.5.
[66] TR01/DR693&786/2006, March 22, 2006.
[67] This sum included €1,800 for compensation for loss of rental income for an adjacent apartment due to the tenants' behaviour. This apartment was also owned by the landlord.
[68] TR02/2006, February 1, 2006.
[69] TR04/DR281/2006, April 5, 2006.
[70] RTA 2004, s.16(i).

in an increase in the premium payable under the insurance policy, the tenant must pay the landlord a sum equal to the amount of that increase. The obligation to pay the increased amount applies in respect of each further premium falling due for payment under the policy that includes the increased element.[71]

8. SUB-LETTING AND ASSIGNMENT

4–23 A tenant is not permitted to sub-let or assign a tenancy to which the RTA 2004 applies without the written consent of the landlord.[72] A landlord may, in his or her discretion, withhold this consent.[73] The landlord is entitled to be reimbursed by the tenant for any costs or expenses reasonably incurred by him or her in deciding upon a request for consent, regardless of whether the consent is granted or refused.[74]

4–24 Before the introduction of the RTA 2004, it was usual to include a covenant in a lease agreement which prohibited assignment and sub-letting. However, this was subject to s.66 of the 1980 Act, which permitted a landlord to withhold consent only if it was reasonable to do so.[75] If consent to an assignment or a sub-let was refused, the onus was on the tenant to prove that it was unreasonably withheld. The RTA 2004 does not impose a "reasonableness" requirement in relation to the landlord's consent. It simply provides that the landlord may, in his or her discretion, withhold consent to an assignment or a sub-let. However, where a landlord refuses to consent, the tenant may terminate the tenancy, even if the tenancy is for a fixed term.[76]

---

[71] RTA 2004, s.16(j). It is not clear, however, how this would operate in practice, in particular as s.16(j) suggests that the tenant's obligation to pay the increase in the premium may extend beyond the termination of the tenancy. There are no recorded PRTB decisions to date on this issue. Also of relevance to the operation of s.16(j) is s.17(4) of the RTA 2004, which provides that if the amount of the insurance premium is subsequently increased or reduced, then the reference to the increased element "shall be construed as a reference to the amount concerned as proportionately adjusted in line with the increase or reduction".

[72] If consent is forthcoming it must be in writing; oral consent will not suffice. An assignment is where a tenant transfers his or her entire interest to a third party. The original tenant then ceases to have any interest or involvement in the tenancy and the assignee becomes the tenant who now owes obligations to the landlord. Sub-letting is somewhat different, in that it involves a sub-grant by the tenant of the tenancy to a third party. The original tenant becomes the head-tenant and still owes the same obligations to the landlord who is now called the head-landlord. The sub-tenant has no relationship with the head-landlord but enters into a separate agreement with the head-tenant, who becomes the landlord of the sub-tenancy. Although the sub-tenant does not enter into a tenancy agreement with the head-landlord, if the sub-tenancy arises out of a Part 4 tenancy, the RTA 2004 imposes obligations on both the head-tenant and the sub-tenant in respect of each other (see para.4 of the Schedule to the RTA 2004).

[73] RTA 2004, s.16(k).

[74] RTA 2004, s.17(3).

[75] Section 66 does not apply to a dwelling to which the RTA 2004 applies—see s.193(d) of the RTA 2004.

[76] RTA 2004, s.186.

9. ALTERATIONS AND IMPROVEMENTS

4–25 The tenant cannot alter or improve the dwelling without the written consent of the landlord.[77] The landlord cannot unreasonably refuse consent if the alteration or improvement consists only of repairing, painting and decorating. In any other case, the landlord may, in his or her discretion, withhold consent. "[A]lter or improve" is defined at s.17(1) of the RTA 2004 as including altering a locking system on a door giving entry to the dwelling and making an addition to, or alteration of, a building or structure, including any building or structure subsidiary or ancillary to the dwelling.[78]

Again, written consent is required from the landlord before making any changes to the dwelling; oral consent will not suffice. The landlord is entitled to be reimbursed by the tenant for any costs or expenses reasonably incurred by him or her in deciding upon a request for consent, regardless of whether the consent is granted or refused.[79]

In *McGuigan v Wiszniewski and Anor*,[80] the tenants were found to be in breach of their obligation not to alter or improve the dwelling by changing the locks of the dwelling without seeking the permission of the landlord.

4–26 For those dwellings which fall outside the remit of the RTA 2004, the 1980 Act is applicable. Section 68 of the 1980 Act concerns covenants which absolutely prohibit the making of any improvement without the consent of the landlord.[81] Section 68 provides that, notwithstanding any such covenant, consent to the making of an improvement cannot be unreasonably withheld.

10. USE OF THE DWELLING

4–27 A tenant cannot use the dwelling for any purpose other than as a "dwelling" (being a self-contained residential unit), without the written consent of the landlord. The landlord may, in his or her discretion, withhold consent to

---

[77] RTA 2004, s.16(l).

[78] "[S]ubsidiary and ancillary" is not defined in the RTA 2004. It has been held with respect to unbuilt-on land in the context of s.46 of the Landlord and Tenant Act 1931 that "subsidiary or ancillary" means such land which is actively beneficial to the buildings in question, rather than merely aesthetically advantageous to them (*Lynch v Simmons* (1954) 88 I.L.T.R. 3). There is no reason why a similar definition would not be given to "subsidiary and ancillary" contained in the RTA 2004. See also Wylie, *Landlord and Tenant Law*, 2nd edn (Dublin: Butterworths, 1998), para.31.07 that considers the meaning of "subsidiary and ancillary" in the context of s.9 of the Landlord and Tenant (Ground Rents) No.2 Act 1978.

[79] RTA 2004, s.17(3).

[80] TR78/DR259/2008, December 9, 2008.

[81] See s.193(d) of the RTA 2004 which excludes the application of s.68 of the 1980 Act to dwellings which fall within the remit of the RTA 2004.

change of use.[82] Similar to the obligations imposed on tenants considered in the previous two paras 4–23 and 4–25, the landlord is entitled to be reimbursed by the tenant for any costs or expenses reasonably incurred by him or her in deciding upon a request for consent, regardless of whether the consent is granted or refused.[83] If a landlord does give written consent to change the use of the dwelling other than for residential purposes, for example, to be changed to a business use, it would then cease to fall within the provisions of the RTA 2004.[84] Again, the written consent of the landlord is required for change of use and oral consent will not be sufficient.

4–28 For those tenancies which fall outside the ambit of the RTA 2004, s.67 of the 1980 Act provides that where there is an absolute prohibition in a lease or tenancy agreement on change of user without the consent of the lessor, the lessor may not unreasonably withhold consent. If consent is not forthcoming from the landlord, the onus of proof is on the tenant to prove that it was unreasonably withheld.[85] Under the RTA 2004, there is no requirement that the landlord's refusal to a request for a change of use of the dwelling be reasonable.

11. Notification of Persons Residing in the Dwelling

4–29 A tenant is required to notify the landlord of the names of all persons ordinarily residing in the dwelling, other than a multiple tenant.[86] This would include a licensee but not a person who stays in the dwelling occasionally. The tenants in *McGuigan v Wiszniewski and Anor*[87] were found to be in breach of their obligation to notify the landlord of persons residing in the dwelling, by failing to notify the landlord that their girlfriends were living in the dwelling concerned for extended periods. In *Ussher v Waters*,[88] the tenant allowed her brother to stay in the dwelling as a guest for a few days. The tenancy tribunal found, contrary to arguments made by the landlord, that she was not entitled to have guests to the dwelling, that the landlord had no justifiable reason to withhold her deposit on this basis.[89]

---

[82] RTA 2004, s.16(m). A "dwelling" for the purposes of the RTA 2004 is defined at s.4(1). See also paras 3–06 to 3–13.

[83] RTA 2004, s.17(3).

[84] RTA 2004, s.3(2). See Ch.3 on the application of the Residential Tenancies Act 2004 that considers the circumstances where a premises may be used for residential and business purposes.

[85] *Rice v Dublin Corporation* [1947] I.R. 425. Section 193(d) of the RTA 2004 excludes the application of s.67 to dwellings falling within the remit of the RTA 2004.

[86] Section 16(n) of the RTA 2004.

[87] TR78/DR259/2008, December 9, 2008.

[88] TR103/DR117/2007, September 28, 2007.

[89] The tenant was entitled to the return of the deposit and compensation of €300 for breach of the landlord's obligation to allow the tenant peaceful occupation of the dwelling.

CHAPTER 5

LANDLORD OBLIGATIONS

1. INTRODUCTION

5–01 Prior to the enactment of the Residential Tenancies Act 2004 (the "RTA 2004"), the principle legislative provisions imposing obligations on landlords of residential dwellings were the Housing (Miscellaneous Provisions) Act 1992, the Housing (Rent Books) Regulations 1993 and the Housing (Standards for Rented Houses) Regulations 1993. The RTA 2004 imposed additional obligations on landlords, in particular through ss.12, 14 and 15. Landlords are also obliged to register every tenancy of a dwelling rented by them with the Private Residential Tenancies Board (the "PRTB").[1]

The RTA 2004 did not consolidate all pre-existing statutory provisions governing residential tenancies but was enacted supplemental to, and runs parallel with, that legislation.[2] Since the introduction of the RTA 2004, the Housing (Standards for Rented Houses) Regulations 2008 and the Housing (Miscellaneous Provisions) Act 2009 have supplemented the obligations owed by landlords to their tenants.[3] Accordingly, in determining the obligations of landlords in any particular circumstance, regard must be had to a number of legislative provisions. The principle obligations of landlords in the private rented sector are considered together at paras 5–02 to 5–62 below.

2. PEACEFUL AND EXCLUSIVE OCCUPATION

A. Prior to the Enactment of the RTA 2004

5–02 Where a tenancy agreement between a landlord and tenant is in writing, the agreement will often contain a covenant requiring the landlord to allow the tenant peaceful occupation of the dwelling, provided that the tenant complies with his or her obligations of the tenancy agreement.[4] Prior to the enactment of

---

[1] Previously, landlords were obliged to register tenancies of the dwellings rented by them with the local housing authority. Landlord's obligations in registering a tenancy of a dwelling, which now apply under the RTA 2004, are considered in detail in Ch.10.

[2] In so far as the pre-existing legislative code was not amended or revoked by the provisions of RTA 2004.

[3] The Housing (Standards for Rented Houses) Regulations 2008, revoked the Housing (Standards for Rented Houses) Regulations 1993, see para.5–07.

[4] See Wylie, *Landlord and Tenant Law*, 2nd edn (Dublin: Butterworths, 1998) para.14.06.

the RTA 2004, if the tenancy agreement did not contain such a covenant, s.41 of the Landlord and Tenant Law Amendment (Ireland) Act 1860 ("Deasy's Act"), implied a covenant that the tenant was to have the quiet and peaceable enjoyment of every lease of lands[5] or tenements without the interruption of the landlord. This covenant could only be invoked by the tenant, so long as the tenant paid the rent and complied with the terms of the agreement.[6] In *Whelan v Madigan*[7] it was held that a tenant could not rely on s.41 because at the time of the disturbance of her enjoyment, the tenant owed a substantial amount of money to the landlord in rent arrears.[8]

B. RTA 2004

5–03 Pursuant to s.12(1)(a) of the RTA 2004 a landlord is obliged to:

> allow the tenant of a dwelling to enjoy peaceful and exclusive occupation of the dwelling.

In contrast to Deasy's Act, this obligation is not subject to a tenant complying with his or her tenancy obligations. Therefore, a landlord must allow the tenant to enjoy peaceful and exclusive occupation of the dwelling, regardless of whether the tenant is in breach of his or her tenancy obligations. In *Boyne v Hanaway*[9] the landlord entered the dwelling without the tenant's permission at a time when the tenant was present in the dwelling. The tenancy tribunal determined that the landlord was to pay the sum of €4,500 in respect of damages for his (and his wife's) unlawful entry into the dwelling, including their threatening behaviour during that episode and for breach of the tenant's right to peaceful and exclusive enjoyment of the dwelling. This award was made by the tenancy tribunal notwithstanding that the tenant was €5,250 in arrears of rent.[10]

5–04 The general rule, prior to the introduction of the RTA 2004, was that there must be some physical interference with the enjoyment of the dwelling the subject of the tenancy, to amount to a breach of an express or implied covenant

---

5   "Lands" is defined at s.1 of Deasy's Act as including houses, messuages, and tenements of every tenure, whether corporeal or incorporeal.

6   Section 41 of Deasy's Act provides that "the tenant shall have quiet and peaceable enjoyment of the said lands or tenements without the interruption of the landlord or any person whomsoever during the terms contracted for, so long as the tenant shall pay the rent and perform the agreements contained in the lease to be observed on the part of the tenant".

7   [1978] I.L.R.M. 136.

8   See also on this issue *Riordan v Carroll* [1996] 2 I.L.R.M. 263; *Fitzpatrick v McGivern Ltd* [1976–7] I.L.R.M. 239; *Solomon v Red Bank Restaurant Limited* [1938] I.R. 793.

9   TR49/DR1262/2008, October 14, 2008.

10   The tenancy tribunal determination also included a direction that the tenant was to pay the arrears of rent of €5,250 to the landlord but that the tenant was entitled to set this sum off against the damages of €4,500 awarded to her, leaving the sum of €750 payable by her to the landlord.

of quiet and peaceful enjoyment.[11] For the purposes of the RTA 2004, it seems that this may no longer be the case. In *Mulvany v Grant*,[12] the tenant submitted an application for dispute resolution to the PRTB, claiming that the landlord sent him text messages demanding payment of rent and threatening to send the sheriff to the property. The tenancy tribunal held that the strategies employed by the landlord to obtain payment of the rent owing were intimidating to the tenant and in breach of s.12(1)(a) of the RTA 2004. The tenancy tribunal directed the landlord to pay to the tenant the sum of €4,000 for the denial by the landlord of the tenant's entitlement to peaceful occupation of the dwelling as prescribed by s.12(1)(a). In *Ryan v Sheridan and Anor*,[13] the landlord sent three letters to the tenant seeking possession of the dwelling at a time when the application for dispute resolution services was before the PRTB. The tenancy tribunal was "satisfied that this correspondence was in breach of the Tenants right to peaceful occupation of the dwelling."[14] The tenant was awarded €3,000 by way of damages for the breach of peaceful enjoyment of the dwelling.[15]

In *Amarat and Anor v Loughnane*,[16] the tenants made an application for dispute resolution services to the PRTB for breach of the landlord's obligation to allow the tenants peaceful enjoyment of the dwelling. It was alleged that the landlord's failure to prevent noise and inconvenience to the tenants from demolition and construction work on a neighbouring property constituted breach of s.12(1)(a) of the RTA 2004. The tenancy tribunal directed the landlord to pay the sum of €5,000 to the tenants, as damages for the landlord's failure to comply with his obligations pursuant to s.12(1)(a).[17]

5–05 A landlord's obligation to allow the tenant of a rented dwelling to enjoy peaceful and exclusive occupation of it is qualified by the tenant's obligation to allow the landlord access to the dwelling at reasonable intervals, for the purpose of inspecting the dwelling and carrying out repairs. If the tenant refuses access,

---

[11] *Whelan v Madigan* [1978] I.L.R.M. 136 at 142, per Kenny J. See also Wylie, *Landlord and Tenant Law*, 2nd edn (Dublin: Butterworths, 1998), para.14.09.

[12] TR08/DR210/2007, March 5, 2007.

[13] TR29/DR710/2007, April 4, 2007.

[14] Tenancy tribunal report, p.8.

[15] See also *Caulfield v Gillen and Anor* (TR64/DR64/2008, October 7, 2008), where the tenant was awarded €400 for breach of the landlord's obligations including the landlord's unauthorised visit to the dwelling.

[16] TR83/DR532/2007, November 30, 2007.

[17] It should be noted that in this case the landlord had accepted in the tenancy tribunal hearing that the tenants had been inconvenienced by the disruption and damage to the property caused by the demolition and construction work next door. Accordingly, the tenancy tribunal was not required to give full consideration to the issue of the extent of a landlord's obligation under s.12(1)(a) of the RTA 2004, where the disruption to the tenant's peaceful and exclusive occupation of the dwelling is caused by the actions of a third party over which the landlord has no control. In *Amarat and Anor v Loughnane*, the landlord had taken High Court proceedings against the owner of the neighbouring dwelling in respect of the damage caused to the rented dwelling; however, these proceedings had not come to trial at the time of the tenancy tribunal hearing.

it does not entitle the landlord to take matters into his or her own hands and enter the dwelling without permission.[18] A tenant's obligation to allow the landlord access to the dwelling is considered in further detail at para.4–10.

3. Repairs and Maintenance

A. Overview

5–06 At common law in the absence of an express provision in the tenancy agreement, the landlord's obligations for carrying out repairs to the rented dwelling were limited—the general rule was that a tenant took the dwelling as he or she found it and the landlord undertook no responsibility for the rented dwelling. There was only one circumstance where the landlord may have had a repair obligation, which arose where the dwelling let was a furnished dwelling. In these circumstances, an implied warranty may have arisen on the part of the landlord that the dwelling was fit for human habitation at the commencement of the tenancy.[19]

5–07 Obligations of repair and maintenance imposed on landlords have been created mainly through statute. Earlier statutory provisions, which implied certain obligations on the landlord to repair the property, included the Public Health (Ireland) Act 1878, that required landlords to ensure the health and safety of premises being let, and s.114 of the Housing Act 1966,[20] that implied into every contract for letting, a condition that the house was at the commencement of the tenancy "in all respects reasonably fit for human habitation".[21] However, the most important statutory provision with regard to a landlord's obligations of repair and maintenance is s.18 of the Housing (Miscellaneous Provisions) Act 1992 (the "1992 Act") as amended by the Housing (Miscellaneous Provisions) Act 2009 (the "Housing Act 2009").[22] Section 18 empowers the Minister[23] to

---

[18] RTA 2004, s.16(c) and (e). The RTA 2004 does not provide for cases where the landlord has been unable to obtain a tenant's consent to enter a dwelling, but requires access because of an emergency situation, for instance to carry out a repair which if unattended to could result in serious damage to the dwelling. In proceedings before the PRTB, such circumstances may be a mitigating factor in determining if an award should be made against the landlord and the nature of any such award.

[19] *Coleman v Dundalk UDC*, unreported, Supreme Court, July 17, 1985; *Brown v Norton* [1954] I.R. 34; *McGeary v Campbell* [1975] N.I. 7. See also Wylie, *Landlord and Tenant Law*, 2nd edn (Dublin: Butterworths, 1998), para.15.04.

[20] See *Siney v Dublin Corporation* [1980] I.R. 400 where it was held that s.114 of the Housing Act 1966 did not apply to housing authorities but that the housing authorities were liable in damages for breach of contract based on the implied warranty as to fitness for human habitation.

[21] Section 114 which is now repealed by s.37 of the 1992 Act.

[22] Section 18 of the 1992 Act is amended as indicated in Sch.2 to the Housing Act 2009.

[23] Minister is defined at s.1(1) of the 1992 Act as the Minister for the Environment (now the Minister for the Environment, Heritage and Local Government).

make regulations prescribing standards for houses. The Housing (Standards for Rented Houses) Regulations 1993[24] (the "1993 Regulations") were enacted under s.18 of the 1992 Act and imposed minimum obligations on landlords in respect of the repair and maintenance of a dwelling. The 1993 Regulations were revoked by the Housing (Standards for Rented Houses) Regulations 2008 (the "2008 Regulations"),[25] with the exception of arts 6 and 7, which remain in force with respect to existing tenancies until February 1, 2013.[26]

5–08 The RTA 2004 also imposes obligations on a landlord with respect to repair and maintenance of the structure and interior of a dwelling.[27] The standards prescribed by the RTA 2004 and the regulations enacted under s.18 of the 1992 Act are the minimum standards that must be complied with by landlords.

B. Structure of the Dwelling

(i) Obligations imposed

5–09 A landlord must carry out to the structure of the dwelling all such repairs that are from time to time necessary and must ensure that the structure of the dwelling complies with any standards for houses for the time being prescribed under s.18 of the 1992 Act.[28] The 2008 Regulations are the principle regulations in force, as enacted under s.18 of the 1992 Act. The 2008 Regulations provide that a landlord of a dwelling must ensure that it is maintained in "a proper state of structural repair."[29]

5–10 A landlord must therefore deal with repairs to the structure of the dwelling when required. Any requirement for repair in the 2008 Regulations shall be construed as requiring a standard of repair that is reasonable in all the circumstances and in determining the appropriate standard of repair, regard shall be had to the age, character and prospective life of the house.[30] A landlord has no obligation to carry out repairs to the structure of the dwelling required because

---

[24] S.I. No. 147 of 1993.
[25] S.I. No. 534 of 2008. The 2008 Regulations were amended by the Housing (Standards for Rented Houses) (Amendment) Regulations 2009 (the "2009 Regulations"). The 2008 Regulations apply to every house let, or available for letting, for rent or other valuable consideration solely as a dwelling. The 2008 Regulations do not apply to holiday lettings and certain dwellings let or available for letting by the Health Service Executive, approved (including voluntary) bodies and local authorities. See art.4 of the 2008 Regulations (as amended by art.2(b) of the 2009 Regulations).
[26] See para.5–14.
[27] RTA 2004, s.12(1)(b).
[28] RTA 2004, s.12(1)(b)(i).
[29] 2008 Regulations, art.5(1).
[30] 2008 Regulations, art.(3).

of the tenant's actions in breach of his or her tenancy obligations, where the deterioration in the condition of the structure is beyond normal wear and tear.[31]

"A proper state of structural repair" is defined in the 2008 Regulations as meaning:

> sound, internally and externally, with roof, roofing tiles and slates, windows, floors, ceilings, walls, stairs, doors, skirting boards, fascia, tiles on any floor, ceiling and wall, gutters, down pipes, fittings, furnishings, gardens and common areas maintained in good condition and repair and not defective due to dampness or otherwise.[32]

This reflects the definition of "a proper state of structural repair" now provided by s.18(8) of the 1992 Act, which was amended by Pt 4 of Sch. 2 to the Housing Act 2009.[33] As originally enacted, s.18(8) of the 1992 Act was less onerous and simply provided that a "proper state of structural repair" was:

> essentially sound, with roof, floors, ceiling, walls and stairs in good repair and not subject to serious dampness or liable to collapse because they are rotted or otherwise defective.[34]

(ii) Cases before the PRTB

5–11 In *Godfrey v Healy-Rae*,[35] the tenant had submitted a complaint to the PRTB against the respondent landlord. The tenant claimed, amongst other things, that the dwelling suffered from water leaks and was damp. The tenant sought compensation because of the failure of the landlord to repair the dwelling. In dealing with the dispute at first instance, the adjudicator inspected the dwelling.

The adjudicator determined there were a number of leaks in the dwelling and there was evidence of dampness, resulting from condensation, which the adjudicator said could be solved with the installation of an extractor fan. The

---

[31] Section 12(2) of the RTA 2004 provides that s.12(1)(b) does not apply to any repairs that are necessary due to the failure of the tenant to comply with s.16(f). While s.12(2) of the RTA 2004 may therefore relieve a landlord from his/her obligation owed to the tenant under s.12(1)(b), a landlord may, however, face liability due to the state of repair of the structure of the dwelling in other instances, for example through an action in tort.

[32] 2008 Regualtions, art.5(2), as amended by art.2(c) of the 2009 Regulations.

[33] Section 18(7) of the 1992 Act provides for a non-exhaustive list of the matters that may be the subject of regulations made under s.18(1). Section 18(7)(b) provides that the regulations may make provision in relation to the maintenance of the house and common areas in a "proper state of structural repair".

[34] This was also the definition of a "proper state of structural repair" originally provided by art.5(2) of the 2008 Regulations. See, "Housing (Standards for Rented Houses) Regulations. S.I. No. 534 of 2008, Technical Guidance Document", Department of the Enviroment, Heritage and Local Government, p.7, which provides guidance as to weather a house will be in a proper state of structural repair in accordance with the 2008 Regulations.

[35] TR35/DR230/2006, August 28, 2006.

adjudicator directed that the landlord should correct the defects in the property but that the tenant was not entitled to compensation. The tenant appealed the adjudicator's determination to a tenancy tribunal that ultimately determined that the tenant was entitled to compensation. It directed the landlord to pay the tenant the sum of €3,000 for his failure to maintain the dwelling in a proper state of structural repair, as required by the 1993 Regulations, and for his failure to comply with his obligation to carry out necessary repairs to the structure of the dwelling as required by s.12(1)(b)(i) of the RTA 2004.

5–12 In *Norris v Rice and Anor*,[36] the tenancy tribunal determined that the landlord was to attend to the repairs required to maintain the property in good repair in accordance with her obligations under s.12(1) of the RTA 2004. It directed that the works required included, inter alia, repairing the malfunctioning shower, eradication of dampness in one bedroom, replacement of loose cork tiles, rectifying sagging doors, and clearing out the sheds as well as attending to a possible leak in the velux windows. The tenancy tribunal directed that this work was to be carried out within three months of the issue of the determination order. In *Walsh v O'Sullivan*,[37] the respondent landlord was directed to pay the tenant the sum of €805, this being compensation for damage caused to the tenant's personal belongings and equipment as a result of a leak in the dwelling caused by a waste water pipe having overflowed.

C. Interior of the Dwelling

5–13 Obligations are also imposed on landlords to maintain the interior of a dwelling rented by him or her. A landlord must carry out to the interior of the dwelling all repairs and replacement of fittings as are from time to time necessary, so that the interior and fittings are maintained in the condition they were in at the commencement of the tenancy and in compliance with any statutory standards prescribed.[38] A landlord has no obligation to carry out repairs to the interior of the dwelling required because of tenant's actions in breach of his or her tenancy, where the deterioration in the condition of the dwelling's interior is beyond normal wear and tear.[39] The 2008 Regulations provide that nothing in the regulations impose an obligation on a landlord to repair or maintain in good repair, working order or in a clean condition anything which a tenant is entitled to remove from the rented dwelling.[40]

---

[36] TR23/DR347/2006, July 25, 2006.
[37] TR41/DR451/2008, November 11, 2008.
[38] RTA 2004, s.12(1)(b)(ii).
[39] RTA 2004, s.12(2).
[40] 2008 Regulations, art.3(4)(b)(ii). The same applied in the context of the 1993 Regulations (art.3(4)(b)(ii)).

D. Facilities within a Dwelling

(i) Interaction of 1993 Regulations and 2008 Regulations

5–14 The 2008 Regulations impose more onerous obligations on landlords in relation to the maintenance of facilities within a dwelling than had been imposed under the 1993 Regulations. The 2008 Regulations allow for a phasing-in period to give landlords a reasonable timeframe to bring their property into compliance with the 2008 Regulations.[41] Accordingly, in respect of an "existing tenancy", arts 6 to 8 of the 2008 Regulations will come into operation on February 1, 2013, while arts 6 and 7 of the 1993 Regulations apply to any such existing tenancy up to that date.[42] An "existing tenancy" for the purposes of the 2008 Regulations means a house let for rent or other valuable consideration solely as a dwelling *at any time* from September 1, 2004 to January 31, 2009.[43] The entirety of the provisions of the 2008 Regulations came into effect on February 1, 2009, for any rental property being let for the first time on or after February 1, 2009.[44]

(ii) Sanitary facilities

5–15 Existing tenancies In the case of an existing tenancy,[45] a landlord is obliged by the 1993 Regulations to ensure that a sink is provided in the habitable area of the house.[46] A watercloset and a fixed bath or shower must also be provided in the habitable area of the house, or where the house is in a part of a building containing more than one house, either in the habitable area of the house or in a part of the building that is either on the same floor as the house or on the floor immediately above or below the house.[47] In the case of a house which is in part of the building, a watercloset and/or the fixed bath or shower cannot be shared between more than two houses, unless the sanitary facility provided is for use by not more than four persons.[48] Each sink, watercloset, fixed bath or shower required to be provided in the case of an existing tenancy must

---

[41] "Housing (Standards for Rented Houses) Regulations, 2008, S.I. No. 534 of 2008, Technical Guidance Document", Department of the Environment, Heritage and Local Government, p.4.

[42] 2008 Regulations, arts 2(b) and 14(2). Article 14(3) of the 2008 Regulations provides that art.7 of the 1993 Regulations shall continue to have effect where the house is let by a housing authority under s.56 of the Housing Act 1966 (as amended) or by a housing body approved under s.6 of the 1992 Act.

[43] 2008 Regulations, art.3(1)(i).

[44] 2008 Regulations, art.2(a).

[45] See para.5–14 for the meaning of an "existing tenancy".

[46] 1993 Regulations, art.6(1).

[47] 1993 Regulations, art.6(2) and (3). See art.6(2)(b)(i), (ii) and (c) for the circumstances where the landlord is not obliged to provide a watercloset in the "habitable area" of the house but in the house only. "House" is defined for the purposes of the 1993 Regulations as including "any building or part of a building used or suitable for use as a dwelling and any out office, yard, garden or other land appurtenant thereto or usually enjoyed therewith" (1993 Regulations, art.3(1)).

[48] 1993 Regulations, art.6(6) and (7).

have an adequate piped supply of water, and a safe and effective means of drainage. For each sink, bath and shower, a facility for the piped supply of hot water must also be provided.[49]

5–16 First lettings and lettings from 2013 In the case of a dwelling let for the first time on or after February 1, 2009 and for all tenancies post-February 1, 2013, a landlord is obliged to provide the following sanitary facilities within the habitable area of the house and *for the exclusive use of the house*:

(a) A watercloset, with dedicated wash hand basin adjacent thereto with a continuous supply of cold water and a facility for the piped supply of hot water, and

(b) A fixed bath or shower with continuous supply of cold water and a facility for the piped supply of hot water.[50]

The landlord is obliged to maintain the watercloset, bath and/or shower in good working order, ensure there is safe and effective means of drainage, that they are properly insulated and secure and have minimum capacity requirements for hot and cold water storage facilities. The watercloset, bath and/or shower must also be provided in a room separated from other rooms by a wall and a door and containing separate ventilation.[51]

(iii) Heating, food preparation and storage and laundry

5–17 Existing tenancies In the case of an existing tenancy,[52] a landlord is obliged by the 1993 Regulations to provide with the house an appliance or appliances capable of providing adequate heating and facilities for the installation of cooking equipment, with provision where necessary for the safe and effective removal of fumes or other products of combustion to the external air. A landlord is also obliged to provide facilities for the hygienic storage of food.[53] No obligations are imposed by the 1993 Regulations for the provision of laundry facilities.

---

[49] 1993 Regulations, art.6(4).

[50] 2008 Regulations, art.6(1). "House", for the purposes of the 2008 Regulations, is defined as including "any building or part of a building used or suitable for use as a dwelling and any outoffice, yard, garden or other land appurtenant thereto or usually enjoyed therewith" (2008 Regulations, art.3(1)(ii)).

[51] 2008 Regulations, art.6(2).

[52] See para.5–14 for the meaning of an "existing tenancy".

[53] 1993 Regulations, art.7. In *Bone v Lojek* (TR12/DR1309/2009, March 6, 2009) the tenant was awarded the sum of €100 for the lack of an adequate fridge and the landlord's failure to maintain dishwasher facilities.

5–18 First lettings and lettings from 2013 In the case of a dwelling let for the first time on or after February 1, 2009 and for all tenancies post-February 1, 2013, a landlord is obliged to provide in every room used, or intended for use by the tenant of the house as a habitable room, a permanently fixed appliance or appliances capable of providing effective heating and capable of being independently managed by the tenant. The landlord is also obliged to provide suitable and adequate facilities for the safe and effective removal of fumes and other products of combustion to the external air.[54]

A landlord must provide the following kitchen facilities within the habitable area of the house and for the exclusive use of the house:

(a) Four-ring hob with oven and grill and suitable facilities for the effective and safe removal of fumes to the external air by means of a cooker hood or extractor fan;

(b) Fridge and freezer or fridge-freezer;

(c) Microwave oven;

(d) Sink with a piped supply of cold water and a facility for the piped supply of hot water and an adequate draining area; and

(e) Suitable and adequate number of kitchen presses for food storage purposes.[55]

A landlord is also obliged to provide, within the habitable area of the house and for the exclusive use of the house, a washing machine or access to a communal washing machine facility and, where the house does not contain a garden or yard for the exclusive use of that house, a dryer or access to a communal dryer facility.[56]

E. Electricity and Gas

5–19 Landlords are obliged to maintain installations for the supply of electricity and gas in good repair and safe working order, with provision where necessary for the safe and effective removal of fumes to the external air.[57] In *Sundarasan (aka Periasamy) v O'Shaughnessy*,[58] the landlord was ordered to pay the tenant €230 for the reimbursement of a gas repair charge.

F. Ventilation and Lighting

5–20 Every room used, or intended for use, by the tenant of a house as a habitable room must have adequate ventilation, which must be maintained by

---

[54] 2008 Regulations, art.7.
[55] 2008 Regulations, art.8(2)(a)–(f).
[56] 2008 Regulations, art.8(2)(g)–(h), as amended by art.2(d)(ii) of the 2009 Regulations.
[57] 2008 Regulations, art.13.
[58] DR1015/2006, determination order dated November 14, 2007.

the landlord in good repair and working order. Adequate ventilation must also be provided for the removal of water vapour from kitchens and bathrooms.[59] Furthermore, every room used or intended for use by the tenant of a house as a habitable room must have adequate natural lighting. Every hall, stairs and landing within the house and every room used or intended for use by the tenant of the house must have a suitable and adequate means of artificial lighting. The windows of every room containing a bath and/or shower and a watercloset must be suitably and adequately screened to ensure privacy.[60]

G. Refuse Facilities

5–21 A landlord of a dwelling is obliged to provide receptacles suitable for the storage of refuse outside the dwelling, except where the provision of such receptacles is not within the power or control of the landlord.[61] This may arise, for instance, in the case of an apartment complex where the management company is in charge of arranging for disposal of waste and the provision of refuse storage facilities.

H. Reimbursement of the Tenant for Repairs

5–22 The obligation to repair and maintain the structure and interior of a dwelling falls on the landlord.[62] A landlord cannot contract out of his or her obligations of repair and maintenance or impose these obligations on the tenant.[63] In *Norris v Rice and Anor*,[64] the landlord claimed that by virtue of clause (g) of the letting agreement, it was the tenants who were obliged to maintain the interior of the dwelling. In the reasons provided for its determination, the tenancy tribunal said that no clause in a letting agreement could override a landlord's statutory obligation to maintain rented properties in a proper state of repair. The tenancy tribunal directed the landlord to attend to the repairs required to maintain the property in good repair in accordance with her obligations under s.12(1) of the RTA 2004.

---

[59] 2008 Regulations, art.9.

[60] 2008 Regulations, art.10.

[61] RTA 2004, s.12(1)(ba), as inserted by s.100(3) of the Housing Act 2009. Article 12 of the 2008 Regulations provides that a house shall have access to suitable and adequate pest and vermin proof refuse storage facilities.

[62] RTA 2004, s.12(1)(b). See also s.18(1) of the 1992 Act, which provides that it shall be the duty of the landlord to ensure that the rented house complies with any regulations enacted under that section.

[63] RTA 2004, s.18(1). Section 18(1) prohibits the parties to a tenancy contracting out of a landlord's obligations contained in s.12 of the RTA 2004. Section 18(3) of the RTA 2004 provides that additional obligations to those contained in s.16 of the RTA 2004 may be imposed on the tenant, but only if those obligations are consistent with the RTA 2004. See also para.5–46.

[64] TR23/DR347/2006, July 25, 2006.

5–23 A tenant may carry out repairs to the structure or interior of a dwelling, subject to the following conditions:

(a) the landlord has refused to carry out the repairs at the time the tenant requests him or her to do so,[65] *and*
(b) the postponement of the repairs to some subsequent date would have been unreasonable having regard to either:
  (i) a significant risk the matters requiring repair posed to the health or safety of the tenant or other lawful occupants in the dwelling, or
  (ii) if the matters requiring repairs caused a significant reduction in the quality of the tenant's or other occupants living environment.[66]

Where the requirements set out at (a) and (b) above are satisfied, a landlord is obliged to reimburse a tenant for all "reasonable and vouched expenses" incurred by the tenant.[67] It is important, therefore, that a tenant who carries out necessary repairs where the landlord has failed or refused to do so, keeps receipts or is otherwise able to prove the expenses that he or she has incurred. In *Costello v Farrell*,[68] the landlord was ordered to reimburse the tenant €1,900 in respect of the supply and installation of a cooker, €1,500 for the supply and fitting of kitchen units and €500 for repairs to the kitchen floor. The evidence that had been submitted to the tenancy tribunal on behalf of the tenant in support of his case consisted of receipts and a general valuation which estimated the cost of carrying out certain works.[69] Persons who had carried out repairs on behalf of the tenant also gave evidence.

I. Enforcement

5–24 Where a landlord has failed to comply with his obligations to repair and maintain a rented dwelling or to reimburse a tenant for carrying out necessary repairs, the tenant's remedy is to submit an application for dispute resolution to the PRTB, complaining of the landlord's failure.[70] The tenant is not allowed to withhold rent or offset the cost of repairs against the amount of rent payable.[71] This is in contrast to the position that existed prior to the enactment of the RTA

---

[65] RTA 2004, s.12(1)(g)(i). While a refusal communicated by a landlord or his or her agent will satisfy the condition prescribed by s.12(1)(g)(i), s.12(5) of the RTA 2004 provides that this condition is also satisfied where, after all reasonable attempts, the landlord or his or her agent could not be contacted to make the request concerned.
[66] RTA 2004, s.12(1)(g)(ii).
[67] RTA 2004, s.12(1)(g).
[68] TR17/DR327/2006, June 19, 2006.
[69] In evidence given by the tenant he said that as he had carried out most of the work himself, the figures given by him were lower than the general valuation.
[70] RTA 2004, s.78(1)(e).
[71] See paras 4–03 to 4–07 which consider a tenant's obligation to pay rent.

2004, where a tenant was entitled to set-off against the rent expenses incurred by doing the repairs himself or herself.[72]

Where a landlord is in breach of his or her obligation to repair or maintain a dwelling contrary to any regulations enacted under s.18(1) of the 1992 Act, the tenant can also make a complaint to the housing authority in the functional area in which the rented dwelling is situated. Housing authorities are empowered to enforce the regulations enacted under s.18(1) of the 1992 Act as set out below.[73] A landlord who contravenes regulations made under s.18 is also guilty of an offence. On conviction, the landlord will be liable to a fine not exceeding €5,000 and/or imprisonment for a term not exceeding six months, in addition to a fine of €400 (on conviction) for each day of a continuing offence.[74]

(i) Improvement notice

5–25 Where a housing authority is of the opinion that a landlord has contravened or is contravening a requirement of a regulation made under s.18(1) of the 1992 Act, it may serve an improvement notice on the landlord of the house concerned. The improvement notice must, amongst other matters, identify the provision of the particular regulation that the housing authority considers that the landlord has contravened or is contravening, and direct the landlord to remedy the contravention within a certain period. The improvement notice may also include directions as to the measures to be taken to remedy the contravention or to otherwise comply with the notice. The local authority must also provide a copy of the improvement notice to the tenant of the house concerned.[75]

5–26 Where an improvement notice has been served on a landlord and the landlord is of the opinion that the improvement notice has been complied with, he or she must confirm in writing to the housing authority that the matters referred to in the notice have been remedied.[76] The landlord must give a copy of this notice to the tenant. Where the housing authority is satisfied that the contravention has been remedied it must give a compliance notice to the landlord within 28 days of receiving the confirmation from the landlord.[77]

5–27 A landlord has the right to object to an improvement notice served on him or her by a housing authority. The landlord must submit an objection to the notice (in the form and manner specified in the improvement notice) within 14

---

[72] Landlord and Tenant (Amendment) Act 1980, s.87.

[73] See paras 4.8.4 and 4.10 of the "Report of the Commission on the Private Rented Residential Sector" (July 2000) which considers the enforcement of the 1993 Regulations by local authorities.

[74] 1992 Act, s.34(1), as amended by Pt 4 (item 6) of Sch.2 to the Housing Act 2009.

[75] 1992 Act, s.18A(1)–(4), as inserted by Pt 4 (item 4) of Sch.2 to the Housing Act 2009.

[76] This must be sent to the local authority before the period contained in the improvement notice expires – 1992 Act, s.18A(5)(A), as inserted by Pt 4 (item 4) of Sch.2 to the Housing Act 2009.

[77] 1992 Act, s.18A(5), as inserted by Pt 4 (item 4) of Sch.2 to the Housing Act 2009.

days, beginning on the day on which the improvement notice is given to him or her. The housing authority is obliged to consider this objection and may, as it sees fit, vary, withdraw, cancel or confirm the notice and must notify the landlord in writing of its decision and the reasons for it within 14 days after the objection.[78] If the landlord is aggrieved by the housing authority's decision, the landlord has a right of appeal to a judge of the District Court in the district court area in which the notice was served. The landlord is obliged to notify the housing authority of his or her appeal and the housing authority will be entitled to participate in the hearing of the appeal. The District Court may confirm, vary or cancel the improvement notice.[79]

(ii) Prohibition notice

5–28 Where a landlord fails to comply with an improvement notice, the housing authority may serve a prohibition notice on the landlord. The notice must state that the housing authority is of the opinion that the landlord has failed to comply with the notice and direct the landlord not to re-let the house for rent or other valuable consideration until the landlord has remedied the contravention specified in the improvement notice. The housing authority is required to provide a copy of the prohibition notice to the tenant of the house concerned.[80] The housing authority must also, in the interests of public health and safety, make such arrangements as it considers necessary to bring the contents of a prohibition notice to the attention of the public.[81]

5–29 Where a prohibition notice has been served on a landlord and the landlord is of the opinion that the prohibition notice has been complied with, he or she must confirm in writing to the housing authority that the matters to which the notice relates have been remedied. The landlord must give a copy of this notice to the tenant. Where the housing authority is satisfied that the matters have been remedied, it must issue a compliance notice to the landlord within 28 days of receiving the confirmation from the landlord.[82]

5–30 A landlord has the right to appeal a prohibition notice to a judge of the District Court in the district court area in which the notice was served. The appeal must be brought within 14 days beginning on the day on which the notice is given to him or her. The landlord is obliged to notify the housing authority of his or her appeal and the housing authority will be entitled to participate in the

---

[78] 1992 Act, s.18A(6) as inserted by Pt.4 (item 4) of Sch.2 to the Housing Act 2009.
[79] 1992 Act, s.18A(7), as inserted by Pt 4 (item 4) of Sch.2 to the Housing Act 2009. The landlord's appeal must be made within 14 days after the housing authority's decision is notified to him or her.
[80] 1992 Act, s.18B(1)–(3), as inserted by Pt 4 (item 4) of Sch.2 to the Housing Act 2009.
[81] 1992 Act, s.18B(10), as inserted by Pt 4 (item 4) of Sch.2 to the Housing Act 2009.
[82] 1992 Act, s.18B(6) and (7) as inserted by Pt 4 (item 4) of Sch.2 to the Housing Act 2009.

hearing of the appeal. The District Court may confirm, vary or cancel the improvement notice.[83]

5–31 Tort In addition to the liability that a landlord may incur for failing to comply with his or her statutory obligations to repair and maintain a dwelling rented by him or her, a landlord may also incur liability in tort. For instance, a landlord may be liable for a nuisance caused by him which affects the tenant. A landlord may also be liable in negligence if he lets a premises that he or she ought to foresee is likely to injure the tenant or damage the tenant's property.[84]

4. Effect and Maintain a Policy of Insurance

5–32 Landlords must take out and maintain a policy of insurance for the *structure* of a dwelling.[85] Section 12(1)(c) of RTA 2004 prescribes that the policy is to:

    (a) insure the landlord against damage to the dwelling and the loss and destruction of the dwelling, and

    (b) indemnify the landlord to a minimum of €250,000 against any liability on his or her part arising out of the ownership, possession and use of the dwelling.

There is one exception to a landlord's obligation to insure, which arises in circumstances where, at any particular time during the term of the tenancy, the landlord cannot obtain a policy of insurance as described at (a) and (b) or cannot obtain such a policy at a "reasonable cost".[86] The RTA 2004 does not provide any guidance in relation to what would be deemed a "reasonable cost" for insurance and there is also a dearth of tenancy tribunal decisions on the issue. In the absence of any such guidance, it seems that it will be a matter to be assessed on a case by case basis, having regard to all relevant circumstances, including the nature of the dwelling concerned.

5–33 The insurance policy, which a landlord is obliged to maintain by reason of s.12(1)(c) of the RTA 2004, relates solely to the dwelling. If a tenant wishes to insure his or her own personal belongings that will be a matter for the tenant.

---

[83] 1992 Act, s.18B(4), as inserted by Pt 4 (item 4) of Sch.2 to the Housing Act 2009.
[84] See McMahon and Binchy, *Irish Law of Torts*, 2nd edn (Dublin: Butterworths, 1990) p.468.
[85] RTA 2004, s.12(1)(c).
[86] RTA 2004, s.12(3).

5. Repayment of Deposit

A. Obligation to Repay Promptly

5–34 A landlord is obliged to return or repay "promptly" any deposit paid by the tenant of a rented dwelling.[87] This obligation is subject to two exceptions, which arise where:

    (a) the tenant is in arrears of rent or has failed to pay any other charges or taxes payable in accordance with the lease or tenancy agreement; or
    (b) where the tenant has caused a deterioration to the condition of the dwelling beyond normal wear or tear.

5–35 Where a tenant is in arrears of rent or has failed to pay any other taxes or charges, a landlord is entitled to deduct the amount of rent or tax or charge owing from the deposit.[88] If the sum owed equals or is greater than the deposit provided by the tenant, the landlord is entitled to withhold the total sum of the deposit.[89] Where a tenant has caused a deterioration in the condition of the dwelling above normal wear and tear, a landlord is entitled to retain part of the deposit to cover the costs that would be incurred by the landlord in taking reasonable steps to restore the dwelling to the condition it was in at the commencement of the tenancy.[90] If the cost of repairing the dwelling equals or is greater than the deposit provided by the tenant, the landlord is entitled to withhold the total sum of the deposit.[91]

In circumstances where the amount of arrears of rent, tax or other charge, or the cost of repairing the dwelling exceeds the deposit, the landlord's means of redress is to submit a dispute to the PRTB for resolution, to recoup the balance of the monies owed to him or her.[92] A landlord of a residential dwelling is not entitled to levy distress for rent.[93]

B. Cases before the PRTB

(i) Determinations

5–36 In *Moroz v Carney*,[94] the landlord was directed to repay the deposit of €2,400 paid by the tenant, less €766.28 for arrears of rent owing and the sum of

---

[87] RTA 2004, s.12(1)(d).
[88] RTA 2004, s.12(4)(b), as amended by s.100(3)(c) of the Housing Act 2009.
[89] RTA 2004, s.12(4)(a)(i), as amended by s.100(3)(b) of the Housing Act 2009.
[90] RTA 2004, s.12(4)(b), as amended by s.100(3)(c) of the Housing Act 2009.
[91] RTA 2004, s.12(4)(a)(ii).
[92] RTA 2004, s.78(1)(d) and (l).
[93] A landlord will levy distress against a tenant where the landlord seizes a tenant's possessions as payment for monies owed to him or her by the tenant. Section 19 of the 1992 Act prohibits distress being levied for the rent (including rent-charge) of any premises let as a residential dwelling.
[94] TR53/DR461/2007, determination order dated November 14, 2007.

€90.01 for repairs to the boiler. The tenancy tribunal also determined that the landlord was to pay the tenant €500 in damages for breach of his obligation to repay the tenant's deposit promptly. Similarly, in *McGrath and Anor v Reddin*,[95] the landlord was directed to pay the tenant the sum of €600, being the balance of the tenant's deposit after an allowance of €100 for damage to the landlord's property was deducted. An award of €100 was also made in favour of the tenant for the landlord's failure to return the deposit promptly.

5–37 In *Hernandez and Anor v Aziz*,[96] the landlord had claimed that he was entitled to retain the full deposit of €1,400 paid by the tenants.[97] The tenancy tribunal directed the landlord to repay to the tenants the sum of €1,020, less the sum of €380 to be retained by the landlord as a contribution towards the cost of carpet cleaning. In *Finlayson v McKeever and Anor*,[98] the landlord had withheld the full deposit of €600 paid by the tenants. The tenancy tribunal found that some minor cleaning was required to restore the dwelling to the condition it was in when it was originally let and determined that the landlord was entitled to retain €100 from the €600 deposit paid by the tenants.

5–38 In the case of *Klatt v Neary*,[99] the tenant referred a dispute to the PRTB for the landlord's failure to return part of a security deposit. There being no reason not to allow the full amount of the security deposit to be repaid to the tenant, the PRTB made a determination order requiring the landlord to repay the outstanding part of the deposit to the tenant.

5–39 As we have seen at para.5–36, in determining disputes on deposit retention, tenancy tribunals have also awarded tenants compensation for the landlord's failure to promptly refund the deposit to the tenant. In *Azad v Sinnathambi*,[100] the landlord was directed to pay the tenant the sum of €900, which was the amount of the deposit, and a further sum of €400 for the landlord's breach of obligation to promptly return the deposit to the tenant. The tenancy tribunal made a similar finding in *Clarke v Gumowska and Anor*,[101] where the sum of €200 was awarded to the tenants for wrongful withholding by the landlord of the deposit.[102]

---

95 TR42/DR27/2008, November 3, 2008.
96 TR51/DR837/2007, August 29, 2007.
97 In that case neither of the tenants were parties to the original agreement but had each taken over from the original tenants. Ms Hernandez gave evidence that she had paid €700 to the former tenants, who in turn had first paid €700 to the landlord as a security deposit.
98 TR40/DR252/2007, August 8, 2007.
99 DR71/2006, determination order dated March 14, 2007.
100 TR16/DR234/2008, October 1, 2008.
101 TR51/DR1195/2009, April 23, 2009.
102 See *Maguire v Kraukle and Anor* (TR129/DR764/2007, March 28, 2008) where the sum of €750 was awarded to the tenants for wrongful retention by the landlord of the deposit monies and in relation to the landlord's failure to provide proper cooking facilities.

(ii) Burden of proof

5–40 The onus is on the landlord to establish why the deposit should be retained.[103] In *Lawlor and Anor v Ryan*,[104] the landlord claimed that he was entitled to retain the deposit to cover the costs of restoring the house to the condition it was in when it was first rented to the tenant. The tenancy tribunal stated that the onus of proof is on the landlord to prove that the security deposit should be retained by him and stated the following:

> "As the Appellant Landlord produced no documentary evidence to support his case, and as the onus is on him to produce compelling reasons why the tenant's money should not be returned to her, the Tribunal finds in favour of the Tenant."[105]

5–41 As discussed at para.5–34 above, where a tenant has caused deterioration in the condition of the dwelling beyond normal wear and tear, a landlord is entitled to retain part or all of a deposit to cover the costs of restoring the dwelling to the condition it was in at the commencement of the tenancy. In these types of cases, it can sometimes be difficult to assess what damage is caused by normal wear and tear, and damage which is not, and to calculate how much can be deducted from the security deposit.[106] However, where a landlord seeks to retain part or all of a deposit paid, it is important that the landlord keeps evidence to support the retention of the deposit, should this be later challenged by the tenant. In *Hernandez and Anor v Aziz*[107] and *Finlayson v McKeever and Anor*,[108] the landlords had retained the deposits paid by the tenants, to cover what they had maintained was a deterioration in the condition of the respective dwellings. The tenancy tribunals in both cases commented on a lack of evidence as to the state of repair of the dwellings and stated that as a result they were not in a position to resolve the conflicts between the parties. In *Finlayson v McKeever and Anor*, the tenancy tribunal noted that in the absence of an agreed inventory of the contents of the dwelling and photographic evidence of the condition of the property at the commencement of the tenancy, the tenancy tribunal was unable to determine whether a deterioration as alleged in the condition of the beds and mattresses had occurred. In *Hernandez and Anor v Aziz*, the tenancy tribunal noted that it would have been of great assistance if the parties had provided some independent witnesses, photographic or video evidence of the condition of the dwelling when it was vacated.

---

[103] See *Keating v Hennelly* (TR11/DR326/2007, March 15, 2007); *Komrakovs v Kenny* (TR20/DR615/2007, April 2, 2007).

[104] TR07/DR711/2007, February 23, 2007.

[105] Tenancy tribunal report, p.4.

[106] See *Early v Chinaka* (TR15/2007/DR1235/2006, April 4, 2007).

[107] TR51/DR837/2007, August 29, 2007.

[108] TR40/DR252/2007, August 8, 2007.

(iii) Reasonable costs

5–42 A landlord is only entitled to his or her reasonable costs in restoring the dwelling to the condition it was in at the commencement of the tenancy. In *McKenna v O'Neill*,[109] on the termination of the tenancy the landlord had retained the full deposit of €1,100 paid by the tenant. The landlord claimed that when the tenant left the property it was in a very dirty condition and that despite an attempt to clean the carpet in the living room, it had to be replaced. The landlord further claimed the cooker was left encrusted with food and she had to replace it, that the washing machine also had to be replaced and that she had to have the property re-painted. The landlord provided receipts to the tenancy tribunal showing that the she had incurred €269 in replacing the cooker, €270 for the washing machine, €830 for wooden flooring she had bought to replace the carpet in the living room and €660 for wooden flooring for the bedrooms. In relation to the latter receipt, the tenancy tribunal noted that it was dated April 2006, being more than 13 months after the tenant had ended the tenancy. Finally, the landlord also submitted into evidence before the tenancy tribunal a receipt (not on headed paper) from an "odd-job man" totalling €900, for various tasks carried out on the property including carpet cleaning, painting, removing dirt and gardening. From the deposit of €1,100 paid, the tenancy tribunal determined that the landlord was entitled to retain €600, being €400 towards the replacement living room carpet, €100 towards the cost of painting the living room and €100 towards general cleaning. The landlord was directed to return the balance of the deposit of €500 to the tenant.

C. Proposed Rental Deposit Board

5–43 Deposit retention cases have consistently been the single largest category of cases submitted to the PRTB for dispute resolution.[110] Submissions were made to the Commission on the Private Rented Residential Sector (the "Commission") that there was a need for regulations providing for the holding of security deposit monies on joint deposits and the return of any interest earned to the tenant. It was also submitted that there was a need for a rental deposit board and in the absence of such a board, the jurisdiction of the Small Claims Court should be reassessed regularly.[111] The Commission, however, made no recommendations in its report in relation to the establishment of a rental deposit board. As enacted, while the RTA 2004 gives the PRTB jurisdiction to deal with disputes in relation to the retention or refund of a deposit, it did not go as far as to establish a rental bond board or to empower the PRTB to hold such deposits. This is in contrast to the situations in other jurisdictions that were considered by

---

[109] TR11/DR91/2006, May 18, 2008.
[110] "Private Residential Tenancies Board, Annual Report & Accounts 2008", p.29.
[111] "Report of the Commission on the Private Rented Residential Sector" (July 2000), appendix B.2.

the Commission.[112] Given that the majority of disputes that have been referred to the PRTB to date relate to the retention or refund of deposits, the establishment of a rental deposit board or the holding of such deposits by the PRTB is a matter that may be revisited in the future.

6. Landlord's Contact Details and Authorised Agents

5–44 If a landlord has authorised an agent to act on his or her behalf in respect of the tenancy of a dwelling, the landlord must notify the tenant of the name of the agent.[113] A landlord of a rented dwelling is also obliged to provide the tenant with details of the means by which the tenant can contact the landlord and his or her authorised agent at all reasonable times.[114]

7. Management Companies

5–45 The RTA 2004 imposes certain limited obligations on landlords with regard to management companies. If the dwelling is one of a number of dwellings comprising an apartment complex,[115] a landlord is obliged to forward to the management company (if any) any written complaint made by the tenant concerning the performance by the management company of its functions.[116] The management company is obliged to have regard to the relevant complaint in performing its functions and must forward to the landlord a written statement of any steps it has taken to deal with the complaint.[117] The landlord must then forward the tenant any initial response and any written statement by the management company of the steps taken to deal with the complaint.[118]

---

[112] For instance in New Zealand by virtue of the provisions of the Residential Tenancies Act 1986 and in New South Wales, Australia under the provisions of the Residential Tenancies Act 1987. See appendix C, A.3.2 of the "Report of the Commission on the Private Rented Residential Sector" (July 2000).

[113] RTA 2004, s.12(1)(e). Section 12(1)(e) refers to the landlord's obligation to notify the tenant of the name of the person authorised by the landlord to act on his or her behalf in relation to the tenancy "for the time being". "[F]or the time being" suggests that a landlord is obliged to keep the tenant updated with any change in the identity of his or her authorised agent.

[114] RTA 2004, s.12(1)(f). The RTA 2004 does not contain any provisions applying directly to landlords' agents, nor does it impose any obligations on agents. The difficulties that have arisen in this regard are considered briefly in the context of the dispute resolution services of the PRTB at para.3–15.

[115] Section 12(1)(h) of the RTA 2004 and the related provisions at s.187 apply specifically to a dwelling which is one of a number of dwellings comprising "an apartment complex". Management companies often, however, also provide services in respect of other forms of "grouped" housing, for instance in the case of a terrace of newly built town houses. In that scenario s.12(1)(h) and s.187 would appear to have no application, as such houses do not comprise dwellings within an "apartment complex".

[116] RTA 2004, s.12(1)(h)(i).

[117] RTA 2004, s.187.

[118] RTA 2004, s.12(1)(h)(ii) and (iii).

The provisions of the RTA 2004 dealing with management companies are arguably of little benefit to tenants. They facilitate the communication of complaints made by tenants in apartment complexes to the management company and oblige the management company to have regard to those complaints. Management companies are also obliged to provide tenants (or landlords), on request, with details in writing of the service charges payable in respect of a dwelling in an apartment complex.[119] Where a management company does not comply with either of these obligations, however, the RTA 2004 does not provide for any sanction or consequence for the management company.

8. No Contracting Out of Landlord's Obligations

5–46 The various obligations that have been imposed on landlords by s.12 of the RTA 2004 have been considered at paras 5–02 to 5–45 above. A landlord to a tenancy cannot contract out of his or her s.12 obligations, even where the tenant agrees that they shall not apply or raises no objection to a provision of a lease or tenancy agreement purporting to exclude their application.[120] A landlord and tenant are not prevented, however, from agreeing more favourable terms for the tenant than those that apply by reason of the obligations imposed on landlords by s.12.[121] Accordingly, while s.12 prescribes a minimum standard, additional obligations can be imposed on the landlord by agreement of the parties.

9. Prohibition on Penalising Tenants

5–47 Section 14(1) of the RTA 2004 provides that a landlord of a dwelling shall not penalise a tenant for[122]:

    (a) referring any dispute between them to the PRTB;

    (b) giving evidence in any proceedings under Part 6 of the RTA 2004 to which the landlord is a party (whether the tenant is a party to those proceedings or not);

    (c) making a complaint to An Garda Síochána or public authority in relation to any matter arising out of or in connection with the occupation of the

---

[119] RTA 2004, s.188

[120] Section 18(1) of the RTA 2004 provides that "no provision of any lease, tenancy agreement, contract or other agreement (whether entered into before, on or after the commencement of [Part 2 of the RTA 2004] may operate to vary, modify or restrict in any way section 12".

[121] RTA 2004, s.18(2).

[122] The Commission in its "Report of the Commission on the Private Rented Residential Sector" (July 2000), records as one of the submissions made to it by third parties the need to eliminate arbitrary evictions in, for example, cases where a tenant has made a complaint under regulations or claimed tax relief (appendix B.2). On this point, see also para.4.8.4.2 of the Report of the Commission.

dwelling or making any application regarding such a matter to a public authority;

(d) the tenant giving notice to the landlord of his or her intention to carry out all or any of the above.[123]

A tenant will be penalised for the purposes of s.14, if the tenant is subjected to any action which adversely affects the tenant enjoying peaceful occupation of the dwelling.[124] Such action may constitute penalisation even though it consists of steps undertaken by the landlord in the exercise of his or her rights, if it can be reasonably inferred that the action was intended to penalise the tenant for doing a thing having regard to:

(a) the frequency or extent to which the right is exercised in relation to the tenant;

(b) the proximity in time of it being so exercised, to the tenant taking any of the steps referred to (a)–(d) above; and

(c) any other relevant circumstance.[125]

5–48 The onus rests with the tenant to prove that he or she has been penalised by the landlord contrary to s.14. In the matter of *Stern v Morris and Anor*,[126] the tenant claimed that he had been penalised by the landlord through the service of a notice of termination, which he maintained the landlord had served as a result of the tenant indicating that he would refer the matter of a rent review to the PRTB. The tenancy tribunial stated that while evidence of a circumstantial nature was presented by the tenant to the tenancy tribunal, and although it could not discount the possibility that the landlord was attempting to penalise the tenant by issuing a retaliatory notice of termination, there was insufficient evidence to reach a conclusive decision on this aspect of the tenant's claim. The tenancy tribunal determined that the landlord was not in breach of s.14(1)(a) of the RTA 2004. In *Ryan v Sheridan and Anor*,[127] the tenant's claim under s.14 also failed, as the tenancy tribunal was of the view that there was no evidence produced in the course of the hearing to prove that the landlord had penalised the tenant when she referred a dispute to the PRTB.

10. Enforce the Obligations of a Tenant

5–49 A landlord has a duty to enforce the obligations of a tenant. This duty is owed to persons who could be potentially affected by the landlord's failure to

---

[123] An allegation that a landlord has contravened s.14 is one of the matters referred to at s.78(1), which may be referred to the PRTB for resolution—RTA 2004, s.78(1)(o).

[124] RTA 2004, s.14(2).

[125] RTA 2004, s.14(3).

[126] TR63/DR193/2006, November 15, 2006.

[127] TR29/DR710/2007, April 4, 2007.

enforce the tenant's obligations.[128] It is one of the most onerous obligations imposed on landlords in the private rented sector and was introduced by s.15(1) of the RTA 2004, which provides:

> A landlord of a dwelling owes to each person who could be potentially affected a duty to enforce the obligations of the tenant under the tenancy.[129]

A "person who could be potentially affected" is defined at s.15(2) as a person who:

> it is reasonably foreseeable, would be directly and adversely affected by a failure to enforce an obligation of the tenant were such a failure to occur and includes any other tenant under the tenancy mentioned in [s.15(1)].

5–50 A common example of a person falling within s.15(2) of the RTA 2004, as a "person who could be potentially affected", is a neighbour of a tenant who lives in close proximity to the rented dwelling and who has been affected by the tenant's behaviour. Section 15(2) also makes clear, however, that a person who could potentially be affected includes any other tenant under the tenancy of the rented dwelling. Therefore, where the breach by one tenant of his or her obligations affects another tenant in the dwelling concerned, the tenant affected has the right to submit a complaint to the PRTB against the landlord, for his or her failure to enforce the obligations of the tenant who has breached them.

5–51 Where a landlord has breached his or her obligation under s.15(1), the sole remedy available to the "person who could be potentially affected" is to refer a complaint to the PRTB in accordance with s.77 of the RTA 2004.[130] A breach of s.15(1) is not actionable in proceedings before the courts or before any other forum.[131] Neighbours of rented dwellings are the parties that most frequently avail of the s.77 procedure, which is considered in detail at paras 9–17 to 9–24.[132] While tenants do not have locus standi to refer applications for dispute resolution against each other to the PRTB, they too, however, may avail of the s.77 procedure, to submit a complaint to the PRTB against a landlord that has failed to enforce another tenant's obligations. Accordingly, the referral of a dispute by a tenant under s.77 is the only time a tenant, albeit indirectly, may

---

[128]   The obligation imposed on landlords by s.15 of the RTA 2004 is considered in further detail at paras 9–17 to 9–24 in the context of dispute resolution.

[129]   RTA 2004, s.15(1).

[130]   RTA 2004, s.15(3). See Ch.9 on dispute resolution which considers s.77 in further detail.

[131]   RTA 2004, s.15(3). Section 15(4) however further provides that nothing in s.15(3) "affects any duty of care, and the remedies available for its breach, that exist apart from [s.15]". Accordingly, the obligation imposed on a landlord by s.15(1) does not impact on any other duty of care that landlords may owe to tenants or third parties outside the ambit of s.15.

[132]   In particular, the pre-conditions that must be satisfied by an applicant prior to referring a dispute to the PRTB for an alleged breach of s.15(1).

avail of the dispute resolution procedures under the RTA 2004, to seek to have issues between him or her and another tenant resolved before the PRTB. If a tenant wishes to take action directly against another tenant of the tenancy concerned, any such proceedings would have to be instituted before the courts.

Any redress granted by the PRTB following the making of an application by an affected party pursuant to s.77 will be as against the landlord and not the tenant whose behaviour is the subject of the complaint. This is because the duty under s.15(1) is owed by the landlord and it is with the landlord therefore that the remedy lies.[133]

5–52 In *Dunne v Farrell*,[134] a third party who was a neighbour of tenants in a rented dwelling made a complaint to the PRTB against the landlord pursuant to s.77 of the RTA 2004, in relation to the tenants' behaviour. The third party alleged that the tenants in the dwelling had engaged in antisocial behaviour, with many cars calling at late hours, by leaving dirt and rubbish in the garden and by being personally intimidating to her. In evidence given by the landlord, he said that he did not dispute that his tenants had engaged in antisocial behaviour but claimed that he had made many attempts to rectify the situation. The landlord said that he had called to the rented dwelling on a number of occasions to ask the tenants not to make noise at antisocial times, that he had spoken to An Garda Síochána and the Residents' Association to whom complaints had been made and that he had issued two notices of termination to the tenants who ultimately vacated the property. Notwithstanding this, on the evidence before it, the tenancy tribunal determined that the landlord had breached his obligations under s.15 of the RTA 2004 and was directed to pay the third party the sum of €1,000 in damages.

5–53 In the matter of *O'Brien and Anor v O'Brien*,[135] the applicants were third parties who referred a dispute to the PRTB under s.77 of the RTA 2004. The applicants' complaint was that they had been continually and persistently denied of their rights to peaceful enjoyment of their home by the actions of the tenants in the adjoining dwelling, who had caused excessive noise, played loud music and were involved in late-night partying. The respondent landlord denied that he was in breach of his duties as a landlord. He gave evidence that he had spoken to the tenants, had offered to pay to have a sound survey carried out and to pay half the costs of any insulation of the walls required. The landlord also gave evidence that following a mediation that had first taken place when the dispute was referred to the PRTB, he had written to the tenants, changed the layout of the living room and paid an electrician so that the TV could be moved to another wall.

---

[133] RTA 2004, s.15(3). See also para.9–22.
[134] TR91/DR736/2008, March 11, 2009.
[135] TR52/DR444/2007, July 13, 2007.

The tenancy tribunal determined that the landlord was in breach of his duty under s.15(1) of the RTA 2004. It found that some of the activities of the tenants were beyond those that would be considered by the tenancy tribunal to be reasonable, irrespective of the quality of the insulation between the properties, in particular, the late-night card parties. The landlord was aware that these activities were a source of distress to the applicants as the adjoining occupiers. The tenancy tribunal determined that the landlord was to pay the applicants the sum of €1,500, as compensation for distress and inconvenience caused by the activities of the tenants.

5–54 In *Egan v Rushe*,[136] a third party referred a dispute to the PRTB, in accordance with s.77 of the RTA 2004, against the landlord of a neighbouring dwelling. The tenancy tribunal in its finding said that close proximity, combined with differing lifestyles, particularly work hours, created tension between the adjacent households. It also found that although the noise from the tenants' household and behaviour of their children was annoying to the third party, they had not behaved in a way that was antisocial as prohibited by s.16(h) of the RTA 2004. The tenancy tribunal considered that the landlord had also taken reasonable steps to investigate the third party's complaints and to ensure the tenants were complying with their obligations under s.16(h). The tenancy tribunal determined that while the tenants and their young children behaved improperly, the landlord had not breached the duty he owed to the third party under s.15(1).

5–55 In *Earls v Askins and Anor*,[137] following an application made under s.77 of the RTA 2004, the landlord was directed to pay the third party applicants the sum of €1,000 in damages. This sum was awarded by way of compensation for the stress, anxiety and other inconveniences suffered by the third parties arising from the tenancy of a dwelling rented by the landlord.

11. RENT BOOKS

A. Rent Book Regulations

5–56 In the simplest of terms, a rent book is a document which records the payments of rent made by a tenant. Landlords in the private rented sector are obliged to provide tenants with rent books and to update them on an ongoing basis. There are no provisions in the RTA 2004 dealing with rent books and regard must still be had to the legislative framework that existed prior to its enactment. Section 17 of the 1992 Act empowers the Minister[138] to make

---

[136] TR04/DR281/2006, April 5, 2006.
[137] TR13/DR529/2006, determination order dated June 28, 2006.
[138] Minister is defined at s.1(1) of the 1992 Act, as the Minister for the Environment (now the Minister for the Environment, Heritage and Local Government).

regulations requiring landlords to provide tenants of houses with rent books. The Housing (Rent Books) Regulations 1993[139] (the "Rent Book Regulations") were enacted under s.17.

The Rent Book Regulations apply to every house let for rent solely as a dwelling, unless the house is let for the purposes of a holiday only or is a dwelling to which Pt II of the Housing (Private Rented Dwellings) Act 1982 applies, namely a controlled dwelling.[140] A landlord of a dwelling to which the Rent Book Regulations apply must provide the tenant of the rented dwelling with a rent book or other document with like effect that complies with the requirements of the Rent Book Regulations. The landlord must provide the tenant with the rent book on the commencement of the tenancy.[141]

B. Particulars Required in Rent Book

5–57 A rent book must contain the following information and it is the landlord's obligation to enter this information in "clearly legible writing"[142]:

    (a) the address of the rented house;
    (b) the name and address of the landlord and his or her agent (if one has been appointed);
    (c) the name of the tenant;
    (d) the term of the tenancy;
    (e) the rent reserved under the tenancy and when and how it is to be paid;
    (f) the amount and purpose of any payments to be made by the tenant to the landlord, in addition to the rent, for services provided by the landlord or otherwise, and when and how each such payment is to be made;
    (g) the amount of any rent paid in advance;
    (h) the amount and purpose of any deposit paid by the tenant and the conditions on which such deposit is repayable[143];
    (i) the date of commencement of the tenancy; and
    (j) particulars of the furnishings and appliances provided by the landlord for the exclusive use of the tenant.[144]

---

[139] S.I. No. 146 of 1993, as amended by the Housing (Rent Books) Regulations 1993 (Amendment) Regulations 2004 (S.I. No. 751 of 2004).

[140] Rent Book Regulations, art.4. Also, art.3(1) of the Rent Book Regulations defines a house as including "any building or part of a building used or suitable for use as a dwelling and any out office, yard, garden or other land appurtenant thereto or usually enjoyed therewith".

[141] Rent Book Regulations, art.5(1). Article 5(1)(b) provides that where a tenancy was in existence on the date the Rent Book Regulations came into force, a landlord was obliged to provide a tenant with a rent book within two months from the date the Rent Book Regulations came into operation.

[142] Rent Book Regulations, art.5(2).

[143] This requirement will be subject to a landlord's obligation under s.12(1)(d) of the RTA 2004, to return or repay any deposit paid by the tenant "promptly" and further the landlord's entitlement to retain part or all of that deposit in accordance with s.12(4) of the RTA 2004 (see para.5–34).

[144] Rent Book Regulations, art.5(2)(a)–(i).

If there is any change in the details referred to at (a) to (j) above, the landlord is obliged to update these details not later than one month after the change comes into effect.[145] The rent book must also contain the statement of information set out in the Schedule to the Rent Book Regulations.[146] This wording is set out in Appendix 2. A tenant must make the rent book available for the purposes of enabling the landlord to make any entry that he or she is required to make under the Rent Book Regulations.[147]

C. Recording of Rent and other Payments

5–58 A landlord must formally acknowledge each payment of rent or other payment made by a tenant and must do so in one of two ways. A landlord must record the payment in the rent book or in the alternative provide the tenant with a written statement or receipt of the payment made.[148]

Where rent is "handed in person" to the landlord by the tenant or another person acting on the tenant's behalf, the landlord must *on receipt* of the payment, either:

    (a) record in the rent book the amount, purpose and date of the payment and the period to which it relates, or

    (b) provide the person making the payment with a receipt stating the amount, purpose and date of the payment and the house and period to which the payment relates.[149]

5–59 Where rent is paid to the landlord other than in person by a tenant or a person acting on his behalf, for instance by way of bank transfer or by leaving it at the dwelling for the landlord to collect, the landlord shall *not more than three months after receipt* of the payment, either:

    (i) record in the rent book the amount, purpose and date of the payment and the period to which it relates, or

    (ii) provide the tenant with a written statement of the amount, purpose and date of the payment.[150]

In both circumstances, that is where the payment is made by the tenant in person or by other means, the landlord must sign each record made in the rent book or sign any receipt provided to the tenant.[151]

---

[145] Rent Book Regulations, art.6(2).
[146] The Schedule to the Rent Book Regulations was amended by art.2 of the Housing (Rent Books) Regulations 1993 (Amendment) Regulations 2004.
[147] Rent Book Regulations, art.6(1).
[148] Rent Book Regulations, art.7.
[149] Rent Book Regulations, art.7(a).
[150] Rent Book Regulations, art.7(b).
[151] Rent Book Regulations, art.7.

E. Enforcement

5–60 Where a landlord fails to provide a tenant with a rent book or receipt or written statement of the rent paid, or fails to comply with the other requirements of the Rent Book Regulations, the tenant may refer the matter to the PRTB for dispute resolution. A tenant may also notify the housing authority in the functional area where the dwelling is situated of the landlord's failure to comply with his or her obligations under the Rent Book Regulations. Housing authorities are empowered with the enforcement of the Rent Book Regulations and any other regulations adopted under s.17 of the 1992 Act. A person authorised by a housing authority may require the tenant to furnish him or her the rent book (if any) and may require the landlord to furnish documents relating to the dwelling or the tenancy of it. That authorised person may also enter and inspect the rented dwelling for the purposes of verifying that the particulars required by any regulations enacted under s.17 are contained in the rent book.[152]

A landlord who contravenes the provisions of the Rent Book Regulations or any other regulations adopted under s.17 of the 1992 Act, or obstructs a housing authority in carrying out its statutory functions pursuant to these provisions, is guilty of an offence. On conviction, the landlord will be liable to a fine not exceeding €5,000 and/or imprisonment for a term not exceeding six months, in addition to a fine of €400 (on conviction) for each day of a continuing offence.[153]

F. Controlled Dwellings

5–61 The Housing (Private Rented Dwellings) Regulations 1982 (the "1982 Regulations")[154] impose obligations on landlords to provide rent books to tenants of dwellings that were previously controlled under the Rent Restrictions Act 1960 (as amended), other than a dwelling held at July 26, 1982 for a term greater than from year to year.[155] Article 10 of the 1982 Regulations requires a landlord of such a dwelling to provide the tenant with a rent book (or similar document) within one month of registration of the tenancy in accordance with the 1982 Regulations. Article 10 also sets out the details that must be included in the rent book. With the decline in the number of controlled dwellings, the 1982 Regulations now have more limited application.[156]

---

[152] 1992 Act, s.17(3). See para.4.10 of the "Report of the Commission on the Private Rented Residential Sector" (July 2000), which considers the enforcement of the Rent Book Regulations.

[153] 1992 Act, s.34(1), as amended by Sch2, Pt.4 (item 6) of the Housing Act 2009.

[154] S.I. No. 217 of 1982, as amended by the Housing (Private Rented Dwellings)(Amendment) Regulations 1983 (S.I. No. 286 of 1983).

[155] 1982 Regulations, art. 4. See also s.8 of the Housing (Private Rented Dwellings) Act 1982 (which commenced on July 26, 1982).

[156] Controlled dwellings are dealt with in further detail at paras 3–29 to 3–34. See also Wylie, *Landlord and Tenant Law*, 2nd edn (Dublin: Butterworths, 1998) para.5.51.

12. FIRE SAFETY

5–62 Landlords also have obligations with regard to fire safety. The house, the subject of the tenancy, must contain a fire blanket and either a mains-wired smoke alarm or at least two 10-year self-contained battery smoke alarms. Each self-contained house in a multi-unit building must contain a mains-wired smoke alarm and a fire blanket. A landlord is also obliged to have in place an emergency evacuation plan for a self-contained house within a multi-unit building and emergency lighting must also be provided in all common areas within the multi-unit building.[157]

---

[157]   2008 Regulations, art.11, as amended by art.2(e) of the 2009 Regulations.

CHAPTER 6

RENT AND RENT REVIEWS

1. BACKGROUND

6–01 The setting of rent in the absence of statutory or other controls on rent has generally depended on supply and demand. One of the issues identified as a concern to tenants prior to the introduction of the Residential Tenancies Act 2004 (the "RTA 2004") was rent control.[1] In assessing what type of rent regulation would be appropriate in the residential sector, the Commission on the Private Rented Residential Sector (the "Commission") considered a wide variety of rent regulation—from total control within the meaning of the former Rent Restriction Acts,[2] where rents were fixed and could not be increased, to a more flexible system of regulated rent reviews by reference to stipulated indices of price movements. The Commission also gave consideration to a "reasonable rent" model.[3]

The Commission was of the view that there was no existing constitutional or legal impediment to recommending the introduction of a system of rent control, provided such a system did not disproportionately interfere with property rights.[4] The Commission considered that as controls on rent would apply to particular tenancies rather than properties, they would be meaningless unless accompanied by a restriction on the landlord's right to recover possession, so that the landlord could not avoid the controls on rent by the termination of the tenancy.[5]

---

[1] Report of the Commission on the Private Rented Residential Sector, July 2000 ("Report of the Commission"), Ch.5 and Appendix B.2.

[2] Parts II and IV of the Rent Restrictions Act 1960 dealing with rent restriction were held to be "unfair and arbitrary" and thus unconstitutional as a reasonable balance between the competing interests had not been struck. The 1960 Act constituted an attack on the property rights of the owners of dwellings to the extent that those provisions rendered ineffective the exercise of such rights by owners. It was held that there is no constitutional impediment to a system of rent control so long as the system is framed within the context of the common good, was fair, not oppressive and had sufficient regard for the interests of both the landlord and the tenant (*Blake and Others v Attorney General* [1982] I.R. 117; *Madigan v Attorney General* [1986] I.L.R.M. 136).

[3] This proposed model provided for an assessment of rent based on what was deemed to be "reasonable". It was considered by the Commission, however, that it would be difficult to define a criterion such as "reasonableness" in such a way as to ensure a clear and unambiguous understanding of what was meant by the concept and which would not be unduly subjective. See the Report of the Commission, para.5.3.9.

[4] Report of the Commission, para.5.3.6.2.

[5] Report of the Commission, para.5.1.3.

6–02 The Commission's final recommendation was that the rent applicable to tenancies in the private rented sector should be the open market rate. It condemned the practice of demanding rent increases greater than the market rate, as a means of forcing tenants to relinquish their tenancies. It further recommended that tenants should not be faced with rent reviews more frequently than once per annum, unless there had been a substantial change in the nature of the accommodation. It was of the view that rent increases should not be greater than that which would bring the rent to the prevailing market rate. The Commission also suggested that if a practice developed whereby landlords terminated tenancies for the purpose of increasing rent more frequently than once a year, the proposed Private Residential Tenancies Board (the "PRTB") should be pro-active in tackling that problem.[6]

6–03 The provisions in the RTA 2004, dealing with the setting of rent and rent reviews, reflect the recommendations of the Commission and provide that rent may not be greater than the open market rate and may normally only be reviewed upward or downward once per annum. The practice of making "market rent" the legal benchmark has been criticised by those in favour of a form of rent regulation or rent control. It was this issue which was intensely debated within the Commission. The overwhelming majority of its members considered market rent to be the most appropriate system, having regard to the negative aspects of rent control, particularly its impact on new supply, on the maintenance of existing rented stock and avoiding the front loading of rent increases on future tenants. Rent control or regulation was considered to prevent tenants from capturing the benefits of falls in market rates.[7]

2. PART 3 OF THE RTA 2004

A. Setting of Rent

6–04 Part 3 of the RTA 2004 imposes restrictions on the setting of rent and rent reviews in the residential sector. A landlord is prohibited from setting the rent for a residential dwelling at a rate above "market rent".[8] This prohibition applies both when the rent is initially being set at the commencement of the tenancy and at the time of any subsequent rent review.[9]

6–05 A "review of rent" for the purposes of Pt 3 of the RTA 2004 is defined broadly. It includes references to any procedure for determining whether and to

---

6 Report of the Commission, para.5.5.
7 Minister Ahern, TD, Seanad Éireann, Vol.177, Col.725, July 2, 2004, second stage.
8 RTA 2004, s.19(1). "Market rent" is defined at s.24(1) of the RTA 2004, see para.6–07 below.
9 RTA 2004, s.19(2)(a) and (b).

what extent a reduction or increase in an amount of rent ought to have effect.[10] It also includes references to the effect of the operation of a provision of a lease or tenancy agreement, providing for a reduction or increase in rent.[11]

6–06 The "setting of a rent" is defined as an agreement made orally or in writing in a lease or tenancy agreement. In the context of a rent review, it is defined as the oral agreeing of rent or the oral or written notification of the rent or where the rent is calculated in accordance with a term contained in a lease or tenancy agreement, the rent being set by the operation of that provision.[12] The RTA 2004 does not specify a formula by which rent is to be calculated or any subsequent rent review is to be carried out. Accordingly, the parties can determine what rent review formula, if any, will apply to their lease or tenancy agreement. The only requirement for the purposes of the RTA 2004 is that the rent set is "market rent".

B. Market Rent

(i) The RTA 2004

6–07 Market rent is defined in s.24 of the RTA 2004 as follows:

> In this Part "market rent", in relation to the tenancy of a dwelling, means the rent which a willing tenant not already in occupation would give and a willing landlord would take for the dwelling, in each case on the basis of vacant possession being given, and having regard to—
> (a) the other terms of the tenancy, and
> (b) the letting values of dwellings of a similar size, type and character to the dwelling and situated in a comparable area to that in which it is situated.

In summary, therefore, market rent is the rent a willing tenant not already in occupation would give and a willing landlord would accept for the dwelling, on the basis of vacant possession being given and having regard to the other terms

---

[10] RTA 2004, s.24(2)(a).

[11] RTA 2004, s.24(2)(b). In *Canty v Private Residential Tenancies Board* [2007] IEHC 243, clause 8 of the tenancy agreement between the tenant and the landlord provided for an extension to the agreement from October 1, 2005 for a period of 12 months without changes in the terms of the tenancy, excepting the right of the landlord to increase the rental charge to a maximum of €750 per calendar month. Laffoy J., in her judgment, considered the operation of clause 8, noting that while the rent increase provided for in that clause was agreed at the outset, it did not come into effect until the happening of an event, being the extension by the tenant of the tenancy beyond October 1, 2005. Laffoy J. held that the effect of the operation of that element of clause 8 fell within the ambit of s.24(2)(b) of the RTA 2004, so that such effect is deemed a review of the rent under Pt 3. Accordingly, s.22 applied when the landlord sought to increase the rent in February 2006 and accordingly, 28 days' notice of the rent review was required (unreported, High Court, August 8, 2007, at pp.3, 4, 20 and 21; [2007] IEHC 243).

[12] RTA 2004, s.24(3).

of the tenancy and the letting values of the dwelling of a similar size, type and character to the dwelling concerned and situated in a comparable area.

6–08 Section 24 of the RTA 2004 defines market rent on the basis of relatively general criteria. Its interpretation, however, is likely to evolve through the determination of disputes relating to rent by the PRTB in particular through the consideration given to the concept in the reports of its tenancy tribunals.[13] In particular, however, the determination of what is market rent for a dwelling is likely to become increasingly dependent on data on rents collected by the PRTB. In that regard, one of the PRTB's functions as prescribed by Pt 8 of the RTA 2004 is "the collection and provision of information relating to the private rented sector, including information concerning prevailing rent levels".[14] The purpose of this provision is to enable the PRTB to compile detailed information on prevailing market rents from the data submitted to the PRTB by landlords, as part of the registration system established by Pt 7 of the RTA 2004. The PRTB's data on prevailing rent levels will be of much assistance in assessing market rent. To date there is no assessment of prevailing market rents available, however, the PRTB does collect the data that will facilitate such an assessment from the tenancy registration forms, which landlords are obliged to submit to the PRTB within one month of the commencement of a tenancy.[15]

(ii) The Landlord and Tenant (Amendment) Act 1980

6–09 The definition of market rent in the RTA 2004 is similar to the definition applying to "gross rent" contained in s.23(5) of the Landlord and Tenant (Amendment) Act 1980 (the "1980 Act"). Section 23(5) defines "gross rent" as "the rent which in the opinion of the Court a willing lessee not already in occupation would give and a willing lessor would take for the tenement, in each case on the basis of vacant possession being given" and having regard to "the letting values of tenements of a similar character to the tenement and situate in a comparable area but without regard to any goodwill which may exist in respect

---

[13]   See paras 6–16 to 6–23 below.

[14]   RTA 2004, s.151(1)(e).

[15]   It was suggested when the Residential Tenancies Bill was going through the Houses of the Oireachtas and in particular at Report stage, that an amendment be inserted to the effect that any annual rent increase would be capped to a 5 per cent increase over the rate of inflation in that year. It was also suggested that a mechanism for assessing market rent could be a book of quantum similar to that contained in the Civil Liability and Courts Act 2004. It was proposed that this would be a fair and reasonable method of ensuring that "rip-off merchants are rooted out of the private rented sector" and overpricing would be regulated. The book of quantum would be amended in accordance with market rent. Both of these proposals were suggested as ways to counteract a potential problem whereby, for example, a desperate tenant looking for accommodation would be forced to accept the amount of rent the landlord charges due to the scarcity of accommodation and could not therefore be considered a "willing tenant". Neither of these options where incorporated into the RTA 2004. (Mr Cuffe, TD and Mr Mogan, TD *Dáil Reports*, Vol.588, Cols 858–859, June 30, 2004, report stage).

of the tenement". There has been judicial criticism of this definition of "gross rent", a variation of which was also used in the Landlord and Tenant Act 1931.[16]

6–10 One of the most important elements of the definition of "gross rent" in the 1980 Act is the "willing lessee". This concept was designed to set as the benchmark the open market letting value with vacant possession.[17] As the hypothetical letting is made with vacant possession, any sub-letting of the premises will be ignored for the purposes of the rent review. The result is that the revised rent will not be considered having regard to the aggregate rent, which could be achieved by sub-letting but relates to the demised premises at the review date let as a whole.[18] *Macey Limited v Tylers Limited*,[19] although relating to a commercial letting,[20] provides some helpful guidance as to how "market rent" has been interpreted in that context. In assessing what factors are to be taken into account, Costello J. referred to the hypothetical situation which an arbitrator must consider when assessing market rent:

> "He is, in my opinion, required to undertake the following exercise. Firstly, he is required to assume (i) that the premises are vacant and (ii) the existence of a willing landlord and a willing lessee. He then must turn to the factual situation at the date of the review and weigh up all the facts relevant for the purposes of ascertaining the open market rent at that date. He will take into account such things as the physical features of the premises and their location; the levels of rent of comparable premises; and any special local conditions which could affect the level of the rent such as the existence of neighbouring occupiers whose interest in the premises might increase competition and thus enhance the open market rent. He should also take into account any legal restrictions which might affect the use of premises. And he must, of course, take into account the terms of the lease itself."[21]

---

[16] *Byrne v Loftus* [1978] I.R. 211, Kenny J. stated in relation to s.29(f) of the Landlord and Tenant Act 1931: "Rarely can a draftsman have produced such an ill-framed paragraph. It contains one economic absurdity and a phrase ('a willing lessor') whose literal meaning makes nonsense of the paragraph … the economic absurdity is that the court must assume that the supply of similar tenements is sufficient to meet the demand as part of the process of determining the rent … to compel the court to fix a rent on the basis that supply equals demand necessarily assumes that the court knows the rent, although the whole purpose of the formula is to determine it. The judges of the High Court and the Circuit Court with their usual good sense have made the formula workable by ignoring this provision." Wylie states that the 1980 Act removed the economic absurdity by requiring the court to assume that the supply of similar tenements was sufficient to meet demand. See Wylie, *Landlord and Tenant Law*, 2nd edn (Dublin: Butterworths, 1998), para.30.55.

[17] Wylie, *Landlord and Tenant Law*, 2nd edn (Dublin: Butterworths, 1998), para.30.55.

[18] *O'Malley Property Ltd v Hynes Limited*, unreported, High Court, November 30, 1987.

[19] [1978] I.L.R.M. 82.

[20] In *Farrelly v Caffrey* [1966] I.R. 170, Teevan J. emphasised that in assessing the letting values of tenements of a similar character, it did not mean that the court could not draw comparisons with properties used for purposes different from those for which the property under consideration was used. See Wylie, *Landlord and Tenant Law*, 2nd edn (Dublin: Butterworths, 1998), para.30.57.

[21] [1978] I.L.R.M. 82 at 84.

Given the similarity of the definition of "gross rent" in the 1980 Act and "market rent" in the RTA 2004, it would not be unreasonable to apply similar principles to a residential letting, falling within the remit of the RTA 2004.

3. FREQUENCY OF RENT REVIEWS

6–11 The RTA 2004 not only places restrictions on the setting of rent above market rent, it also limits the frequency with which rent reviews may occur. Section 20(1) of the RTA 2004 provides that a review of rent may not occur more than once in each 12-month period, nor during the first 12 months from the commencement of the tenancy. Any provision of a lease or tenancy agreement which purports to allow for the occurrence of a rent review on a more frequent basis will have no application and cannot be relied upon by the landlord or tenant to alter the rent.[22]

The RTA 2004 provides for one exception to the restrictions imposed by s.20(1) on the frequency with which a review of rent is permitted. This exception arises where there has been a substantial change in the nature of the accommodation provided under the tenancy and by virtue of that change, the market rent for the tenancy would be different to the rent that had originally been set for the dwelling.[23]

4. PROCEDURE FOR SETTING REVISED RENT

6–12 If a landlord intends to set a new rent for the tenancy, he or she is obliged to serve a notice in writing on the tenant, not less than 28 days before the date the new rent is to have effect. The notice served by the landlord must state the amount of the new rent and the date from which it is to have effect.[24] If these conditions are not complied with, the rent review shall not have effect.[25] In addition, the landlord is required to notify the PRTB of the revised rent so that the PRTB can make the relevant amendment to the registration details for the tenancy.[26] A sample rent review notice for landlords is contained at Appendix 3.

5. DISPUTE RESOLUTION

A. Jurisdiction

6–13 Since the enactment of the RTA 2004, the PRTB is the appropriate forum for resolving disputes between landlords and tenants relating to rent reviews and

---

[22] RTA 2004, s.20(2).
[23] RTA 2004, s.20(3).
[24] RTA 2004, s.22(2).
[25] RTA 2004, s.22(1).
[26] RTA 2004, s.139. See also para.10–20.

rent generally.[27] Where a valid notice of a review in rent has been served by a landlord and a dispute arises between the parties, one or more of them must refer the dispute to the PRTB before the new rent is to have effect or before the expiry of 28 days from receipt by the tenant of the landlord's notice.[28] However, the PRTB has the discretion to extend this time limit where a person shows "good grounds" for such an extension of time.[29]

It is important to note that the RTA 2004 imposes no time limitations on the referral of a dispute to the PRTB where no valid notice has been served on a tenant, notifying the tenant of the rent review. Accordingly, it seems that a tenant has a longer period in which to refer a dispute relating to a rent review, if the landlord has failed to serve a valid notice of a review in rent, giving the tenant 28 days' notice of the change in the rate of rent payable under the tenancy. Subject to the provisions of the Statute of Limitations 1957 and the other jurisdictional limitations of the PRTB,[30] such a dispute can be referred to the PRTB at any stage.

6–14 For a dispute to fall within the jurisdiction of the PRTB, a tenancy must be or have been in existence.[31] Accordingly, in circumstances where a prospective landlord and tenant cannot agree an initial rent, such a dispute will not fall within the jurisdiction of the PRTB, unless the complainant is in a position to prove that a tenancy was in fact in being.[32]

6–15 Section 86(1) of the RTA 2004 provides that the existing rent for a tenancy of a dwelling continues to be payable pending the determination of any dispute referred to the PRTB for resolution. It also provides that if the dispute relates to the amount of rent payable, no increase in the amount of rent may be made pending a determination. However, it is open to the parties to agree to suspend the rent or to agree to a rent increase.[33] Section 120 of the RTA 2004 provides that circumstances, financial or otherwise, of either the landlord or the tenant cannot be taken into account by the PRTB when dealing with a dispute relating to the issue of rent.

---

[27] This is subject to any limitations that may apply to the PRTB's jurisdiction. See Chs 3 and 9.

[28] RTA 2004, s.22(3).

[29] RTA 2004, s.88. See also para.9–50.

[30] See Chs 3 and 9.

[31] Section 3(1) of the RTA 2004 provides that, "[s]ubject to subsection (2), this Act applies to every dwelling, the subject of a tenancy (including a tenancy created before the passing of this Act)." See also para.3–04.

[32] Note also that the payment of rent or a letting for valuable consideration is an essential characteristic of a "dwelling" for the purposes of the RTA 2004. Where no rent or valuable consideration is payable, the RTA 2004 will have no application. See para.3–07.

[33] RTA 2004, s.86(2). See also paras 9–105 to 9–109 on s.86 of the RTA 2004.

B. Tenancy Tribunal Determinations

6–16 Rent increases and allegations of unfair rent have been the subject of a number of determinations made by the PRTB. However, as the RTA 2004 was only enacted in September 2004, with its dispute resolution provisions in force since December 2004, the jurisprudence of the PRTB on market rents is still limited. In addition, it would seem that the PRTB's data on rents, which is in its embryonic stage at present, will become a significant factor in determining whether rents have been set above the market rate.

(i) Market rent

6–17 An assessment as to what is market rent has to be made by an adjudicator or a tenancy tribunal at the time of the particular dispute. In the matter of *Stern v Morris and Anor*,[34] the tenant made an application for the dispute resolution services of the PRTB pursuant to s.78(1)(c) and (f) of the RTA 2004. In this case, the landlords sought an increase in the rent, to be implemented 12 months after the commencement of the tenancy. The tenant alleged, inter alia, that the landlords failed to follow proper procedures to carry out a rent review and had demanded rent above prevailing market levels.

In evidence given by the tenant before the tenancy tribunal, the tenant conceded that that he was relying on anecdotal evidence and had not consulted local valuers or letting agents in relation to the market rent for the rented dwelling. The solicitor, on behalf of the landlords, produced to the tenancy tribunal a letter from a firm of letting agents giving details of market rents in the locality of the rented dwelling in June 2005.[35] It was contended on behalf of the landlords that this letter, which gave details on rent levels in other comparable local properties, was evidence that the landlords were not demanding rent above market levels and therefore they were not in breach of s.19(1) of the RTA 2004. Furthermore, the landlords claimed they did not breach s.21 of the RTA 2004 by denying the tenant's right to a rent review.[36]

On the issue of the rent review, the tenancy tribunal determined that:

> "The notice of rent increase issued by Town and Country Lettings on the 9th May 2005 and due to take effect on 31st May 2005 was invalid: it did not allow for 28 days notice for a rent increase as required under section 22 of the Residential Tenancies Act 2004."[37]

---

[34] TR63/DR193/2006, November 15, 2006.
[35] The tenancy tribunal report also records that copies of letting advertisements on the "Daft" website were submitted in evidence. The tenancy tribunal report does not specify, however, which party sought to rely on the particulars provided in these letting advertisements, nor does its report consider specifically the probative nature of such evidence.
[36] The tenancy tribunal did not make a determination in relation to s.21 of the RTA 2004.
[37] Tenancy tribunal report, p.6.

6–18 The report of the tenancy tribunal, also in *Stern v Morris and Anor,* recorded a number of "findings of fact". In particular in relation to the issue of market rent, the tenancy tribunal found that neither party presented sufficient evidence to allow it to make a determination on whether the rent payable under the tenancy agreement was the market rent. In addition, the tenancy tribunal stated that one of the reasons for its determination was that there were no supporting witnesses and no compelling evidence provided by either party to enable it to reach a decision as to what was the market rent.

6–19 The findings of the tenancy tribunal in *Stern v Morris and Anor* suggest that there is a relatively high onus on parties to produce sufficient evidence to support or refute the allegation that rent has been set above market rent and that at least in certain circumstances, it is necessary that documentary evidence produced is supported by direct oral evidence. In *Devlin v MacDermot-Roe,*[38] the tenancy tribunal accepted the direct evidence from an auctioneer who appeared on behalf of the landlord in relation to the market rent of the dwelling. He gave evidence that rents in the area of a similar size to the dwelling rented by the tenant were in the region of €800–€850 per month. The tenancy tribunal accepted this evidence (which was not expressly disputed by the tenant) and determined that the tenant was to pay market rent of €800 per month for the appropriate period.

6–20 Where a dispute arises in relation to the level of rent set for a tenancy, the status quo will remain unless the applicant for dispute resolution services can prove their case that the rent is or is not set at the market rate. As it will generally be the tenant and not the landlord who will be contesting the level of rent as being above the market rate, the onus of proof in the large majority of cases will lie with the tenant to establish that the rent is above market rent. The determinations of the PRTB's tenancy tribunals to date, however, demonstrate that the respondent must also be prepared to provide sufficient evidence by way of rebuttal as to the appropriate level of market rent.

(ii) Rent review procedures

6–21 If a landlord fails to follow the procedures set out in Pt 3 of the RTA 2004, the rent review will have no effect and the old rent will continue to apply. In the matter of *Canty v Connelly,*[39] a rent increase was notified to the tenant, by way of letter dated February 23, 2006. It was stated in this correspondence that rent at the rate of €750 per month was to be payable by the tenant in respect of the tenancy from March 1, 2006, to the date of vacation by him of the rented dwelling. The tenant referred the matter of the rent increase, amongst other issues, to the PRTB. The tenancy tribunal determined that:

---

[38] TR30/DR511/2007, April 26, 2007.
[39] TR22/DR259/2006, July 11, 2006.

> "The rent increase notified to the tenant by way of correspondence dated the
> 23rd February 2006 is a valid increase of rent pursuant to the Lease
> Agreement between the parties. Rent at the rate of €750 per month shall be
> payable by the tenant in respect of the tenancy from the 1st March 2006 to the
> date of vacation by him of the premises, this is without prejudice to any right
> the landlord may have under the Residential Tenancies Act 2004 to any
> increased amount of rent or other charges."[40]

The tenant appealed this determination of the tenancy tribunal to the High Court
on a point of law pursuant to s.123 of the RTA 2004, on the basis (inter alia) that
the landlord had failed to comply with the provisions of Pt 3 of the RTA 2004
by not giving 28 days' notice to the tenant of the rent increase. The matter came
before Laffoy J. in the High Court and judgment was handed down on August
8, 2007.[41] In considering the validity of the rent increase, Laffoy J. had regard
to the provisions of ss.19, 20, 21 and 22 of the RTA 2004. In relation to s.22,
she stated that it required a landlord to give 28 days' notice of a rent increase
and failure to give such notice will mean that the rent increase has no effect:

> "Therefore s. 22 applied when the landlord sought to increase the rent in
> February, 2006 and 28 days' notice was required under s. 22. As the required
> notice was not given, the rent increase did not have effect".[42]

6–22 In *Treacy and Anor v Curran*,[43] the landlord wrote to the tenants on March
3, 2006 informing them that the rent would be increased by €150 per month and
would take effect from March. On April 3, 2006, the tenants informed the
landlord that they would be moving out in four weeks. It was agreed between
the parties that the lease would expire on May 1, 2006. The landlord withheld
€300 from the deposit to take into account the rent increase for the two months
of March and April. The tenancy tribunal found that the rent increase was invalid
as it failed to comply with s.22 of the RTA 2004, which requires 28 days' notice
in writing of the setting of a new rent:

> "Given that the lease ended on 1st May 2006, the landlord's withholding of
> €300 from the security deposit for rent increases indicates that he intended the
> rent increase, notified on the 3rd March 2006, to come into effect immediately
> for the rents covering March and April 2006. Since the rent in this tenancy
> was paid in advance, the March rent would have been due on the 28th
> February. Therefore the notice of rent increase did not give the tenants a notice
> in writing 28 days before the date from which the rent was to have effect as
> required under the Act, making it a defective notice."[44]

---

[40]　Tenancy tribunal report, p.12.
[41]　Unreported, High Court, August 8, 2007; [2007] IEHC 243.
[42]　Unreported, High Court, August 8, 2007, at p.11.
[43]　TR24/DR96/2008, August 25, 2008.
[44]　Tenancy tribunal report p.6. See also *Boateng v Glackin and Anor* (TR74/DR363&DR927/2008,

6–23 The determination of the tenancy tribunal in *Kelly and Anor v O'Loughlin*[45] dealt with s.20(1)(a) of the RTA 2004. As referred to at para.6–11 above, s.20(1)(a) provides that a rent review cannot take place more frequently than once in each period of 12 months, unless there is substantial change in the nature of the accommodation provided under the tenancy.[46] In that case the landlord attempted to alter the rent within a 12-month period when no change in the nature of the accommodation had taken place. The tenancy tribunal determined that the landlord was not permitted to do so by reason of s.20(1)(a).

C. Determinations at Adjudication

6–24 The majority of disputes on the setting of rent and the validity of rent reviews have been dealt with by the PRTB by way of adjudication. As adjudication is a confidential process,[47] it is only the determination orders made by the PRTB in accordance with s.121(1)(b) of the RTA 2004, that can be considered in the context of the disputes dealt with at adjudication. As these determination orders record the final decision of the PRTB only, they are of limited value in developing the PRTB's jurisprudence on what is "market rent" and how it is determined. A number of the PRTB's determinations, adopted under s.121(1)(b) have, however, been highlighted below.

6–25 In the matter of *Ralph v Flannery*,[48] the determination order of the PRTB recorded that, "[t]he Respondent Landlord shall pay to the Applicant Tenant, within 7 days of the date of issue of this Order, the sum of €200 as refund of the unlawful rent increase applied by the Respondent Landlord".[49] In *Youf v Branagan*[50] it was determined that, "[t]he Applicant Tenant's claim for €1,400 in respect of rent paid in excess of the market rent for the . . . . . . dwelling is dismissed".[51]

6–26 In the matter of *O'Callaghan v Corcoran and Anor*,[52] it was determined that the landlords were not entitled to increase the rent unless certain remedial works were carried out to the dwelling. The determination order of the PRTB records as follows:

November 28, 2008), where the rent review was deemed invalid as the notice of rent increase was not in accordance with s.22(2) of the RTA 2004.

[45] TR72/DR605/2008, November 3, 2008.
[46] RTA 2004, s.20(3).
[47] See para.9–70.
[48] DR232/2005.
[49] Determination order, January 18, 2006.
[50] DR809/2005.
[51] Determination order, September 1, 2006.
[52] DR14/2006.

"[t]he Applicant Landlord is not entitled to increase the rent to €800 per month
in respect of the tenancy of the dwelling . . . . . . until the following remedial
works are satisfactorily completed –
• repairs to the central heating boiler
• repairs to the chimney to alleviate dampness
• repairs to kitchen tiles and lino
• replace the hessian backed carpets".[53]

This decision illustrates how the PRTB's assessment of market rent in certain
circumstances may relate to the state of the dwelling itself. In *O'Callaghan v
Corcoran and Anor*, as the landlord was in breach of his obligation to repair, the
landlord could not increase the rent until the remedial works as set out above
were carried out. In contrast, in *Waldron and Anor v O'Shea and Anor*,[54] a
determination order issued from the PRTB in the following terms:

"The rent of €500 per month in respect of the tenancy of the dwelling . . . . . .
. . . . . which was agreed between the Applicant Tenants and the Respondent
Landlords was not above the market rate. The Applicant Tenants were aware
of the standard and maintenance of the property prior to paying the deposit."[55]

---

[53] Determination order, October 18, 2006.
[54] DR844/2005.
[55] Determination order, November 15, 2006.

CHAPTER 7

SECURITY OF TENURE

1. INTRODUCTION

A. The Landlord and Tenant (Amendment) Act 1980

7–01 Prior to the enactment of the Residential Tenancies Act 2004 (the "RTA 2004"), tenants of residential dwellings in the private rented sector had limited security of tenure. A tenant could apply for a new tenancy, where the lease itself gave a right of renewal at the expiration of the initial agreement. In terms of statutory protection, Pt II of the Landlord and Tenant (Amendment) Act 1980 (the "1980 Act") was the main legislative provision that gave security of tenure to tenants. Under the 1980 Act, residential tenants had the right to apply for a new tenancy in two limited circumstances. The first was where the tenant had carried out improvements to the premises, which were equivalent to at least one half of the letting value. This provision was rarely invoked, in particular with most improvements made to rented accommodation not reaching the threshold of half the letting value. The second situation under the 1980 Act, where a tenant was entitled to apply for a new tenancy, was after 20 years of occupation.[1] However, it was very easy in practice for a landlord to prevent a tenant qualifying for a new tenancy on this basis, by terminating the existing tenancy before the tenant acquired 20 years user.[2]

B. Review of the Law on Security of Tenure

7–02 A Working Group on Security of Tenure (the "Working Group") was established in November 1994 by the Minister for Justice, Equality and Law Reform. The Working Group was set up to examine and report on the position of security of tenure in the private rented sector, with particular focus on any changes desirable to the provisions of the 1980 Act.[3] Amongst the findings of

---

[1] Occupation by a predecessor in title could also be taken into account for the purposes of calculating this 20-year period. See para.7–45.

[2] Although s.85 of the 1980 Act provides that a landlord could not contract out of its provisions, this did not affect the right of a landlord to terminate a tenancy, so long as this was done in accordance with the legislative code having application at that time.

[3] The Working Group reported to the Minister for Justice, Equality and Law Reform in July 1996 and its report (The Housing Market: An Economic Review and Assessment) was published in February 1999. The Government announced on March 9, 1999, as one of the range of measures

the Working Group was that the long occupation equity user available under Pt II of the 1980 Act, a provision which was designed to improve security of tenure for tenants, actually militated against it. The Working Group recommended that there be an amendment of the 1980 Act, so as to allow tenants opt out of any entitlement to a lease of up to 35 years.[4]

7–03 The Commission on the Private Rented Residential Sector (the "Commission") was launched on July 22, 1999. Its first term of reference was to:

> "examine the working of the landlord and tenant relationship in respect of residential tenancies in the private rented sector and to make such recommendations, including changes to the law, as the Commission considers proper, equitable and feasible with a view to:
>
> • improving the security of tenure of tenants in the occupation of their dwellings."[5]

The Commission ultimately proposed that there should be a new legislative framework for providing security of tenure to tenants. The Commission recommended that where a tenancy had lasted a minimum period of six continuous months, all tenants should (subject to specified conditions), be statutorily entitled to continue in occupation of the dwelling for a period of up to four years from the date of the commencement of the tenancy. The Commission further recommended that during the initial six months of the tenancy, the landlord should be able to terminate it by giving 28 days' notice. However, if the landlord wished to terminate the tenancy after the initial six months, he or she could only do so in certain circumstances and would be required to give the tenant a specific period of notice, which would depend on how long the tenancy had existed at that time. The Commission recommended that the tenant, on the other hand, should be able to terminate the tenancy without giving a reason, as long as the requisite period of notice was given.[6]

---

in response to the report its decision to establish a commission to examine issues relating to security of tenure.

[4] Report of the Commission on the Private Rented Residential Sector, July 2000 ("Report of the Commission"), para.1.4.4.2. Note that 35 years is the maximum term of a tenancy that may be granted under Pt II of the 1980 Act on the basis of an improvements equity or long occupation equity (1980 Act, s.23(2) as amended by s.5 of the Landlord and Tenant (Amendment) Act 1994).

[5] Report of the Commission, "Introduction", p.1. It was initially envisaged that the Commission would only deal with the issue of security of tenure. However, Mr Robert Molloy TD, the Minister for Housing and Urban Renewal who launched the Commission, was of the view that the issue of security of tenure could not appropriately be considered in isolation from other key issues, such as supply and quality of accommodation, investment return and market considerations and constraints to develop the sector. See the Report of the Commission, "Introduction", p.1.

[6] Report of the Commission, para.8.5.

C. The RTA 2004

7–04 In introducing the Residential Tenancies Bill 2003 to the Dáil, Mr Noel Ahern TD, Minister for State, stated that the Bill was "one of the most important Housing Bills to have been brought before this House in many years and the most comprehensive reform of the residential private rented sector in Ireland in almost 150 years."[7] In addressing the pre-existing right of a tenant under the 1980 Act, to a renewable lease of up to 35 years after 20 years in occupation, he reiterated the view of the Commission that this "well-intentioned provision has proved counter-productive, prompting eviction of those approaching 20 year occupancy."[8]

7–05 The recommendations of the Commission on the issue of security of tenure were incorporated into the RTA 2004. As enacted, one of the most significant amendments it has made for dwellings falling within its jurisdiction was to abolish, from September 1, 2009, a tenant's right to a new tenancy on the basis of the so-called improvements equity and long occupation equity.[9] Accordingly, Pt II of the 1980 Act no longer applies to a dwelling to which the RTA 2004 applies. However, for all dwellings which fall outside the remit of the RTA 2004, Pt II still has application. Part II of the 1980 Act is considered in further detail later on in this chapter.[10]

2. PART 4 OF THE RTA 2004

A. General Rule

7–06 Part 4 of the RTA 2004 radically changed the pre-existing law on security of tenure. The provisions of Pt 4 place on a statutory footing a minimum period of security of tenure for tenants that cannot be contracted out of and which is implied into every tenancy or lease agreement.

The basic security of tenure principle under Pt 4 is contained in s.28 of the RTA 2004. This section provides that where a tenant has been in occupation of a dwelling for a continuous period of six months and a notice of termination has not been served during that period,[11] the tenant will be entitled to what has been termed by the legislation as a "Part 4 tenancy".[12] A Part 4 tenancy entitles a

---

7   Dáil Éireann, Vol.568 Col.1143, June 17, 2003, second stage.
8   Dáil Éireann, Vol.568, Col.1151, June 17, 2003, second stage.
9   RTA 2004, s.192. See also paras 7–53 to 7–54.
10 See paras 7–43 to 7–52. The 1980 Act is also dealt with in greater detail in Wylie, *Landlord and Tenant Law*, 2nd edn (Dublin: Butterworths, 1998).
11 Section 28(4) of the RTA 2004 provides that if a notice of termination has been served but is subsequently withdrawn, it will not interfere with the right to a Part 4 tenancy pursuant to s.28(1).
12 RTA 2004, s.29.

tenant to remain in occupation of the dwelling for a further period of three and a half years. That entitlement to stay on in the dwelling is subject to s.34 of the RTA 2004, which lists six different grounds on which a landlord may terminate a Part 4 tenancy. It is important to bear in mind that these grounds set out in s.34 comprise an exhaustive list and certain conditions must be adhered to strictly before a landlord may rely on any of them to terminate a tenancy. The grounds and procedures for the termination of a Part 4 tenancy are dealt with in Ch.8 on Termination of Tenancies.

B. Requirement for Continuous Occupation

7–07 As referred to above, a Partt 4 tenancy will come into being after a tenant has been in occupation of a dwelling for a continuous period of six months. Section 31 of the RTA 2004 provides that a "continuous period of occupation" under a tenancy as referred to in s.28 includes a reference to a continuous period of occupation under a series of two or more tenancies. Therefore, a tenant could enter into two consecutive fixed-term tenancies for a period of three months each and still qualify for Part 4 tenancy rights. The entire period of occupation would be counted for the purposes of establishing whether the tenant has been in occupation for a continuous period of six months.

In the case of a tenancy with multiple occupants, if one of those occupants is a licensee but subsequently becomes a tenant of the dwelling, any continuous period of occupation, whether as a licensee or a tenant, may be counted for the purposes of calculating the continuous period of occupation required by s.28.[13]

7–08 If a tenancy was in being prior to the enactment of the RTA 2004, a period of occupation prior to the commencement of Pt 4 will not be counted for the purposes of establishing a Part 4 tenancy.[14] Part 4 commenced on September 1, 2004.[15] Accordingly, the four-year tenancy cycle would have started from that date, for all tenancies in existence at that time falling within the jurisdiction of the RTA 2004.

---

[13] RTA 2004, s.50(5). See also para.2–25 which considers the circumstances where a licensee may become a tenant of a dwelling.

[14] Section 27 of the RTA 2004 provides that in Pt 4 a "continuous period of 6 months" means "a continuous period of 6 months that commences on or after the relevant date". "Relevant date" is defined at s.5(1) of the RTA 2004 as the date on which Pt 4 is commenced.

[15] Residential Tenancies Act 2004 (Commencement) Order 2004 (S.I. No. 505 of 2004).

C. Terms of a Part 4 Tenancy

7–09 We have considered above how a Part 4 tenancy comes into existence, if the tenancy continues after the initial six months without termination. The terms of that Part 4 tenancy will be the same as the terms of the tenancy during that initial six-month period.[16] Section 30(2) of the RTA 2004 provides that at any time during the Part 4 tenancy, the parties may agree to vary the terms of the tenancy. Any variation in the terms, however, will have no effect if inconsistent with Pt 4 or any other Part of the RTA 2004.[17]

D. More Beneficial Rights

7–10 Section 26 of the RTA 2004 is an important provision of Pt 4. It provides that nothing in Pt 4 operates to derogate from any rights the tenant enjoys that are more beneficial for the tenant than those created by Pt 4. Therefore, if the tenancy agreement provides security of tenure rights of 30 years, those more beneficial rights will supersede Pt 4. Part 4 is only intended to be a minimum standard which is implied into every tenancy or lease agreement and which cannot be derogated from. However, the more beneficial rights that may be enjoyed over Part 4 security of tenure rights, are now subject to limitation as provided by s.100(2)(b) of the Housing (Miscellaneous Provisions) Act 2009 (the "Housing Act 2009"). Section 100(2)(b) is considered below.

7–11 The issue of more beneficial security of tenure rights arose in the Circuit Court case of *S & L Management Limited v Mallon and Private Residential Tenancies Board*.[18] In that case the lease agreement between the management company and the lessee was for a period of 500 years. The Circuit Court was satisfied that this arrangement was not affected by Pt 4 of the RTA 2004 and that the lease came within the jurisdiction of the PRTB.[19] However, since the Circuit Court decision in *S & L Management Limited*, the Housing Act 2009 has been enacted amending the provisions of the RTA 2004, so that it no longer applies to tenancies which are longer than 35 years. Section 100(2)(b) of the Housing Act 2009 provides that "notwithstanding the definition of 'tenancy' in s. 5(1)[20]

---

[16] RTA 2004, s.30(1).

[17] RTA 2004, s.30(3).

[18] Unreported, Circuit Court, Linnane J., April 3, 2009; unreported, High Court, Budd J., April 23, 2010.

[19] The PRTB argued that "long leases" where the lessee pays substantial consideration for a residential lease (€200,000 in that case), were never intended by the legislature to come within the remit of the RTA 2004. The PRTB brought judicial review proceedings to quash the decision of Linnane J. which were unsuccessful. Budd J. in the High Court held that the Circuit Court was correct in its findings that if the provisions of s.3(1) of the RTA 2004 were not to apply to long leases of an owner occupied apartment, then the legislation shown have expressly excluded such dwellings just as other dwellings are excluded in s.3(2)(a)–(i) inclusive.

[20] Section 5(1) of the RTA 2004 defines a "tenancy" as including "a periodic tenancy and a tenancy for a fixed term, whether oral or in writing or implied, and, where the context so admits, includes a sub-tenancy and a tenancy or sub-tenancy that has been terminated".

[of the RTA 2004], in this section[21] a reference to a tenancy does not include a tenancy the term of which is more than 35 years".[22] Therefore, the RTA 2004 only applies to tenancies where the agreed term is less than 35 years.[23]

E. No Contracting Out

7–12 It is not possible to contract out of any of the provisions of Pt 4 of the RTA 2004. No lease, tenancy agreement, contract or other agreement may operate to vary or modify in any way the provisions of Pt 4.[24] This, however, is without prejudice to s.26 of the RTA 2004, which allows more beneficial rights for a tenant. Therefore, if parties to a lease agree to a term giving more security of tenure to the tenant, that will be permitted.[25]

F. Further and Successive Further Part 4 Tenancies

7–13 If a Part 4 tenancy lasts for four years without a notice of termination being served by the landlord or the tenant, then on the expiry of the four years, a further Part 4 tenancy will come into being between the parties. This tenancy is referred to in the RTA 2004 simply as a "further Part 4 tenancy".[26] The further Part 4 tenancy commences on the expiration of the first four-year period of the tenancy and it continues in being for four years, unless validly terminated by the landlord or tenant.[27]

7–14 The rights provided by Pt 4 of the RTA 2004 are to be "regarded as being of a rolling nature."[28] Accordingly, once a further Part 4 tenancy comes to an end, another further Part 4 tenancy will automatically come into existence and this will continue on at the expiration of each further four-year period, unless the landlord or tenant terminates the tenancy.[29] A successive further Part 4 tenancy is also referred to in the RTA 2004 as a "further Part 4 tenancy".[30]

---

[21]   RTA 2004, s.3(3), as inserted by s.100(2)(b) of the Housing Act 2009.
[22]   Section 100 of the Housing Act 2009 commenced on July 15, 2009.
[23]   See para.3–62.
[24]   RTA 2004, s.54(1).
[25]   RTA 2004, s.54(2). Note, however, paras 3–62 and 7–11, which consider how a tenancy for an agreed term of more than 35 years falls outside the jurisdiction of the RTA 2004 (Housing Act 2009, s.100(2)(b)).
[26]   RTA 2004, s.41(2).
[27]   RTA 2004, s.41(3) and (4). A further Part 4 tenancy may be terminated in accordance with s.34 and s.42 of the RTA 2004 in the case of a landlord and s.36 of the RTA 2004 in the case of a tenant. See Ch.8.
[28]   RTA 2004, s.43.
[29]   RTA 2004, s.43 and s.45.
[30]   RTA 2004, s.45(2).

7–15 The terms of a further Part 4 tenancy shall be those of the preceding Part 4 tenancy or as the case may be, the preceding further Part 4 tenancy.[31] At any time during the period of any further Part 4 tenancy, the parties may agree to vary its terms provided any variations are in accordance with the RTA 2004.[32]

G. Termination of Part 4 Tenancy Rights on a Tenant's Death

7–16 The general rule is that a Part 4 tenancy terminates on the death of a tenant.[33] However, there are certain circumstances where this rule does not apply and the Part 4 tenancy will continue in being as if the tenant did not die.[34] If the dwelling at the time of the death of the tenant was occupied by–

    (a) a spouse of the tenant;
    (b) a person who was not a spouse of the tenant but who cohabited with the tenant as husband and wife in the dwelling for a period of at least six months ending on the date of the tenant's death;
    (c) a child of the tenant being 18 years or more[35]; or
    (d) a parent of the tenant,

the Part 4 tenancy will continue in being, if any one of those persons elects in writing to become a tenant of the dwelling.[36] The RTA 2004 does not prescribe what kind of notice the person is required to give the landlord when electing to become a tenant, but presumably the notice should specify the relationship between the person and the deceased tenant of the dwelling, state that the person concerned resided with the deceased in the dwelling at the time of the deceased's death and the length of time he or she resided there.

The RTA 2004 does not make any specific provision for a landlord to object to a person becoming a tenant of the dwelling in the circumstances described above. However, s.76(3) of the RTA 2004 does provide that a landlord may refer a dispute to the PRTB between the landlord and another, not being the tenant but who is claiming an entitlement to the rights of a tenant through a person who is or was the tenant.

7–17 Where a person elects to and becomes a tenant in the circumstances described at para.7–16 above, the Part 4 tenancy will not continue in being any longer than it would have, had the original tenant not died. If the person who elected to become a tenant also dies, any other person who resided with that deceased tenant and who falls within the categories described at (a) to (d) of

---

[31] RTA 2004, s.46(1).
[32] RTA 2004, s.46(2) and (3).
[33] RTA 2004, s.39(1).
[34] RTA 2004, s.39(2).
[35] Child also includes a stepchild, foster child or an adopted child (RTA 2004, s.39(3)(iii)).
[36] RTA 2004, s.39(3).

para.7–16 above, may also elect to become a tenant of the dwelling. Again, however, the Part 4 tenancy will not continue in being any longer than it would have had the original tenant not died.[37]

H. Exclusion from Part 4 of the RTA 2004

7–18 There are three types of tenancies that are subject to the provisions of the RTA 2004 but fall outside the provisions of Pt 4.[38]

7–19 The first exception to Pt 4 arises in the case of a dwelling occupied by a tenant, which is one of two dwellings within a building that originally comprised a single dwelling. Part 4 will have no application where the landlord resides in the other of the two dwellings and serves a notice in writing on the tenant before the commencement of his or her tenancy, stating that Pt 4 will not apply to the tenant's tenancy.[39] Accordingly, if a landlord wishes to avail of this exception to Pt 4, it is imperative for the landlord to serve the notice on the tenant before the commencement of the tenancy. A notice served at a later date will be ineffective in precluding the application of Pt 4.

7–20 The second exception to Pt 4 arises in the context of s.50 of the Finance Act 1999, which provides for a scheme of tax relief for rented residential accommodation for third level students. In this regard, Pt 4 has no application to a tenancy of a dwelling where the landlord is entitled to a deduction of the kind referred to in s.380B(2), s.380C(4) or s.380D(2) (inserted by s.50 of the Finance Act 1999) of the Taxes Consolidation Act 1997, in relation to expenditure incurred on the construction, conversion into or refurbishment of the dwelling.[40] In other words, Pt 4 of the RTA 2004 has no application to what has been termed "s.50 student accommodation".[41]

7–21 The last circumstance where Pt 4 has no application to a tenancy is where a tenant's entitlement to reside in a dwelling is connected with his or her continuance in any office, appointment or employment.[42] This exception to Pt 4 prevents the unworkable situation that could arise if the employee (as a tenant)

---

[37] RTA 2004, s.39(5).

[38] For consideration of the application of the RTA 2004, see Ch.3.

[39] RTA 2004, s.25(1), (2) and (3).

[40] RTA 2004, s.25(4)(a). Sections 380B(2), 380C(4) and 380D(2) of the Taxes Consolidation Act 1997 were repealed by s.24 of the Finance Act 2002 with effect from January 1, 2002; see now Taxes Consolidation Act 1997, Pt 10 Ch.11 (ss.372AK–AV) (as subsequently amended by the Finance Act 2003) which codified with effect from January 1, 2002, reliefs for lessors and owner occupiers in respect of expenditure incurred on the provision of certain residential accommodation on construction, conversion and refurbishment.

[41] See the Explanatory Memorandum to the RTA 2004, s.25. Also, see "Student Accommodation Scheme", Office of the Revenue Commissioners, May 2007.

[42] RTA 2004, s.25(4)(b).

acquired Part 4 tenancy rights, however, the contract of employment under which the employee was provided with accommodation was later terminated.

3. Multiple Occupants, Licencees and Part 4 Tenancy Rights

A. Multiple Occupants

(i) Definition

7–22 Chapter 6 of Pt 4 of the RTA 2004 deals with multiple occupants. Multiple tenants are defined at s.48 as:

> 2 or more persons who are tenants of the dwelling (whether as joint tenants, tenants-in-common or under any other form of co-ownership) and "multiple tenant" means any one of them.

Chapter 6 makes clear that its provisions apply regardless of the fact that the dwelling concerned is occupied at the particular time by either or both –

> (a) multiple tenants;
> (b) one or more persons who are lawfully in occupation of the dwelling as licensees of the tenant or the multiple tenants, as the case may be.[43]

(ii) Rights under Part 4

7–23 One multiple occupant, who may not have acquired Part 4 tenancy rights, can benefit from the Part 4 tenancy rights of another tenant. Section 49(2) provides that:

> In particular, the fact that the continuous period of occupation, as respects a particular dwelling, by one or more of the multiple tenants is less than 6 months at a particular time does not prevent a Part 4 tenancy coming into existence at that time in respect of the dwelling if –
> (a) another of the multiple tenants has been in continuous occupation of the dwelling for 6 months, and
> (b) the condition in section 28(3) is satisfied.

The condition in s.28(3) is that no notice of termination has been served in relation to the tenancy. Therefore, if one tenant acquires Part 4 tenancy rights, having been in occupation of the dwelling for a period of six months without a notice of termination being served, a Part 4 tenancy comes into existence in respect of the *dwelling*. It is therefore not necessary for all occupants of a dwelling to have been in occupation of the dwelling for a continuous period of

---

[43] RTA 2004, s.49(1).

six months before a Part 4 tenancy in respect of the dwelling comes into existence.[44]

A multiple tenant will, however, only be entitled to the rights afforded by Pt 4 when they themselves have been in occupation of the dwelling for a continuous period of six months. This applies to a multiple tenant who occupies the dwelling before the Part 4 tenancy comes into being and to a multiple tenant who occupies the dwelling on or after the Part 4 tenancy has commenced.[45] Therefore, the rights and obligations under Pt 4 will apply equally to a multiple tenant once he or she has been in occupation for six months, as they apply in relation to the multiple tenant whose continuous occupation gave rise to the Part 4 tenancy's existence.

7–24 A Part 4 tenancy will commence with the first tenant having been in continuous occupation for six months. Therefore, Part 4 protection will last less than four years for those who join in at a later stage. The Part 4 tenancy will continue for four years[46] as long as there is at least one person who has acquired six months' occupancy and this need not be one of the original tenants.[47] If a person is a licensee immediately before becoming a tenant of the dwelling, any continuous period of occupation, whether as a licensee or a tenant, may be counted for the purposes of calculating the continuous period of occupation.[48]

7–25 It is important to note that the provisions relating to multiple occupants do not bring into existence a separate Part 4 tenancy for the benefit of each person residing in the dwelling. Section 53 of the RTA 2004 makes it very clear that where a multiple tenant acquires Part 4 tenancy rights, this shall not operate to bring into existence a separate Part 4 tenancy in his or her favour. Where a Part 4 tenancy arises, it comes into existence in respect of the dwelling, and a multiple occupant who may not previously have had Part 4 tenancy rights can benefit from this.

(iii) Vacating or death of a multiple tenant

7–26 If a tenant whose occupation gave rise to the Part 4 tenancy vacates the dwelling or dies, this does not act to deprive the other multiple tenant or tenants of the protection of that Part 4 tenancy.[49]

---

[44]   See also para.7–24 below.
[45]   RTA 2004, s.50(2) and (3).
[46]   Unless terminated earlier.
[47]   RTA 2004, s.52. See para.7–26.
[48]   RTA 2004, s.50(5).
[49]   RTA 2004, s.52.

(iv) Acts of multiple tenants

7–27 The act of one tenant cannot prejudice or affect the rights of another tenant. A common example of this is where one multiple tenant may be engaging in antisocial behaviour or have caused a deterioration in the condition of the dwelling beyond normal wear and tear but a co-tenant has not engaged in that activity.[50] The Part 4 tenancy rights of the multiple tenant who is not at fault in relation to such behaviour may not be prejudiced. This is established by s.51 of the RTA 2004, which provides that no act done by one or more of the multiple tenants of a dwelling, which could bring about the termination of the Part 4 tenancy, shall have that result for the tenant who is blameless. This is subject to the condition that an explanation or information is furnished to the landlord by the "innocent" tenant, from which a landlord, acting reasonably in the circumstances, would conclude that the act was done without the innocent tenant's consent.[51] The RTA 2004 defines what acting "reasonably" would be in that situation. A landlord acts reasonably if he or she requires the tenant who claims that he or she is blameless in relation to the particular act concerned to provide such information or assistance to the landlord, as he or she may reasonably need to ascertain with whose consent (if any) and by whom the act concerned was done. If the tenant fails to provide this assistance to the landlord, the landlord may conclude that the act concerned was done with that tenant's consent.[52]

In summary, therefore, a tenant will not be prejudiced by the acts of another tenant in the dwelling if he or she cooperates with the landlord in providing information or assistance to the landlord and the landlord is in a position to conclude from this information that the tenant was not complicit in the actions complained of. If the tenant fails to provide such assistance, the landlord can conclude that the act concerned was done with the consent of the tenant.

7–28 It is important to bear in mind that the provisions of s.51 discussed above also apply equally to the omissions of a multiple tenant.[53] Therefore, a failure of a multiple tenant to do something in accordance with his or her obligations as imposed by s.16 of the RTA 2004, which could bring about the termination of the tenancy, shall not prejudice a tenant who is not at fault in relation to that omission.

---

[50] Section 16 of the RTA 2004 imposes obligations on tenants. Section 16 is considered in detail in Ch.4.

[51] RTA 2004, s.51(1).

[52] RTA 2004, s.51(2). See *Griseto v O'Driscoll and Anor* (TR154/DR231/2007, September 18, 2008). See also s.17(2) of the Intoxicating Liquor Act 2003 which also deals with the issues of privity and consent. It provides that "a licensee is guilty of an offence if, with the licensee's privity or consent, intoxicating liquor supplied by the licensee in a closed container for consumption off the premises is consumed in a place which is within 100 metres of those premises". Similarly, under the RTA 2004, a tenant can be held responsible for the conduct or behaviour of another tenant if he consented to the conduct.

[53] RTA 2004, s.51(7).

B. Licensees

7–29 A person who is lawfully in occupation of a dwelling as a licensee of a tenant or a multiple tenant during the subsistence of a Part 4 tenancy may request the landlord of the dwelling to allow him or her to become a tenant of the dwelling.[54] If a licensee makes a request to become a tenant, the landlord may not unreasonably refuse to accede to such a request.[55] Where the landlord does accede to the licensee's request, the landlord must acknowledge in writing that the licensee has now become a tenant of the dwelling.[56]

7–30 A licensee who becomes a tenant of the dwelling in the circumstances described above will hold the dwelling on the same terms, or as appropriately modified, as those on which the existing tenant or multiple tenants hold the dwelling.[57] The new tenant can then avail of the provisions of s.50(3), which allows a licensee-turned-tenant to benefit from an already existing Part 4 tenancy, as that person has been in continuous occupation of the dwelling for a period of six months.[58] The new tenant can count the time spent as a licensee for the purposes of making up the six-month period.[59]

3. SUB-TENANCIES, ASSIGNMENTS AND PART 4 TENANCY RIGHTS

A. Sub-Tenancies

(i) General

7–31 A tenant of a dwelling must first obtain the written consent of the landlord before creating a sub-tenancy.[60] Where a Part 4 tenancy is in existence, the creation of a sub-tenancy of part only of the dwelling is prohibited. Any such sub-tenancy purported to be created is void.[61]

---

[54] RTA 2004, s.50(7).

[55] If the landlord refuses a licensee's request to become a tenant, he or she must be satisfied that such refusal was not unreasonable. If a licensee is aggrieved that the landlord has refused his or her request, the licensee has locus standi to make an application for dispute resolution services to the PRTB pursuant to s.76(4) of the RTA 2004. See *Galik v Oberneier* (TR93/DR472/2007, April 11, 2008). See also para.9–16.

[56] Section 50(8) of the RTA 2004. See paras 2–22 to 2–27 that consider licensees and the RTA 2004 in further detail.

[57] RTA 2004, s.50(8). Section 50(8)(b) provides that the terms will be the same, other than terms comprising the rights, restrictions and obligations which arise by virtue of a Part 4 tenancy being in existence in respect of the dwelling.

[58] See para.7–07.

[59] RTA 2004, s.50(5).

[60] RTA 2004, s.16(k).

[61] RTA 2004, s.32(2) and (3).

Sub-tenants are also protected by Pt 4 and accordingly they too can acquire Part 4 tenancy rights.[62] The Schedule to the RTA 2004 is titled "Protection for Sub-Tenancies Created out of Part 4 Tenancies". It sets out in detail the rights afforded to a sub-tenant under Pt 4. In summary, where the head-tenant has acquired Part 4 tenancy rights, the sub-tenant can benefit from these rights. If the written consent of the landlord to the creation of the sub-tenancy is not obtained, the provisions contained in the Schedule will not apply.[63]

(ii) Protection for sub-tenants

7–32 A sub-tenancy shall continue in being for so long as the Part 4 tenancy (being the head-tenancy) continues to exist, unless it is terminated sooner under the provisions of Pt 4.[64] Paragraph 4 of the Schedule to the RTA 2004 establishes that although a head-landlord may not have a contractual relationship with the sub-tenant, he or she will still owe the sub-tenant duties pursuant to s.12(1)(a) and (b) of the RTA 2004.[65] The sub-tenant also owes obligations to the head-landlord pursuant to s.16(f) and (g) of the RTA 2004.[66] The obligations owed between the head-landlord and the sub-tenant shall exist for as long as the sub-tenancy continues in being. Any dispute between the sub-tenant and the head-landlord that arises in relation to the sub-tenant's obligations may be referred to the PRTB for dispute resolution under Pt 6 of the RTA 2004.[67] Similarly, a dispute in relation to obligations owed by the head-landlord to the sub-tenant may also be referred to the PRTB.[68]

(iii) Sub-tenants' Part 4 tenancy rights after termination of the head-tenancy

7–33 If a landlord serves a notice of termination in respect of a Part 4 tenancy (which is a head-tenancy) but does not require the sub-tenancy to be terminated, the sub-tenant will become the tenant of the landlord and the sub-tenancy will be deemed to be converted into the Part 4 tenancy.[69] This will also occur where the head-tenant terminates the head-tenancy and does not terminate the sub-tenancy.[70] In both instances, the terms of the Part 4 tenancy under which the sub-tenant (turned tenant) will then hold the dwelling shall be those on which he or she held it under the sub-tenancy, unless the parties agree to vary its terms. The

---

[62] RTA 2004, s.32(1).

[63] RTA 2004, para.2(1) of the Schedule.

[64] RTA 2004, para.2(2) of the Schedule.

[65] RTA 2004, para.4(1) of the Schedule. None of the other obligations in s.12 are owed by a head-landlord to a sub-tenant. See Ch.5 on Landlord Obligations.

[66] RTA 2004, para.4(2) of the Schedule. None of the other obligations in s.16 are owed by the sub-tenant to the head-landlord. See Ch.4 on Tenant Obligations

[67] RTA 2004, para.4(2)(c) of the Schedule.

[68] RTA 2004, para.4(1)(b) of the Schedule.

[69] RTA 2004, para.5(a) of the Schedule. See also paras 8–111 to 8–117 which consider the procedural requirements for terminating head-tenancies and sub-tenancies.

[70] RTA 2004, para.6 of the Schedule.

duration of that Part 4 tenancy shall be the same as if the head-tenancy had not been terminated.[71]

Where a sub-tenant assumes Part 4 tenancy rights on the termination of a head-tenancy by the head-landlord or the head-tenant, this will not affect the liabilities that may have arisen between the sub-tenant and the head-tenant by virtue of the sub-tenancy.[72]

B. Assignment and Part 4 Tenancy Rights

(i) General

7–34 A tenant may not assign a tenancy of a dwelling without the consent of the landlord.[73] Where a Part 4 tenancy is in existence, the assignment of part only of a dwelling is prohibited. Any such assignment purported to be created is void.[74]

(ii) Assignment to a person other than a sub-tenant

7–35 If a tenant assigns a Part 4 tenancy to a person other than a sub-tenant, the protection provided by Pt 4 will cease. The assignee will require six months of continuous occupation in the dwelling before qualifying for Part 4 tenancy rights.[75]

(iii) Assignment to a sub-tenant

7–36 If a tenant assigns a dwelling to a sub-tenant, the Part 4 tenancy will continue in being in favour of the assignee for the period that it would have continued in being had the assignment not been made. The assignee's sub-tenancy of the dwelling merges with the Part 4 tenancy and the assignee becomes the tenant of the landlord under the Part 4 tenancy. The terms of the Part 4 tenancy shall continue to be those under which the assignor held the tenancy, unless the assignee and the landlord agree to a variation of them.[76] Where an assignee's sub-tenancy merges with a Part 4 tenancy, this will not affect any liabilities that may have arisen between the assignee and the assignor by virtue of the sub-tenancy concerned.[77]

---

[71] RTA 2004, para.5(b) and (c) and para.6 of the Schedule.

[72] S.I. No. 272 of 1980. See Appendix 16.

[73] RTA 2004, s.16(k).

[74] RTA 2004, s.38(4) and (5).

[75] Section 38(1)(a) of the RTA 2004 provides that if a Part 4 tenancy is assigned by a tenant with the written consent of the landlord and the assignment is to a person other than a sub-tenant of the dwelling, the assignment shall operate to convert the Part 4 tenancy of the dwelling into a periodic tenancy of the dwelling and the protection provided by s.28 for the assignor will cease.

[76] RTA 2004, s.38(2).

[77] RTA 2004, s.38(3).

4. FIXED TERM TENANCIES AND PART 4 TENANCY RIGHTS

A. Interaction of Fixed Term Tenancies and Part 4

7–37 A fixed term tenancy is a tenancy that the landlord and tenant agree will last for a specified period of time. As discussed above, a Part 4 tenancy affords a tenant the right to remain in occupation of a dwelling for a total period of four years.[78] The issue arises as to how fixed term tenancies interact with Part 4 tenancies. This is considered below.

7–38 It is not possible to contract out of the provisions of Pt 4 or to include a clause in a lease or tenancy agreement which attempts to modify or vary the provisions of Pt 4.[79] Accordingly, although a landlord and tenant may agree to enter into a fixed term tenancy, this will not affect a tenant acquiring Part 4 tenancy rights after six months of occupation. In effect, the fixed term tenancy simply runs with the Part 4 tenancy.

7–39 Before the enactment of the RTA 2004, it was common to enter into leases or tenancy agreements for 12-month periods. On the expiration of the 12 months, the tenancy terminated. While 12-month contracts are still common, the tenancy will not necessarily terminate after the expiry of the term in circumstances where the tenant relies on his Part 4 tenancy rights to remain in occupation. As Pt 4 gives a tenant security of tenure for a further three and a half years after six months of continuous occupation, the tenant will still have a right to remain in occupation for a further three years, on the expiry of the 12-month fixed-term agreed.[80]

7–40 If the tenant has a fixed term tenancy for a period of at least six months, the tenant must notify the landlord if he/she wishes to stay on in the dwelling once the fixed term tenancy expires. This notification is required by s.195 of the RTA 2004. Section 195 does not state, however, whether or not the notice to be given by the tenant to the landlord is to be in writing. As the burden will rest with the tenant to prove notice was given of his or her intention to stay on in the dwelling, it is preferable from the tenant's perspective that it is in writing.[81] In *O'Connor and Others v Naughton*[82] the tenancy tribunal found that the tenants had not claimed a Part 4 tenancy nor had they indicated to the landlord that they

---

[78] In addition to such subsequent periods that may arise by reason of the coming into being of a further Part 4 tenancy. See para.7–13.

[79] RTA 2004, s.54.

[80] This is subject to the right of the landlord to terminate the tenancy. See Ch.8 on Termination of Tenancies.

[81] See also para.8–110.

[82] TR97/DR684/2007, August 21, 2007.

intended to stay in occupation beyond the period specified in the letting agreement, as they were required to do under s.195 of the RTA 2004.

B. More Beneficial Rights than Part 4

7–41 It is not possible to contract out of the provisions of Pt 4 of the RTA 2004. However, it is permissible to include in a lease or tenancy agreement a clause which provides more beneficial rights for a tenant than those created by Part 4.[83] For example, a fixed term tenancy for a period of say, five years, will give a tenant greater security of tenure than a Part 4 tenancy.[84]

7–42 In certain circumstances, fixed term tenancies can also give tenants more security of tenure than afforded by Part 4 tenancies, by reason of the fact that a fixed term tenancy can only be terminated by the landlord where the tenant has breached his or her tenancy obligations. Accordingly, while a landlord of a Part 4 tenancy can terminate it by relying on the grounds set out at paras 2 to 6 of the Table to s.34 of the RTA 2004, the landlord of a fixed term tenancy cannot do so unless specific provision is made in the fixed term lease or tenancy agreement that these grounds will apply. The result is that while a landlord can terminate a Part 4 tenancy if, for example, he or she wishes to take up occupation of the rented dwelling, a landlord of a fixed term tenancy cannot rely on this ground to terminate the tenancy, unless the fixed term lease or tenancy agreement provides it may be terminated on this basis.[85]

Furthermore, the limited circumstance in which a landlord can terminate a fixed term tenancy gives tenants greater security of tenancy during the first six months of a tenancy when Pt 4 has no application. During this six-month period, a landlord of a tenancy that is not for a fixed term can terminate the tenancy without reason and by simply serving a notice of termination. On the other hand, a landlord of a fixed term tenancy cannot terminate the tenancy at any time during the fixed term period unless there has been a breach of obligation by the tenant or as considered at para.8–109, possibly where the lease or tenancy agreement provides it can be terminated in the limited circumstances described at that paragraph. Therefore, if the term of the tenancy is for a fixed term during the six-month period, the tenant will have greater security of tenure than where the tenancy is not for a fixed term.

---

[83] RTA 2004, s.26. See also para.7–10.

[84] As considered at paras 8–53 to 8–54, however, during the six-month period immediately following the expiration of the first four years of a tenancy, a landlord may terminate the further Part 4 tenancy arising even if none of the grounds set out in the Table to s.34 of the RTA 2004 exist.

[85] See paras 8–28 to 8–55 which consider the grounds on which a landlord can terminate a Part 4 tenancy.

5. Security of Tenure for Tenants of Dwellings Falling Outside the Jurisdiction of the RTA 2004

A. The Right to a New Tenancy under the 1980 Act

(i) Overview

7–43 Where the tenancy of a dwelling falls outside the jurisdiction of the RTA 2004, a tenant may make an application for a new tenancy under Pt II of the 1980 Act. Under Pt II a tenant is entitled to apply for a new tenancy of the rented dwelling if the tenant can establish any of the following: (1) a business equity, (2) a long occupation equity and (3) an improvements equity.[86] For the purpose of this text, which deals with residential tenancies in the private rented sector, consideration is given to the equities at (2) and (3) only.[87]

(ii) Tenement

7–44 For a tenant to be entitled to apply for a new tenancy under Pt II of the 1980 Act, the tenant must be in occupation of a "tenement".[88] Tenement is defined at s.5 of the 1980 Act, which provides as follows–

In this Act "tenement" means –
(a) premises complying with the following conditions:
  (i)   they consist either of land covered wholly or partly by buildings or of a defined portion of a building;
  (ii) if they consist of land covered in part only by buildings, the portion of the land not so covered is subsidiary and ancillary to the buildings;
  (iii) they are held by the occupier thereof under a lease or other contract of tenancy express or implied or arising by statute;
  (iv) such contract of tenancy is not a letting which is made and expressed to be made for the temporary convenience of the lessor or lessee ... ; and
  (v)   such contract of tenancy is not a letting made for or dependant on the continuance in any office, employment or appointment of the person taking the letting;
or
(b) premises to which section 14 or 15 applies.

Accordingly, in determining whether a premises is a tenement under the 1980 Act, it is essential to ascertain what the main purpose of the property is and this main purpose must then attach to the buildings and not the land. The portion of

---

[86]   1980 Act, s.16.

[87]   1980 Act, s.13(1)(b) and s.13(1)(c) respectively.

[88]   A tenant is defined in s.3 of the 1980 Act as "the person for the time being entitled to the occupation of premises and where, the context so admits, includes a person who has ceased to be entitled to that occupation by reason of the termination of his tenancy."

the land not covered by buildings must be subsidiary and ancillary to the buildings.[89]

B. Long Occupation Equity

7–45 Under s.13(1)(b) of the 1980 Act a tenant has a long occupation equity if:

> the tenement was, during the whole period of twenty years ending at that time, continuously in the occupation of the person who was the tenant immediately before that time or of his predecessors in title.

Therefore, if a tenant can prove that he or she was in occupation of a dwelling for 20 years, the tenant will be entitled to apply for a new tenancy under the 1980 Act. Occupation by a predecessor in title can also be taken into account in the calculation of that 20-year period.[90]

C. Improvements Equity

7–46 Under s.13(1)(c) of the 1980 Act a tenant has an improvements equity if:

> improvements have been made on the tenement and the tenant would, if this Part did not apply to the tenement, be entitled to compensation for those improvements under Part IV [of the 1980 Act] and not less than one-half of the letting value of the tenement at that time is attributable to those improvements.

Improvement is defined in s.45 of the 1980 Act as:

> any addition to or alteration of the buildings comprised in the tenement and includes any structure erected on the tenement which is ancillary or subsidiary to those buildings and also includes the installation in the tenement of conduits for the supply of water, gas or electricity but does not include work consisting only of repairing, painting and decorating, or any of them.

---

[89] See *Mason v Leavy* [1952] I.R. 40; *Kenny Homes & Co. v Leonard*, unreported, Supreme Court, June 18, 1998; *Terry v Stokes* [1993] 1 I.R. 204.

[90] Section 55(1) of the RTA 2004 makes clear that occupation under a Part 4 tenancy is to be counted for the purposes of calculating 20 years' occupancy to establish a long occupation equity. However, s.55 is subject to s.192 of the RTA 2004. Except in one limited circumstance, s.192(2) abolishes from September 1, 2009, the right of a tenant to make an application for a new tenancy under Pt II of the 1980 Act, where the dwelling concerned is one to which the RTA 2004 applies. In practice therefore, s.55 of the RTA 2004 now has limited application. See also para.7–53 and para.7–54 where s.192 is considered in further detail. See also para.7–47 that considers the application of s.55(2).

Therefore, for an improvements equity to arise, the tenant must be entitled to compensation for improvements under Pt 4 of the 1980 Act and such improvements must account for half or more than half of the letting value of the tenement. An improvements equity entitles a tenant to apply for a new tenancy under the 1980 Act.

D. Restrictions on the Right to a New Tenancy under the 1980 Act

7–47 A tenant will lose his or her entitlement to a new tenancy on the basis of a long occupation equity or an improvements equity if any of the circumstances described in s.17(1) of the 1980 Act exist.[91] Section 17(1) provides that a tenant shall not be entitled to a new tenancy if—

   (a) the tenancy has been terminated because of non-payment of rent;
   (b) the tenancy has been terminated on account of a breach by the tenant of a covenant of the tenancy;
   (c) the tenant has terminated the tenancy by notice of surrender or otherwise;
   (d) the tenant has completed and signed a renunciation of his or her entitlement to a new tenancy in the tenement and has received independent legal advice;
   (e) the tenancy has been terminated by notice to quit given by the landlord for good and sufficient reason;
   (f) the tenancy terminated otherwise than by notice to quit and the landlord either refused for good and sufficient reason to renew it or would, if he had been asked to renew it, have had good and sufficient reason for refusing.

"Good and sufficient reason" for the purposes of s.17(1) means a reason which emanates from some action or conduct of the tenant and which "having regard to all the circumstances of the case, is in the opinion of the Court a good and sufficient reason for terminating or refusing to renew (as the case may be) the tenancy."[92]

Section 55(2) of the RTA 2004 provides that the termination of a Part 4 tenancy under the RTA 2004 shall not be regarded as a termination for the purposes of s.17(1)(a) of the 1980 Act, unless the tenancy has been terminated because the tenant has breached his or her tenancy obligations. Section 55(2) is, however, subject to s.192 of the RTA 2004. Section 192(2) abolishes from September 1, 2009, the right of a tenant to make an application for a new tenancy under Pt II of the 1980 Act, where the dwelling concerned is one to which the RTA 2004 applies.[93] Accordingly, s.55(2) now has limited application.[94]

---

[91] As amended by s.4 of the Landlord and Tenant (Amendment) Act 1994 and s.191 of the RTA 2004.
[92] 1980 Act, s.17(1)(b).
[93] Note however that s.192(3) of the RTA 2004 provides that s.192(2) does not have effect where the tenant served a notice of intention to claim relief under the 1980 Act prior to September 1, 2009. See paras 7–53 and 7–54, where s.192 of the RTA 2004 is considered in further detail.
[94] See also fn.90 above at para.7–46.

7–48 Section 17(2) of the 1980 Act sets out a number of grounds on which a landlord can rely to refuse to grant a new tenancy. They are—

    (a) the landlord intends to pull down and rebuild or reconstruct the buildings or part of the buildings and has planning permission for the work to be carried out;

    (b) The landlord required vacant possession for the purposes of carrying out a scheme of development of property which includes the tenement and has planning permission for the work;

    (c) The landlord being a planning authority and the tenement is situate in an area in respect of which the development plan indicates objectives for its development or renewal as being an obsolete area;

    (d) The landlord being a local authority, requires possession within a period of five years after termination of the existing tenancy for any purpose for which the local authority is entitled to acquire property compulsorily;

    (e) For any reason the creation of a new tenancy would not be consistent with good estate management.[95]

E. Procedure and the Terms of a New Tenancy under the 1980 Act

7–49 If a tenant is in a position to establish a long occupation equity or an improvements equity, this does not give the tenant an automatic right to a new tenancy. To claim a new tenancy, the tenant must serve a "notice of intention to claim relief" in the prescribed form on the landlord pursuant to s.20 of the 1980 Act. The prescribed form for such a notice is that comprising Form 1, which is annexed to the Landlord and Tenant Regulations 1980.[96]

Once a notice of intention to claim relief has been served, a tenant will then only be granted a new tenancy where the landlord consents to this or, in the absence of any such agreement, where a new tenancy is granted by the court.[97]

7–50 Where a tenant is entitled to a new tenancy on the basis of an improvements equity or long occupation equity, the terms of the new tenancy will be those as may be agreed between the landlord and the tenant or in default of agreement, as fixed by the court.[98] Where the court fixes the terms of the new tenancy, it is required to fix the duration of the tenancy at 35 years or such lesser term as the tenant may nominate.[99] The rent fixed by the court must be the

---

[95] This ground has been the subject of much litigation. See *Gallagher v Earl of Leitrim* [1948] Ir. Jur. Rep. 23; *Dolan v Corporation of the Corn Exchange Buildings Company of Dublin* [1973] I.R. 269; *Ryan v Bradley* [1956] I.R. 31.

[96] S.I. No. 272 of 1980.

[97] 1980 Act, s.16.

[98] See s.18 of the 1980 Act which applies where the court fixes the terms of the new tenancy. In particular, s.18(4) makes clear that the tenant is not entitled to compensation in respect of the termination of his previous tenancy.

[99] 1980 Act, s.23(2), as amended by s.5 of the Landlord and Tenant (Amendment) Act 1994. Note

"gross rent" reduced, where appropriate, by an allowance for improvements.[100] Gross rent is defined as:

> the rent which in the opinion of the Court a willing lessee not already in occupation would give and a willing lessor would take for the tenement, in each case on the basis of vacant possession being given, and having regard to the other terms of the tenancy and to the letting values of tenements of a similar character to the tenement and situate in a comparable area but without regard to any goodwill which may exist in respect of the tenement.[101]

Therefore, the court must determine the level of rent payable based on market rates.[102] The court cannot insert a rent review clause into a lease granted under the 1980 Act but both the landlord and tenant are entitled to apply to the court for a review of the rent at five-yearly intervals.[103]

F. Alternative Rights to a New Tenancy under the 1980 Act

(i) Compensation for improvements

7–51 If a tenant is not entitled to a new tenancy under the 1980 Act (or perhaps decided not to apply for one) but the tenant has during the course of the tenancy made improvements to the dwelling, the tenant can instead apply for compensation for improvements.

Section 46 of the 1980 Act provides that where a tenant quits a tenement because a landlord terminates the tenancy, he or she is entitled to be paid compensation by the landlord for every improvement made on the tenement by him or her or any of his or her predecessors in title. This right to compensation is subject to the improvements adding to the letting value of the tenement and being suitable to its character. No compensation is payable if the tenant himself or herself had terminated the tenancy by notice of surrender or otherwise, or the tenancy is terminated because of non-payment of rent.

---

that this 35-year period only applies in the case of a tenancy granted on the basis of a long occupation or an improvements equity.

[100] 1980 Act, s.23(4). The allowance for improvements shall be such proportion of the gross rent as is, in the opinion of the court, attributable to improvements made by the tenant or his predecessors in title and in respect of which the tenant would have been entitled to compensation for improvements if (as the case may be) Pt II of the 1980 Act did not apply to the tenement or the new tenancy had not been created (1980 Act, s.23(6)).

[101] 1980 Act, s.23(5). See also para.6–09 which deals with "gross rent", in the context of rent reviews.

[102] The definition of market rent in the 1980 Act is largely the same as "market rent" for the purposes of Pt 3 of the RTA 2004 that deals with rent and rent reviews. See paras 6–07 to 6–10.

[103] Landlord and Tenant (Amendment) Act 1984, s.15.

(ii) Compensation for disturbance

7–52 Prior to the RTA 2004 when a landlord terminated a tenancy, compensation for disturbance was only available to business tenants pursuant to s.58 of the 1980 Act. Section 58(1) provides that where the court is satisfied that a tenant would be entitled to a new tenancy but for s.17(2) of the 1980 Act,[104] the tenant in lieu of a new tenancy is entitled to be paid compensation for disturbance by the landlord.[105] Section 199(1) of the RTA 2004 amends s.58(1)(b) of the 1980 Act and extends the right to compensation for disturbance to tenants holding a long occupation equity. This relief applies only to tenancies of dwellings falling within the ambit of the 1980 Act.

6. INTERACTION OF THE RTA 2004 AND THE 1980 ACT

A. Abolition of Long Occupation Equity and Improvements Equity

7–53 A tenant's right to a new tenancy on the basis of a long occupation equity and an improvements equity under Pt II of the 1980 Act has been abolished for all dwellings which fall within the jurisdiction of the RTA 2004. Section 192(2) of the RTA 2004 provides that from the fifth anniversary of the commencement of Pt 4,[106] Pt II of the 1980 Act shall not apply to a dwelling to which the RTA 2004 applies.[107] Accordingly, tenants can no longer make an application for a new tenancy on the basis of a long occupation equity or improvements equity if the rented dwelling falls within the ambit of the RTA 2004.[108] There is one exception to this and that is where the tenant had served a notice of intention to claim relief in accordance with s.20 of the 1980 Act prior to September 1, 2009.[109]

---

[104] See para.7–48 above.

[105] Section 58(2) of the 1980 Act provides that the measure of compensation that a tenant is entitled to is the monetary or pecuniary loss, damage or expense which the tenant sustains or incurs by reason of his quitting the tenement and which is the direct consequence of that quitting.

[106] Part 4 of the RTA 2004 commenced on September 1, 2004 (Residential Tenancies Act 2004 (Commencement) Order 2004 (S.I. No. 505 of 2004)). See also s.5 of the RTA 2004 that defines the "relevant date" for the purposes of that legislation, as the date on which Pt 4 is commenced.

[107] Note also s.191 of the RTA 2004 which provides that a tenant may renounce his or her right to a long occupation equity, where the dwelling is one to which the RTA 2004 applies, the tenant has received independent legal advice and the renunciation is in writing. The intention of s.191 was that if a tenant was coming up to 20 years' occupancy of the tenement and the landlord intended to terminate the tenancy to prevent the tenant acquiring the right to a long occupation equity, the tenant could have renounced that right, in return for the landlord allowing the tenancy to continue. As a tenant of a dwelling to which the RTA 2004 applies no longer has a right since September 1, 2009 to apply for a long occupation equity, s.191 is now of less significance.

[108] For dwellings which fall outside the jurisdiction of the RTA 2004, the statutory reliefs available under the 1980 Act still apply.

[109] RTA 2004, s.192(3).

7–54 The abolition of the long occupation equity was the result of recommendations made by the Commission. It considered it necessary to abolish the equity to facilitate the new security of tenure proposals recommended by it.[110]

B. The Application of the RTA 2004 and Continuing Rights under the 1980 Act

7–55 As noted at para.7–43 above, a tenant's right to claim a new tenancy under Pt II of the 1980 Act still applies in respect of dwellings which do not fall within the jurisdiction of the RTA 2004. However, the question arises as to whether a person who has been granted a tenancy under Pt II of the 1980 Act may also apply for a new tenancy under the 1980 Act when that tenancy expires? Alternatively, is it the case that once a tenancy granted under the 1980 Act expires any time after September 1, 2009, the dwelling will fall instead within the jurisdiction of the RTA 2004.[111]

Section 192 of the RTA 2004 provides that Pt II of the 1980 Act no longer applies to a dwelling to which the RTA 2004 applies, unless the tenant had served a notice of intention to claim relief in accordance with s.20 of the 1980 Act prior to September 1, 2009. Section 3(2)(i) of the RTA 2004 provides that the RTA 2004 has no application if:

> A dwelling the subject matter of a tenancy *granted*[112] under Part II of the Landlord and Tenant (Amendment) Act 1980 or under Part III of the Landlord and Tenant Act 1931 or which is the subject of an application made under section 21 of the Landlord and Tenant (Amendment) Act 1980 and the court has yet to make its determination in the matter.

It could be argued that the abolition of an entitlement to a long occupation equity or improvements equity only applies to those tenants who have never previously claimed the right to a new tenancy under Pt II of the 1980 Act or who never made an application for such a right prior to September 1, 2009.[113] The alternative interpretation is that once a tenancy granted under the 1980 Act expires, the right to apply for a new tenancy under the 1980 Act after September 1, 2009 no longer exists. The tenancy granted under the 1980 Act will have expired, while s.192(2) provides that the Pt II of the 1980 Act shall not apply after September 1, 2009.[114]

---

[110] Report of the Commission, para.8.5.13.

[111] Assuming that there is no other reason why the RTA 2004 would have no application. See Ch.3 on the Application of the Residential Tenancies Act 2004.

[112] Emphasis added.

[113] This is the view of the authors in Brennan, *Landlord and Tenant Law*, 4th edn (Dublin: Law Society of Ireland, 2007) and of the Department of the Environment Heritage and Local Government in an information leaflet "Private Rented Sector – Tenants of 20 or More Years Occupancy".

[114] See O'Riordan, M., *Consolidated Landlord and Tenant Legislation* (Dublin: Clarus Press,

This issue has not yet been the subject of judicial consideration. As such, the correct interpretation of s.192 of the RTA 2004 and the application of Pt II of the 1980 Act remains unclear.

2007), where the author opines at p.105 that, "section 192 of the Residential Tenancies Act 2004 states that as and from the fifth anniversary of the relevant date ... Part II of [the 1980 Act] shall not apply to a dwelling to which the 2004 Act applies. However, this does not have effect in relation to a dwelling where the tenant has served a notice of intention to claim relief before the fifth anniversary of the relevant date". This reflects the position that if a claim for a new tenancy under Pt II of the 1980 Act has not been made before September 1, 2009, the tenancy will come within the jurisdiction of the RTA 2004. It also seems to suggest, however, that further applications for relief under 1980 Act may not be made even though a tenancy may previously have been granted under that legislation.

CHAPTER 8

TERMINATION OF TENANCIES

1. INTRODUCTION

A. Law on Termination of a Tenancy prior to the RTA 2004

8–01 Before the enactment of the Residential Tenancies Act (the "RTA 2004"), there were well-established common law and statutory rules that were applicable to terminating a tenancy.[1] Section 16 of the Housing (Miscellaneous Provisions) Act 1992 provided that a tenancy could be terminated by serving a notice to quit giving a minimum period of four weeks' written notice to the other party. This requirement to give four weeks' notice applied to both landlords and tenants. In relation to a fixed term tenancy agreement, the tenancy expired automatically at the end of the fixed term, without either party having to take any action.

Where the tenant failed or refused to vacate the property, the most common remedy invoked by landlords was to institute ejectment proceedings for overholding and seek an order for vacant possession. Ejectment proceedings for non-payment of rent was the remedy availed of by landlords where a tenant failed to pay rent or other charges.[2] Forfeiture and re-entry was the other remedy available to landlords where a tenant was in breach of the tenancy agreement. Each of these remedies still apply to tenancies which fall outside the remit of the RTA 2004.[3]

B. Report of the Commission on the Private Rented Residential Sector

8–02 The Commission on the Private Rented Residential Sector (the "Commission")[4] made a number of recommendations in relation to the termination of tenancies.[5] The Commission recommended that the notice periods for the termination of a tenancy should be based on the length of the tenancy itself. However, in cases of breach of the tenancy agreement, the Commission

---

[1] See generally Wylie, *Landlord and Tenant law*, 2nd edn (Dublin: Butterworths, 1998), Ch.23.

[2] Landlord and Tenant (Amendment) (Ireland) Act 1860 ("Deasy's Act"), ss.52, 66 and 72.

[3] See paras 8–121 to 8–129.

[4] The Commission was launched on July 22, 1999 by Mr Robert Molloy TD, Minister for Housing and Urban Renewal. It was charged with examining the workings of the landlord and tenant relationship. See para.1–03.

[5] Report of the Commission on the Private Rented Residential Sector, July 2000 ("Report of the Commission"), para.8.5.

recommended that the landlord or tenant should be permitted to terminate the tenancy giving shorter periods of notice. It recommended that the minimum statutory notice which should be given to a tenant should be 28 days. That minimum standard would apply where the tenancy was for a period of six months or less, with the landlord being required to give longer periods of notice as the duration of the tenancy increased.

In relation to the newly proposed "Part 4 tenancy",[6] it recommended that a landlord could only terminate a Part 4 tenancy on the following grounds:

- "The tenant has not fulfilled his/her obligations under the agreement, (e.g. has not paid the rent, has not looked after the property properly, has been guilty of anti-social behaviour, etc.)
- The accommodation is no longer suitable to the tenant's circumstances by reference to the number of bedspaces (i.e. no. of occupants is greater than no. of bedspaces)
- The landlord wishes to sell or substantially refurbish/renovate the property in a way which requires the property to be vacated, change its business use or requires it for own or family member occupation."[7]

Most of the recommendations of the Commission concerning termination of tenancies are contained in the RTA 2004.

C. The RTA 2004

(i) Overview

8–03 The RTA 2004 fundamentally changed the way in which a landlord or tenant could terminate a residential tenancy in the private rented sector. The pre-existing statutory provisions and common law rules in force prior to the enactment of the RTA 2004 no longer apply to residential tenancies which come within the ambit of the RTA 2004.[8] Accordingly, landlords are no longer able to utilise means such as forfeiture and re-entry to recover possession of a dwelling.[9] Even the common law rule, that at the end of a fixed term tenancy the tenancy expired automatically without either party having to take any action, no longer has application to tenancies which fall within the ambit of the RTA 2004.[10] In

---

[6] As proposed by the Commission and ultimately enacted in the RTA 2004, a Part 4 tenancy is a tenancy that comes into being after the tenant has been in continuous occupation of a dwelling for six months. The effect of a Part 4 tenancy is to give a tenant security of tenure for a further period of three and a half years after the tenancy has been in existence for that initial six-month period. Part 4 tenancies, their meaning and effect, are considered in detail in Ch.7.

[7] Report of the Commission, para.8.5.2.

[8] By way of example, s.16 of the 1992 Act no longer has application to residential tenancies falling within the remit of the RTA 2004.

[9] Section 58 of the RTA 2004 provides that a tenancy may not be terminated by means of a notice of forfeiture, a re-entry or any other procedure not provided by Pt 5.

[10] RTA 2004, s.59. See paras 8–102 and 8–104.

relation to those residential tenancies which fall outside the jurisdiction of the RTA 2004, the rules and the law in force prior to its enactment still have application.[11] These rules are considered later on in this Chapter.[12]

8–04 The principal change brought about by the RTA 2004 is that a tenancy can only be terminated by serving a valid notice of termination in accordance with the provisions of Pt 5.[13] Where a landlord or tenant seeks to terminate the tenancy, they are required to give specific periods of notice. In line with the Commission's recommendations, Pt 5 introduced set notice periods, linked to the duration of the tenancy.

Strict compliance with the RTA 2004 is necessary if a landlord or a tenant wishes to terminate a tenancy. If the landlord fails to serve a valid notice of termination, the tenant will have no obligation to vacate the premises. If an invalid notice of termination is served towards the end of the first six months of the tenancy, the tenant may secure a Part 4 tenancy, which will give the tenant security of tenure for a further three and a half years.[14] Similarly, if a tenant fails to serve a valid notice of termination and vacates the premises, this may result in the tenant forfeiting his or her deposit. It is therefore imperative that both landlords and tenants are aware of the rules that must be followed to terminate a tenancy of a dwelling to which the RTA 2004 applies. It is an offence for a landlord or tenant to take any action in reliance on an invalid notice of termination that he or she knew or ought to have known was invalid.[15]

(ii) Interaction of Part 4 and Part 5 of the RTA 2004

8–05 Part 5 of the RTA 2004 specifies the procedures which must be followed to validly terminate a tenancy falling within the jurisdiction of the RTA 2004. Part 4 of the RTA 2004 deals with security of tenure for tenants. As outlined in the preceding paragraph, the security of tenure provisions of Pt 4 provide that after six months of occupation, the tenant will secure a Part 4 tenancy, entitling the tenant to remain in occupation for a further three and a half years.[16]

8–06 Although Pt 5 of the RTA 2004 deals with the termination of tenancies, Pt 4 contains additional provisions that apply where a landlord seeks to terminate a Part 4 tenancy. By way of summary, for a landlord to terminate a

---

[11] Certain dwellings and tenancies are excluded from the jurisdiction of the RTA 2004 by s.3(2) and s.3(3). See Ch.3 on the Application of the RTA 2004.

[12] See paras 8–121 to 8–129.

[13] RTA 2004, ss.57 and 58. Section 57 of the RTA 2004 makes clear that Pt 5 applies to all tenancies to which the RTA 2004 applies, including those tenancies to which Pt 4 has no application.

[14] See Ch.7 on Security of Tenure.

[15] RTA 2004, s.74.

[16] See Ch.7 on Security of Tenure.

Part 4 tenancy, one of the six grounds set out in the Table to s.34 of the RTA 2004 must exist first.[17] The landlord must also comply with any requirements to terminate a tenancy that attaches to that particular ground.[18] Once the provisions of s.34 are satisfied, the landlord must then comply with the procedural requirements for the termination of a tenancy contained in Pt 5.

Accordingly, if a landlord is terminating a Part 4 tenancy, the landlord must have regard to and comply with the applicable provisions of both Pt 4 and Pt 5 of the RTA 2004.[19] A landlord need only have regard to Pt 5 if terminating a tenancy that is not a Part 4 tenancy.[20] In contrast, where a tenant terminates a tenancy to which the RTA 2004 applies, the tenant is only required to have regard to Pt 5, regardless of whether the tenancy is a Part 4 tenancy or not.

(iii) Complex nature of termination rules

8–07 Prior to the enactment of the RTA 2004, the rules governing the termination of the landlord and tenant relationship were at times complex and difficult to follow. However, the provisions of the RTA 2004 that have replaced those rules have been described as unnecessarily technical and confusing.[21] In so far as possible, this chapter seeks to summarise comprehensively the provisions of the RTA 2004 dealing with the termination of tenancies.

2. Termination by a Landlord—Overview of Procedure

8–08 If a landlord wishes to terminate a tenancy to which the RTA 2004 applies, the landlord must consider a number of issues before doing so. These issues are as follows:

---

[17] RTA 2004, Table to s.34, para.1–6.

[18] These additional requirements are also set out in the Table to s.34 of the RTA 2004.

[19] This position is not so clear if the provisions of Pt 4 and 5 of the RTA 2004 are considered separately. Section 33 of Part 4 states that, "a Part 4 tenancy may not be terminated by the landlord save in accordance with s. 34." However, s.57(b) of Pt 5 makes it clear that Part 4 requirements are "in addition" to the requirements of Pt 5. It is important therefore, when terminating a Part 4 tenancy, to have regard to both the provisions of Pt 4 and Pt 5. See also *Canty v Private Residential Tenancies Board* [2007] IEHC 243; unreported, High Court, August 8, 2007, where at pp.22–23, Laffoy J. considers this issue in the context of the notices under Pts 4 and 5 that a landlord must give to a tenant prior to terminating a tenancy for the tenant's failure to pay rent.

[20] A tenancy to which the RTA 2004 applies will not be a Part 4 tenancy during the first six months of its existence or in circumstances where s.25 excludes the application of Pt 4. Section 25 provides for three circumstances where the provisions of Pt 4 has no application—1) where the dwelling is one of two dwellings that comprised a single dwelling when originally constructed and the landlord resides in the other dwelling, 2) "s.50 student accommodation" or 3) if the entitlement of the tenant to occupy the dwelling is connected with his or her continuance in any office, appointment or employment. See paras 7–18 to 7–21.

[21] Laffoy J. in *Canty v Private Residential Tenancies Board* [2007] IEHC 243, unreported, High Court, August 8, 2007, p.23.

(a) Is a notice of termination required?

(b) If so, has the notice of termination been drafted correctly in compliance with all the requirements of the RTA 2004?

(c) Does the landlord need a reason to terminate the tenancy?

(d) Are there any statements which need to be included in the notice of termination?

(e) If the landlord is terminating the tenancy because the tenant has failed to comply with his or her tenancy obligations, does the landlord need to give the tenant an opportunity to remedy this breach before terminating the tenancy?

(f) Is the landlord terminating the tenancy because the tenant is in arrears of rent? If so, does the landlord need to serve a warning letter before serving a notice of termination?

(g) Is the tenancy a fixed term tenancy?

(h) Has the tenancy been sub-let? If so, does the landlord also require that the sub-tenancy be terminated?

(i) What is the appropriate notice period which the landlord must give to the tenant?

This is a useful checklist for landlords in ensuring that they comply with all of the requirements of the RTA 2004 for terminating a tenancy. Each of these issues are considered in turn below.

A. Notice of Termination

8–09 A notice of termination must be served by a landlord in all cases, including on the expiry of a fixed term tenancy.[22] There are certain cases, however, where the tenancy will simply be deemed to have terminated. In those instances the tenancy will be at an end, without any action required of the landlord, including the service of a notice of termination.[23]

B. Valid Notice of Termination

8–10 The notice of termination served by the landlord must comply with and contain all of the details required by s.62 of the RTA 2004. The requirements of s.62 include that the notice of termination is in writing, is signed by the landlord or his or her authorised agent, states the termination date and the date of service. Section 62 and the requirements for a valid notice of termination are considered in detail at paras 8–04 to 8–71.

---

[22] See paras 8–102 and 8–110 that considers the issues that arise on the expiry of a fixed term tenancy.

[23] See para.8–56 that considers the circumstances where a tenancy will be deemed to have terminated. In summary, these will arise where the tenant vacates the dwelling and is in arrears of rent.

C. Reason for Termination

8–11 A landlord must always state the reason for the termination of the tenancy in the notice of termination. The only exception to this is where the tenancy has not yet lasted six months and accordingly is not a Part 4 tenancy.[24]

If the tenancy is a Part 4 tenancy, the landlord may only terminate it if one of the six grounds in the Table to s.34 of the RTA 2004 exist. The ground on which the landlord relies to terminate the Part 4 tenancy must then be stated in the notice of termination.[25] These grounds are considered in further detail at paras 8–28 to 8–51.

8–12 If a landlord wishes to terminate a Part 4 tenancy but none of the grounds in the Table to s.34 exist, there are two limited circumstances where the landlord can terminate the Part 4 tenancy. These are considered at para.8–52.

D. Accompanying Statements

8–13 In certain circumstances, the notice of termination served on the tenant must be accompanied by or contain a statement prescribed by the RTA 2004. These circumstances arise only in the case of a Part 4 tenancy and where the landlord's reason for terminating the tenancy is that:

    (a) the landlord or a member of the landlord's family wishes to reside in the dwelling;
    (b) the landlord wishes to carry out refurbishment or renovation to the dwelling; or
    (c) the landlord wishes to change the use of the dwelling.[26]

In any of those cases, the notice of termination must also contain or be accompanied by the appropriate statement set out in paras 4, 5 or 6 of the Table to s.34 respectively.[27] Each of these statements is considered in detail at paras 8–39 to 8–46.

E. Opportunity to Remedy Breach of Obligation

8–14 If the landlord is terminating a Part 4 tenancy due to the tenant's failure to comply with his or her tenancy obligations, the landlord must notify the

---

[24] RTA 2004, s.62(1)(e).
[25] RTA 2004, s.34(a)(ii) and s.62(1)(e).
[26] RTA 2004, Table to s.34, paras 4, 5 and 6.
[27] Under para.4 the landlord must identify the person who will be residing in the dwelling and the expected length of time of the occupancy; under para.5, the landlord must identify the nature of the works which are being carried out on the dwelling; and under para.6, the landlord must identify the nature of the change of use of the dwelling.

tenant of that failure in writing. The landlord must then also give the tenant an opportunity to remedy that failure.[28] The only exception to this is where the tenant has engaged in certain antisocial behaviour.[29] The procedure that a landlord must follow and the rules applying to the termination of tenancies where the tenant is in breach of obligation are considered in detail at paras 8–75 to 8–83.

F. 14-Day Warning Letter

8–15 If the landlord is terminating a tenancy due to the tenant's failure to pay rent, a warning letter must be served by the landlord giving the tenant 14 days to pay outstanding rent arrears. The letter must set out the amount of rent due.[30] The procedure that must be followed to terminate a tenancy where the tenant is in arrears of rent is considered in detail at para.8–82.

G. Fixed Term Tenancies

8–16 If the tenancy is for a fixed term the landlord cannot terminate the tenancy during the fixed term period, unless the tenant has breached his or her tenancy obligations or the other limited circumstances considered at para.8–105 exist. The termination of fixed term tenancies is considered at paras 8–102 to 8–109.

H. Sub-Tenancies

8–17 If a rented dwelling has been sub-let by the tenant, there are additional requirements that a landlord must comply with whereby the landlord seeks to terminate the tenancy. These rules vary depending on whether the landlord wants to terminate the head-tenancy only or requires both the head-tenancy and the sub-tenancy to be terminated. The procedures that a landlord must follow to terminate a tenancy that has been sub-let are considered at paras 8–111 to 8–117.

I. Notice Period

8–18 To terminate a tenancy the landlord must give the tenant the correct period of notice. The notice periods for terminating a tenancy are set down in ss.66 and 67 of Pt 5 of the RTA 2004. The notice period that a landlord is required to give a tenant will depend on the length of the tenancy and the reason for termination of the tenancy. In summary:

---

[28] RTA 2004, Table to s.34, para.1.
[29] Namely, that described at s.17(1)(a) and (b) of the RTA 2004. See paras 8–76 to 8–81.
[30] RTA 2004, s.67(3).

    (a) If the tenant has <u>*not* breached</u> his or her tenancy obligations, the longer notice periods contained in s. 66 apply.[31]

    (b) if the tenant <u>*has* breached</u> his or her tenancy obligations, the shorter notice periods contained in s.67 apply.

The notice periods contained in ss.66 and 67 are considered in detail at paras 8–73 to 8–83.

3. Termination by the Tenant—Overview of Procedure

8–19 If a tenant wishes to terminate a tenancy to which the RTA 2004 applies, the tenant must also consider a number of issues before doing so. These issues are as follows:

    (a) Is a notice of termination required?

    (b) If so, has the notice of termination been drafted correctly, in compliance with all the requirements of the RTA 2004?

    (c) Does the tenant need a reason to terminate the tenancy?

    (d) If the tenant is terminating the tenancy because the landlord has failed to comply with his or her tenancy obligations, does the tenant need to give the landlord an opportunity to remedy this breach before terminating the tenancy?

    (e) Is the tenancy a fixed term tenancy?

    (f) Has the tenancy been sub-let? If so, does the tenant also require that the sub-tenancy be terminated?

    (g) What is the appropriate notice period which the tenant must give to the landlord?

This is a useful checklist for tenants in ensuring compliance with all of the requirements of the RTA 2004 for terminating his or her tenancy. Each of these issues are considered in turn below.

A. Notice of Termination

8–20 A notice of termination must be served by a tenant in all cases including on the expiry of a fixed term tenancy. The termination of fixed termed tenancies is considered in further detail at paras 8–105 to 8–109.

---

[31] Section 66 of the RTA 2004 also applies where a *tenant* is terminating a tenancy and the landlord is not in breach of his or her obligations. See para.8–73.

B. Valid Notice of Termination

8–21 The notice of termination served by the tenant must comply with and contain all the details required by s.62 of the RTA 2004. The requirements of s.62 include that the notice of termination is in writing, is signed by the tenant, states the termination date and the date of service. Section 62 and the requirements for a valid notice of termination are considered in detail at paras 8–64 to 8–71.

C. Reason for Termination

8–22 There is no obligation on a tenant to provide a reason in the notice of termination for terminating the tenancy. This applies regardless of whether the tenancy is a Part 4 tenancy or not.[32]

D. Opportunity to Remedy Breach of Obligation

8–23 If the tenant is terminating a tenancy due to the landlord's failure to comply with his or her tenancy obligations, the tenant must notify the landlord of that failure in writing. The tenant must then also give the landlord an opportunity to remedy that failure.[33] The procedure that a tenant must follow and the rules applying to the termination of tenancies where the landlord has breached his or her tenancy obligations are considered in detail at paras 8–84 to 8–86.

E. Fixed Term Tenancies

8–24 If the tenancy is for a fixed term the tenant cannot terminate the tenancy during the fixed term period, unless the landlord has breached his or her tenancy obligations or has refused to consent to the tenant assigning or sub-letting the tenancy or in the limited circumstances described at para.8–105. The termination of fixed term tenancies is considered at paras 8–102 to 8–109.

F. Sub-Tenancies

8–25 Where a tenant has sub-let a dwelling, he or she (then referred to as the head-tenant) assumes the role of landlord in respect of the sub-tenancy. Should the head-tenant wish to terminate the sub-tenancy he or she will be obliged to comply with all the requirements for terminating a tenancy imposed on landlords by the RTA 2004. These requirements are considered at paras 8–115 to 8–117 below.

---

[32] RTA 2004, s.36(1) and s.62(1)(e).
[33] RTA 2004, s.68(3).

8–26 It may also be the case that a head-landlord seeks to terminate a tenancy that has been sub-let. In these circumstances, additional rules must be complied with by both the head landlord and the head tenant. The rules which apply depend on whether the head landlord, in terminating the head-tenancy, also requires the sub-tenancy to be terminated or whether the head landlord simply wishes to terminate the head-tenancy. The requirements of the RTA 2004 in both of these instances, including the obligations that arise for head tenants and sub-tenants, are considered at paras 8–112 to 8–114.

G. Notice Period

8–27 To terminate a tenancy, the tenant must give the landlord the correct period of notice. The notice periods for terminating a tenancy are set down in ss.66 and 68 of Pt 5 of the RTA 2004. The notice period that a tenant is required to give a landlord will depend on the length of the tenancy and the reason for terminating it. In summary:

    a. If the landlord has *not* breached his or her tenancy obligation, the longer notice periods contained in s.66 apply.[34]

    b. If the landlord *has* breached his or her tenancy obligations,the shorter notice periods contained in s.68 apply.

The notice periods contained in ss.66 and 68 are considered in detail at paras 8–73 and 8–84 to 8–86.

4. GROUNDS PERMITTING A LANDLORD TO TERMINATE A PART 4 TENANCY

8–28 A Part 4 tenancy is a tenancy that comes into being after the tenant has been in continuous occupation of a dwelling for six months. The effect of a Part 4 tenancy is to give a tenant security of tenure for a further period of three and a half years after the tenancy has been in existence for that initial six-month period. Part 4 tenancies are considered in detail in Ch.7.

The circumstances where a landlord can terminate a Part 4 tenancy are limited. A landlord can only terminate a Part 4 tenancy on the basis of one of the six grounds set out in the Table to s.34 of the RTA 2004.[35] If the landlord seeks to rely on one of the six grounds, he or she must comply with any

---

[34] Section 66 of the RTA 2004 also applies where a *landlord* is terminating a tenancy and the tenant is not in breach of his or her obligations. See para.8–73.

[35] RTA 2004, Table to s.34, paras 1–6. Section 34 does not apply to tenants. Tenants may terminate a Part 4 tenancy without giving any reason, provided the other procedural requirements of Pt 5 have been complied with. See para.8–55.

additional requirement imposed by that particular ground before proceeding to terminate the tenancy.[36] The landlord must also comply with all the procedural requirements of Pt 5 of the RTA 2004; in particular, the landlord must serve a notice of termination giving the tenant the required notice period.[37]

Each of the six grounds on which a landlord may terminate a Part 4 tenancy are considered in turn at points A–F below.

A. Breach of Tenant's Obligations

(i) Procedure

8–29 A landlord may terminate a Part 4 tenancy where the tenant has breached his or her tenancy obligations.[38] This is permitted by para.1 of the Table to s.34 of the RTA 2004. However, if a tenant has failed to comply with his or her obligations that does not automatically give the landlord a right to terminate the Part 4 tenancy.[39] The landlord must first notify the tenant of the tenant's breach of obligation. This notice must state:

(a) the obligation the tenant has failed to comply with;
(b) the period of time (which must be reasonable) within which the tenant has to remedy his or her failure to comply with the tenancy obligation[40];
(c) that the landlord is entitled to terminate the tenancy if the tenant fails to remedy that breach of obligation within the period specified.

A common mistake made by landlords in terminating a Part 4 tenancy because the tenant has failed to comply with his or her tenancy obligations is one in which they do not give the tenant the warning notice as outlined above. A sample notice is contained at Appendix 4.[41]

8–30 In *Barrington-Martin and Anor v O'Neill and Anor*,[42] the landlords sought to terminate a Part 4 tenancy on the ground that the tenants had failed to comply with their tenancy obligations. In that case the tenancy tribunal stated that:

---

[36] A landlord is entitled to invoke one or more of the grounds for termination provided for in the Table to s.34. See *Canty v Private Residential Tenancies Board* [2007] IEHC 243; unreported, High Court, August 8, 2007, at p.38.

[37] Accordingly, to terminate a Part 4 tenancy a landlord must first comply with the requirements of Pt 4 and then follow the procedural requirements prescribed by Pt 5.

[38] RTA 2004, Table to s.34, para.1. See also Ch.4 on Obligations of Tenants.

[39] Unless the failure is deemed an "excepted basis" for termination, which arises in certain cases of antisocial behaviour. See paras 8–76 to 8–81.

[40] "Remedy the failure" in this context is defined in s.35 of the RTA 2004. See para.8–31.

[41] Note that the RTA 2004 does not state whether such a notice need be in writing or not, although this is arguably implied by the use of the phrase "notification states" at para.1 of the Table to s.34. It is advisable however, for a landlord to put such a notice in writing to avoid any dispute that may arise at a later date in relation to whether the landlord complied with the requirements of para.1.

[42] TR66/DR695/2007, July 9, 2007.

"Section 34 of the Residential Tenancies Act 2004 requires that where a landlord is terminating a tenancy on the ground that a tenant has failed to comply with any of his or her obligations in relation to the tenancy, unless the failure provides an excepted basis for termination (i.e. anti-social behaviour described in sub-s 16(h)), the tenant must be notified of the failure by the landlord and that notification must state that the landlord is entitled to terminate the tenancy if the failure is not remedied within a reasonable time specified in the notification and the tenant does not remedy the failure within a reasonable time."[43]

The tenancy tribunal found that there was no evidence that the landlords served such a notice prior to serving the notice of termination on the tenants. On this basis, the tenancy tribunal determined that the notice of termination served was invalid.

8–31 "Remedy the failure" As we have considered in the preceding paragraphs, a landlord is not permitted to terminate a Part 4 tenancy where a tenant has failed to comply with his or her tenancy obligations, unless the landlord has first afforded the tenant an opportunity to remedy that failure. "Remedy the failure" for the purposes of para.1 of the Table to s.34 is defined as follows:

(a) to desist from the conduct that constitutes the failure or, if the failure consists of an omission to comply with an obligation, to comply with that obligation, and

(b) In the case of failure that results in financial loss or damage to the landlord or his or her property –
   i. to pay adequate compensation to the landlord (or if the failure consists of the non-payment of rent, pay the arrears of rent) or to fully repair any damage caused to the premises, and
   ii. to desist from the conduct that constitutes the failure or comply with the obligation concerned.[44]

It is only if the tenant fails to remedy his or her breach of obligation, within the time specified in the warning notice given to the tenant by the landlord, that the landlord is then permitted to proceed to terminate the tenancy in accordance with the provisions of Pt 5 of the RTA 2004.

---

[43] Tenancy tribunal report, p.9.
[44] RTA 2004, s.35(2).

8–32 "Reasonable time" to remedy the failure The landlord must give the tenant "a reasonable time" to remedy the tenant's failure to comply with his or her tenancy obligations. Paragraph 1 of the Table to s.34 does not give any guidance as to what constitutes "a reasonable time" but the decision of Laffoy J. in *Canty v Private Residential Tenancies Board*[45] considered the question of what is a reasonable time.

In *Canty*, the landlord had served a notice on the tenant, giving the tenant three days to remedy his failure to comply with his tenancy obligations. In that case the tenant had failed to pay rent in accordance with the tenancy agreement. Laffoy J. held that the notice of termination subsequently served by the landlord was invalid because three days was not a reasonable period to satisfy the requirements of the RTA 2004 in that instance. Laffoy J. was of the view that the landlord should have given the tenant 14 days to pay the rent arrears. She also stated that on the facts of a particular case that period might not constitute a "reasonable time" within the meaning of para.1 of the Table to s.34.[46]

8–33 Accordingly, in each individual case and having regard to all the relevant circumstances, a landlord will be required to make a decision as to what is "a reasonable time" to give to a tenant to remedy a breach of a tenancy obligation. What is sufficient to constitute a "reasonable time" is a judgement (and often a difficult one) that landlords have to make. For instance, it may not be unreasonable to give the tenant seven days to pay an outstanding ESB charge of, say, €150. On the other hand, it may be unreasonable to give the tenant just 14 days to carry out a substantial repair required to a dwelling.[47]

(ii) Procedure specific to rent arrears

8–34 Where a landlord seeks to terminate a Part 4 tenancy because the tenant has failed to pay rent, a more complex procedure applies. The landlord must serve the tenant with the notice considered in the preceding paragraphs, which informs the tenant of his or her breach of obligation and affords the tenant a reasonable time to remedy that breach. In addition, however, the landlord must also serve the tenant with a 14-day warning letter in relation to the rent arrears.[48] Accordingly, to terminate a Part 4 tenancy where a tenant is in arrears of rent, the following three-step procedure must be followed:

---

[45] [2007] IEHC 243.

[46] Page 24 of the judgment.

[47] If a tenant has caused a deterioration in the condition of the dwelling beyond normal wear and tear, the tenant is obliged to takes steps to restore the dwelling to the condition it was at the commencement of the tenancy or to compensate the landlord for doing so (RTA 2004, s.16(g)).

[48] RTA 2004, s.67(3). It is clear from the decision in *Canty* (see below) that the notice in para.1 of the Table to s.34 is a separate and distinct notice from the 14-day warning letter required pursuant to s.67(3). The 14-day warning letter is only required to be served where the tenant has failed to pay rent.

    (1) The landlord must serve a notice on the tenant, which states:
        a. the tenant is in arrears of rent;
        b. the period of time within which the tenant has to remedy that breach
           of obligation.[49]
    (2) If the tenant fails to pay the arrears of rent, the landlord must serve a
        second notice on the tenant informing him or her that an amount of rent
        is due.[50] The landlord must then give the tenant 14 days to pay those rent
        arrears.
    (3) If the tenant fails to pay the rent due within 14 days of receipt of the
        notice referred to at (2), the landlord may proceed to terminate the
        tenancy by serving a notice of termination. The landlord is only required
        to give the tenant a period of 28 days notice of the termination of the
        tenancy in these circumstances.[51]

Accordingly, to terminate a Part 4 tenancy where a tenant is in arrears of rent, the landlord must serve three separate notices on the tenant.[52] In *Canty v Private Residential Tenancies Board*, Laffoy J. stated that in her view:

> "the provisions of the Act of 2004 for the valid termination of a Part 4 tenancy for non-payment of rent are very technical and confusing. It is difficult to understand why, in relation to non-payment of rent, the notification required by para. (a) of ground 1 in s.34 could not have been made co-terminous with the notification under s. 67(3). As it has not been, it seems to me that prudence dictates that a landlord invoking ground 1 should serve notice in the form required by para.(a) on the tenant allowing at least fourteen days for remedying the breach, that is to say, discharging the outstanding rent, although, on the facts of a particular case, that period might not constitute a 'reasonable time' within the meaning of para.(a)".[53]

(iii) Exception to the requirement for notice to be given of breach of obligation

8–35 We have considered in the preceding paragraphs that where a landlord wants to terminate a tenancy because the tenant has failed to comply with his or her tenancy obligations, the landlord must first serve a notice on the tenant informing the tenant of that breach of obligation. The landlord must then also give the tenant a reasonable time to remedy that breach. There is one instance where

---

[49] This is the notice required by para.1 of the Table to s.34. See para.8–29 that outlines the required contents of such a notice.

[50] RTA 2004, s.67(3). The RTA 2004 does not specify that the landlord is to state the actual amount of rent arrears, rather that "an amount of rent" has not been paid. However, to properly identify the tenant's breach of obligation and facilitate compliance, it seems the better approach would be to provide details of the arrears of rent in the notice.

[51] RTA 2004, s.67(2).

[52] If the tenancy is not a Part 4 tenancy, the landlord is only required to serve the latter two notices on the tenant, namely the 14-day warning letter and the notice of termination.

[53] [2007] IEHC 243; unreported, High Court, August 8, 2007, at pp.23–24.

these requirements do not have to be complied with. This exception arises where the tenant engages in certain anti-social behaviour. Antisocial behaviour is defined for the purposes of the RTA 2004 at s.17(1) as follows:

(a) Behaviour that constitutes an offence[54];
(b) Behaviour that causes (or could cause) fear, danger, injury, damage or loss to any person living, working or otherwise lawfully in the dwelling concerned or its vicinity[55];
(c) Persistent behaviour that prevents or interferes with the peaceful occupation of another person residing in the rented dwelling or its vicinity.[56]

Where the tenant's behaviour falls within categories (a) or (b) above, the landlord is neither required to serve a notice on the tenant informing the tenant of the breach of tenancy obligation nor required to afford the tenant an opportunity to "remedy the failure". The landlord may instead proceed to terminate the tenancy by simply serving a notice of termination and by following the procedure for termination as required by Pt 5 of the RTA 2004.[57] If, however, the tenant's behaviour falls within category (c) above, the landlord must serve the tenant with the notice required under para.1 of the Table to s.34 and must afford the tenant an opportunity to remedy the behaviour that has caused the tenant to be in breach of his or her tenancy obligations.

8–36 It is important, therefore, for a landlord to ascertain what type of antisocial behaviour a tenant is engaging in before proceeding to terminate the tenancy. Antisocial behaviour has been the subject of a number of determinations made by the PRTB's tenancy tribunals. These determinations demonstrate that there is a high threshold to be met to establish antisocial behaviour. The approach of the tenancy tribunals has been to reserve classifying behaviour as antisocial for the more serious of cases.[58] Therefore, in assessing whether the conduct of a tenant constitutes antisocial behaviour, one should bear in mind this approach of the tenancy tribunals to date. If the behaviour does not reach the threshold of being antisocial as defined at s.17(1)(a) and (b) of the RTA 2004, and the landlord does not give the tenant notice as required by para.1 of the Table to s.34 or does not give the tenant an opportunity to remedy the failure, the termination of the tenancy will be invalid. The termination of a tenancy because the tenant

---

[54] Being an offence which, if committed, would be reasonably likely to directly affect the well-being or welfare of others (RTA 2004, s.17(1)(a)).
[55] This behaviour is defined as including violence, intimidation, coercion, harassment or obstruction of, or threats to the person. (RTA 2004, s.17(1)(b)).
[56] RTA 2004, s.17(1)(c).
[57] This procedure is outlined at paras 8–08 to 8–18.
[58] See paras 8–76 to 8–81, which deal with cases of antisocial behaviour. See also the consideration of antisocial behaviour in the context of the obligations of tenants at paras 4–20 to 4–21 and also in the context of dispute resolution at paras 9–18 to 9–23.

has engaged in antisocial behaviour is considered in greater detail at paras 8–76—8–81.

B. The Dwelling is no Longer Suitable

8–37 A landlord may terminate a Part 4 tenancy where the dwelling is no longer suitable for the accommodation needs of the tenant and of any persons residing with the tenant, having regard to the number of bed spaces contained in the dwelling and the size and composition of the occupying household.[59] Where a landlord seeks to terminate a tenancy on this basis, the landlord must cite this reason in the notice of termination and follow the procedural requirements to terminate a tenancy prescribed by Pt 5.[60]

C. The Landlord Intends to Sell the Property

8–38 A landlord may terminate a Part 4 tenancy where the landlord intends to sell the property within three months after the termination of the tenancy. To rely on this ground, the landlord must intend to enter into an enforceable agreement to transfer the whole of his or her interest in the dwelling for its full consideration.[61] Accordingly, the tenancy may not be terminated if the landlord intends to sell part only of his or her interest in the dwelling or to sell the dwelling for anything less than its full consideration.[62]

If a landlord intends to terminate the tenancy on the basis that he or she intends to enter into an enforceable agreement to sell the dwelling, the landlord must cite this ground in the notice of termination and follow the procedural requirements to terminate a tenancy prescribed by Pt 5.[63]

In *O'Gorman v Slattery and Anor*,[64] the landlords served a notice of termination on the tenant on the basis that they wished to sell the property. The tenant failed to vacate and was also in arrears of rent. The landlords, under

---

[59] RTA 2004, Table to s.34, para.2.

[60] This procedure is outlined at paras 8–08 to 8–18.

[61] RTA 2004, Table to s.34, para.3. If a tenant challenges an attempt by the landlord to terminate the tenancy on this ground, the landlord may be required to adduce evidence to show his or her intention to sell the dwelling. In these circumstances, the landlord may be able to demonstrate that he or she has taken steps to sell the dwelling, such as where it has been placed on the market or where negotiations have been progressed with potential purchasers. See, however, *Collins v O'Connor and Anor* (TR02/DR329/2007, February 26, 2007) considered at para.8–43 which considers a tenant's right to query the bona fides of a landlord's stated intention for terminating a tenancy.

[62] The circumstances where a dwelling might be sold for less than its full consideration could arise where the landlord's interest in the property is sold to a family member. The requirement for "full consideration" prevents a situation arising where title to a dwelling is transferred to a family member to facilitate the termination of a tenancy of that dwelling.

[63] This procedure is outlined at paras 8–08 to 8–18.

[64] TR36/DR236/2007, March 28, 2007.

pressure to complete the sale, changed the locks of the dwelling, preventing the tenant from gaining access. The tenancy tribunal determined that changing the locks constituted an unlawful termination of the tenancy and awarded the tenant €9,000 in compensation for the inconvenience caused to him.[65]

D. The Landlord Requires the Dwelling for his or her own Use

8–39 A landlord is permitted to terminate a Part 4 tenancy if the landlord requires the dwelling, or the property containing the dwelling, for the purposes of his or her own occupation or for occupation by a family member.[66] If the landlord seeks to rely on this ground to terminate the tenancy, he or she must do the following:

1) Serve a notice of termination which states that the reason for termination of the tenancy is that the landlord requires the dwelling for his or her use or for use by a family member[67];
2) Furnish the tenant with a statement either contained in the notice of termination or accompanying it, stating –
   a. the intended occupant's identity and if it is not the landlord, the intended occupant's relationship with the landlord[68];
   b. the expected duration of the landlord's or family member's occupation[69];
   c. that the landlord is required to offer to the tenant a tenancy of the dwelling if the dwelling becomes available for re-let (i) within six months from the expiry of the notice period that the landlord is required to give to the tenant to terminate the tenancy; or (ii) within six months from the final determination of any dispute referred to the PRTB in relation to the validity of a notice of termination[70] and the following conditions have been satisfied:
      • the tenant notifies the landlord in writing of his or her contact details within 28 days from the service of the notice of termination

---

[65] See also the tenancy tribunal decision of *Boyne v Hanaway* (TR49/DR1262/2008, October 14, 2008), where the landlord sought to terminate the tenancy on the grounds that he wished to sell the property. The tenancy tribunal upheld this as a valid ground for terminating the tenancy in the circumstances. See also paras 8–87 to 8–99 on Unlawful Termination.

[66] RTA 2004, Table to s.34, para.4. The reference to a member of the landlord's family is a reference to any spouse, child, stepchild, foster child, grandchild, parent, grandparent, step parent, parent-in-law, brother, sister, nephew or niece of the landlord or a person adopted by the landlord under the Adoption Acts 1952 to 1998 (RTA 2004, s.35(4)).

[67] RTA 2004, s.34(a)(ii) and s.62(1)(e). The procedural requirements of Pt 5 of the RTA 2004 for the termination must also be complied with (see paras 8–08 to 8–18 which considers this procedure). In particular, the notice of termination must contain all the information required by s.62 and the correct notice period (set out in s.66 in this instance) must be given to the tenant.

[68] RTA 2004, Table to s.34, para.4(a)(i).

[69] RTA 2004, Table to s.34, para.4(a)(ii).

[70] RTA 2004, Table to s.34, para.4(b)(i).

> or from the final determination of any dispute referred to the PRTB relating to the validity of the notice of termination[71];
> - the tenant notifies the landlord in writing of any change in the tenant's contact details as soon as practical after that change occurs[72];
> - the tenancy has not been terminated by virtue of the grounds set out at paras 1, 2, 3 or 6 of the Table to s. 34 of the RTA 2004.[73]

8–40 In *Barrett v Ward*,[74] the landlord terminated the tenancy on the basis that he required the dwelling for his own use. The landlord, however, failed to occupy the dwelling and did not offer the tenant a tenancy of the dwelling when he decided not to take up occupation. The tenancy tribunal determined that this invalidated the original notice of termination that the landlord had served. Accordingly, as the tenant had vacated the dwelling due to what transpired to be an invalid notice of termination, and as a result lost the benefit of his Part 4 tenancy, the tenant was awarded €3,300 in compensation.

8–41 In *Barrington-Martin and Anor v O'Neill and Anor*,[75] the landlords claimed that they were entitled to terminate the tenancy because the dwelling was required by the landlords for occupation by a family member. The tenancy tribunal noted that these circumstances had arisen subsequent to the date of the notice of termination that had been served by the landlords. There was also no other notice of termination before the tenancy tribunal that purported to terminate the tenancy on the basis of family need. Accordingly, the landlords failed in their attempt to rely on para.4 of the Table to s.34 as a valid reason for the termination of the tenancy. The tenancy tribunal found that it was not sufficient to state a reason which had not in fact arisen at the time of service of the notice of termination but which only arose subsequently.

8–42 In *McDermott and Anor v Quinn*,[76] a notice of termination was served by the landlord to terminate a Part 4 tenancy, giving six months to vacate the dwelling. The notice stated that the reason for termination of the tenancy was because the landlord wished to re-occupy the dwelling. The notice did not, however, state the expected duration of the occupation of the landlord. The tenant argued that the notice of termination was invalid on the basis that it failed to refer to the intended occupation of the landlord and that as the landlord was suffering from ill-health at the time, the landlord was not in a position to return

---

[71] RTA 2004, s.35(5)(a).

[72] RTA 2004, s.35(5)(b).

[73] RTA 2004, Table to s.34, para.4(b)(ii). The grounds specified in paras 1, 2, 3 and 6 are, respectively: breach of the tenant's obligations; the dwelling is no longer suitable for the occupants; the landlord intends to sell the property within three months of the termination of the tenancy; and the landlord intends to change the use of the dwelling. See paras 8–29 to 8–38 and 8–46.

[74] TR135/DR963/2007, March 31, 2008.

[75] TR66/DR695/2007, July 9, 2007.

[76] TR15/DR1154/2008, September 30, 2008.

and occupy the dwelling. The tenancy tribunal accepted both of these arguments and determined that the notice of termination was invalid.[77]

8–43 The tenancy tribunal decision of *Collins v O'Connor and Anor*[78] considered whether the Table to s.34 prescribes merely procedural requirements which must be adhered to when terminating a tenancy or whether there are in fact evidential burdens placed on a landlord in proving his or her intention to reside in the property itself. In that case the tenant submitted that if a landlord seeks to terminate a tenancy on the basis that a family member wishes to occupy the premises, a tenant is entitled to query the bona fides of the landlord and the landlord should be put on proof as to the veracity of his or her intended action. The tenancy tribunal found that as no evidence was introduced which would undermine the bona fides of the landlord, the bona fides of the landlord could not be called into question. In its finding, the tenancy tribunal stated that:

> "It is not the intention of the Act that the Landlord should be put on proof of their stated intention, but rather that the Tenant would have a right of redress, including reinstatement in the dwelling should it be proven after a reasonable period that the Section 34 notice was fraudulently or improperly served."[79]

Therefore, if a landlord states that he or she intends to occupy the dwelling as the ground relied on for the termination of the tenancy, his or her bona fides will not be called into question unless there is evidence to the contrary.

E. The Landlord Intends to Substantially Refurbish or Renovate the Dwelling

8–44 A landlord is permitted to terminate a Part 4 tenancy where he or she wishes to substantially refurbish or renovate the dwelling (or the property containing the dwelling) in a way that requires the dwelling to be vacated to facilitate this.[80] Where planning permission is required for the works to be carried out, that planning permission must already have been obtained before service of the notice of termination. If the landlord seeks to rely on this ground to terminate the tenancy, he or she must do the following:

---

[77] See also *Barrett v Ward* (TR135/DR963/2007, March 31, 2008).

[78] TR02/DR329/2007, February 26, 2007.

[79] Tenancy tribunal report, p.13. See, however, the wording in para.8(4)(b) of the Schedule to the RTA 2004, which relates to a sub-tenant's right to refer a dispute to the PRTB concerning the validity of a notice of termination served by the head-tenant and in particular to the right of the sub-tenant "to put in issue, in a dispute in relation to the validity of the notice of termination referred to the [PRTB] under Part 6, the *bona fides of the intention of the head-tenant* to do or, as appropriate, permit to be done the thing mentioned in the notice" (emphasis added).

[80] RTA 2004, Table to s.34, para.5.

(1) Serve a notice of termination which states the reason for the termination of the tenancy is that the landlord intends to substantially refurbish or renovate the dwelling (or the property containing the dwelling) in a way that requires the dwelling to be vacated[81];

(2) Furnish the tenant with a statement either contained in the notice of termination or accompanying it, stating –

(a) the nature of the intended works, and

(b) that the landlord is required to offer the tenant a tenancy of the dwelling if the dwelling becomes available for re-letting[82] the following conditions have been satisfied:

- the tenancy has not been terminated on the basis of the grounds described at paras 1, 2, 3 or 6 of the Table to s.34 of the RTA 2004[83];
- the tenant notifies the landlord in writing of his or her contact details within 28 days from the service of the notice of termination or from the final determination of any dispute referred to the PRTB relating to the validity of the notice of termination[84];
- the tenant notifies the landlord in writing of any change in the tenant's contact details as soon as practical after that change occurs.[85]

8–45 In *Hewer and Anor v Williams and Anor*,[86] the landlords terminated the tenancy on the basis that they intended to carry out substantial refurbishment to the dwelling. The required statement that accompanied the notice of termination failed to state that the tenant would be offered the option to renew the tenancy when the refurbishment work was completed. The tenancy tribunal was of the

---

[81] RTA 2004, s.34(a)(ii) and s.62(1)(e). The procedural requirements of Pt 5 of the RTA 2004 for the termination must also be complied with (see paras 8–08 to 8–18, which consider this procedure). In particular, the notice of termination must contain all the information required by, s.62 and the correct notice period (set out in s.66 in this instance) must be given to the tenant.

[82] RTA 2004, Table to s.34, para.5(b)(i). It is interesting to note that pursuant to paras 4 and 6 of the Table to s.34, the landlord is only required to offer a further tenancy to the tenant if the dwelling becomes available for letting within six months from either the date of termination of the tenancy, or, if a dispute is referred to the PRTB in relation to the notice of termination, within six months from the final determination of the PRTB. However, there is no such time period stipulated in relation to para.5 of the Table to s.34, where the landlord requires possession of the dwelling to refurbish or renovate it. Consequently, where a landlord is refurbishing or renovating a dwelling, the obligation placed on the landlord to offer a tenancy to a former tenant will continue at least until the works have been completed and the dwelling becomes available to re-let.

[83] RTA 2004, Table to s.34, para.5(b)(ii). The grounds specified in paras 1, 2, 3 and 6 are, respectively: breach of the tenant's obligations; the dwelling is no longer suitable for the occupants; the landlord intends to sell the property within three months of the termination of the tenancy; and the landlord intends to change the use of the dwelling.

[84] RTA 2004, s.35(5)(a).

[85] RTA 2004, s.35(5)(b).

[86] TR21/DR427&1252/2008, July 30, 2008.

view that the notice of termination was valid as it "conforms to the relevant sections of the Act and is therefore a valid notice" but that a proviso should have been included to state that the tenant would be offered the option to renew occupation once the refurbishment work was complete.[87] This approach is inconsistent with the tenancy tribunal decision of *McDermott and Anor v Quinn*,[88] where it found that as the accompanying statement did not state the expected duration of the occupation of the landlord, the notice of termination was invalid. *Hewer and Anor v Williams and Anor* is also inconsistent with the approach generally of tenancy tribunals, which is to interpret the provisions of the RTA 2004 dealing with the termination of tenancies very strictly. This approach is particularly apparent in the tenancy tribunal determinations in relation to the requirements of s.62 of the RTA 2004, which are considered at paras 8–64 to 8–71.

F. The Landlord Intends to Change the Use of the Dwelling

8–46 A landlord is permitted to terminate a Part 4 tenancy where he or she intends to change the use of the dwelling or the property containing the dwelling.[89] Where planning permission is required for the change of use, that permission must have been obtained prior to the service of the notice of termination. If the landlord seeks to rely on this ground to terminate the tenancy, he or she must do the following:

1) Serve a notice of termination, which states that the reason for the termination of the tenancy is that the landlord intends to change the use of the dwelling[90];
2) Furnish the tenant with a statement either contained in the notice of termination or accompanying it, stating –
   (a) the nature of the intended use[91];
   (b) that the landlord is required to offer the tenant a tenancy of the dwelling if the dwelling becomes available for re-letting: (i) within six months from the expiry of the notice period that the landlord is required to give to the tenant of the termination of the tenancy; or (ii) within six months from the final determination of any dispute referred to the PRTB in relation to the validity of a notice of termination[92] and the following conditions have been satisfied:

---

[87] Tenancy tribunal report, p.6.
[88] TR15/DR1154/2008, September 30, 2008.
[89] RTA 2004, Table to s.34, para.6.
[90] RTA 2004, s.34(a)(ii) and s.62(1)(e). The procedural requirements of Pt 5 of the RTA 2004 for the termination must also be complied with (see paras 8–08 to 8–18 which consider this procedure). In particular, the notice of termination must contain all the information required by s.62 and the correct notice period (set out in s.66 in this instance) must be given to the tenant.
[91] RTA 2004, Table to s.34, para.6(a).
[92] RTA 2004, Table to s.34, para.6(b)(i).

- the tenant notifies the landlord in writing of his or her contact details within 28 days from the service of the notice of termination or from the final determination of any dispute referred to the PRTB relating to the validity of the notice of termination[93];
- the tenant notifies the landlord in writing of any change in the tenant's contact details as soon as practical after that change occurs[94];
- the tenancy has not been terminated on the basis of the grounds set out at paragraphs 1, 2 or 3 of the Table to s. 34 of the RTA 2004.[95]

G. Additional Considerations Relevant to the Termination of a Part 4 Tenancy by a Landlord

(i) Where offer to re-occupy accepted

8–47 A landlord is required to offer a tenant a right to re-occupy a dwelling if it becomes available for re-let where the tenancy was terminated on the basis of paras 4–6 of the Table to s.34 of the RTA 2004. These grounds for termination are that the landlord[96]:

- required the dwelling for his or her occupation or that of a family member;
- intended to substantially refurbish or renovate the dwelling; or
- intended to change the use of the dwelling.

The landlord's obligation to offer the tenant a right to re-occupy a dwelling is subject to the tenant furnishing the landlord with his or her contact details and keeping the landlord updated with these details.[97]

8–48 If an offer to re-occupy a dwelling is accepted by a tenant, this will result in an enforceable agreement between the parties.[98] Occupation by the tenant under the new tenancy shall, together with his or her occupation under the former tenancy, be regarded as a continuous period of occupation by the tenant under the one tenancy.[99] This means that a tenant's Part 4 tenancy rights are protected and the termination of a Part 4 tenancy pursuant to paras 4–6 of the Table to s.34 cannot cut short a tenant's Part 4 tenancy rights.

---

93 RTA 2004, s.35(5)(a).
94 RTA 2004, s.35(5)(b).
95 RTA 2004, Table to s.34, para.6(b)(ii). The grounds specified in paras 1, 2 and 3 are, respectively: breach of the tenant's obligations; the dwelling is no longer suitable for the occupants; and the landlord intends to sell the property within three months of the termination of the tenancy. See paras 8–29 to 8–38.
96 RTA 2004, Table to s.34, paras 4, 5 and 6.
97 RTA 2004, s.35(5). A landlord has no obligation to ascertain the tenant's whereabouts.
98 RTA 2004, s.35(6)(a).
99 RTA 2004, s.35(6)(b).

8–49 Where a tenant re-occupies a dwelling subsequent to the original tenancy being terminated for any of the reasons set out at paras 4–6 of the Table to s.34, the RTA 2004 is silent as to whether the terms of the new agreement are to be the same as the terms which existed under the previous tenancy. Section 35(6) of the RTA 2004 deals with the circumstances where an offer to reoccupy made to a tenant is accepted. In this context s.35(6)(a) refers to the "resulting agreement", which suggests that the parties will not be bound by the terms of the previous tenancy.

(ii) Redress for abuse of the procedure for terminating a Part 4 tenancy

8–50 Where a tenant disputes the validity of a notice of termination served in reliance on one of the six grounds set out in the Table to s.34 of the RTA 2004, the tenant may refer a dispute to the PRTB. The RTA 2004 makes specific provision for awards of damages and other orders where a tenant has vacated the dwelling on one of the grounds set out at paras 3–6 of the Table to s.34 and the landlord has failed to carry out what was intended to be done or has failed to offer a new tenancy to the tenant.[100] If the tenant considers that he or she has been unjustly deprived of possession, the tenant may refer a dispute to the PRTB. On the hearing of such a complaint, the adjudicator or tenancy tribunal dealing with the matter may make a determination that:

(a)   the landlord must pay damages to the tenant for depriving the tenant of possession of the dwelling, and/or;
(b)   the tenant be permitted to resume possession of the dwelling.[101]

In *Collins v O'Connor and Anor*,[102] the tenancy tribunal stated that, "the Tenant would have a right of redress, including reinstatement in the dwelling should it be proven after a reasonable period that the Section 34 notice was fraudulently or improperly served."[103] Where an order for possession is made, a tenancy tribunal or adjudicator may also make a declaration that any period of interruption in possession that has occurred is to be disregarded for one or more purposes.[104]

8–51 The decision by an adjudicator or tenancy tribunal to make an order allowing the tenant to resume possession of a dwelling is discretionary and is subject to s.118 of the RTA 2004. Section 118 provides that if a determination permitting the tenant to resume possession of a dwelling would cause hardship

---

[100]   Provided the tenant provides the landlord with his or her contact details and keeps the landlord updated with any changes to these details (RTA 2004, s.35(5)).
[101]   RTA 2004, s.56(3).
[102]   TR02/DR329/2007, February 26, 2007.
[103]   Tenancy tribunal report, p.13.
[104]   RTA 2004, s.115(2)(g). See also para.8–48 above.

or injustice to a person not a party to the dispute but who is now in occupation of that dwelling, the adjudicator or tenancy tribunal dealing with the dispute may refuse an order for possession.

In deciding whether a direction to resume possession would cause hardship or injustice to a person in occupation of the dwelling, the adjudicator or tenancy tribunal must have regard to the following:

(a)   the length of time the "second tenant" has been in possession of the dwelling;

(b)   the involvement the "second tenant" may have had in depriving the original tenant of possession of the dwelling; and

(c)   any knowledge the "second tenant" may have had before he or she took possession of the dwelling of the existence of a dispute concerning the right of the original tenant to possession of the dwelling.[105]

The second tenant must be afforded an opportunity by the adjudicator or tenancy tribunal dealing with the dispute to make submissions as to whether a determination should be made permitting the original tenant to resume possession of the dwelling. If necessary, the proceedings will be adjourned to notify the second tenant of the matter.[106] In circumstances where an adjudicator or tenancy tribunal is satisfied that an order for possession may cause hardship to the second tenant, it may instead make a determination which includes a declaration that the original tenant was wrongfully deprived of possession, in addition to a direction that the landlord is to pay damages to the original tenant by way of compensation.

5. Termination of a Part 4 Tenancy by a Landlord where no Permitted Grounds Exist

8–52 If the landlord cannot satisfy one of the grounds set out in the Table to s.34 of the RTA 2004, there are two circumstances where the landlord can terminate a Part 4 tenancy. These circumstances are where:

(1)   The landlord serves a notice of termination giving the required period of notice[107] and where that notice expires on or after the end of the Part 4 tenancy (that is a date that falls on or after the 4th year from when the tenancy commenced).[108]

---

[105]   RTA 2004, s.118(2).

[106]   RTA 2004, s.118(3).

[107]   The longer notice periods as prescribed by s.66 of the RTA 2004 will apply. See para.8–73.

[108]   RTA 2004, s.34(b).

(2) The landlord serves a notice of termination during the first 6 months of the further Part 4 tenancy (being the period between 4–4½ years of the tenancy's existence).[109]

If a notice of termination is served in either of these circumstances, there is no requirement that one of the grounds in the Table to s.34 exists. However, as the duration of the tenancy will have been for more than six months, the landlord is required to state a reason for the termination of the tenancy in the notice of termination.[110]

6. TERMINATION OF FURTHER PART 4 TENANCIES BY A LANDLORD

A. Identical Procedure to Terminating a Part 4 Tenancy

8–53 A further Part 4 tenancy comes into being after the end of the first four-year cycle of a tenancy. The further Part 4 tenancy will also last for a four-year period and the tenant shall continue to enjoy his or her Part 4 tenancy rights during that time.[111]

The same rules that apply to terminating a Part 4 tenancy,[112] also apply to the termination of a further Part 4 tenancy (and each successive further Part 4 tenancy) that arises in respect of the dwelling.[113] Accordingly, a further Part 4 tenancy can only be terminated if one of the grounds set out in the Table to s.34 exist. If a landlord cannot rely on any of these grounds, the only way a landlord can terminate the further Part 4 tenancy is by serving a notice that expires on or after the end of the further Part 4 tenancy[114] or by serving a notice of termination during the first six months of the further Part 4 tenancy, giving 112 days notice.[115]

B. Termination during first six Months of a Tenancy and during the first six Months of a Further Part 4 Tenancy

8–54 It is not necessary that one of the grounds in the Table to s.34 exists to terminate a tenancy during the first six months after its commencement or

[109] RTA 2004, s.42. Section 42(2) makes clear that in these circumstances the landlord must give the tenant 112 days notice of the termination of the tenancy (see also para.8–53).
[110] RTA 2004, s.62(1)(e).
[111] See paras 7–13 to 7–15 that consider the nature of further and successive further Part 4 tenancies.
[112] As considered at paras 8–28 to 8–51.
[113] RTA 2004, s.47(1).
[114] RTA 2004, ss.34(b) and 47. See also para.8–54.
[115] RTA 2004, ss.42 and 47. See also para.8–54.

during the first six months of a further Part 4 tenancy. The procedure, however, for termination does differ as follows:

(a) 28 days notice must be given to terminate a tenancy during the first six months.[116]

(b) 112 days notice must be given must be given to terminate a further Part 4 tenancy during the first six months.[117]

7. TERMINATION OF A PART 4 TENANCY BY THE TENANT

8–55 A tenant may terminate a Part 4 tenancy by serving the landlord with a notice of termination. A tenant does not have to give a reason for terminating a tenancy in any circumstance[118] but must give the appropriate notice period as prescribed by Pt 5 of the RTA 2004.[119] However, where a tenant is terminating a tenancy because the landlord has failed to comply with his or her tenancy obligations, the tenant must first afford the landlord an opportunity to remedy that failure before serving a notice of termination.[120] If the landlord does not take appropriate action, the tenant may then proceed to serve the notice of termination giving one of the shorter notice periods permitted by s.68(2) of the RTA 2004.

8. DEEMED TERMINATION OF A PART 4 TENANCY

A. Circumstances where a Tenancy will be Deemed to Have Terminated

8–56 There are two situations where the RTA 2004 will deem a tenancy to have terminated, notwithstanding the fact that a notice of termination may not have been served or, if it has been served is invalid.[121] This applies to Part 4 tenancies and to tenancies to which Pt 4 has no application.[122] A tenancy shall be deemed to have terminated in the following circumstances:

---

[116] RTA 2004 s.66.

[117] RTA 2004, s.42.

[118] Section 34 of the RTA 2004 applies to landlords only. Section 62(1)(e) of the RTA 2004 only requires the landlord to serve a notice of termination.

[119] See paras 8–73 to 8–74 and 8–84 to 8–86.

[120] RTA 2004, s.68(3).

[121] RTA 2004, s.37.

[122] RTA 2004, s.194. Part 4 does not apply to a tenancy during the first six months from its commencement and also in the circumstances outlined at paras 7–18 to 7–21.

(1) The tenant vacates the dwelling but serves a notice of termination which fails to give the required period of notice and the tenant is in arrears of rent[123]; or

(2) The tenant vacates the dwelling having failed to serve a notice of termination and is in arrears of rent for a period of 28 days or more.[124]

If a tenant is in arrears of rent and the tenancy is deemed to have terminated in the circumstances described above, the tenant may still be liable for the rent for the period that would have elapsed had a notice of termination been served giving the required period of notice. Further consideration is given to this matter at paras 8–58 and 8–63.

8–57 It is important to note that the provisions of the RTA 2004 which deem a tenancy to have terminated are subject to the provisions relating to multiple tenants in Ch.6 of Pt 4.[125] Accordingly, although a tenant may have vacated a dwelling in one of the circumstances outlined above, this does not result in the tenancy being "deemed" to have terminated for the other tenants. It is also important to note that the provisions of the RTA 2004 on deemed termination have no effect where the tenancy has been assigned or sub-let.[126]

B. Deemed Termination or Unlawful Termination?

8–58 If a tenancy is deemed to have terminated by reason of the circumstances described at (1) or (2) at para.8–56, the tenancy will be at an end and the landlord will be entitled to take possession of the dwelling. It is important, however, that the landlord is satisfied that the tenant has in fact vacated the dwelling before taking possession. If the tenant has not vacated the dwelling and the landlord changes the locks, the landlord may be liable to pay damages to the tenant for illegal eviction. This is more likely to arise in cases where no notice of termination has been served by the tenant. If the tenant had served a notice of termination, albeit an inadequate one, it will be clear at least that the tenant intended to vacate the dwelling at some stage.

8–59 In *Gallagher and Anor v Oladunjoye*[127] the landlord served a notice of termination. At a later date she called to the property to collect the keys and take possession. As no one was present and over one month had passed since the service of the notice of termination, she entered the dwelling. The tenant alleged that on his return to the flat he found that all his belongings were placed in plastic bags and left outside under a stairs. He also maintained that the locks

---

[123] RTA 2004, s.37(1).
[124] RTA 2004, s.37(2).
[125] RTA 2004, s.37(5).
[126] RTA 2004, s.37(3).
[127] TR40/DR1173/2008, October 9, 2008.

were changed and he was therefore locked out of the premises. The tenancy tribunal was satisfied that an illegal eviction had taken place and made a determination requiring the landlord to pay the tenant compensation for the loss of the property and for distress and inconvenience resulting from the illegal eviction.

8–60 In *Coote and Anor v Arisekola*[128] the landlords attempted to rely on the provisions of the RTA 2004 which deem a tenancy to have terminated in certain circumstances. The landlords argued that the tenant had not been in the dwelling since March 2006. They maintained that a number of people called to the dwelling looking for him and that they themselves had sent a number of text messages to the tenant but got no response. Around the end of April 2006, the landlords entered the dwelling. There were a number of personal items belonging to the tenant still in the dwelling but the landlords concluded that the tenant had given up vacant possession. The tenant maintained that he had not abandoned the dwelling and had merely gone abroad which he did on a regular basis. The tenancy tribunal accepted that the landlords believed that the tenant had abandoned the dwelling but considered that it had not been given any compelling evidence to show what steps, if any, were taken by the landlords to establish that the tenant had left on a permanent basis. The tenancy tribunal awarded the tenant the sum of €2,000 in compensation for the unlawful termination of his tenancy.

C. Tenant's Personal Belongings left in the Dwelling

8–61 The RTA 2004 does not deal with the situation where a tenant may have vacated a dwelling but has left some of his or her belongings behind. The question arises as to whether the landlord is permitted to remove these belongings or whether he or she is required to keep the belongings for the tenant (at least for a certain period) until the tenant collects them. The matter becomes more difficult where larger items such as furniture are left behind in the dwelling by the tenant.

8–62 In *Coote and Anor v Arisekola*[129] one of the landlords gave evidence that she had cleaned out the apartment, recycled some of the contents and removed others to her own house. She brought what she thought might be valuable items to the Garda Station. These items included a computer hard drive, three passports and personal documents. In the report of the tenancy tribunal it is recorded that other than the items admitted by the landlords, there was no agreement reached between the parties as to what goods and belongings were present in the apartment at the time the landlords took possession. The tenancy tribunal concluded that in not keeping a proper record of items kept and/or

---

[128]   TR128/DR709/2007, March 27, 2008.
[129]   TR128/DR709/2007, March 27, 2008.

disposed of, the landlords failed to take adequate care of the tenant's belongings. The tenancy tribunal awarded the tenant €1,000 compensation for the inconvenience and loss of personal possessions.

In *Gallagher and Anor v Oladunjoye*[130] the landlord took possession of the dwelling and initially placed the tenant's belongings under a stairs outside the dwelling. She then removed the belongings to a charity organisation for safe keeping. The tenant alleged that on checking the plastic bags containing his personal belongings, items were missing. Although the tenancy tribunal accepted that the tenant had been deprived of possession of some of his belongings, as the tenant did not produce into evidence any receipts or invoices relating to the missing property, the tenancy tribunal awarded the tenant a sum of only €500 in compensation.

8–63 As outlined above, the RTA 2004 provides no guidance to landlords as to how they should deal with a tenant's personal belongings that are left in a dwelling. It appears that the safest course for landlords would be to attempt to make contact with the tenant to arrange for the return of his or her property and to retain these items for a reasonable period to allow the tenant to collect them. The landlord should also keep a list of the items removed by him or her from the dwelling. Nevertheless, as the RTA 2004 does not impose any specific obligations on landlords in this regard, the reasonableness of the landlord's actions will be assessed on a case by case basis. Section 19 of the Housing (Miscellaneous) Provisions Act 1992 makes clear, however, that no distress shall be levied for the rent of any premises let solely as a dwelling. Accordingly, where a tenant is in arrears of rent the landlord cannot sell the tenants belongings and offset the proceeds of the sale against the rent due.

9. NOTICES OF TERMINATION

A. Requirement for a Notice of Termination

8–64 If a landlord *or* a tenant wishes to terminate a tenancy, he or she must serve a notice of termination.[131] In no circumstance can a party notify the other orally that he or she is or intends to terminate the tenancy.[132] A notice of termination must comply with s.62 of the RTA 2004 in all cases. If any of the requirements of s.62 are not complied with, the notice of termination will be deemed invalid, with the result that when served, it will not effect the

---

[130] TR40/DR1173/2008, October 9, 2008.

[131] See Appendices 6–13 for example notices of termination.

[132] RTA 2004, s.62(1)(a); See *McKenna and Anor v Nabeal Anor* (TR52/DR651/2008, November 14, 2008) where the landlord attempted to terminate the tenancy by giving oral notification to the tenant. The tenancy tribunal determined that as no written notice of termination was served on the tenant, the tenancy had not been validly terminated.

termination of the tenancy. There is no obligation on a landlord or tenant to have regard to or to vacate a dwelling on the basis of a notice of termination, unless it complies with the provisions of s.62. The reason for the termination of the tenancy is irrelevant. In *Kelly v Kearns*[133] the tenancy tribunal was satisfied that the tenant was engaging in antisocial behaviour. The tenant had assaulted a co-tenant for which he was subsequently charged and convicted of an offence. As the other tenants of the dwelling complained to the landlord that they were suffering from anxiety as a result of the tenant's behaviour, the landlord served a seven day notice of termination on the basis of antisocial behaviour. However, as the notice of termination did not comply with s.62 of the RTA 2004, the tenancy tribunal determined that the tenancy had not been validly terminated.

B. Contents of a Notice of Termination

8–65 Section 62(1) of the RTA 2004 lists the requirements for a notice of termination. For a notice of termination to be valid, it must:

- (a) be in writing;
- (b) be signed by the landlord or his or her authorised agent or, as appropriate, the tenant;
- (c) specify the date of service of it[134];
- (d) be in such form (if any) as may be prescribed[135];
- (e) state the reason for termination if the duration of the tenancy is for a period of more than 6 months and the termination is by the landlord;
- (f) specify the termination date. If the notice of termination is served by the tenant, the termination date is the day, month and year on which the tenancy will terminate. If the notice of termination is served by the landlord, the termination date is the day, month and year:
  - On which the tenancy will terminate, <u>and</u>
  - On or before which the tenant must vacate the dwelling.

  Section 63 makes clear that the day that is to be specified as the termination date is the last day of the notice period.[136] The notice period commences on the day following service of the notice of termination.[137]

---

[133] TR119/DR822/2007, February 27, 2008.

[134] See also para.8–69 below.

[135] There is currently no prescribed form but a sample notice of termination is available on the PRTB's website at *www.prtb.ie*. Sample notices of termination are also contained at Appendices 6–13.

[136] RTA 2004, s.63. The duration of the notice period is the number of days' notice that the landlord or tenant is required by Pt 5 to give or such longer period as agreed between the parties. If the duration of the tenancy is less than six months, a period of notice of more than 70 days may not be given. However, if a tenancy or lease agreement requires a greater period of notice to be given than that required by Pt 5, that greater period shall be given. See paras 8–72 to 8–86 below.

[137] RTA 2004, s.61(1).

(g) state (if the notice of termination is served by the landlord) that the tenant has the whole of the 24 hours of the termination date to vacate the dwelling;

(h) state that any issue as to the validity of the notice of termination or the right of the landlord or tenant, as appropriate, to serve it, must be referred to the PRTB under Pt 6 within 28 days from the date of receipt of it.

8–66 As highlighted above, the notice of termination must state the date of service of it. The notice of termination will not be valid if any relevant steps in the service of the notice have not been taken on the day specified as the date of service.[138] For example, if the notice of termination stated that service took place on a certain date but the notice was not served for a number of days after that date specified as the service date, the notice of termination will be invalid.

8–67 It is an offence to purport to serve an invalid notice of termination and then rely on it in a way that adversely affects the interests of the person on whom it was served. However, it is a defence to any prosecution for such an offence, if it is shown that the defendant neither knew nor could reasonably have been expected to know that the notice of termination was invalid.[139]

C. Multiple Tenants

8–68 Where there are multiple tenants and they wish to terminate their tenancy, it suffices for one tenant to sign the notice of termination on behalf of the others. However, the notice must state that one tenant signs on his or her behalf and on behalf of the other tenant or tenants. Each of the tenants must also be named in the notice.[140]

D. Service

8–69 A notice of termination must be addressed to the person concerned by name and may be served by one of the methods set out in s.6 of the RTA 2004.[141] The methods of service are as follows:

- By delivering it to the person;
- By leaving it at the address at which the person ordinarily resides or in the case in which an address for service has been furnished, at that address;

---

[138]   RTA 2004, s.64(1). Section 64(2) provides that for a step to be deemed "untaken" it must first be in the power or control of the landlord and tenant to take it.

[139]   RTA 2004, s.74. Also, see s.9 of the RTA 2004 sets out the relevant provisions relating to offences under the RTA 2004.

[140]   RTA 2004 s.73.

[141]   See also paras 9–132 to 9–133 which considers s.6 in the context of the dispute resolution provisions of Pt 6 of the RTA 2004.

- By sending it by post in a prepaid letter to the address at which the person ordinarily resides or, in a case in which an address for service has been furnished, to that address.[142]

For the purposes of service, a company shall be deemed to be ordinarily resident at its registered office and every other body corporate and every unincorporated body shall be deemed to be ordinarily resident at its principal office or place of business.[143]

E. Approach of the PRTB

8–70 A large number of disputes referred to the PRTB concern the validity of notices of termination served by either the landlord or the tenant. In considering whether or not a notice is valid, the PRTB has interpreted s.62(1) of the RTA 2004 strictly. This is apparent from its determination orders and tenancy tribunal decisions. The consequences for a landlord if an invalid notice of termination is served within the first six months of the tenancy, is that the tenant (having occupied the tenancy for six months), will acquire a Part 4 tenancy with all its associated rights. In particular, the tenant will be entitled to remain in the property for a further three and a half years.[144] If a tenant serves an invalid notice of termination, the tenant may forfeit all or part of the deposit he or she has paid. For example, if the tenant vacates a property without giving notice as required by Pt 5 of the RTA 2004, an amount may be deducted from his or her deposit to the extent necessary to cover the period of notice the tenant should have given. If the tenant does not vacate the property at the end of any notice period given, he or she will be required to serve another notice of termination to validly terminate the tenancy. The tenant will then have to stay on in the dwelling and continue to pay rent so as the required notice can be given to the landlord. If, however, the tenant cannot continue in occupation, in lieu of paying the landlord rent for the full notice period, the tenant may forfeit part or all of the deposit that he or she has paid.

8–71 In *MacCarthy v Sweeney and Anor*[145] the landlord claimed to have terminated the respondent's tenancy by notice of termination and brought a claim for possession and arrears of rent. The PRTB determined that the notice of termination was invalid for a number of reasons. It failed to contain a statement of the date on which the tenancy would terminate or to state the date on or before which the tenant was to vacate possession of the dwelling. It also

---

[142] RTA 2004, s.6(1)(a)–(c).

[143] RTA 2004, s.6(3).

[144] Unless of course the tenancy is validly terminated during that period. There are however limited grounds on which a Part 4 tenancy may be terminated by the landlord. See paras 8–28 to 8–46.

[145] DR14/2005, determination order dated July 8, 2005.

failed to state that the tenant had the whole of the 24 hours of the termination date to give up vacant possession. In *McKay v Hughes*,[146] *Kershaw v English*[147] and *O'Sullivan v Burdon*,[148] the PRTB found that the termination notices served were invalid as they either did not specify the date of service or a termination date as required by s.62(1)(c) and s.62(1)(f) respectively.[149]

In *Barrington-Martin and Anor v O'Neill and Anor*[150] the landlords served a notice of termination but the notice failed to comply with s.62(1)(f) of the RTA 2004, as it did not state the day, month and year on which the tenancy was to terminate. Neither did it state that the tenants had the whole of the 24 hours of the termination date to vacate possession of the dwelling. The tenancy tribunal also found that as the tenancy was a Part 4 tenancy, its purported termination was invalid because the landlords had failed to notify the tenants of their breach of their tenancy obligations. There was no evidence put before the tenancy tribunal that the formalities of s.34 of the RTA 2004 had been complied with.[151]

In *Byrne and Anor v Reddington and Anor*[152] the first-named applicant (a tenant) argued that a notice of termination served by the landlords was invalid. He challenged the validity of the seven days' notice given by the landlords and the termination of the tenancy on the grounds of antisocial behaviour. He said he had been given no warning prior to service of the notice of termination. The tenancy tribunal determined that there had been no conduct on the part of the tenants which amounted to antisocial behaviour and on that basis the notice of termination was invalid. The tenancy tribunal came to a similar conclusion in respect of alleged antisocial behaviour in *Long v Donnellan*.[153]

10. RELEVANT NOTICE PERIODS

A. Overview

8–72 Ironically there is no requirement to actually state the period of notice which is being given in a notice of termination.[154] Compliance with s.62 of the RTA 2004 is satisfied if the termination date is identified.[155]

---

[146] DR86/2005, determination order dated August 19, 2005.
[147] DR199 and 200/2005, determination order dated August 19, 2005.
[148] DR09/2005, determination order dated June 24, 2005.
[149] See also *Ryan v Gleeson & Anor* (DR37/2005, determination order dated August 29, 2005).
[150] TR66/DR695/2007, July 9, 2007.
[151] A landlord may terminate a Part 4 tenancy where the tenant has failed to comply with his or her tenancy obligations. However, the landlord is first required to notify the tenant of the breach of obligation and give the tenant an opportunity to remedy that breach (RTA 2004, Table to s.34, para.1). See paras 8–29 to 8–34.
[152] TR02/2006, February 1, 2006.
[153] TR06/DR244&753/2006, February 28, 2006.
[154] RTA 2004, s.65(2).
[155] RTA 2004, s.62(1)(f). See also para.8–65 for an explanation of the termination date.

The RTA 2004 requires both landlords and tenants to give specific periods of notice to terminate a tenancy. The length of notice that a party is required to give will depend on the length of the tenancy and the reason for terminating the tenancy. Shorter notice periods apply where the landlord or tenant is in breach of their tenancy obligations. Longer notice periods apply where there is no breach. A landlord and tenant may agree to a longer period of notice being given than that required by the RTA 2004, except in the case of a tenancy the duration of which is less than six months. If a notice of termination is served during the first six months of the tenancy a period of more than 70 days' notice cannot be given.[156]

There is one further situation where the longer notice periods will apply also. If a landlord or tenant is attempting to rely on the shorter notice periods but the procedural requirements of ss.67 and 68 are not strictly complied with, the longer notice periods as prescribed by s.66 will apply instead.[157]

B. Standard Notice Periods (No Breach of Tenancy Obligation)

(i) Statutory minimum

8–73 Section 66 of the RTA 2004 specifies the standard periods of notice that must be given when terminating a tenancy. These notice periods apply except in circumstances where the tenancy is being terminated because the landlord or tenant has failed to comply with their obligations under the tenancy.

The notice periods required by s.66 are set out in the table below. These notice periods vary depending on the period the tenancy has been in existence and also on whether it is the landlord or tenant seeking to terminate the tenancy.

Duration of Tenancy	Notice by Landlord	Notice by Tenant
Less than 6 months	28 days	28 days
6 months or more months but less than 1 year	35 days	35 days
1 year or more but less than 2 years	42 days	42 days
2 years or more but less than 3 years	56 days	56 days
3 years or more but less than 4 years	84 days	56 days
4 years or more	112 days	56 days

---

[156] RTA 2004, s.65(3) and (4).
[157] RTA 2004 s.66(1)(b).

(ii) Lesser notice periods

8–74 The landlord and tenant may agree to a shorter period of notice but only at the stage where one party gives notice to the other party of his or her intention to terminate. The landlord and tenant are not permitted to agree to a shorter notice period being given at the commencement of the tenancy or at any other time until one of them intends to terminate the tenancy.[158]

In *Rushe v Kelly and Others*[159] the tenancy tribunal stated that:

> "Section 69 of the Act does allow for shorter notice to apply where there is agreement by both parties. However, no evidence was available to the Tribunal that such an agreement had been reached ... The Landlord was at a loss for 2 months rent as a result of the Tenants' decision to leave the Dwelling before the expiry of the full 12 months."[160]

The tenancy tribunal determined that the landlord was entitled to retain the balance of the tenants' deposit.

C. Notice Periods where Tenant in Breach of Tenancy Obligations

8–75 The notice periods prescribed by s.67 of the RTA 2004 apply where the tenancy is being terminated by the landlord as a result of the tenant's failure to comply with any of his or her tenancy obligations.

(i) Antisocial behaviour

8–76 A landlord is only required to give a tenant seven days' notice if the tenancy is being terminated as a result of the tenant's antisocial behaviour as defined at s.17(1) (a) or (b),[161] namely:

a) Behaviour that constitutes an offence[162];
b) Behaviour that causes (or could cause) fear, danger, injury, damage or loss to any person living, working or otherwise lawfully in the dwelling concerned or its vicinity.[163]

---

[158] RTA 2004, s.69.

[159] TR149/DR982/2007, September 15, 2008.

[160] Tenancy tribunal report, p.3.

[161] RTA 2004, s.67(2)(a). Note that s.17(1)(c) of the RTA 2004 also includes in the definition of antisocial behaviour: persistent behaviour that prevents or interferes with the peaceful occupation of another person residing in the rented dwelling or in its vicinity. Different rules, including longer notice periods apply to the termination of a tenancy in these circumstances. See para.8–83.

[162] Being an offence which if committed, would be reasonably likely to directly affect the well-being or welfare of others (RTA 2004, s.17(1)(a)).

[163] This behaviour is defined as including violence, intimidation, coercion, harassment or obstruction of, or threats to the person. (RTA 2004, s.17(1)(b)).

If a landlord seeks to terminate a tenancy giving seven days' notice, it is important that the landlord is satisfied that the tenant is engaging in activity which falls within category (a) and (b) above. If only seven days' notice is given to a tenant to vacate a dwelling and the tenant's behaviour does not meet that threshold of antisocial behaviour, the termination of that tenancy will be invalid.

8–77 Strict interpretation of "antisocial" behaviour Antisocial behaviour has been interpreted narrowly by tenancy tribunals in determining disputes. In this regard, landlords should attempt to satisfy themselves in so far as possible that the behaviour complained of is antisocial within the meaning of s.17(1)(a) and (b) of the RTA 2004, before serving a notice of termination giving seven days' notice. In *Brooks and Anor v Finnerty*,[164] the tenancy tribunal stated that:

> "an allegation of anti-social behaviour has serious implications for the character, person and good name of a citizen as well as their accommodation. Where anti-social behaviour is alleged, a heavy burden of proof rests on those parties bringing such an allegation."[165]

This was re-iterated in *Sweeney v O'Reilly*[166] where the tenancy tribunal made the following comments:

> "The Tribunal is fully aware that losing one's home at notice as short as 7 days is a particularly serious life event and would require a heavy burden of proof to be justified."[167]

8–78 In *Sweeney v O'Reilly*[168] the tenant made an application to the PRTB challenging the validity of a notice of termination served on him, which gave the tenant seven days to vacate the property. The notice stated that it was being served as a result of complaints that the tenant's behaviour was threatening and disruptive. These complaints were made by other residents of the property in which the tenant's dwelling was situate. The behaviour they complained of included keeping the residents awake at night and making threats to harm other residents personally and to burn the property down.

---

[164] TR23/DR64/2007, March 9, 2007.
[165] Tenancy tribunal report, p.4
[166] TR37/2007, DR995&1148/2006, April 18, 2007.
[167] Tenancy tribunal report, p.5. Also note the comments of the tenancy tribunal in *Horgan v Walsh and Anor* (TR84/DR719/2007, April 17, 2008) where it stated that "It should be noted that an allegation of anti-social behaviour has serious implications for the character, person and good name of a citizen as well as their accommodation, and where it is alleged, a heavy burden of proof rests on the person making the allegation" (tenancy tribunal report, p.9). See also para.9–23 where this decision is considered in the context of s.77 of the RTA 2004.
[168] TR37/2007, DR995&1148/2006, April 18, 2007.

The tenancy tribunal determined from the evidence before it that the tenant had behaved in a way that was antisocial within the meaning of s.17(1)(b) of the RTA 2004. The tenant had threatened the landlord, his son and other tenants in the property in a manner that caused sufficient fear to justify the service of a notice of termination giving seven days' notice. In these circumstances, the tenancy tribunal determined that the notice of termination served by the landlord on the tenant was valid.

8–79 Landlord must produce sufficient evidence The landlord must have sufficient evidence that the tenant is engaging in antisocial behaviour. In *Jordan and Anor v Trofimovs and Anor*,[169] the landlord had served a seven-day notice of termination on the tenants for antisocial behaviour. The tenancy tribunal was not satisfied that the landlord had produced sufficient evidence to prove that the tenant's behaviour was of a persistent nature which interfered with other people's peaceful occupation of the property. The tenancy tribunal stated in its findings that:

> "One letter from a management company, unsupported by witnesses cannot be accepted as proof of such a serious charge as anti-social behaviour. Nor can the landlords evidence of hearing loud music played twice during the day time discharge the burden of proof in such circumstances".[170]

8–80 In the tenancy tribunal decision of *Leader v Metcalfe*[171] the tenancy tribunal was satisfied that the tenant was engaging in antisocial behaviour. The tenancy tribunal accepted the landlord's evidence that he was in fear and felt intimidated by the tenant's behaviour. It was satisfied that the tenant had acted in a way which "causes or could cause fear, danger, injury, damage or loss to any person".[172]

8–81 A single incident may constitute antisocial behaviour A single incident can constitute antisocial behaviour. If the conduct is sufficiently serious it will be deemed antisocial. This is likely to arise where the behaviour relates to the commission of an offence. In the tenancy tribunal decision of *Kelly v Kearns*[173]

---

[169] TR89/DR153/2008, February 27, 2009.
[170] Tenancy tribunal report, p.4.
[171] TR19/DR1158/2008, July 29, 2008.
[172] Tenancy tribunal report, p.6. The RTA 2004 does not state whether this test is subjective or objective but it would seem from this decision that the test under s.17(1)(b) is a subjective one. It is noteworthy that the tenancy tribunal in coming to its conclusion did have regard to the fact that the landlord had to have a second person attend the house with him when he collected the rent, which supported the fact that he was in fear and felt intimidated.
[173] TR119/DR822/2007, February 27, 2008.

the tenancy tribunal was satisfied that the tenant had engaged in antisocial behaviour arising from one incident of assault on another tenant.

(ii) Failure to pay rent

8–82 Where a tenant has failed to pay rent due under the tenancy, the tenant must be notified in writing by the landlord that an amount of rent due has not been paid. If 14 days elapse from receipt of that notice and the rent remains unpaid, the landlord may then serve a notice of termination giving 28 days' notice.[174] A sample 14-day notice is contained in Appendix 5.

If the tenancy is a Part 4 tenancy the landlord must first take the additional step of serving a notice giving the tenant an opportunity to remedy the failure before serving the 14-day warning letter. If the tenant fails to remedy the failure, the landlord may then serve the 14-day warning letter. See para.8–34 above which deals with terminating a Part 4 tenancy where the tenant is in arrears of rent.

(iii) Other breach of tenant's tenancy obligation

8–83 Where a tenant's breach of his or her tenancy obligations does not amount to antisocial behaviour[175] or relate to arrears of rent, the tenancy may be terminated giving 28 days notice. An example of where a tenancy may be terminated in these circumstances could arise for instance where the tenant has caused a deterioration in the condition of the dwelling beyond that of ordinary wear and tear.[176] Another example that may arise, is where the tenant has refused to allow the landlord reasonable access to the dwelling for the purposes of carrying out repairs for which the landlord is responsible.[177]

If the tenancy is a Part 4 tenancy, the landlord must first notify the tenant in writing of his or her breach of obligation before serving a notice of termination. The landlord must also give the tenant a reasonable opportunity to remedy that breach.[178] If the tenant fails to do so, only then may the landlord serve a notice of termination giving 28 days notice.[179]

D. Notice Periods where Landlord in Breach of Tenancy Obligations

8–84 The notice periods set out in s.68 of the RTA 2004 apply where the tenant is terminating the tenancy because the landlord has breached his or her tenancy obligations.

---

[174]   RTA 2004, s.67(2) and (3).
[175]   Within the meaning of s.17(1)(a) and (b) of the RTA 2004.
[176]   This constitutes a breach of a tenant's obligation imposed by s.16(f) of the RTA 2004.
[177]   This constitutes a breach of a tenant's obligation imposed by s.16(e) of the RTA 2004.
[178]   RTA 2004, Table to s.34, para.1. See paras 8–29 to 8–33.
[179]   RTA 2004, s.67(2) and (3).

(i) Breach of obligation

8–85 If a landlord has breached his or her tenancy obligations, the tenant must terminate the tenancy giving at least 28 days' notice. Before a tenant can serve a notice of termination giving 28 days' notice, the tenant must first:

(a) notify the landlord in writing of his or her failure to comply with his or her tenancy obligations;

(b) afford the landlord a reasonable time[180] to remedy that failure.[181]

Only if the landlord fails to remedy his or her breach of obligation, within a reasonable period of time after receiving the tenant's notification, can the tenant then proceed to terminate the tenancy giving 28 days' notice. The RTA 2004 defines the circumstances where a landlord will be considered to have remedied his or her failure to comply with the obligations of the tenancy. These circumstances are as follows:

(a) if the landlord desists from the conduct that amounts to a breach of the tenancy obligation concerned or in the case of an omission, the landlord complies with the tenancy obligation, and

(b) in the case of a failure which results in financial loss or damage to the tenant or his or her property –

    (i) to pay adequate compensation to the tenant or repair the damage fully, and

    (ii) unless the failure is not of a continuing nature, to desist from the conduct that amounts to the breach of tenancy obligation or (as appropriate) comply with the obligation concerned.[182]

(ii) Imminent danger

8–86 The tenant must give seven days' notice if he or she is terminating the tenancy by reason of the fact that the behaviour of the landlord:

"poses an imminent danger of death or serious injury or imminent danger to the fabric of the dwelling or the property containing the dwelling".[183]

In these circumstances there is no obligation on the tenant to give the landlord an opportunity to remedy his or her behaviour.

---

[180] See *Canty v Private Residential Tenancies Board* [2007] IEHC 243; unreported, High Court, August 8, 2007, at p.24 which gives consideration to what may be deemed a reasonable period to remedy a breach of obligation. See also paras 8–32 to 8–33.

[181] RTA 2004, s.68(3).

[182] RTA 2004, s.68(4).

[183] RTA 2004, s.68(2)(a).

11. Unlawful Termination

A. Act of the Landlord

(i) Examples of unlawful termination

8–87 If a landlord serves a notice of termination which is invalid or fails to serve a notice of termination at all and changes the locks of a dwelling to prevent the tenant access to the dwelling, both of those acts will be deemed an illegal eviction and the tenant will be compensated accordingly. The PRTB can make an order under s.115 of the RTA 2004 directing that "a specified amount of damages or costs or both be paid" to the tenant and can also make an order directing that a tenant has a "right to return to, or continue in, occupation of a dwelling".[184]

8–88 In the matter of *Harpur and Anor v Kelly*[185] the landlord served a five-day notice requesting the tenant to vacate the dwelling. As the tenant did not vacate within the five-day period, the landlord changed the locks of the dwelling. The tenancy tribunal made a finding that the landlord had placed the tenants under considerable pressure to vacate the property, effectively leaving the family homeless. The manner in which the tenancy was terminated resulted in considerable inconvenience and distress for the young family with no alternative accommodation in place. The tenants were awarded €5,000 in damages for the unlawful termination of the tenancy.

8–89 In *Komoni v Dunne and Anor*[186] the landlords changed the locks and left all of the tenant's belongings in plastic bags outside of the dwelling, some of which were subsequently stolen. The tenant was required to stay in hostel accommodation with her two young children until she found alternative accommodation. She also had acquired a Part 4 tenancy which she had been deprived of by the landlord's actions. In making its award, the tenancy tribunal stated that it was "appalled at the actions of the respondent landlord against such a vulnerable person".[187]

8–90 Even if the landlord has served a valid notice of termination and the tenant fails to vacate on the expiry of such a notice, the landlord does not have a right

---

[184] See para.9–93 that considers s.115 in further detail.

[185] TR03/DR69/2007, February 16, 2007.

[186] TR64/DR322/2007, June 6, 2007.

[187] Tenancy tribunal report, p.6. In *Komoni v Dunne and Anor* the tenant was awarded €10,000 in compensation. See also *Callely v Cooney* (TR110/DR1226/2007, November 16, 2007) where the tenant was locked out of her house with two young children. The tenant was awarded €8,500 for the loss of her Part 4 tenancy and the distress and inconvenience suffered by her and her children. As the tenant owed a substantial amount of rent, these arrears were off-set against the award made for the illegal eviction.

to change the locks of the dwelling so as to deny the tenant access to the dwelling. In *O'Gorman v Slattery and Anor*[188] the landlord wished to terminate the tenancy as he wanted to sell the property. The landlord had served a notice of termination which was valid but as the tenant failed to vacate the dwelling on the expiry of the notice period, the landlords changed the locks and effected a re-entry of the dwelling contrary to s.58 of the RTA 2004. The tenancy tribunal noted that "they had not done so in ignorance of the Act".[189] The tenant had suffered loss not just of accommodation but of an educational opportunity.[190] The tenant was awarded compensation in the amount of €9,000 in respect of the unlawful termination and retention of goods.[191]

(ii) Liability to an order for damages

8–91 The level of damages which can be awarded against a landlord for illegal eviction will vary depending on the individual circumstances of each case.[192] In determining the appropriate level of damages, tenancy tribunals have had regard to a number of factors such as, whether the tenant had acquired a Part 4 tenancy when the illegal eviction took place, what the landlord did with the tenant's belongings, whether the tenant had a family and also whether the tenant had to look for temporary emergency accommodation.

In *Partridge v Watson*[193] the sum of €12,000 was awarded against the landlord for illegally evicting the tenant. In that particular case, the tenant returned home to find that the locks of the dwelling had been changed. The landlord had left the tenant's belongings and furniture in the back garden of the dwelling which were substantially damaged due to the bad weather. The tenancy tribunal found that the "trauma and shock of the manner in which [the tenant] was removed from the dwelling caused her and her family great distress".[194]

8–92 In *Devenney and Anor v Nolan*[195] the landlord had attended the dwelling but refused to take the rent from the tenant and told the tenant and his family to

---

[188] TR36/DR236/2007, March 28, 2007.
[189] Tenancy tribunal report, p.8.
[190] The tenant gave evidence that as a result of events he had missed his final examinations at the end of a two-year course.
[191] See *Sokolov v McGuinness* (TR50/2007/DR558/2006, August 20, 2007) where the tenant was awarded €3,500 for illegal eviction, notwithstanding the service of a valid notice of termination. The tenancy tribunal concluded that it is not lawful to change the locks unless the tenant has vacated the dwelling.
[192] See *Gallagher and Anor v Oladunjoye* (TR40/DR1173/2008, October 9, 2008), where €2,000 was awarded for illegal eviction; *Wall v Cullen and Anor* (TR17/DR487/DR655/2008, October 29), where €2,850 was awarded for illegal eviction; *Griseto v O'Driascoll and Anor* (TR154/DR231/2007, September 18, 2008), where €3,000 was awarded for an illegal eviction. The sum of €3,000 was awarded in the case of *O'Sullivan v Hogan* (TR26/DR396/2007 May 4, 2007).
[193] TR109/2007, January 7, 2008.
[194] Tenancy tribunal report, p.11.
[195] TR63/2007/DR1107/2006, June 6, 2007.

vacate the dwelling. The landlord turned off the water and the electricity and along with two friends began to remove the tenant's goods.[196] The sum of €15,000 was awarded to the tenant and his family as a result of the illegal eviction.

8–93 If an unlawful termination gives rise to a number of tenants being deprived of possession of the property, the tenancy tribunal may make individual awards in favour of each tenant. This is what occurred in the decision of *Leonard v McHugh and Anor*[197] where the landlord changed the locks contrary to s.58 of the RTA 2004. The tenancy tribunal awarded €5,000 to each tenant for the illegal eviction.

(iii) Orders for repossession

8–94 The tenancy tribunal has not only awarded compensation to tenants for the unlawful termination of a tenancy but has made Orders allowing the tenant to retake possession of the dwelling. In *Sneyd v Coote*,[198] the landlord changed the locks because the tenant was not paying rent in accordance with the lease agreement and the tenant was forced to move into temporary accommodation. The tenancy tribunal determined that the behaviour of the tenant in relation to the payment of rent would not alter the fact that the termination of a tenancy in the manner used was clearly in breach of the provisions of the RTA 2004. The tenancy tribunal made a finding that the tenant was entitled to continue in occupation of the dwelling until the tenancy was lawfully terminated in accordance with the RTA 2004. The tenant was also awarded the sum of €5,000 in compensation.

B. Cases which do not Amount to an Unlawful Termination

8–95 To claim damages for illegal eviction, a tenant cannot have left a dwelling voluntarily. In the tenancy tribunal decision of *Walsh v O'Sullivan*[199] it was found that there was no evidence that an illegal eviction had taken place as the tenant had left voluntarily and could therefore not claim to have been evicted. Similarly in *O'Connor and Others v Naughton*[200] the tenancy tribunal determined that the tenants had not claimed a Part 4 tenancy and neither had they indicated to the landlord that they intended staying on in the dwelling after the expiry of the fixed term tenancy.[201] The tenants therefore could not claim they had been illegally evicted.

---

[196] For the purposes of demonstrating the impact of the legal eviction on the tenants, evidence was also given of how the children had attended local schools near the rented dwelling.
[197] TR44/DR476/2007, June 29, 2007.
[198] TR56/2007/DR286/2006, May 16, 2007.
[199] TR41/DR451/2008, November 11, 2008.
[200] TR97/DR684/2007, August 21, 2007.
[201] As required by s.195 of the RTA 2004.

In *Haaer v Rowlands*[202] the tenant had begun to move out her personal belongings from the rented dwelling having been served with a valid notice of termination to vacate. However, in the course of removing her belongings she was refused access to the dwelling. The tenancy tribunal determined that it was not an illegal eviction as the tenant was leaving in any event. Nevertheless, the tenancy tribunal upheld an adjudicator's award to the tenant of the sum of €850 in damages for the upset and embarrassment she sustained by being locked out of the property.

C. Constructive Termination

8–96 An unlawful termination of a tenancy will not only have occurred in circumstances where a landlord has physically removed a tenant or prevented him or her from gaining entry to a dwelling. A tenancy may also be unlawfully terminated where the tenant leaves a dwelling because he or she feels forced to do so because of the behaviour of the landlord. Turning off the electricity or water supply can amount to unlawful termination as can verbally abusing or harassing a tenant.

In *Wall v Cullen and Anor*[203] the tenant entered into a 12-month fixed term lease agreement. The landlord cut off the electricity supply to the dwelling to force the tenants to vacate. The tenancy tribunal determined that the landlord attempted to invalidly terminate the tenancy by having the electricity supply cut off "causing distress and inconvenience to the tenants."[204] The tenancy tribunal awarded the tenants €2,850 as compensation for the distress and inconvenience caused by the landlord. In a similar decision in *Bruce v Ross and Anor*,[205] the landlord cut the electricity off and served an invalid notice of termination. The tenant said he was ignorant in relation to his rights and felt he had to move out on foot of the notice. The tenancy tribunal accepted that the tenant was not aware of his rights, particularly when the notice of termination failed to state that the tenant had a right to refer the validity of the notice to the PRTB within 28 days of receipt. The tenancy tribunal also accepted that in "acting on foot of th[e] invalid notice the Tenants [sic] suffered costs in excess of normal outgoings in securing alternative accommodation."[206] The tenancy tribunal awarded the tenant €650 by way of compensation for distress.

8–97 In *Brereton v Smyth*[207] the tenancy tribunal found that the agent of the landlord had behaved in an abusive and threatening manner towards the tenant putting her in fear that she would be evicted from the premises and that her belongings would be thrown out. The tenant was nine months pregnant at the

---

[202] TR86/DR582/2007, May 7, 2008.
[203] TR17/DR487/DR655/2008, October 29, 2008.
[204] Tenancy tribunal report, p.5.
[205] TR125/DR1012/2007, February 29, 2008.
[206] Tenancy tribunal report, p.4.
[207] TR130/DR1007/07, March 28, 2007.

time and in accordance with the evidence presented to the tenancy tribunal, "was terrified and could no longer stay in the property although she was entitled to do so".[208] The tenancy tribunal concluded as follows:

> "The Tribunal concludes that the [agent's] actions ... resulted in an unlawful termination of the tenancy by compelling the Tenant to vacate the premises through intimidation and harassment in contravention of Section 58 of the Act in so far as the said unlawful termination was constructively affected. The tenant's right of peaceful occupation of the property was also contravened contrary to Section 12(1) of the Act."[209]

The tenant was awarded €3,000 in compensation for the inconvenience and distress caused to her.

D. Mitigating Circumstances and Unlawful Termination

8–98 Where a tenancy has been unlawfully terminated, the landlord's liability may be reduced if there are mitigating circumstances. In *Hemat v Donnolly*,[210] the tenancy tribunal accepted that the landlord had illegally evicted the tenant as an invalid notice of termination was served on the tenant and the locks of the dwelling were changed. However, the behaviour of the tenant was taken into account in assessing the amount of damages. The tenancy tribunal found that in:

> "determining the amount of damages awarded against [the Landlord] for the illegal eviction, the Tribunal has borne in mind that [the Tenant] has been obstructive towards [the Landlord] in his attempts to register the tenancy with the PRTB".[211]

The tenant was awarded €1,500 in compensation for the unlawful termination of the tenancy.

8–99 In *Monaghan and Anor v Woods*,[212] the landlord alleged that the tenant had been engaging in intimidating behaviour and served a notice of termination. The landlord acknowledged that the notice of termination was not technically in accordance with s.62 of the RTA 2004 but requested that if the tenancy tribunal was to impose any penalty in respect of technical difficulties with the notice of termination, that penalty should be mitigated substantially by the behaviour of the tenant and the feelings of fear which the landlord and his family had in their home as a result of the tenant's conduct.[213]

---

[208]　Tenancy tribunal report, p.8.
[209]　Tenancy tribunal report, p.9.
[210]　TR32/2007/DR 981/2007, March 16, 2007.
[211]　Tenancy tribunal report, p.8.
[212]　TR18/DR1411/2008, September 30, 2008.
[213]　The extent to which the tenancy tribunal took these mitigating factors into account is not

12. Duty to Mitigate Loss

8–100 Where a tenant has not validly terminated a tenancy, the landlord may be entitled to retain the deposit, or a portion of it, paid by the tenant. For example, where the tenant has failed to give the required notice period, the general rule is that the landlord will be entitled to retain the portion of the deposit attributable to the appropriate notice period. However, a landlord does not have an entitlement to double rent and once a dwelling has been re-let, the liability of the former tenant ceases. The landlord is required to mitigate his or her loss and to rent out the dwelling as soon as practicable. The landlord will be entitled to retain the deposit while he or she is making attempts to re-let and the appropriate deduction can be made depending on the length of time it has taken to secure another tenant to occupy the dwelling. In *Kinney and Anor v O'Doherty*[214] the tenants had vacated a dwelling but the landlord made no effort to minimise his losses. The tenancy tribunal stated that, "[t]he Landlord failed to convince the Tribunal that he had made serious efforts to minimise his losses by endeavouring to obtain replacement tenants, particularly as Term had only just started."[215] The landlord was required in those circumstances to return the deposit to the tenants.

8–101 In *Kervick v Walsh*[216] the landlord had changed the locks to the dwelling and put the tenant's belongings onto the pavement outside the dwelling. The tenant maintained that as a consequence of these actions, he had lost a number of his possessions. The tenancy tribunal refused to accept the landlord's submission that the tenant having been locked out of the dwelling, had a duty to mitigate his losses which included the duty to return and collect all his belongings placed on the pavement.

13. Termination of Fixed Term Tenancies

A. Overview

8–102 Prior to the commencement of the RTA 2004, a fixed term tenancy terminated on the expiry of the fixed term. This common law rule no longer applies to a tenancy which comes within the scope of the RTA 2004. A fixed

---

evident from the tenancy tribunal decision. The tenancy tribunal awarded the tenant €3,000 for the landlord's behaviour, which included locking the tenant out of the dwelling. As that award is substantially less than other awards made where a landlord has prevented a tenant from gaining access to a dwelling, it may have been one of the factors which the tenancy tribunal had regard to when determining the amount of the award.

[214] TR26/DR1039/2008, September 19, 2008.

[215] Tenancy tribunal report, p.6.

[216] TR68/DR255/2007, July 19, 2007.

term tenancy to which the RTA 2004 applies will continue on the expiry of the fixed term.[217]

A fixed term tenancy can only be terminated during the fixed term period in the three limited circumstances. These circumstances are considered at paras 8–105 to 8–109 below.[218]

B. Non-Application of s.34 of the RTA 2004

8–103 Section 34 of the RTA 2004 does not apply to fixed term tenancies. Therefore, it is not possible for a landlord to terminate a fixed term tenancy at any stage during the fixed term because he or she wishes to sell the dwelling, reoccupy it or, for any other reason set out in the Table to s.34. As we shall see below, the only exception to this is if the landlord and tenant agree that one of the grounds permitted to terminate a Part 4 tenancy in s.34, is to be a specific term of the lease agreement.[219] Laffoy J. in *Canty* stated that:

> "The obvious purpose of s. 58(3) is to ensure that contractual rights of a tenant which are more beneficial than the statutory rights conferred by the Act of 2004 are not interfered with, an objective which is also given effect to in s.26, which provides that nothing in Part 4 shall derogate from rights enjoyed by the tenant which are more beneficial for the tenant than Part 4 rights".[220]

In *Glynn v Mannion*[221] the landlord of a fixed term tenancy served a notice of termination on the tenant stating that he required the dwelling for the occupation of his daughter. The tenancy tribunal found that the notice of termination was invalid because the tenancy was for a fixed term and therefore could not be terminated under s.34. The tenant was awarded €5,000 in damages for the distress and upset caused to her.

8–104 As discussed in Ch.7 on Security of Tenure, if a tenant enters into a fixed term tenancy, the tenant will still acquire Part 4 tenancy rights (after six months of occupation). The Part 4 tenancy rights apply to the fixed term tenancy but only to the extent that they may provide further benefit to the tenant over and above the rights afforded to him or her by virtue of the fixed term tenancy

---

[217] Section 59 of the RTA 2004 provides as follows—"(a) any rule of law, nor (b) provision of any enactment in force immediately before the commencement of this Part ... shall apply in relation to the termination of a tenancy of a dwelling". A tenancy to which the RTA 2004 applies may only be terminated by service of a notice termination that complies with Pt 5 (RTA 2004, s.58(2)).

[218] See para.8–65 above. A valid notice of termination must also be served pursuant to s.62 of the RTA 2004.

[219] See para.8–109 below.

[220] *Canty v Private Residential Tenancies Board* [2007] IEHC 243; unreported, High Court, August 8, 2007, at pp.34–35.

[221] TR89/DR242/2007, December 12, 2007.

agreement.[222] Once a fixed term tenancy expires and has not been terminated by a notice of termination, the tenancy will continue.[223] The landlord and tenant (unless the fixed term tenancy is renewed) may then rely on s.34 of the RTA 2004 to terminate the tenancy.

C. Circumstances where a Fixed Term Tenancy may be Terminated

8–105 There are only three situations in which a fixed term tenancy may be terminated. They are as follows:

(1) where there has been a breach of obligation by either the landlord or the tenant[224];

(2) where a landlord refuses his or her consent to an assignment or sub-letting of the tenancy by the tenant[225];

(3) where the lease or tenancy agreement provides for specific grounds for the termination of the fixed term tenancy and that ground is not in contravention with Part 4 of the RTA 2004.[226]

(i) Where the landlord or tenant is in breach of the tenancy agreement

8–106 Section 58(3) of the RTA 2004 provides that a fixed term tenancy can be terminated if there has been a breach of obligation by either the tenant or the landlord. Accordingly, if there has been a failure by a landlord or tenant to comply with any obligations of the tenancy, the fixed term tenancy may be terminated. Where a party seeks to terminate a fixed term for breach of the tenancy agreement, the procedures set out at paras 8–29 to 8–36 apply.

(ii) Landlord's refusal to allow the tenancy be sub-let or assigned

8–107 The second situation where a fixed term tenancy can be terminated is contained in s.186 of the RTA 2004. This section provides that if a landlord refuses his or her consent to an assignment or sub-letting of the tenancy by the tenant, the tenant can terminate the tenancy by serving a notice of termination giving the appropriate period of notice to the landlord.[227] It is interesting to note that s.186 applies regardless of whether the landlord's refusal is reasonable or not. Prior to the introduction of the RTA 2004, a landlord could not unreasonably withhold consent to an assignment or sub-let.[228]

---

[222] See paras 7–41 to 7–42, which considers this issue in the context of security of tenure.

[223] See para.8–102 above and paras 7–37 to 7–40.

[224] RTA 2004, s.58(3)(c).

[225] RTA 2004, s.186.

[226] See para.8–109.

[227] Section 16(k) of the RTA 2004 imposes an obligation on the tenant not "to assign or sub-let the tenancy without the written consent of the landlord (which consent the landlord may, in his or her discretion, withhold)." See Ch.4 on Tenant Obligations.

[228] *Rice and Kenny v Dublin Corporation* [1947] I.R. 425. Also, s.66 of the Landlord and Tenant

8–108 In *Kelleher v McAuliffe*[229] the tenant entered into a fixed term tenancy for successive 12-month periods. The tenant informed the landlord that he wished to vacate the dwelling but that he had a replacement tenant. However, the landlord required the tenant to produce either a bank reference or work reference for the prospective tenant. The tenant failed to do so and the tenant vacated the dwelling as he was not in a position to continue paying the rent. The tenancy tribunal found that, "the landlord was within his rights to insist on references in advance of agreeing to allow a replacement tenant to reside in the dwelling."[230] The landlord was allowed to retain the deposit in the circumstances. The tenancy tribunal report does not expand on the reasons why the landlord was within his rights to insist on references. Arguably, on a strict reading of s.186 of the RTA 2004 and given that its provisions are not subject to any requirement of "reasonableness", the tenant should have been entitled to terminate the tenancy once the landlord had refused consent to the sub-let or assignment.

(iii) Terms of the tenancy agreement

8–109 If parties agree on the circumstances in which either party can terminate a fixed term lease, that will be permitted but those grounds must be one of the grounds set out in the Table to s.34 of the RTA 2004.[231] In *Canty v Private Residential Tenancies Board*, the parties had agreed that if the landlord wished to re-occupy the dwelling that would constitue a permitted ground to terminate the agreement, which Laffoy J. was of the view "was the bargain between the parties freely entered into".[232] In *Canty*, the fixed term tenancy was a Part 4 tenancy. Both the judgment in *Canty* and the RTA 2004 do not address the issue of whether a fixed term tenancy which is not a Part 4 tenancy can be terminated using a ground under s.34. [233]

D. Required Notice for Continued Occupation

8–110 A tenant must notify the landlord if he or she wishes to stay on in the dwelling once the fixed term of the tenancy has expired.[234] The tenant is required to notify the landlord not later than one month and not sooner than three months before the expiration of the fixed term period.[235] If a tenant fails to comply with

---

(Amendment) Act 1980 (by virtue of s.193(d) of the RTA 2004, s.66 does not apply to a dwelling to which the RTA 2004 applies).

[229] TR10/DR564/2008, September 12, 2008.

[230] Tenancy tribunal report, p.4.

[231] RTA 2004, Table to s.34, para.1–6. See also para.8–28.

[232] [2007] IEHC 243; unreported, High Court, August 8, 2007, at p.33.

[233] A fixed term tenancy will not be a Part tenancy if it is for less than six months or if it is a tenancy to which s.25 of the RTA 2004 applies. See paras 7–18 to 7–20.

[234] RTA 2004, s.195.

[235] RTA 2004, s.195(3).

this requirement and the landlord suffers loss or damage as a result of that failure, the landlord may make a complaint to the PRTB under Pt 6 of the RTA 2004 that he or she has suffered such loss or damage.[236]

In *Clarke v Gumowska and Others Anor*[237] the tenancy tribunal refused to accept an argument submitted by a tenant that the tenants were not obliged to give notice of the termination of the tenancy as required by s.66 of the RTA 2004 because they had not expressed an intention pursuant to s.195 to stay on in the dwelling after the expiration of the fixed term tenancy. The tenancy tribunal stated that it "does not accept that the tenants' actions in not informing the landlord that they intended to stay on after the expiration of the fixed term can have the effect of avoiding the notice requirements set out in Section 66."[238]

In *Flynn v Ikponmwosa*[239] the tenancy tribunal found that:

> "Although [the tenant] neglected to notify the Landlord of her intentions regarding her Part 4 tenancy in accordance with section 195 of the Act, this omission on her part did not entitle the Landlord to turn up at the dwelling and force her and her family to leave."[240]

The tenant was entitled to general damages for the pain and upset that the unlawful eviction caused to her and her family and was awarded €6,250 in damages.

14. TERMINATION OF SUB-TENANCIES

8–111 There are additional requirements that a landlord must comply with where the landlord seeks to terminate a tenancy that has been sub-let. Sections 70–72 of the RTA 2004 deal with sub-tenancies and set out the procedures which must be followed where the tenancy is being terminated and the tenancy is sub-let. These procedures are considered in detail below.[241]

A. Head-Landlord Serving Notice of Termination on the Head-Tenant

(i) Termination of both the sub-tenancy and the head-tenancy

8–112 Where a landlord wishes to terminate a tenancy that has been sub-let, the landlord must stipulate in the notice of termination served on the head tenant[242]

---

[236] RTA 2004, s.195(4).
[237] TR51/DR1195/2009, April 23, 2009.
[238] Tenancy tribunal report, p.4.
[239] TR10/DR1463/2009, March 2, 2009.
[240] Tenancy tribunal report, p.3.
[241] A substantial amount of cross-referencing is necessary to establish what is required under RTA 2004 legislation in relation to sub-tenancies. See also the Schedule to the RTA 2004 specifically dealing with sub-tenancies.
[242] The notice of termination must comply with s.62 of the RTA 2004. See para.8–65.

whether he or she also requires the sub-tenancy to be terminated.[243] Where the landlord wishes the sub-tenancy to be terminated, s.70(3) of the RTA 2004 requires that a copy of the notice of termination is also served on the sub-tenant.[244] Section 70(3) does not state who is required to serve the notice on the sub-tenant and whether it is in fact the head-tenant or the head-landlord. The Explanatory Memorandum to the RTA 2004 provides, however, that it is the landlord who must serve the notice of termination on the sub-tenant.

8–113 Where the landlord requires the head-tenancy and the sub-tenancy to be terminated and the head-tenant does not dispute the termination of the head-tenancy, the head-tenant must within 28 days of the receipt of the notice of termination from the landlord, serve a separate notice of termination on the sub-tenant.[245] (This notice of termination served by the head-tenant, is in addition to the copy of the head-landlord's notice of termination which must also be served on the sub-tenant pursuant to s.70(3) as referred to above).

Where the head-tenant *does* dispute the termination of the tenancy, the head-tenant must also serve a notice of termination on the sub-tenant. This notice of termination must include a statement that the sub-tenant is to inform the head-tenant within 10 days of receipt of the notice, whether he or she also intends to refer a dispute to the PRTB about the termination of the tenancy.[246] The head-tenant may not refer his or her dispute to the PRTB until 15 days have elapsed from service of the head-tenant's notice of termination on the sub-tenant.[247]

(ii) Where the landlord wishes to terminate the head-tenancy but not the sub-tenancy

8–114 Where the landlord wishes to terminate the head-tenancy but does not require the sub-tenancy to be terminated the landlord must also state this in the notice of termination. However, a different procedure must be followed depending on whether the head tenant disputes the termination of the tenancy.

If the head-tenant *does not* object to the termination of the head-tenancy and does not refer any dispute to the PRTB in relation to its termination, the head-tenant must within 28 days from receipt of the landlord's notice of termination, notify the sub-tenant of the contents of that notice.[248] The RTA 2004 does not

---

[243]   RTA 2004, s.70(2).
[244]   RTA 2004, s.70(3).
[245]   RTA 2004, s.71(1).
[246]   RTA 2004, s.81(2) and (3). If the head-tenant does not include this statement in the notice of termination, he shall be prohibited from referring a dispute to the PRTB (RTA 2004, s.81(5)(a) and see also para.9–42). Similarly, if the sub-tenant fails to inform the head-tenant that he or she wishes to refer a dispute to the PRTB within 10 days, the sub-tenant will also be prohibited from referring a dispute to the PRTB (RTA 2004, s.81(4) and see also para.9–42).
[247]   RTA 2004, s.81(5)(b).
[248]   RTA 2004, s.72(1).

stipulate whether the head-tenant must provide this notification to the sub-tenant in writing or not.

If the head-tenant *does* dispute the termination of the head-tenancy and refers the matter to the PRTB under Pt 6 of the RTA 2004, the head-tenant must notify the sub-tenant of the contents of the notice of termination served by the landlord within 28 days from receiving it.[249] The head-tenant must also notify the sub-tenant of the fact that a dispute has been referred to the PRTB.[250] Again the RTA 2004 does not specify whether this notice must be in writing or not. Finally, once the dispute has been determined by the PRTB, the head-tenant must notify the sub-tenant of the terms of the determination order within 14 days from receiving it.[251]

B. Head-tenant Terminating Sub-Tenancy to which Part 4 Applies

8–115 At paras 8–28 to 8–46 above, the Table to s.34 of the RTA 2004 and the six grounds permitted to terminate a Part 4 tenancy have been considered. Three of these grounds only apply to sub-tenancies and may be relied upon by the head-tenant to terminate a sub-tenancy the subject of a Part 4 tenancy.[252] These grounds are as follows:

1) breach by the sub-tenant of the tenancy agreement[253];
2) the dwelling is no longer suitable for the accommodation needs of the sub-tenant or any persons residing with him or her[254]; and
3) the head-tenant wishes to use the property for his or her occupation or for the occupation by a family member.[255]

8–116 Where a sub-tenant disputes the validity of a notice of termination served in reliance on any of these three grounds, the sub-tenant may refer the dispute to the PRTB. The same rules that apply to the termination of a Part 4 tenancy also apply to the termination of a sub-tenancy the subject of a Part 4 tenancy. These rules are dealt with at paras 8–29 to 8–37 and 8–39.

---

[249] RTA 2004, s.72(2)(i).
[250] RTA 2004, s.72(2)(ii).
[251] RTA 2004, s.72(3).
[252] RTA 2004, para.3(d) of the Schedule. Paragraphs 3, 5 and 6 of the Table to s.34 of the RTA 2004 are not included amongst the grounds on which a head-tenant may terminate a sub-tenancy. Principally this can be said to be because these grounds involve matters over which the head-tenant has no control or matters for which the head-tenant would at first instance require the consent of the head-landlord. The grounds for termination contained in paras 3, 5 and 6 of the Table to s.34 are respectively—the landlord intends to sell the property within three months of the termination of the tenancy; the landlord intends to substantially refurbish or renovate the dwelling; the landlord intends to change the use of the dwelling.
[253] RTA 2004, Table to s.34, para.1.
[254] RTA 2004, Table to s.34, para.2.
[255] RTA 2004, Table to s.34, para.4.

C. Notice of Termination Served Directly between Head-Tenant and Sub-Tenant

8–117 Where a tenant has created a sub-tenancy of the tenancy granted to him or her, the head-tenant assumes the role of landlord in respect of the sub-tenancy. Accordingly, where the head-tenant seeks to terminate a sub-tenancy, he or she is acting in the capacity of a landlord. In these circumstances, the head-tenant will be obliged to comply with all the procedural requirements for terminating a tenancy imposed on landlords by the RTA 2004. These requirements have been considered at paras 8–08 to 8–18. Similarly, if the sub-tenant seeks to terminate the sub-tenancy he or she will also be required to comply with all the procedural requirements for terminating a tenancy imposed on tenants by the RTA 2004. These requirements have been considered at paras 8–19 to 8–27.

15. CONTRACTING OUT OF PART 5

8–118 The procedure set down in Pt 5 is mandatory and must be followed by a landlord or tenant who wishes to terminate a tenancy of a dwelling that falls within the jurisdiction of the RTA 2004. Section 58 of Pt 5 provides:

> a tenancy of a dwelling may not be terminated by the landlord or the tenant by means of a notice of forfeiture, a re-entry <u>or any other process or procedure not provided by this Part</u>.

Section 54(1) of RTA 2004 as contained in Pt 4 also states that "no provision of any tenancy agreement may operate to vary, modify or restrict in any way a provision of this Part." Accordingly, the provisions of Pt 4 that deal with the termination of Pt 4 tenancies must be complied with by landlords and tenants and cannot be contracted out of.

16. OFFENCES

8–119 Section 74 of the RTA 2004 provides that a person is guilty of an offence if:

(a) a notice of termination that is invalid purports to be served by that person (or on his or her behalf) in respect of a tenancy, and

(b) that person does any act in reliance on the notice, that affects adversely, or is calculated to affect adversely, any interest of the person on whom the notice is served.

An act is done by a person "in reliance" on a notice of termination if:

(1) the act when carried out is accompanied or preceded by a statement made by the person (in writing or otherwise) that it is being carried out or will be carried out in reliance on the notice, or

(2) in all the circumstances it is reasonable to infer that the act is carried out in reliance on the notice.[256]

8–120 It is a defence to an offence under s.74 to show that the defendant neither knew nor reasonably could be expected to have known of the existence of any fact that gave rise to the notice of termination being invalid.[257]

17. TERMINATION OF TENANCIES FALLING OUTSIDE OF THE JURISDICTION OF THE RTA 2004

8–121 The law governing the termination of residential tenancies prior to the enactment of the RTA 2004 still applies to tenancies that fall outside its jurisdiction.[258] The two primary methods for terminating tenancies to which the RTA 2004 has no application, is to serve a notice to quit or a forfeiture notice. In the case of a fixed term tenancy, the tenancy will automatically terminate on the expiry of the fixed term.[259]

A. Notice to Quit

(i) Form

8–122 If the tenancy is a periodic tenancy,[260] the tenancy may be terminated by serving a notice to quit in accordance with the Housing (Miscellaneous Provisions) Act 1992 (the "1992 Act"). The notice to quit must be in writing,[261] otherwise there is no prescribed form that the notice to quit must follow. It must be clear from the notice however that the landlord or tenant wishes to terminate the tenancy of the dwelling. Details of the tenancy should be given in the notice including, the term of the tenancy, the parties to the tenancy, the amount of rent payable and a description of the dwelling.[262]

---

[256] RTA 2004, s.74(3).

[257] RTA 2004, s.74(2).

[258] See Ch.7 on the application of the RTA 2004. The law that applied to the termination of tenancies prior to the enactment of the RTA 2004 is dealt with in great detail in other texts. See for example, Wylie, *Landlord and Tenant Law*, 2nd edn (Dublin: Butterworths, 1998).

[259] This is in contrast to the position under the RTA 2004, see para.8–104.

[260] Periodic tenancies are tenancies that run for successive periods, for example week to week, month to month, year to year. Prior to the 1992 Act, a tenancy could be terminated giving notice according to the length of the successive period, for example in the case of a weekly tenancy only seven days' notice was required.

[261] 1992 Act, s.16(1).

[262] See *Gorty Estates Ltd v Mooney*, unreported, High Court, May 13, 1971 at pp.5–6 where

A periodic tenancy can be terminated without giving a reason. However, where a landlord is serving a notice to quit, the tenant may also be entitled to apply for a new tenancy under the Landlord and Tenant (Amendment) Act 1980.[263]

(ii) Notice period

8–123 The 1992 Act prescribes a minimum statutory notice period of four weeks when terminating a tenancy[264] but the parties are permitted to agree to a longer period of notice.[265] Subject to these rules, the notice that must be given of the termination of a tenancy will depend on the tenancy itself. If a tenancy is weekly, four weeks' notice must be given, which is the statutory minimum. If a tenancy is a monthly tenancy, one month's notice is required, three months' notice is required to terminate a quarterly tenancy and if a yearly tenancy is being terminated, 183 days' notice is required.[266]

In the case of a periodic tenancy, the notice period must expire on a gale day, as there is a presumption that this day coincides with the commencement date of the tenancy. A gale day is the day on which a periodic payment of rent is due. If the notice expires after the gale day, then another period of the periodic tenancy begins and this will have to expire before the notice becomes effective to terminate the tenancy.

(iii) Service

8–124 A notice to quit must be served on the recipient before the commencement of the notice period. Unless there is specific provision in the lease agreement itself in relation to service of the notice, personal service is the safest method of service as it ensures that the notice is received prior to the notice period commencing. A notice can be served by post but again the party serving the notice must ensure that the recipient receives the notice prior to the commencement of the notice period.

(iv) Fixed term tenancies

8–125 A notice to quit has no application in the termination of fixed term tenancies. Either the tenancy expires on the last date of the tenancy or if the tenancy is being terminated early, forfeiture is the appropriate procedure.[267] If

---

O'Higgins C.J. stated: "It is true that the premises are incorrectly described and the rent wrongly stated. I am satisfied on authority that where the Defendant has not been misled these defects are not fatal. Here there has been no confusion as to what was referred to". See Appendix 14 for a Sample Notice to Quit.

[263] See Ch.7 on Security of Tenure, in particular paras 7–43 to 7–52.
[264] 1992 Act, s.16(1)
[265] 1992 Act, s.16(3).
[266] *Wright v Tracey* (1874) I.R. 8 C.L. 478; *Kane v McCabe* [1952] Ir. Jur. Rep. 41; *Kemp v Derrett* (1814) 3 Cam. 510.
[267] See paras 8–126 to 8–128.

the circumstances which give rise to forfeiture do not exist, the fixed term tenancy may not be terminated by the landlord or the tenant during the fixed period.

B. Forfeiture

(i) Appropriate circumstances for forfeiture

8–126 Forfeiture is the appropriate means to terminate a tenancy where the tenant is in breach of his or her tenancy obligations. If there has been no breach of obligation, the landlord has no right to terminate the tenancy by means of forfeiture. Forfeiture is appropriate where:

    (a) the tenant disclaims the landlord's title;
    (b) there has been breach of a condition of the tenancy agreement[268];
    (c) there has been a breach of covenant.[269]

(ii) Procedure

8–127 The landlord is required to follow specific statutory procedures when relying on forfeiture as a remedy. If the landlord fails to do so, he or she may lose the right to forfeit the lease. As forfeiture is an equitable remedy, the court has a wide discretion to grant relief to the tenant on such terms as it sees fit.

Before forfeiture can take place, a notice must be served by the landlord on the tenant under s.14 of the Conveyancing Act 1881.[270] One exception to this is where the tenant is in arrears of rent.[271] In such cases a s.14 notice is not required but as forfeiture is an equitable remedy (which the courts are reluctant to grant), it is advisable that a demand for rent is made by the landlord.[272] A section 14 notice served by a landlord should:

---

[268] A condition is a covenant preceded by the words "provided that" or "upon condition that". See Wylie, *Landlord & Tenant Law*, 2nd edn (Dublin: Butterworths, 1998) at para.24.07.

[269] This ground can only be relied on where there is a forfeiture clause providing that if a covenant is breached, the tenant is liable to forfeiture. See *Spencer v Godwin* (1815) 4 M&S 265.

[270] Section 14(1) of the Conveyancing Act 1881 provides "a right of re-entry or forfeiture under any proviso or stipulation in a lease, for a breach of any covenant or condition in the lease, shall not be enforceable, by action or otherwise, unless and until the lessor serves on the lessee a notice specifying the particular breach complained of and, if the breach is capable of remedy, requiring the lessee to remedy the breach, and, in any case, requiring the lessee to make compensation in money for the breach, and the lessee fails, within a reasonable time thereafter, to remedy the breach, if it is capable of remedy, and to make reasonable compensation in money, to the satisfaction of the lessor, for the breach." See Appendix 15 for a sample s.14/Forfeiture Notice.

[271] The exceptions to s.14(1) are set out in s.14(6) of the Conveyancing Act 1881, as amended by the Conveyancing Act 1892, s.2(2) and s.35 of the Landlord and Tenant (Ground Rents) Act 1967.

[272] At common law a landlord had to make a formal demand for rent before he or she could invoke a right of re-entry, although this requirement was often overwritten by lease agreements which provided that such a demand for rent was not necessary.

1) specify the particular covenant that was breached[273];
2) require the tenant to remedy the breach.[274]

The landlord should serve the section 14 notice and wait a reasonable period for the tenant to remedy the breach of covenant. If the tenant fails to remedy that breach, the landlord can make a demand for possession and re-entry may be effected only if it can be done peaceably.[275] The landlord must physically re-enter the premises with the intention of determining the tenancy.[276] Service of the s.14 notice is not sufficient—an attempt must be made by the landlord to re-enter the dwelling. If re-entry cannot be effected peaceably,[277] the landlord will be required to issue proceedings to recover possession based upon the forfeiture.[278]

(iii) Relief against forfeiture

8–128 A tenant may seek relief against forfeiture by relying on s.14(2) of the Conveyancing Act 1881, which allows a tenant to oppose ejectment proceedings brought by a landlord before the Circuit Court. However, statutory relief is not available to a tenant if the landlord has entered into possession unless the tenant can argue that the landlord re-entered without complying with the statutory rules on forfeiture (if for example the landlord did not serve a s.14 notice when required to do so, or the tenant had remedied the breach of covenant within the time specified in the notice).

The tenant can also seek equitable relief against forfeiture. In these circumstances, the court will decide whether to exercise its equitable jurisdiction to grant relief where it would be just and equitable to do so. The courts have demonstrated a reluctance to grant forfeiture.[279] The court may refuse forfeiture, particularly if it is the first occasion the tenant has been in breach of the tenancy. The court may, however, consider it appropriate to make other orders, such as directing the tenant to pay outstanding rent arrears, or remedy the breach of tenancy by appropriate means.[280]

---

[273] See *The Mercers Co. v McKeefrey* (1896) 30 I.L.T.R. 41; *Minister for Local Government and Public Health v Kenny* (1940) 75 I.L.T.R. 26.

[274] Although this is only necessary if the breach is capable of remedy—*Rugby School v Tannahill* [1935] 1 K.B. 87.

[275] See *Sweeney v Powerscourt Shopping Centre* [1985] I.L.R.M. 442.

[276] See *Bank of Ireland v Lady Lisa Ireland Limited* [1992] 1 I.R. 404, at 408–9.

[277] See s.2 of the Prohibition of Forcible Entry and Occupation Act 1971, which makes it a criminal offence to use force to enter a dwelling.

[278] See para.8–129.

[279] See *Whipp v Mackey* [1927] I.R. 406; *Public Trustee v Westbrook* [1965] 1 W.L.R. 1160.

[280] See *Ennis v Rafferty* (1938) 72 I.L.T.R. 56.

C. Application to Court

8–129 If a tenant fails to vacate after a notice to quit has been served or an attempt has been made by the landlord to peaceably re-enter the dwelling following the service of a section 14 notice, a landlord will be required to make an application for ejectment before the courts.[281] There are four types of proceedings which the landlord may bring:

(1) Ejectment Civil Bill on Title based on Forfeiture—this is the appropriate remedy where the tenant will not vacate the dwelling notwithstanding the fact that the tenancy has been terminated by forfeiture.

(2) Ejectment for Non-Payment of Rent—these proceedings are instituted pursuant to s.52 of Deasy's Act. The disadvantage to this procedure is that the tenant must be in arrears for a period of one year before bringing proceedings. In addition, a landlord is not entitled to eject the tenant for six months after the order for possession is made and if the tenant makes payment within that period of time, the order of the court will lapse.

(3) Ejectment Civil Bill for Overholding—this procedure is utilised where a notice to quit has been served but the tenant has failed to vacate or the original lease has expired and the tenant is still in the dwelling.[282]

(4) Ejectment for Deserted Premises—where a dwelling has been deserted and a half year's rent is due—the landlord will have a right to recover possession.[283]

---

[281] See Ord.51, Ord.1 r.6 and Ord.37 rr.1–3, Rules of the Superior Courts 1986, Rules of the Circuit Court 2001, and District Court Rules 1948 Form XXI.

[282] Deasy's Act, s.72. Order 51, Rules of the Circuit Court 2001; District Court Rules.

[283] Deasy's Act, s.78. See Ch.27 of Wylie, *Landlord and Tenant Law*, 2nd edn (Dublin: Butterworths, 1998) for a more detailed consideration of these reliefs.

CHAPTER 9

DISPUTE RESOLUTION

1. INTRODUCTION

A. The Commission on the Private Rented Residential Sector

9–01 The resolution of disputes between landlords and tenants was an issue of central focus in the review carried out by the Commission on the Private Rented Residential Sector (the "Commission"). It considered that a necessary pre-requisite to a vibrant private rented residential sector, was access to a much speedier dispute resolution process than was likely to be available before the courts.[1] The Report of the Commission recorded that many of the disputes between tenants and landlords concerned different perceptions of the conditions of the physical accommodation; fittings and fixtures; levels of rent; behaviour and the right to the return of deposits paid. It was the Commission's view that these disputes did not require legal experience to determine but often would benefit from mediation, an expert opinion or just simply an independent third party view.[2]

In examining the legal and regulatory framework in the residential sector, in place at the time of carrying out its review, the Commission found that the law surrounding the landlord and tenant relationship was complex and rooted in Victorian legislation, with court procedures being complicated and time consuming. These factors contributed to a reluctance on both the parts of landlords and tenants to pursue legal action and become involved in court proceedings.[3] The Commission said it followed that the landlord and tenant relationship would be improved considerably, if tenancy disputes were dealt with in a more speedy, informal and confidential manner. The Commission

---

[1] Report of the Commission on the Private Rented Residential Sector, July 2000 (the "Report of the Commission"), para.8.3.1.

[2] Report of the Commission, para.8.3.2.

[3] Report of the Commission, Ch.4, Pt III, p.98. See also para.2.6.2 of the Report of the Commission, where "disputes" were identified as one of the issues of concern to tenants, who considered that there should be a cost-effective rapid dispute resolution framework and legal structures accessible by tenants and landlords should be established. "Dispute resolution" was also identified as an issue of concern to landlords in the context of operational/regulatory matters. The general view of landlords was that minor disputes should be handled by the Small Claims and District Courts and that there should be provision for the payment of rent pending a court hearing (see Report of the Commission, para.2.6.3.).

208

concluded that there were strong arguments for the establishment of a board to deal with disputes arising from the landlord and tenant relationship.[4]

B. Residential Tenancies Act 2004

9–02 The long title to the Residential Tenancies Act 2004 (the "RTA 2004") states that it was enacted with the aim of allowing disputes between landlords and tenants to be resolved cheaply and speedily, for the establishment of a body to be known as the Private Residential Tenancies Board (the "PRTB") and for the conferral on it of powers and functions of a limited nature in relation to the resolution of such disputes.

The PRTB was established with effect from September 1, 2004.[5] Its functions relating to dispute resolution subsequently commenced on December 6, 2004, with the coming into force of Pt 6 of the RTA 2004.[6] Since that time the PRTB has largely replaced the function of the courts in dealing with landlord and tenant disputes in the residential sector. Disputes are dealt with by the PRTB through mediation, adjudication or by way of a tenancy tribunal hearing. During 2005 almost 900 applications for dispute resolution were referred to the PRTB.[7] This figure had risen to almost 1,650 during 2008.[8]

9–03 This chapter explores Pt 6 of the RTA 2004, in particular the restrictions imposed on the PRTB's jurisdiction in dealing with disputes, the practical steps in making an application for dispute resolution and the dispute resolution process before the PRTB.[9]

---

[4] Report of the Commission, para.8.3.2. The Commission also considered the less formal procedures that existed in other jurisdictions, namely New Zealand, Ontario in Canada and New South Wales and Queensland in Australia (see Report of the Commission, para.3.4).

[5] Residential Tenancies Act 2004 (Establishment Day) Order 2004 (S.I. No. 524 of 2004).

[6] Residential Tenancies Act 2004 (Commencement) (No.2) Order 2004 (S.I. No. 750 of 2004).

[7] "Private Residential Tenancies Board, Annual Report, 1/9/2004–31/12/2005", p.16. Other statistics made available through the PRTB's annual reports show that during 2006 almost 1,300 applications for dispute resolution services were made to the PRTB ("Private Residential Tenancies Board, Annual Report 2006", p.17.), while during 2007 almost 1,500 applications were made ("Private Residential Tenancies Board, Annual Report & Accounts 2007", p.17).

[8] "Private Residential Tenancies Board, Annual Report & Accounts 2008", p.27.

[9] On November 4, 2009, Michael Finneran TD, Minister for Housing and Local Services, announced the preliminary results of a review of the RTA 2004. The review was stated to have made recommendations in a number of key areas with an overall emphasis on streamlining and simplifying the RTA 2004 and reducing delays in the provision of the PRTB's services. The Minister outlined his intention to introduce amending legislation. A number of the main issues that the Minister indicated would be addressed in an amending enactment, related to the dispute resolution process before the PRTB. Where appropriate the amendments proposed as a result of the review, have been referenced throughout this chapter. See Press Release, "Minister Michael Finneran announces significant changes to Private Residential Tenancies Board (PRTB) legislation", November 4, 2009, *www.environ.ie*.

2. SECTION 109 PROCEDURAL RULES

9–04 The PRTB is empowered by s.109(1) of the RTA 2004, to make procedural rules with the consent of the Minister,[10] in relation to the procedure to be followed under Pt 6 in dealing with disputes. Section 109(2) provides for a non-exhaustive list of the type of procedural rules that the PRTB may make. It includes rules relating to the type of form that must be completed by applicants when referring a dispute to the PRTB, the fee that must be paid for the referral, the period within which a mediator or adjudicator must furnish their report to the PRTB and the time by which a tenancy tribunal must make its determination in relation to a dispute.

The PRTB has exercised its powers under s.109 to prescribe certain rules for the dispute resolution procedure under Pt 6. These rules do not reflect all of the matters dealt with at s.109(2) but they do deal with a number of the practical issues that arise during the dispute resolution process. The "Section 109 Rules, Private Residential Tenancies Board Dispute Resolution Procedure" agreed by the PRTB on August 19, 2009 (the "Procedural Rules 2009") are referred to where relevant throughout this chapter.[11]

3. PRACTICAL STEPS IN MAKING AN APPLICATION TO THE PRTB

A. Application Form

9–05 To refer a dispute to the PRTB, the applicant must complete an application form for dispute resolution.[12] The most up-to-date version of this form can be downloaded from the PRTB's website. The form requires the applicant to provide the following details[13]:

    (a) a description of the applicant, that is whether the applicant is a tenant or landlord (or an agent or representative of either) or a third party;

    (b) the type of dispute resolution service the applicant is seeking – mediation or adjudication[14];

---

[10] The Minister for the purposes of the RTA 2004 is the Minister for the Environment, Heritage and Local Government (RTA 2004, s.4(1)).

[11] "Section 109 Rules, Private Residential Tenancies Board Dispute Resolution Procedure", agreed by the PRTB on August 19, 2009. The Procedural Rules 2009 are available on the PRTB's website (*www.prtb.ie*). Regard should be had to the PRTB's website for any amendment or update to these rules.

[12] 2009 Procedural Rules, para.1.

[13] The application form and the details to be provided by the party applying for dispute resolution services, have been amended from time to time by the PRTB. For the most up to date version of the application form, see *www.prtb.ie*.

[14] Tenancy tribunals provide another forum of dispute resolution before the PRTB. However, there are only very limited circumstances in which a dispute referred to the PRTB may be dealt with by a tenancy tribunal at first instance. See para.9–78.

(c) details of the tenant(s), including name, address, telephone number, and personal public service number ("PPSN");

(d) details of the landlord(s), including name, address, telephone number, PPSN and tenancy registration number[15];

(e) if a landlord or tenant is being represented by an agent or another person, that agent's or person's details, including name, address, telephone number and company registration number if appropriate;

(f) if a dispute is being referred by a third party under s.77 of the RTA 2004, the third party's details, including his or her name, address, telephone number and details of the steps taken by the third party to resolve the dispute before referring it to the PRTB[16];

(g) the tenancy commencement date and tenancy end date (if applicable);

(h) the address of the rented dwelling;

(i) the applicant's reason for seeking dispute resolution services;

(j) the type of documents (if any) being enclosed with the application form;

(k) whether an alternative legal remedy has already been sought in respect of the matter the subject of the application; and

(l) the signature of the applicant.

Documents which are frequently enclosed with application forms for dispute resolution, include tenancy agreements, notices of termination (or purported notices of termination), rent books, correspondence and receipts. All relevant documents that are submitted with the application form for dispute resolution are copied to the other party to the dispute.[17] The application form with any accompanying documentation must be sent with the prescribed fee to the PRTB. The PRTB's website provides up-to-date details on submitting applications, including the fee payable.[18] The PRTB is not permitted to deal with a dispute where the application fee is not paid.[19]

9–06 Where a dispute relates to more than one matter, these matters may be included in the same reference to the PRTB.[20] In practice this means that the party referring a dispute to the PRTB will not be required to complete an application form for dispute resolution in respect of each issue that has arisen in relation to the tenancy and may simply provide details of all complaints in one application form.

---

[15] Where a tenancy of a dwelling is registered with the PRTB it is assigned a tenancy registration number ("TR" number) (see para.10–11). The PRTB is not permitted to deal with a dispute submitted by a landlord where the tenancy of the dwelling concerned has not been registered with the PRTB (RTA 2004, s.83(2) and see also paras 9–38 and 10–22). On registration generally, see Ch.10.

[16] See para.9–17 which considers the pre-conditions that must be satisfied by a third party before referring a dispute to the PRTB under s.77 of the RTA 2004.

[17] This is made clear on the application form for dispute resolution services. See also para.9–56 below.

[18] *www.prtb.ie.*

[19] RTA 2004, s.83(1). See also para.9–37.

[20] RTA 2004, s.79.

B. Pre-conditions and Limitations on Jurisdiction—Checklist

9–07 Paragraphs 9–10 to 9–53 below consider the conditions which a party must comply with prior to referring a dispute to the PRTB and also the limitations imposed on the PRTB's jurisdiction in dealing with disputes. For a party referring a dispute to the PRTB, a useful summary checklist is as follows:

(a) Is the dwelling the subject of the tenancy one to which the RTA 2004 applies?[21]

(b) Am I a party who may refer a dispute to the PRTB?[22]

(c) Are there any procedural requirements that must be satisfied before referring the dispute to the PRTB or is the nature of the dispute such that additional conditions must first be satisfied before the dispute can be referred?[23]

(d) Does the amount of damages or arrears of rent or other charges I am claiming fall within the monetary jurisdiction of the PRTB?[24]

(e) Must my dispute be referred to the PRTB within any particular time period?[25]

4. DISPUTES REFERRED TO THE PRTB

A. Nature of most Common Disputes

9–08 The PRTB deals with a wide-ranging nature of tenancy disputes. Annual Reports published by the PRTB show that the majority of disputes that have been referred to it by tenants relate to deposit retention, while arrears of rent make up the majority of cases referred by landlords.[26] To date deposit retention cases have consistently been the single largest category of cases referred to the PRTB on an annual basis.[27]

---

[21] See Ch.3 on the Application of the Residential Tenancies Act 2004.

[22] See paras 9–10 to 9–27.

[23] See paras 9–36 to 9–42 and para.9–17 in relation to applications made by third parties under s.77 of the RTA 2004.

[24] See para.9–43.

[25] See paras 9–45 to 9–53.

[26] "Private Residential Tenancies Board, Annual Report, 1/9/2004–31/12/2005", pp.17, 35 and 36; "Private Residential Tenancies Board, Annual Report 2006", pp.18, 35 and 36; "Private Residential Tenancies Board, Annual Report & Accounts 2007", pp.19 and 20; "Private Residential Tenancies Board, Annual Report & Accounts 2008", pp.28–31.

[27] "Private Residential Tenancies Board, Annual Report & Accounts 2008", p.29. It was recommended in the preliminary results of the review of the RTA 2004 that there should be fixed fines where deposits are illegally retained by landlords (see Press Release, "Minister Michael Finneran announces significant changes to Private Residential Tenancies Board (PRTB) legislation", November 4, 2009, *www.environ.ie*). See also para.5–43 that considers the submissions that were made to the Commission in relation to the need for a rental deposit board.

B. Specific Disputes

9–09 Section 78 of the RTA 2004 lists a number of particular matters that may be referred to the PRTB for resolution. This is a non-exhaustive list and does not limit in any way the type of disputes that parties to a tenancy or certain other third parties may submit to the PRTB. The matters listed at s.78 are, however, typical of some of the more common disputes that the PRTB deals with. They are as follows:

(a) The retention or refund of a deposit[28];

(b) The setting of rent or rent reviews[29];

(c) A claim by the landlord for arrears of rent or other charges[30];

(d) Breach of obligation by the landlord or the tenant and any claim for costs and/or damages by the landlord or the tenant that may arise from such a breach[31];

(e) Invalid termination of a tenancy by the landlord or tenant and any claim for costs and/or damages that may arise from such a breach[32];

(f) Failure of the tenant or sub-tenant to vacate a dwelling having been validly served with a notice of termination by the landlord or head-tenant as appropriate[33];

(g) The landlord has not complied with an agreement arising under s.35(6) of the RTA 2004 to re-let the dwelling to the tenant, when following the termination of the tenancy, the dwelling concerned has become available for re-letting[34];

(h) Whether a tenancy is terminated in circumstances where the tenant has allegedly vacated but where no notice of termination was served by the tenant[35];

(i) An allegation that the landlord has penalised the tenant for doing or giving notice of his or her intention to do any of the following:

i. referring a dispute against the landlord to the PRTB;

ii. giving evidence in any proceedings to which the landlord is a party before the PRTB; or

iii. making a complaint arising out of the occupation of the rented dwelling to An Garda Síochána or a public authority[36];

(j) An alleged failure by a person to comply with a determination order made by the PRTB.[37]

---

[28] RTA 2004, s.78(1)(a).

[29] RTA 2004, s.78(1)(b) and (c).

[30] RTA 2004, s.78(1)(q).

[31] RTA 2004, s.78(1)(d), (e) and (l).

[32] RTA 2004, s.78(1)(f)–(h) and (m).

[33] RTA 2004, s.78(1)(j) and (k).

[34] RTA 2004, s.78(1)(p). See also paras 8–48 to 8–49 which consider s.35(6) of the RTA 2004.

[35] RTA 2004, s.78(1)(i). See also paras 8–56 to 8–60 which consider the circumstances where a tenancy will be deemed to have terminated.

[36] RTA 2004, s.78(1)(o). Section 14 of RTA 2004 imposes an obligation on a landlord not to penalise a tenant for any of the matters described at (i) of para.9–09 above. See paras 5–47 to 5–48 which consider s.14 of the RTA 2004.

[37] RTA 2004, s.78(1)(n). Although a person may refer a complaint to the PRTB in relation to the

5. The Parties who have a Right to Refer a Dispute

9–10 The PRTB has jurisdiction to deal only with disputes[38] between parties to a tenancy and certain other persons. The right of these parties to refer a dispute to the PRTB may be subject to other jurisdictional limitations which are dealt with at paras 9–28 to 9–52 below.

A. Landlords and Tenants

9–11 A landlord or tenant to an existing or terminated tenancy of a dwelling may individually or jointly refer a dispute between them to the PRTB concerning any matter relating to the tenancy.[39] Where both a landlord and tenant submit separate applications for dispute resolution services, it has generally been the practice of the PRTB to deal with both applications together. Annual Reports published by the PRTB show that the majority of applications for dispute resolution services made to the PRTB are by tenants. For example in 2008, 69 per cent of disputes were referred by tenants, as opposed to 28 per cent referred by landlords.[40]

---

non-compliance by a party with a determination order, pursuant to s.124 of the RTA 2004 an application for enforcement of a determination order may be made to the Circuit Court. If a person does refer a complaint to the PRTB alleging non-compliance with a determination order under s.78(1)(n), the PRTB may make a further determination order requiring the party in default to comply with the first determination order. If there is non-compliance with that further determination order, the matter may ultimately be the subject of an application under s.124 of the RTA 2004 for enforcement. There would seem little utility therefore in referring a complaint to the PRTB where there has been non-compliance with the initial determination order made, when the remedy under s.124 of the RTA 2004 is available to the aggrieved party in the first instance.

[38] A "dispute" for the purposes of Pt 6 includes a "disagreement" and for the purposes of certain sections, a "complaint" (RTA 2004, s.75(2)). Section 75(3) of the RTA 2004 specifically provides that a "disagreement" for the purposes of Pt 6 shall be deemed to include any issue arising between a landlord and tenant with regard to their legal relations, including compliance with their respective tenancy obligations and any claim by the landlord for arrears of rent that the tenant does not dispute but has failed to pay.

[39] RTA 2004, s.76(1). Note that "tenancy", "landlord" and "tenant" are each defined in the RTA 2004 as including (respectively) a terminated tenancy and a former landlord and a tenant of a tenancy that has terminated (RTA 2004, s.5(1) and see also paras 3–14 to 3–18). Accordingly, just because a tenancy has terminated does not mean that the PRTB has no jurisdiction to deal with a dispute relating to it (although time limits for the referral of particular disputes may apply, as considered at paras 9–45 to 9–53).

[40] "Private Residential Tenancies Board, Annual Report & Accounts 2008", p.27. Other statistics made available through the PRTB's annual reports show that in 2006 almost 67 per cent of all cases referred were by the tenant, as opposed to 28 per cent by landlords ("Private Residential Tenancies Board, Annual Report 2006", p.18). In 2007 almost 66 per cent of cases were referred by tenants and 29 per cent by landlords ("Private Residential Tenancies Board, Annual Report & Accounts 2007", p.18).

9–12 The PRTB has no jurisdiction to deal with disputes arising between tenants of a tenancy. A referral of a dispute under s.77 of the RTA 2004 is the only context in which this may indirectly arise. Section 77 is considered at paras 9–17 to 9–24.

B. Landlords and Another

9–13 A landlord may also refer a dispute to the PRTB relating to a claim by a person not being the tenant but who is claiming an entitlement to the rights of a tenant, through an existing or former tenant of the dwelling.[41] This may occur for instance where on the death of a tenant, his or her spouse who occupied the dwelling at the time of the tenant's death, elects in writing to become the tenant of the dwelling.[42] If the landlord disputes the spouse's entitlement to do so, the landlord may make an application for dispute resolution services to the PRTB and the respondent to that application will be the spouse.

C. Sub-Tenancies

(i) Head-tenant/sub-tenant

9–14 The referral of a dispute to the PRTB by a sub-tenant against a head-tenant or a head-tenant against a sub-tenant, is no different to the referral of a dispute by a tenant against a landlord where no sub-tenancy arrangement exists.[43]

(ii) Head-landlord/sub-tenant

9–15 At common law, there is neither privity of estate between sub-tenants and head-landlords nor privity of contract (unless created).[44] Under the RTA 2004 where a sub-tenancy has been created out of a Part 4 tenancy,[45] with the consent of the landlord, certain tenancy obligations are imposed between the then head-landlord and the sub-tenant. The head-landlord is obliged to allow the sub-tenant of the dwelling to enjoy peaceful and exclusive occupation of it and must also

---

[41] RTA 2004, s.76(3). See also s.76 of the Explanatory Memorandum to the RTA 2004.

[42] RTA 2004, s.39. See para.7–16 where s.39 is considered in further detail.

[43] The fact that a sub-tenancy has been created, does not affect a head-landlord's right to refer a dispute to the PRTB against the head-tenant and visa versa. See, however, para.9–42 that considers the conditions imposed on the referral of a dispute to the PRTB, in circumstances where a notice of termination has been served by the head-landlord on the head-tenant, in the context of a sub-tenancy arrangement.

[44] See Wylie, *Landlord and Tenant Law*, 2nd edn (Dublin: Butterworths, 1998), para.22.06.

[45] A Part 4 tenancy arises after a tenant has resided in a dwelling for six months. The effect of a Part 4 tenancy is to give a tenant security of tenure for a further period of three and a half years, after the tenancy has been in existence for that initial six-month period. Part 4 tenancies, their meaning and effect, are considered in detail in Ch.7.

carry out any necessary repairs to the structure and interior of the dwelling.[46] If the head-landlord breaches any of these obligations that he owes to the sub-tenant, the sub-tenant may refer a dispute to the PRTB for resolution.[47]

The sub-tenant owes an obligation to the head-landlord not to cause a deterioration in the condition of the dwelling beyond normal wear and tear. If the tenant does cause damage to the dwelling beyond normal wear and tear, the tenant is obliged to repair the dwelling or compensate the head-landlord for doing so.[48] If the sub-tenant breaches any of these obligations that he owes to the head-landlord, the head-landlord may refer a dispute to the PRTB.[49]

D. Licensees

9–16 Generally, licensees are not afforded rights under the RTA 2004 and do not come within its jurisdiction. There is one limited exception to this, which arises in the context of s.50(7) of the RTA 2004. Section 50(7) provides that a licensee of a tenant may request the landlord to allow him or her to also become a tenant of the dwelling.[50] Where the landlord unreasonably refuses to accede to this request,[51] the licensee may make an application for dispute resolution to the PRTB.[52] This is the only time where a licensee may have recourse to the dispute resolution services of the PRTB, unless the nature of any other dispute that arises, is such that a licensee may make a referral under s.77 of the RTA 2004. Section 77 is discussed at paras 9–17 to 9–24 below.

E. Third Parties

(i) Right of referral of third parties

9–17 A landlord owes to "each person who could be potentially affected" a duty to enforce the obligations of a tenant under a tenancy. This duty is imposed on landlords by s.15(1) of the RTA 2004.[53] It is a duty that may be owed to a third party who has no relationship with the tenancy concerned. However, it is also a duty that is owed to any other tenant of the tenancy, who may be affected by a landlord's failure to enforce the obligations of another tenant.[54] Where it is

---

[46] RTA 2004, para.4(1) of the Schedule.
[47] RTA 2004, para.4(1)(b) of the Schedule.
[48] RTA 2004, para.4(2) of the Schedule.
[49] RTA 2004, para.4(2)(c) of the Schedule.
[50] Note that for s.50(7) of the RTA 2004 to apply, a Part 4 tenancy must be in existence.
[51] Section 50(8) of the RTA 2004, provides that a landlord may not unreasonably refuse to accede to such a request made by a licensee to become a tenant of the dwelling.
[52] RTA 2004, s.76(4).
[53] See paras 5–49 to 5–55 that also consider a landlord's obligation under s.15(1) of the RTA 2004 and the parties to whom that duty is owed.
[54] The RTA 2004 does not provide for any procedure to facilitate directly the resolution of disputes that arise between the tenants of a dwelling (see para.9–12).

alleged that a landlord has breached his or her duty under s.15(1), the affected party has a right to refer a complaint against the landlord to the PRTB pursuant to s.77 of the RTA 2004.[55] Before such a complaint may be referred to the PRTB, the following conditions must first be satisfied:

(a) the referrer of the complaint is or was directly *and* adversely affected by the landlord's alleged breach of duty of s.15(1)[56]; and

(b) before submitting the complaint the referrer took all reasonable steps to resolve the matter by communicating or attempting to communicate with the relevant parties or former parties[57] of the tenancy concerned. This condition does not require the referrer to institute or threaten to institute legal proceedings against the parties or former parties of the tenancy.[58]

To facilitate compliance with the condition outlined at (b), the PRTB may furnish to the person who proposes to submit a dispute, the name of the landlord (or former landlord) or that of his or her agent.[59] The PRTB may exercise this discretion if it appears to the PRTB that the party proposing to refer a dispute is a person who may submit a complaint to it under s.77 of the RTA 2004.

In the matter of *Horgan v Walsh and Anor*,[60] a third party referred a dispute to the PRTB against the owners of a neighbouring dwelling. In its decision the

---

[55] Section 15(3) of the RTA 2004 makes clear that a third party's remedy for breach of a landlord's duty under s.15(1), is to refer a complaint to the PRTB under s.77 of the RTA 2004. Section 15(4), however, provides that nothing in s.15(3) affects any duty of care and the remedies available for its breach that exist apart from s.15.

[56] RTA 2004, s.77(2)(a).

[57] The RTA 2004 does not explicitly state who the "relevant parties or former parties" to the tenancy will be—that is whether it is just the offending tenant or also the landlord. The better view it seems, which is supported by the determinations of tenancy tribunals, is that the third party is obliged to communicate with both the offending tenant and the landlord. In certain circumstances, however, where the behaviour of a tenant is so intimidating that the third party is in fear of communicating or attempting to communicate with the tenant, it may be difficult to satisfy this pre-condition as far as the tenant is concerned. In *Horgan v Walsh and Anor* (TR84/DR719/2007, April 17, 2008) the third party's application failed because the tenancy tribunal determined that the third party did not comply with s.77(2)(b), as he did not communicate with the offending tenants directly. Section 77(2)(b) does not specify however how communications with the parties to a tenancy are to be made. Therefore, in cases where the behaviour of the tenant is of a violent or threatening nature, it seems that the pre-condition in s.77(2)(b) could be satisfied if the communication was made in writing, so long as it was sufficient to convey to the offending tenant, the issue or concerns of the third party. Ultimately, it will be an issue to be determined in each case having regard to the circumstances, whether a third party satisfies the obligation imposed by s.77(2)(b), to take "all reasonable steps" to resolve a matter "by communicating or attempting to communicate" with the tenant concerned.

[58] RTA 2004, s.77(2)(b). The PRTB's application form for dispute resolution requires a third party to outline the steps taken by the him or her to resolve the matter before referring the dispute to the PRTB.

[59] RTA 2004, s.77(3).

[60] TR84/DR719/2007, April 17, 2008.

tenancy tribunal said that it did not consider that the third party had complied with s.77(2)(b) of the RTA 2004, in that he did not take all reasonable steps to resolve the matter and in particular did not approach the tenants directly, in whose hands the tenancy tribunal said that the remedy for the third party's complaints lay.

(ii) Common examples and PRTB cases

9–18 The most common example of the operation of ss.15 and 77 in practice arises where a neighbour of a rented dwelling is affected by the behaviour of a tenant residing in that dwelling. For instance, a tenant may be causing noise late at night or engaging in antisocial behaviour. As there is no procedure under the RTA 2004 for the neighbour to refer a dispute to the PRTB directly against the tenant, the dispute referred by him or her will be that the landlord has failed in his or her obligation to enforce the obligations of the tenant under s.15 of the RTA 2004.[61]

9–19 In *Dunne v Farrell*[62] a neighbour to a rented dwelling made a complaint to the PRTB in relation to the behaviour of the tenants of that dwelling. The neighbour alleged that the tenants in the dwelling had engaged in antisocial behaviour, with many cars calling at late hours to the house, by leaving dirt and rubbish in the garden and by being personally intimidating to her. In evidence given by the landlord, he said that he did not dispute that his tenants had engaged in antisocial behaviour but claimed that he had made many attempts to rectify the situation. The landlord said that he had called to the rented dwelling on a number of occasions to ask the tenants not to make noise at anti-social times, that he had spoken to An Garda Síochána and the Resident's Association to whom complaints had been made and that he had issued two notices of termination to the tenants who ultimately vacated the property. Notwithstanding this, the tenancy tribunal determined on the evidence before it that the landlord had breached his obligations under s.15 of the RTA 2004 and was directed to pay the third party the sum of €1,000 in damages.

9–20 In the matter of *O'Brien & Anor v O'Brien*[63] the neighbours to a rented dwelling referred a dispute to the PRTB under s.77 of the RTA 2004. The neighbours' complaint was that they had been continually and persistently denied their rights to peaceful enjoyment of their home by the actions of the tenants in the adjoining dwelling, who had caused excessive noise, played loud music and were involved in late-night partying. The landlord denied that he was

---

[61] The remedy available to a third party under s.15 of the RTA 2004, is without prejudice to any other remedy that the third party may have against the tenant that exists outside the scope of the RTA 2004. See para.9–24.

[62] TR91/DR736/2008, March 11, 2009.

[63] TR52/DR444/2007, July 13, 2007.

in breach of his duties as a landlord. He gave evidence that he had spoken to the tenants, had offered to pay to have a sound survey carried out and to pay half the costs of any insulation of the walls required. The landlord also gave evidence that following a mediation that had first taken place when the dispute was referred to the PRTB, he had written to the tenants, changed the layout of the living room and paid an electrician so that the TV could be moved to another wall.

The tenancy tribunal determined that the landlord was in breach of his duty under s.15(1) of the RTA 2004. It found that some of the activities of the tenants were beyond those that would be considered by the tenancy tribunal to be reasonable, irrespective of the quality of the insulation between the properties, in particular, the late night card parties. The landlord was aware that these activities were a source of distress to the neighbours who had submitted the dispute to it, as the adjoining occupiers. The tenancy tribunal directed the landlord to pay the neighbours the sum of €1,500, as compensation for distress and inconvenience caused by the activities of the tenants.

9–21 In *Egan v Rushe*[64] a dispute was referred to the PRTB against the landlord of a rented dwelling by the occupier of a neighbouring dwelling pursuant to s.77 of the RTA 2004. The rented dwelling was leased to a family with children. The tenancy tribunal found that close proximity combined with differing lifestyles, particularly work hours, created tension between the adjacent households. Although, the noise from the tenants' household and behaviour of their children was annoying to the third party, they had not behaved in a way that was anti-social as prohibited by s.16(h) of the RTA 2004. The tenancy tribunal also found that the landlord had taken all reasonable steps to investigate the third party's complaints and to ensure the tenants were complying with their obligations under s.16(h). While the tenants and their young children behaved improperly, the tenancy tribunal determined that the landlord had not breached the duty he owed to the occupier of the neighbouring dwelling under s.15(1) of the RTA 2004.

(iii) Duty under s.15(1) and effectiveness of section 77 procedure

9–22 Where a third party is successful in his or her case against a landlord and has established a breach of s.15(1) of the RTA 2004, the result for the third party can nevertheless be unsatisfactory in certain instances (notwithstanding that an order for compensation may also be made). A determination of the PRTB that a landlord has failed to enforce certain obligations of the tenant, may do little in practice to provide a remedy to the third party who has referred the dispute to the PRTB. As a dispute referred under s.77 of the RTA 2004, is between the landlord and the third party, the PRTB cannot order the tenant directly to do a certain thing or refrain from engaging in certain behaviour (even if the tenant

---

[64] TR04/DR281/2006, April 5, 2006.

does partake in the hearing).[65] There are also a number of tenancy tribunal decisions where it has been decided that the landlord has done all he or she can to deal with the tenant. From a third party's perspective, the problem at hand will remain unsolved.

9–23 In the matter of *Horgan v Walsh and Anor*,[66] a third party referred a dispute to the PRTB against the owners of a dwelling three properties apart from the third party's house. The owners of that dwelling had rented it to a family, namely a husband, wife and their four children. Before the tenancy tribunal the third party outlined the various complaints he had made against the tenants, including trespass by two of the younger children, a lack of maintenance by the tenants of the rear garden of the property, the dumping of rubbish there and abusive and threatening behaviour by the tenants towards himself and other neighbours. In evidence, one of the landlords said that he had received about three complaints from the third party in 2005 and 2006. The landlord had informed the third party that he would speak with his tenants, which he then did and told the tenants to keep away from the third party's property. He also said that he had reacted to complaints by another neighbour in a similar prompt fashion. The landlord gave further evidence that he had made enquiries with An Garda Síochána as to whether there was any substance to the complaints made by the third party and was told there was no substance and that it was all "just kids". He also gave evidence that he and his wife had on a number of occasions driven from their home in the evenings to check out the tenants' behaviour and the state of the rear laneway, when they had received complaints.

The tenancy tribunal found that the third party had not demonstrated to the tenancy tribunal that the behaviour of the tenants constituted antisocial behaviour as defined in s.17 of the RTA 2004[67] and that the behaviour of their younger children did not prevent or interfere in any real way with the peaceful occupation of the third party's dwelling. It determined that while the corroborative evidence of some neighbours certainly told of intermittent disputes

---

[65] Section 77 of the RTA 2004 is silent on the involvement a tenant may have in the hearing of a dispute concerning an alleged breach by a landlord of his or her obligation under s.15(1). Although the duty imposed by s.15(1), arises between the affected person and the landlord only, it seems that a tenant's constitutional right to fair procedures mandates at the very least that he or she is informed of the hearing and is afforded an opportunity to partake in the hearing if he or she wishes.

[66] TR84/DR719/2007, April 17, 2008.

[67] To "behave in a way that is anti-social" (contrary to a tenant's obligations under s.16(h) of the RTA 2004) has been interpreted strictly by tenancy tribunals. When seeking relief on the grounds of antisocial behaviour, a party should ensure in so far as possible that such behaviour meets the required threshold for antisocial behaviour as defined at s.17(1) of the RTA 2004. Tenancy tribunal decisions interpreting s.17(1) provide useful guidance in this regard. If there is a question over whether the behaviour complained of is "anti-social" for the purposes of the RTA 2004, it may be appropriate for the party seeking a remedy to do so on the basis of additional or other grounds. See Chs 4 and 8 which consider antisocial behaviour further in the context of tenancy obligtions and the termination of tenancies respectively.

between the new tenants and the long-standing residents in the area, which were undoubtedly upsetting to the parties concerned, the frequency of these incidents and the manner in which the landlord had dealt with them were not such as to constitute a failure by the landlords to comply with their obligations under the RTA 2004. The tenancy tribunal determined that the third party had failed to prove his case.

9–24 Accordingly, a third party will be left with no remedy under the RTA 2004, if it can be shown that the landlord has not failed to enforce a tenant's obligations, notwithstanding that the tenant's behaviour complained of may still impact on the third party. In this context, it is interesting to note the results of a comparative study with other jurisdictions on third party complaints of anti-social behaviour, which was carried out on behalf of the PRTB. The overall conclusion that emerged from this analysis was that Irish legislation dealing with third party antisocial behaviour disputes in the private rented sector, is not currently replicated in other countries.[68]

Section 182 of the RTA 2004 makes clear that proceedings cannot be commenced before the courts, if the PRTB has jurisdiction to deal with the dispute.[69] However, s.182 cannot prevent a third party instituting court proceedings directly against a tenant, whose behaviour is adversely affecting the third party, as this is not a dispute that may be referred to the PRTB for resolution. By way of example, proceedings could be instituted before the courts by a third party against a tenant in the form of a nuisance claim or under s.108 of the Environmental Protection Agency Act 1992 in respect of loud and continuous noise. Such proceedings are different from a complaint that may be referred by a third party to the PRTB under s.77, namely that a landlord has breached his or her obligation under s.15(1) to enforce a tenant's obligations.

F. Personal Representatives

(i) Rent or charges

9–25 The personal representative[70] of a deceased landlord or tenant may refer a dispute to the PRTB where it relates to a claim to recover rent or other charges.[71]

---

[68] "Third Party Complaints of Anti-Social Behaviour in the private residential sector", Candy Murphy and Associates, February 2007, p.9.

[69] See also paras 9–43 to 9–44.

[70] A "personal representative" is defined in s.4(1) of the RTA 2004, as having the same meaning given to it by the Succession Act 1965. Section 3(1) of the Succession Act 1965 defines "personal representative" as meaning "the executor or the administrator for the time being of a deceased person".

[71] RTA 2004, s.75(4)(b).

(ii) Others causes of action

9–26 A personal representative may also refer a dispute to the PRTB where the claim is a cause of action, within the meaning of the Civil Liability Act 1961 (the "Civil Liability Act"), which would have survived for the benefit of or against the estate of the landlord or the tenant.[72]

Section 7(1) of the Civil Liability Act provides that on the death of a person, all causes of action (other than excepted causes of action)[73] vested in him or her, shall survive for the *benefit of* his or her estate. An example of such a cause of action that may arise in the context of a residential tenancy, is where a landlord seeks to recover the costs incurred by him or her in carrying out repairs to the dwelling, which are required because of the tenant's actions in breach of the tenancy agreement. If the landlord dies without this claim being satisfied, it shall survive for the benefit of his or her estate.

Section 8(1) of the Civil Liability Act provides that on the death of a person, all causes of action (other than excepted causes of action) *subsisting against* him or her shall survive against his or her estate. Another example of such a cause of action that may arise in the context of a residential tenancy, is a claim by a tenant for the return of a deposit which the landlord has withheld but where the landlord dies before the dispute is resolved.

(iii) PRTB cases

9–27 In the matter of *Kelly v Warnham*[74] the respondent made an application to the PRTB for dispute resolution services. The respondent sought the return of some of her sister's belongings from the appellant. Her sister had resided in a dwelling owned by the appellant and had died while residing there. The respondent submitted that s.75(4) of the RTA 2004, permitted her to make an application to the PRTB, as the personal representative of her late sister. She maintained that there was a subsisting cause of action as required by that section, though it might not have been prosecuted prior to her sister's death, which related to the detention of her sister's goods and chattels. The appellant on the other hand argued that there was no cause of action in being prior to the death of the respondent's sister and therefore the respondent could not be regarded as a person with standing before the PRTB. Furthermore, she could not claim to be a personal representative as referred to in s.75 of the RTA 2004. The appellant maintained that the RTA 2004 did not provide for this type of situation which came before the tenancy tribunal and in particular it did not provide for issues concerning the goods of a tenant after his or her death.

---

[72]　RTA 2004, s.75(4)(c).

[73]　Part II of the Civil Liability Act, deals with the survival of certain causes or action on death. For the purposes of Pt II "excepted cause of action" is defined at s.6 of the Civil Liability Act as meaning: (a) a cause of action for breach of promise to marry or for defamation or for seduction or for inducing one spouse to leave or remain apart from the other or for criminal conversation, or (b) any claim for compensation under the Workmen's Compensation Act 1934.

[74]　TR147/DR20/2007, June 4, 2008.

The tenancy tribunal considered that the question that it was required to address was whether the respondent was entitled to invoke the dispute resolution procedures of the RTA 2004, as a person entitled to administer the estate of the deceased tenant. In considering the evidence of the parties, the tenancy tribunal noted that at the date of the hearing the respondent had not yet obtained a grant of administration, although it understood the respondent's solicitor was actively seeking such a grant. It had regard to s.27(3) of the Succession Act 1965 and Ord.79 r.5 of the Rules of the Superior Courts 1986 which provide that in the absence of a will, the persons having a beneficial interest in the estate are entitled to a grant of administration in a specified order of priority.

In considering the locus standi of the respondent, the tenancy tribunal found that there was no provision under the RTA 2004 for a person entitled to a grant of administration of a deceased tenant (but to whom a grant had not yet issued) to invoke the dispute resolution procedures of the PRTB. It said that there were limited provisions for a personal representative to avail of the PRTB's dispute resolution service, being claims in respect of arrears of rent and a cause of action that would have survived after the death of the tenant or landlord. The tenancy tribunal found that neither of these limited circumstances applied. It also found that the respondent was not a "personal representative" for the purposes of the RTA 2004, which meant the executor or administrator for the time being of a deceased person.[75] Until the respondent obtained a grant of administration, she was not a personal representative. The tenancy tribunal ultimately determined that the respondent was not entitled to make an application for dispute resolution services to the PRTB, as the intended personal representative of her late sister.[76]

6. RIGHT OF PRTB NOT TO DEAL WITH CERTAIN APPLICATIONS

A. Right to Refuse an Application

9–28 The PRTB has a right not to deal with certain applications made to it for dispute resolution services, which fall within any of the categories described at s.84(1) of the RTA 2004. These categories are considered at paras 9–29 to 9–33 below. Adjudicators and tenancy tribunals may also refuse to deal with any dispute that they consider falls within s.84(1).[77]

---

[75] RTA 2004, s.4(1).

[76] Although the tenancy tribunal was not required to make a determination on this issue in *Kelly v Warnham*, it is worth noting its comments in relation to s.13 of the Succession Act 1965. Section 13 provides that where a person dies intestate, the deceased's "real and personal estate, until administration is granted in respect thereof, shall vest in the President of the High Court". The tenancy tribunal said that as a consequence of this provision, it appeared that the landlord should not have disposed of any of the property of the deceased tenant without the permission of the President of the High Court (tenancy tribunal report, p.8).

[77] RTA 2004, s.85(1). Section 85(1) is, however, subject to the exceptions set out in s.85(2) of the

(i) Dwelling not within the PRTB's jurisdiction

9–29 The PRTB has no jurisdiction to deal with a dispute, where the dwelling concerned is not one to which the RTA 2004 applies.[78] A dwelling for the purposes of the RTA 2004 is defined at s.4(1), while s.3(2) lists the type of dwellings which fall outside its scope. Both s.4(1) and s.3(2) of the RTA 2004 are considered in detail in Ch.3.

(ii) Dispute not within the PRTB's jurisdiction

9–30 The PRTB has the right to refuse to deal with a dispute if (for any other reason than that described at para.9–29 above) the dispute does not come within the PRTB's jurisdiction.[79] A dispute will also be considered as falling outside of the jurisdiction of the PRTB, where a person has failed to comply with any condition that must be satisfied before the PRTB is permitted to deal with their complaint.[80] An example of such a "pre-condition" is the requirement that a tenancy must be registered by a landlord or the application fee for dispute resolution services must be paid, before the application can be processed by the PRTB.[81] A further example is the requirement that a party is first obliged to take reasonable steps to resolve an issue arising with the tenant of a rented dwelling, before he or she refers a complaint to the PRTB in accordance with s.77 of the RTA 2004.[82]

(iii) Dispute is statute-barred

9–31 The RTA 2004 imposes time limits on the referral of certain disputes to the PRTB. These are dealt with at paras 9–45 to 9–49 and cover the type of cases that are most frequently referred to the PRTB. In all other cases the Statute of Limitations 1957–1991 (the "Statute of Limitations")[83] will apply, as if the referral of a dispute to the PRTB were proceedings that were being instituted before a court.[84] An example of where the Statute of Limitations will apply is where a tenant carries out necessary repairs to a dwelling that the landlord has failed to carry out but the landlord does not subsequently discharge the tenant's

---

RTA 2004. Section 85(2) provides that an adjudicator or tenancy tribunal must deal with a dispute where the PRTB has previously held a similar opinion to that held by the adjudicator or tenancy tribunal (that it had a right not to deal with a a dispute under s.84(1)), however, the PRTB having gone through the process at s.84(2)–(4), decided that its initial opinion was not well founded. The adjudicator or tenancy tribunal must also proceed to deal with the dispute, where the PRTB has been directed by the Circuit Court to deal with the dispute under s.84(6).

[78]   RTA 2004, s.84(1)(a).
[79]   RTA 2004, s.84(1)(b). For example, the applicant may be a person who does not have a right to refer a dispute to the PRTB (see paras 9–10 to 9–17).
[80]   RTA 2004, s.84(1)(b).
[81]   RTA 2004, s.83. See also paras 9–37 and 9–39.
[82]   RTA 2004, s.77(2)(b). See para.9–17.
[83]   The Statute of Limitations 1957–1991, as amended by the Civil Liability and Courts Act 2004.
[84]   RTA 2004, s.84(1)(c) and s.84(7).

reasonable and vouched expenses incurred in carrying out those repairs.[85] The tenant may refer a complaint to the PRTB, however, as the RTA 2004 does not impose any specific time limits for the referral of such a dispute, regard must be had to the Statute of Limitations. Accordingly, the tenant will be required to refer the dispute to the PRTB before the expiry of six years from the accrual of the cause of action. If the tenant fails to do so, the dispute will be statute barred and the PRTB shall have no jurisdiction to deal with the dispute.

(iv) Trivial or vexatious matter

9–32 The PRTB has the right to refuse to deal with an application for dispute resolution services, where it is of the opinion that the matter the subject of the application is "trivial or vexatious".[86] The RTA 2004 provides no guidance as to what type of complaints will be considered trivial or vexatious. There is also limited authority on this issue, as the PRTB is not obliged to publish its reasons for refusing to deal with disputes that it considers fall within s.84 of the RTA 2004.

9–33 In *McAlister v Lonergan*[87] the landlord of the dwelling served a notice of termination dated February 11, 2005 on the tenants. One of the tenants contested the validity of the notice and applied to the PRTB for dispute resolution services. An adjudication hearing took place on July 19, 2005 and the PRTB made a determination order on September 28, 2005, determining that the notice of termination served was not valid. Prior to the making of that determination order, the landlord had in fact served a further notice of termination dated September 6, 2005 on the tenants, stating that the tenancy would terminate on November 1, 2005. On September 22, 2005 the tenants referred another dispute to the PRTB concerning the validity of that second notice of termination.[88] Their challenge to the validity of the second notice was based on the contention that s.86(1)(c) of the RTA 2004,[89] prohibits the service of a notice of termination at a time when there is an unresolved dispute before the PRTB relating to a tenancy.

---

[85] See s.12(1)(g) of the RTA 2004 which (subject to certain conditions) obliges a landlord to reimburse a tenant for repairs carried out to a dwelling.

[86] RTA 2004, s.84(1)(d).

[87] DR98/2005, determination order dated September 28, 2005.

[88] This application for dispute resolution services is referred to in the matter of *Lonergan v McAlister and Anor* (TR31/DR742/2006, May 10, 2006), which related to an application made by the landlord to the PRTB on foot of the tenants' failure to vacate the premises having been served with the notice of termination dated September 6, 2005. (The tenancy tribunal hearing in that case was postponed by the PRTB pending the outcome of an application made by one of the tenants to the Circuit Court under s.84(5) of the RTA 2004. See below *McAlister v Private Residential Tenancies Board*, unreported, Circuit Court, ex tempore, Linnane J., March 30, 2006).

[89] Section 86 of the RTA 2004, prescribes the status quo that must be maintained pending the determination of a dispute that has been referred to the PRTB.

Section 86(1)(c) of the RTA 2004 provides that, "pending the determination of a dispute that has been referred to the [PRTB] … (c) a termination of the tenancy concerned may not be effected". The tenants argued that the second notice of termination of September 6, 2005 was invalid because it was served prior to the date on which the PRTB made its determination in relation to the first dispute (September 28, 2005). In contrast, the PRTB was of the opinion that s.86(1)(c) did not operate to prevent the service of a notice of termination where there was another undetermined dispute before the PRTB. On this basis and given the only ground provided for disputing the validity of the notice of termination of September 6, 2005, was that it was served prior to the making of the determination order of September 28, 2005, the PRTB formed the view that this application was trivial or vexatious within the meaning of s.84(1)(d) of the RTA 2004. The PRTB then notified the applicants accordingly.[90]

On September 27, 2005 the tenants made a further application for dispute resolution services to the PRTB, which was supplemental to their earlier application of September 22, 2005. In this supplemental application the tenants stated that s.86 of the RTA 2004 prevented the specification of a termination date, and therefore, prevented the service of a notice of termination where there was an unresolved dispute before the PRTB. The PRTB maintained its view that a complaint made on the issue of the effect of s.86 was trivial or vexatious. Accordingly, pursuant to s.84(1)(d) of the RTA 2004, it served a notice on the tenants informing them of its decision not to deal with the tenants' application for dispute resolution services. One of the tenants appealed this decision of the PRTB to the Circuit Court pursuant to s.84(5) of the RTA 2004.[91]

In *McAlister v Private Residential Tenancies Board*[92] the tenant argued before the Circuit Court that the matter of whether a notice of termination could be served when another dispute was before the PRTB, was at least arguable and consequently could not be "trivial or vexatious". She submitted that it was not clear from s.86(1) of the RTA 2004, whether a notice of termination could be served when a matter was before the PRTB.[93] The tenant also relied on s.62(1)(f) of the RTA 2004, which provides that a notice of termination must specify a termination date. She submitted that if a dispute was before the PRTB, no *certain* termination date could be specified. The PRTB on the other hand argued that s.86(1) of the RTA 2004 was clear. It provided for circumstances where the

---

90   The PRTB's decision not to deal with the tenants' second application on the basis of s.84(1)(d) of the RTA 2004, is also recorded in the tenancy tribunal report in the matter of *Lonergan v McAlister and Anor* (TR31/DR742/2006, May 10, 2006).

91   See tenancy tribunal report in the matter of *Lonergan v McAlister and Anor* (TR31/DR742/2006, May 10, 2006). See also paras 9–34 to 9–35 on appeals to the Circuit Court under s.84(5).

92   Unreported, Circuit Court, ex tempore, Linnane J., March 30, 2006.

93   In support of this submission the tenant also relied upon s.58(2) of the RTA 2004. Section 58(2) provides that the termination of a tenancy by a landlord must be "*effected* by means of a notice of termination that complies with this Part" (emphasis added). The tenant argued that in light of s.58(2) of the RTA 2004, the meaning of "effected" in s.86(1)(c) of the RTA 2004 was not entirely unambiguous.

termination of a tenancy may not be *effected* when a dispute relating to the tenancy was before the PRTB, however, this did not prohibit the service of a notice of termination.[94] In response to the tenant's contention made in relation to s.62(f), the PRTB submitted that the termination date is calculated by reference to the notice periods required pursuant to s.66 of the RTA 2004. In an ex tempore judgment, Linnane J. dismissed the tenant's application and upheld the PRTB's decision that the matter referred to it was trivial or vexatious.

B. Procedure where Application Refused

(i) Before the PRTB

9–34 Where the PRTB is of the opinion that a dispute referred to it falls within any of the categories described at paras 9–29 to 9–32 above,[95] the PRTB must serve a notice on the applicant informing him or her of the PRTB's opinion. The notice must also state that the PRTB shall not deal with the dispute, unless the applicant is in a position to establish that the PRTB's opinion is not well founded.[96] The applicant will then be afforded an opportunity to make submissions to the PRTB to establish his or her case.[97] The RTA 2004 does not prescribe any particular procedure for the making of submissions in this situation, other than that they are to be made within the period stated in the notice served by the PRTB.[98] It is also clear from s.84(4) of the RTA 2004 that submissions may be made in writing or orally.

Having considered the applicant's submissions, if the PRTB is satisfied that it does have a right to refuse to deal with the dispute by reason of s.84(1), it shall inform the applicant of this and shall not process the dispute. If on the other hand, it considers that its initial decision to refuse to deal with the dispute was not in fact well founded, it must proceed to process the application. In these circumstances, the PRTB must notify the other party to the dispute of this decision. On the request of that other party, the PRTB must furnish to him or her a copy of the submissions made by the applicant party. Where the submissions made by the applicant are not in writing, a written summary of the submissions must be prepared by the PRTB.[99]

Both the applicant and the respondent party to an application for dispute resolution services made to the PRTB, has the right to appeal the PRTB's decision to deal with or refuse to deal with the matter, on the basis of any of the

---

[94] This issue was later considered in the High Court in *Canty v Private Residential Tenancies Board* [2007] IEHC 243. See paras 9–108 to 9–109.

[95] RTA 2004, s.84(1)(a)–(d).

[96] RTA 2004, s.84(1).

[97] RTA 2004, s.84(2).

[98] RTA 2004, s.84(2). Procedural rules may, however, be adopted by the PRTB under s.109 of the RTA 2004 to prescribe an appropriate procedure.

[99] RTA 2004, s.84(4).

grounds listed in s.84(1). This right of appeal is to the Circuit Court and is permitted by s.84(5) of the RTA 2004.

(ii) Before the Circuit Court

9–35 An appeal brought under s.84(5) of the RTA 2004 must be made in accordance with the Ord.51A r.1A of the Circuit Court Rules 2001.[100] An appeal must be made within 21 days of the date of issue of the PRTB's decision to deal or not to deal with a dispute in response to the submissions made to it by either the applicant or respondent party.[101] The appeal must be brought in the County in which the tenancy or dwelling is or was situate and must be made by way of notice of motion and grounding affidavit.[102] The notice of motion must be in accordance with Form 44A of the schedule of forms to the Circuit Court Rules 2001, a copy of which is attached at Appendix 17. The person appealing the PRTB's decision under s.84(5) shall be the plaintiff and both the PRTB and the other party to the dispute must be joined as the defendants.[103] The notice of motion must be served no later than 14 days prior to the return date assigned to it by the Circuit Court office.[104]

As referred to at para.9–33 an appeal was made to the Circuit Court under s.84(5) of the RTA 2004 in the matter of *McAlister v Private Residential Tenancies Board*.[105] Linnane J. upheld the PRTB's decision to refuse to deal with the dispute on the grounds that it was trivial or vexatious.

7. Pre-Conditions to the Referral of a Dispute

9–36 The RTA 2004 prescribes certain pre-conditions that must be satisfied before a party may refer a dispute to the PRTB. If the party does not satisfy these

---

[100] The Circuit Court Rules (Residential Tenancies) 2006 (S.I. No. 410 of 2006), amended the Circuit Court Rules (Residential Tenancies Act 2004) 2005 (S.I. No. 388 of 2005) by inserting rules dealing with the procedure that must be followed in an application made pursuant to s.84(5) and s.88(4) of the RTA 2004.

[101] Procedural Rules 2009, para.5. (Order 51A r.1A.(1) of the Circuit Court Rules provides that the notice of motion must issue within such period as may be specified in rules made by the PRTB in accordance with s.109 of the RTA 2004).

[102] Circuit Court Rules 2001, Ord.51A r.1A(1) and (2).

[103] Circuit Court Rules 2001, Ord.51A r.1A(1).

[104] Circuit Court Rules 2001, Ord.51A r.1A(3). See also Ord.51A r.1A(4) and (5), which provide respectively that the notice of motion is to be issued and filed by the plaintiff in the appropriate Circuit Court office no later than 21 days before the commencement of the sittings at which it is intended that the action shall be listed for hearing, except in the case of Dublin Circuit, where the notice of motion is to be issued and filed by the plaintiff no later than 21 days from the date upon which it is intended that the action shall be listed for hearing.

[105] Unreported, Circuit Court, ex tempore, Linnane J., March 30, 2006.

pre-conditions, the PRTB is not permitted to deal with the dispute, notwith-standing that the application may otherwise fall within its jurisdiction.[106]

A. Fee for Application not Paid

9–37 There is a fee payable for the PRTB's dispute resolution services, which must accompany the application form.[107] The PRTB has no jurisdiction to deal with a dispute where the application fee has not been paid.[108] The PRTB does have a discretion, however, to afford the party who referred the dispute a reasonable opportunity to make the payment. If the party does pay the application fee within a reasonable time, the PRTB shall proceed to deal with his or her application.[109]

B. Unregistered Tenancy

9–38 The PRTB has no jurisdiction to deal with an application for dispute resolution services made to it by a *landlord*, if the tenancy concerned is not registered in accordance with Pt 7 of the RTA 2004.[110] This limitation on the PRTB's jurisdiction applies only to applications made by landlords because it is a landlord's (and not a tenant's) obligation to register a tenancy.[111] Where a tenancy has not been registered, the PRTB may afford the landlord a reasonable opportunity to register the tenancy and if the landlord does so within a reasonable time, the PRTB shall then proceed to process the dispute.[112]

9–39 Prior to the amendment of s.135 of the RTA 2004 by the Housing (Miscellaneous Provisions) Act 2009 (the "Housing Act 2009"),[113] it was possible for tenants to easily disrupt the dispute resolution process, where a landlord only took steps to register the tenancy at the time a dispute arose with

---

[106] Section 84(1)(c) of the RTA 2004 prescribes that a dispute will also be considered as falling outside of the jurisdiction of the PRTB, where a person has failed to comply with any condition that must be satisfied before the PRTB is permitted to deal with their complaint.

[107] The PRTB's website (*www.prtb.ie*) provides up to date details of the application fee that must be paid.

[108] RTA 2004, s.83(1).

[109] RTA 2004, s.83(3). No guidance is given in s.83(3) as to what is considered a "reasonable opportunity" or "a reasonable time" to pay the application fee. The applicant would, however, at least be required to act promptly and to pay the application fee as soon as possible.

[110] RTA 2004, s.83(2).

[111] RTA 2004, s.134(1).

[112] RTA 2004, s.83(3). Again, no guidance is given in s.83(3) as to what is considered a "reasonable opportunity" or "a reasonable time" to register the tenancy. At a minimum this would at least have to take into account the time it takes the PRTB to process an application for the registration of a tenancy of a dwelling.

[113] Housing Act 2009, s.100(4).

the tenant. Section 135(2) had required as a condition of registration that the tenant sign the application form for registration known as the Form PRTB1.[114] In a number of cases tenants thwarted the registration process by refusing to sign the Form PRTB1. As the tenancy could not be registered without the tenant's signature and the landlord could not refer a dispute to the PRTB unless the tenancy was registered, the result was that the landlord was left without a remedy under the RTA 2004. This was of particular detriment to a landlord where the tenant remained in occupation of the dwelling without paying rent. Section 100(4) of the Housing Act 2009 deleted s.135(2) of the RTA 2004, which had required a tenant's signature on the Form PRTB1 as a pre-condition to the registration of a tenancy.

Although tenants are no longer in a position to easily hinder registration and consequently the dispute resolution process, where a landlord fails to register a tenancy within one month of its commencement, he or she will be in breach of his or her obligations under the RTA 2004. The landlord will also be required to pay the higher registration fee applicable to tenancies which are not registered on time.[115]

C. Alternative Remedy Pursued

9–40 A person may not make an application for dispute resolution services to the PRTB, where he or she has taken any steps to avail of an alternative remedy.[116] (For ease of reference in this paragraph we shall presume a tenant has availed of an alternative remedy). If, however, the other party to the dispute (say the landlord) makes an application for dispute resolution services to the PRTB, in so far as the landlord's application relates to the tenant's dispute for which the alternative remedy is being pursued, the PRTB may take into account[117] the existence of that alternative remedy in determining the relief that should be granted to the landlord.[118] To the extent, however, that a legally enforceable remedy of the issues in dispute in the tenant's case has actually been granted through the alternative forum, the principle of res judicata would require the PRTB to have regard to that remedy and it would be prohibited from determining the issues in the landlord's case, to the extent that they had already been determined by the alternative forum.[119]

9–41 Since the commencement of Pt 6 of the RTA 2004, the alternative remedies available for resolving disputes relating to residential tenancies in the

---

[114]   See para.10–07.
[115]   See Ch.10 on Registration of Tenancies.
[116]   RTA 2004, s.91(1).
[117]   To the extent it is considered just (see RTA 2004, s.91(2)).
[118]   RTA 2004, s.91(2).
[119]   Presuming of course the alternative forum is one recognised by law and its decisions are legally enforceable.

private sector are limited.[120] This is because the RTA 2004 gives the PRTB jurisdiction to deal with the majority of landlord and tenant disputes and limits the extent to which such disputes can be the subject of court proceedings.[121] Further, the PRTB's jurisdiction cannot be ousted in circumstances where a tenancy agreement contains a provision that the parties are to arbitrate in the event of a dispute.[122] The one exception to this arises where the tenant *at* or *after* the time the dispute arises, consents to the dispute being referred to arbitration.[123]

D. Termination of Tenancies and Sub-Tenancies

9–42 The PRTB has no jurisdiction to deal with certain disputes referred to it by a head-tenant or sub-tenant in relation to the termination of their respective tenancies, where s.81 of the RTA 2004 applies and the head-tenant or sub-tenant has not satisfied the pre-conditions contained in that section. Section 81 applies in circumstances where:

- a landlord in terminating a tenancy that has been sub-let, requires the head-tenant to terminate the sub-tenancy[124]; and
- the head-tenant intends to refer a dispute to the PRTB about the termination of the head-tenancy.

Where a landlord in terminating the head-tenancy also requires the sub-tenancy to be terminated, the head-tenant must serve a notice of termination on the sub-tenant[125] (which is in addition to the copy of the landlord's notice of termination

---

[120] Note that s.89 of the RTA 2004 provides that any dispute that had been the subject of proceedings instituted in any court before the commencement of Pt 6 and which were discontinued by agreement of the parties after the commencement of Pt 6 but before the court made its final determination, may be the subject of a reference to the PRTB. As Pt 6 commenced on December 6, 2004, there will be limited circumstances in which s.89 is now likely to have application.

[121] Section 182 of the RTA 2004 provides that where a dispute falls within the jurisdiction of the PRTB it cannot (except in limited circumstances) be the subject of court proceedings. See para.9–43.

[122] RTA 2004, s.90(1). Section 90(1) also provides that no enactment will operate to preclude the PRTB's jurisdiction because of an arbitration agreement. For the purposes of s.90 "arbitration agreement" has the same meaning as it has in the Arbitration Act 1954 (RTA 2004, s.90(2)).

[123] RTA 2004, s.90(1). Section 90(1) is silent on a situation that may arise where the tenant wishes the dispute to be resolved by arbitration but the landlord wishes to submit the matter to the PRTB for dispute resolution services. As s.90 speaks in terms of the tenant's "consent", it seems that the provision was drafted to envisage a situation where the landlord seeks to rely on the arbitration clause (as opposed to the tenant) and is therefore required to obtain the tenant's consent.

[124] See paras 8–111 to 8–114 which deals with the conditions that a landlord must comply with when terminating a tenancy where the tenancy has been sub-let and also the obligations of the head-tenant in these circumstances.

[125] See para.8–113.

that must also be served on the sub-tenant).[126] Where the head-tenant intends to refer a dispute to the PRTB about the termination of the head-tenancy, the head-tenant must include a statement in the notice of termination that he or she serves on the sub-tenant. This statement is that the sub-tenant must inform the head-tenant within 10 days of receipt of the notice of termination, whether the sub-tenant also intends to refer a dispute about the termination of the tenancy to the PRTB.[127] The head-tenant may not refer his or her dispute to the PRTB until 15 days have elapsed from service of the head-tenant's notice of termination on the sub-tenant.[128]

If the head-tenant or sub-tenant do not comply with their respective obligations outlined above, they have no right to refer a dispute concerning the termination of the tenancy to the PRTB. Accordingly, if the head-tenant does not state in the notice of termination that the sub-tenant must inform him or her whether the sub-tenant also intends to refer a dispute to the PRTB, the head-tenant is not permitted to make an application for dispute resolution services to the PRTB concerning the termination of the tenancy.[129] Similarly, if the sub-tenant does not inform the head-tenant whether he or she intends to refer a dispute to the PRTB in relation to the termination of the tenancy (within 10 days from the receipt of the head-tenant's notice of termination), the sub-tenant will also be prohibited from making an application for dispute resolution services to the PRTB relating to the termination of tenancy.[130]

8. MONETARY JURISDICTION

9–43 A dispute falling within the PRTB's jurisdiction may not be the subject of court proceedings.[131] There is, however, one exception to this which arises where one or more of the following reliefs is claimed in the proceedings:

(a) damages of more than €20,000[132];
(b) the recovery of arrears of rent or other charges is in excess of €20,000 or twice the annual rent, whichever is greater and in all cases where such a claim exceeds €60,000.[133]

---

[126] RTA 2004, s.70(3). See also para.8–112.
[127] RTA 2004, s.81(2) and (3).
[128] RTA 2004, s.81(5)(b).
[129] RTA 2004, s.81(5)(a).
[130] RTA 2004, s.81(4).
[131] Section 182 of the RTA 2004 is an important section to be considered to determine the appropriate remedy and forum for obtaining a remedy for certain disputes. The provisions of s.182, however, are curiously not included in Pt 6 of the RTA 2004, which deals with "Dispute Resolution" but in Pt 9 which is titled "Miscellaneous".
[132] RTA 2004, s.182(1)(a).
[133] RTA 2004, s.182(1)(b).

If a party's claim for damages or rent or other charges exceed these amounts, that party may institute proceedings before the courts to recover the damages or losses that the party claims to have suffered. As each of these amounts exceed the District Court's jurisdiction, the appropriate forum will be the Circuit Court or the High Court depending on the amounts claimed.

9–44 Section 182 of the RTA 2004 imposes the monetary limits as described at para.9–43 above, which must be exceeded before a dispute may be the subject of court proceedings. Section 182 does not, however, explicitly state that where such reliefs are claimed, a party is precluded from referring a dispute to the PRTB but rather s.182 provides that the dispute may be the subject of court proceedings. That said, if a dispute is referred to the PRTB and a party seeks the recovery of damages and/or rent or other charges in excess of the amounts referred to in s.182, the PRTB will have no jurisdiction to make an award for the full amount claimed. This is because the PRTB's jurisdiction to award damages and/or rent or other charges is limited to the amounts prescribed by s.115(3) of the RTA 2004, which reflect the amounts contained in s.182. Section 115(3) provides that an award made by the PRTB shall not exceed €20,000 in damages or for a claim for arrears of rent or other charges, an amount in excess of €20,000 or twice the annual rent (whichever is higher) but subject to a maximum award of €60,000. Therefore, if a party has a claim that exceeds these limits and he or she wishes to recover the full amount, the party will be required to institute court proceedings. If a party does, however, wish to refer a dispute to the PRTB, there is nothing to stop the party waiving the amount of his or her claim that exceeds the PRTB's jurisdiction.

9. Time Limits for the Referral of Particular Disputes

A. Time Limits Prescribed

9–45 There are a number of time limits imposed by the RTA 2004, for the referral of particular disputes to the PRTB. A party who is referring a matter to the PRTB should consider whether these time limits apply to his or her dispute. The specific time limits imposed by the RTA 2004 are dealt with at paras 9–46 to 9–49 below. In all other cases the Statute of Limitations will apply.[134]

(i) Rent increase

9–46 A dispute relating to a new rent being set by a landlord must be referred to the PRTB before:

---

[134] See para.9–31.

(a) the date from which the new rent is to have effect; or
(b) the expiry of 28 days from receipt by the tenant of the notice informing him or her of the new rent,

whichever date occurs later.[135] These time limits are only imposed where a landlord has complied with the procedure for setting a new rent as required by s.22 of the RTA 2004. This procedure is considered in detail at para.6–12 but in summary it requires a landlord to serve a notice on the tenant 28 days before the date from which the new rent is to have effect, informing him or her of the new rent and the date from which it will begin to be payable. If the landlord does not follow this procedure and fails to serve such a notice on the tenant and/or fails to give the tenant 28 days notice of the new rent, the time limits for the referral of a dispute as set out at (a) and (b) above will not apply.

(ii) Rent dispute following termination of a tenancy

9–47 If a tenancy has been terminated and the former tenant wishes to refer a dispute to the PRTB in relation to the amount of rent that had been agreed to or was paid by the former tenant, he or she must do so within 28 days from the termination of the tenancy.[136]

(iii) Notice of termination

9–48 A dispute relating to the validity of a notice of termination which has been served or purported to be served may not be referred to the PRTB at any time after 28 days has elapsed from the date of receipt of that notice.[137]

(iv) Deceased persons

9–49 A personal representative of a deceased landlord or tenant may refer a dispute to the PRTB relating to the recovery of rent or other charges and in relation to any other matter, if it is a cause of action within the meaning of the Civil Liability Act, which would have survived for the benefit of or against the estate of the deceased landlord or tenant.[138]

The time limits imposed by the RTA 2004, or if there are no such time limits, the Statute of Limitations, will apply with regard to a cause of action vested in a person on their death that survives for the *benefit* of his or her estate and which is a claim that falls within the PRTB's jurisdiction. A claim made *against* a deceased person's estate however, shall not be maintainable unless either:

---

[135] RTA 2004, s.22(3).
[136] RTA 2004, s.76(2).
[137] RTA 2004, s.80. It is presumed that the reference to "purported to be served", is a reference (at least) to circumstances where the service of a notice of termination may not have been effected in accordance with s.6 of the RTA 2004.
[138] RTA 2004, s.75(4)(b) and (c). See paras 9–25 to 9–27.

(a) the proceedings against the deceased landlord or tenant were commenced within the period prescribed by the RTA 2004 or the Statute of Limitations (whichever applies in the circumstances)[139] and the proceedings were pending at the date of the landlord's or tenant's death[140]; or

(b) the proceedings are commenced within the period prescribed by the RTA 2004 or the Statute of Limitations (whichever applies in the circumstances) or within two years after the date of the death of the landlord or tenant, whichever period expires first.[141]

B. Extension of Time Limits

(i) At the discretion of PRTB

9–50 The PRTB may extend any time limit imposed by the RTA 2004, for the referral of a dispute to it for resolution.[142] The PRTB is empowered to do so by s.88 of the RTA 2004. The party seeking the extension must make an application to the PRTB explaining why the extension is required.[143] The PRTB shall not grant an extension unless the applicant has shown "good grounds" for why the time should be extended.[144]

The PRTB may also extend any time limit imposed by the RTA 2004, for fulfilling a condition precedent that must be satisfied before a dispute can be referred to the PRTB.[145] There are few circumstances where this applies in practice. One example arises in the context of the pre-conditions imposed on head-tenants and sub-tenants by s.81 of the RTA 2004, for the referral of a dispute to the PRTB.[146] Section 81 applies where a landlord seeks to terminate a tenancy and the landlord also requires the head-tenant to terminate a sub-tenancy that was granted by the head-tenant. In these circumstances, the head-tenant must serve a notice of termination on the sub-tenant and if the head-tenant intends to refer a dispute to the PRTB in relation to the termination of the tenancy, he or she must include a statement in the sub-tenant's notice of termination. This statement is that the sub-tenant must inform the head-tenant within 10 days of receipt of the notice of termination, whether the sub-tenant also intends to refer a dispute about the termination of the tenancy to the PRTB. If the sub-tenant fails to inform the head-tenant that he or she intends to refer a dispute to the PRTB within 10 days, the sub-tenant is not permitted to make an

---

[139] See paras 9–45 to 9–48 above.

[140] Civil Liability Act, s.9(2)(a).

[141] Civil Liability Act, s.9(2)(b).

[142] RTA 2004, s.88(1). This discretion relates only to time limits imposed by the RTA 2004 for the referral of disputes to it and does not extend to any time limits imposed by other enactments including the Statute of Limitations (RTA 2004, s.88(1)).

[143] RTA 2004, s.88(1).

[144] RTA 2004, s.88(2).

[145] RTA 2004, s.88(3).

[146] See para.8–113 that considers s.81 of the RTA 2004 in further detail.

application for dispute resolution services to the PRTB.[147] The sub-tenant may, however, rely on the provisions of s.88 for the purposes of seeking an extension to that 10-day time limit.

9–51 Section 88 applies only to the time limits imposed for *referring* a dispute to the PRTB or to the time limits imposed for fulfilling a condition precedent that is required to be satisfied before a dispute is referred.[148] Section 88 has no application in respect of any other time limits imposed throughout the dispute resolution process under Pt 6. Accordingly, where an application for dispute resolution services has been accepted and is being processed by the PRTB, a party cannot rely on s.88 to seek to extend a time limit that applies during the dispute resolution process itself. For instance, s.88 will have no application where a party who wishes to appeal a determination of an adjudicator, fails to do so within 21 days from the date the PRTB serves the adjudicator's report on that party.[149]

(ii) Right of appeal where extension granted or refused

9–52 The decision of the PRTB to grant or refuse to grant an extension of time for the referral of a dispute to it, may be appealed to the Circuit Court pursuant to s.88(4) of the RTA 2004. Further, a decision by the PRTB to grant or refuse to grant an extension of time to fulfil a condition precedent for the referral of a dispute, may also be appealed to the Circuit Court. An appeal under s.88(4) must be made in accordance with the Circuit Court Rules 2001.[150] The appeal must be brought in the County in which the tenancy or dwelling is or was situate and must be made by way of notice of motion and grounding affidavit.[151] The notice of motion must be in accordance with Form 44B of the schedule of forms to the Circuit Court Rules 2001,[152] a copy of which is attached at Appendix 18. An appeal of a decision of the PRTB to grant or not to grant an extension of time under s.88 must be made within 21 days of the date of issue of the PRTB's decision.[153] The person appealing the PRTB's decision pursuant to s.88(4) shall be the plaintiff and both the PRTB and the other party to the dispute must be joined as the defendants.[154] The notice of motion must be served no later than 14 days prior to the return date assigned to it by the Circuit Court office.[155]

---

[147] RTA 2004, s.81(4).
[148] RTA 2004, s.88(1) and (3). See also s.88 of the Explanatory Memorandum to the RTA 2004, which makes clear that s.88 only empowers the PRTB to extend time limits imposed by the RTA 2004 for referring disputes to it.
[149] RTA 2004, s.100. See para.9–76.
[150] Order 51A. See also fn.100 at para.9–35 above.
[151] Order 51A r.1A.(1) and (2).
[152] Form 44B was inserted into the schedule of forms annexed to the Circuit Court Rules 2001, by the Circuit Court Rules (Residential Tenancies) 2006 (S.I. No. 410 of 2006).
[153] Procedural Rules 2009, para.4. (Order 51A r.1A.(1) provides that the notice of motion must issue within such period as may be specified in rules adopted by the PRTB under s.109 of the RTA 2004).
[154] Order 51A r.1A.(1).
[155] Order 51A r.1A.(3). See also Ord.51A r.1A.(4) and (5), which provide respectively that the

9–53 In *O'Connor v Private Residential Tenancies Board*[156] the applicant (a landlord) instituted judicial review proceedings against the PRTB seeking orders of certiorari, including in relation to a decision of the PRTB to allow the notice party (a tenant) an extension of time to make a complaint. The PRTB had submitted that the High Court should refuse the application before it on the grounds that the applicant should have used an alternative remedy to judicial review, including the appeal process under s.88(4) of the RTA 2004. Although the High Court determined the application before it on other grounds, Hedigan J. stated that:

> "It is clear that the applicant had the opportunity to appeal the [PRTB's] decision to extend the time for the notice party to bring his application to it. He did not avail of this when he became aware of it ... In short he had an adequate remedy and did not avail of it".[157]

Accordingly, where a party is aggrieved by a decision of the PRTB to grant (or to refuse to grant) an extension of time within which to make an application for dispute resolution services, the appropriate remedy for the aggrieved party is to appeal the PRTB's decision to the Circuit Court pursuant to s.88(4) of the RTA 2004.

10. The Dispute Resolution Process

A. Preliminary Steps

9–54 Once a dispute is referred to the PRTB, it may (but is not obliged to) communicate with the applicant and respondent parties to ensure that they are fully aware of the issues the subject of the application.[158] Where the PRTB considers the dispute is due to some basic misunderstanding between the parties as to the rights or obligations of landlords and tenants, it may communicate with the parties with a view to resolving the issues between them by agreement at the earliest possible stage, without the need for recourse to the full mechanisms of the dispute resolution process before the PRTB.[159]

In relation to the preliminary communications that may be made by the PRTB to the applicant and respondent parties, the RTA 2004 provides:

---

notice of motion is to be issued and filed by the plaintiff in the appropriate Circuit Court office no later than 21 days before the commencement of the sittings at which it is intended that the action shall be listed for hearing, except in the case of Dublin Circuit, where the notice of motion is to be issued and filed by the plaintiff no later than 21 days from the date upon which it is intended that the action shall be listed for hearing.

[156] [2008] IEHC 205; unreported, High Court, Hedigan J., June 25, 2008.
[157] [2008] IEHC 205; unreported, High Court, Hedigan J., June 25, 2008 at p.6.
[158] RTA 2004, s.92(1)(a).
[159] RTA 2004, s.92(1)(b) and (2).

(a) where it would be of assistance to the parties, the PRTB may provide them with an indication of the typical determination before the PRTB, of the issues that are in dispute between them. This indication must be based on appropriate assumptions which must be stated by the PRTB to the parties[160];

(b) any such indication must be communicated equally to both parties[161]; and

(c) in its communications the PRTB is obliged to bear in mind the right of the parties to invoke all the procedures under Part 6 of the RTA 2004.[162]

In more complex cases, it is likely to be difficult for the PRTB to indicate a "typical outcome" of certain issues based on appropriate assumptions in the preliminary stages. However, the fact that the PRTB may communicate with the parties in the early stages, embodies the informal nature of the dispute resolution process and reflects one of the purposes of the PRTB, that being to facilitate the cheap and speedy resolution of disputes between landlords and tenants.[163]

B. Forums for Dispute Resolution

(i) Overview

9–55 There are three alternative forums that facilitate dispute resolution before the PRTB:

(a) mediation;
(b) adjudication; and
(c) tenancy tribunal.

The PRTB generally operates its dispute resolution service in two stages. Stage 1 consists of the parties engaging in either mediation or adjudication. In the event that mediation is not successful or an appeal of an adjudicator's decision is made, the dispute resolution process will move to stage 2 which is a hearing by a tenancy tribunal. There are certain circumstances, usually involving more urgent cases, where a matter may be heard at first instance by a tenancy tribunal.[164] Mediation, adjudication and tenancy tribunals are considered in turn at paras 9–61 to 9–90.

---

[160] RTA 2004, s.92(3).
[161] RTA 2004, s.92(4). Adherence to this requirement is of particular importance, to avoid any prejudice that may otherwise arise.
[162] RTA 2004, s.92(4), which curiously does not require the PRTB to communicate this fact to the parties.
[163] See the long title to the RTA 2004.
[164] RTA 2004, s.104(1)(a). See para.9–78.

C. Issues Common to Mediation, Adjudication and Tenancy Tribunals

(i) Documents submitted copied to other parties

9–56 Documents submitted with an application form for dispute resolution will be copied to the other party to the dispute.[165] The PRTB will also circulate to the applicant or the respondent any other papers submitted by either of them in advance of the hearing date. The adjudicator, mediator or tenancy tribunal as appropriate will be provided with copies of any such documents. The Procedural Rules 2009 place the burden on the party submitting the documents, to take any steps necessary to protect sensitive information the documents may contain. For example, this may require the party to mask the sensitive information or to obtain any consent necessary from third parties for the disclosure of particular information.[166] PRTB management may specify and the adjudicator, mediator or tenancy tribunal may enforce, certain deadlines to be complied with by parties in submitting documentation for consideration at PRTB hearings or at a paper-based adjudication.[167]

(ii) Adjournments

9–57 The general practice of the PRTB is not to grant adjournments of a mediation, adjudication or tenancy tribunal hearing, unless there is special reason for doing so.[168] The Procedural Rules 2009 provide that applications by parties prior to a hearing, to adjourn or defer a mediation, adjudication or a tenancy tribunal hearing to another date, may only be considered in "very limited circumstances".[169] The party applying for the adjournment may be required to provide vouching documentation to "verify substantive reasons" for their non-availability on the scheduled hearing date.[170]

9–58 In *O'Shea v Plunkett*,[171] a tenancy tribunal hearing convened with less than one week's notice to the parties,[172] was adjourned following an application made by the tenant. She had applied for an adjournment on the grounds that she

---

[165] The current version of the application form for dispute resolution services in use at the time of publication, indicates that the documents submitted with it, will be copied to the other party.

[166] Procedural Rules 2009, para.10.

[167] Procedural Rules 2009, para.11.

[168] Section 107 of the RTA 2004 specifically empowers tenancy tribunals to grant adjournments. The RTA 2004 does not contain a similar provision in respect of mediation or adjudication. Also, note also that para.7 of the Procedural Rules 2009 provides that instead of seeking to adjourn a matter, the parties may alternatively nominate a representative to attend a hearing in their place and/or submit a written statement for consideration by the adjudicator/mediator at the hearing (no reference is made to a tenancy tribunal in the latter context).

[169] Procedural Rules 2009, para.7. In relation to tenancy tribunals, see also RTA 2004, s.104(4)(e).

[170] Procedural Rules 2009, para.7.

[171] TR101/DR963/2007, September 3, 2007.

[172] See para.9–81 that considers the circumstances where a tenancy tribunal hearing may be convened with less than 21 days notice.

had a hospital appointment for the ongoing treatment of an illness on the day of the hearing. In addition, she said that she felt intimidated by the number of people who attended at the hearing on behalf of the landlord and that she wanted to obtain assistance for the purposes of the hearing, either from a solicitor or Threshold. The landlord on the other hand submitted that he was extremely concerned at any delay to the hearing of his application because he considered there to be a serious danger to the welfare and safety of himself, his family and other tenants in occupation of the premises in which the flat rented by the tenant was situated. Having considered the submissions of both parties the tenancy tribunal granted an adjournment of the hearing but to the following day only.

(iii) Inspection of dwellings

9–59 A mediator, an adjudicator, a member of a tenancy tribunal or the PRTB, may inspect the dwelling to which an application for dispute resolution services relates. Twenty four hours notice of an inspection must be given to a person who is in occupation of the dwelling but not involved in the dispute resolution process. The mediator, adjudicator, tenancy tribunal or the PRTB may authorise a person with particular expertise relevant to the dispute to inspect the dwelling (for example an engineer, valuer or surveyor). A person who obstructs or impedes an inspection is guilty of an offence.[173]

(iv) Certain proceedings and Acts privileged

9–60 Any report or other document prepared or communication made by a mediator, adjudicator, tenancy tribunal or the PRTB in connection with proceedings that are being dealt with under Pt 6, enjoy absolute privilege for the purposes of the law of defamation.[174] Any report, document or communication made in connection with the performance of the functions of a mediator, adjudicator, tenancy tribunal or the PRTB under the RTA 2004 generally (but which are not connected to an actual proceeding before it), enjoy qualified privilege.[175]

11. Mediation

A. Invitation to Mediate

9–61 The parties to a dispute submitted to the PRTB for resolution, shall first be invited by the PRTB to resolve the matter through mediation.[176] The PRTB

---

[173] RTA 2004, s.111.
[174] RTA 2004, s.114(1).
[175] RTA 2004, s.114(2).
[176] RTA 2004, s.93(1). Only a small number of applicants in dispute cases referred to the PRTB

currently uses the application form for dispute resolution services to ascertain whether the party submitting the complaint is willing to enter the mediation process. The form contains a section requesting the referring party to confirm the type of dispute resolution service sought (either mediation or adjudication) and where the party wishes to mediate, he or she must sign an agreement to mediation. All parties must consent to engaging in mediation for this process to proceed. Accordingly, if a party to the dispute does not agree to engage in mediation or fails to respond to a request made by the PRTB in relation to whether he or she wishes to mediate, the matter will be referred to adjudication by the PRTB.[177] The adjudication process is dealt with at paras 9–69 to 9–77 below.

9–62 There are two instances where the PRTB is not obliged to invite the parties to mediate at first instance. These arise where:

(a) An application for interim or interlocutory relief in aid of the dispute resolution process has been made by the PRTB to the Circuit Court under s.189 of the RTA 2004[178]; or

(b) The PRTB considers that in the circumstances of the case, it would be more appropriate for the matter to be referred directly to a tenancy tribunal for determination.[179]

In the circumstances as described at (a) above, where an application has been made for interim or interlocutory relief under s.189, the PRTB may arrange for the full hearing of the matter to be dealt by an adjudicator or a tenancy tribunal. In relation to the scenario at (b), a common example of the type of dispute which is often deemed appropriate for a direct referral to a tenancy tribunal is cases involving allegations of serious antisocial behaviour.

B. The Mediation Process

(i) *The mediation*

9–63 Where the parties to a dispute elect to mediate, a mediator will be appointed by the PRTB from its panel of mediators.[180] The PRTB shall inform

---

choose to avail of mediation. The preliminary results of the review of the RTA 2004 that were announced by the Minister for Housing and Local Services, identified as one of the main issues to be addressed in proposed amending legislation, was the introduction of measures that would encourage the greater use of mediation as a means of settling disputes. See Press Release, "Minister Michael Finneran announces significant changes to Private Residential Tenancies Board (PRTB) legislation", November 4, 2009, *www.environ.ie*.

[177] RTA 2004, s.93(3).
[178] RTA 2004, s.94(a). See paras 9–111 to 9–117 that considers the section 189 process.
[179] RTA 2004, s.94(b).
[180] RTA 2004, s.93(2). See also s.164 of the RTA 2004 which deals with the appointment of mediators and their terms and conditions of appointment.

the parties of the date on which the mediation shall take place. A mediation will not be deferred to another date at the request of a party, except in very limited circumstances.[181] During the mediation, the mediator will inquire fully into the relevant aspects of the dispute, with the objective of having the issue or issues between the parties resolved by agreement. In aid of this process, the mediator may provide to and receive from each party such information as he or she believes appropriate.[182] The mediation process is confidential[183] and while the conduct of the mediation will generally be at the discretion of the mediator, he or she is obliged to ensure the mediation is conducted without undue formality.[184] This reflects the informal first stage of the dispute resolution process envisaged by the Commission in its report.[185]

(ii) Procedure after mediation

9–64 After a mediation has concluded, the mediator must prepare a report which will include a summary of the matters (if any) agreed between the parties. If agreement on certain issues is reached at mediation, the summary of these matters must be set out in a document and signed by the parties.[186] Once the mediator has prepared a report the mediator must furnish a copy of the report to the Director of the PRTB.[187] The Director in turn then provides to the PRTB, the document setting out the matters agreed between the parties or if no agreement has been reached, a statement to that effect.[188] The complete mediator's report is not furnished to the PRTB on foot of the confidential nature of the mediation process.[189]

9–65 Following receipt by the PRTB of a document from the Director that sets out the terms of an agreement, the PRTB shall serve that document on each of the parties to the dispute, together with a notice asking the parties to confirm

---

[181] See para.9–57.

[182] RTA 2004, s.95(2) and (3). See also para.9–56 that deals with the circulation by the PRTB of documents submitted by the parties to a dispute in advance of mediation or an adjudication or tenancy tribunal hearing.

[183] See also ss.101(1)(c) and 112 of the RTA 2004. These provisions impose obligations of confidentiality on mediators with respect to the mediation, statements or information received by the mediator during this process and the report prepared by the mediator. These provisions also deal with the limited circumstances where disclosure of such confidential information can be made.

[184] RTA 2004, s.101(4). The manner in which a mediation is conducted by a mediator, is subject to any procedural rules that may be adopted by the PRTB under s.109 of the RTA 2004.

[185] Report of the Commission, para.8.4.3.2.

[186] RTA 2004, s.95(4).

[187] RTA 2004, s.95(5).

[188] RTA 2004, s.95(6).

[189] See s.95 of the Explanatory Memorandum to the RTA 2004. Further if the mediation is not successful the matter shall, at the request of the parties, be referred to a tenancy tribunal hearing. Tenancy tribunals are constituted from members of the dispute resolution committee, some of whom are also members of the PRTB (see para.9–79).

within 21 days from receipt of the notice whether the agreement still exists.[190] In the alternative, if the PRTB receives a statement from the Director that no agreement was reached, this statement shall instead be served on each of the parties, together with a notice asking the parties to confirm within 21 days from receipt of the notice, if they have reached an agreement since the mediation.[191]

If the PRTB is informed by the parties that an agreement exists between them (either reached at mediation or subsequently), the PRTB shall issue a determination order incorporating the terms of that agreement.[192] Importantly, in circumstances where an agreement was reached at mediation but where one or more of the parties fails to inform the PRTB that the agreement no longer exists or fails to do so within 21 days, the PRTB is still required to issue a determination order incorporating the terms of that agreement.[193] Accordingly, if any agreement reached at mediation subsequently breaks down, the parties must notify the PRTB of this within the 21 days required. If notified after this period, the PRTB's hands are tied and it is obliged to issue a determination order incorporating the terms that had been agreed between the parties.[194]

(iii) Determination orders

9–66 Where the PRTB proceeds to issue a determination order, incorporating an agreement reached between the parties as a result of the mediation process, it must do so no later than 28 days and no earlier than 21 days after the service of the notice on the parties as referred to at para.9–65 above.[195] The PRTB will not issue a determination order if, within that 21 days from the service of the notice, one or more of the parties to the dispute informs the PRTB that an agreement no longer exists between them.[196]

9–67 A determination order resulting from an agreement reached at mediation is binding on the parties when issued and cannot be the subject of an appeal or further consideration before the PRTB.[197]

---

[190] RTA 2004, s.96(1) and s.96(2)(a). Also, see comments at fn.199 at para.9–68 below.

[191] RTA 2004, s.96(1) and s.96(2)(b).

[192] RTA 2004, s.96(3)(a). The determination order must be issued in accordance with s.121 of the RTA 2004. Note, however, that s.121 of the RTA 2004 provides for the making of a determination order in respect of an agreement mentioned in s.95(4), that is an agreement reached at mediation. Section 121 does not deal with the making of a determination order in cases where an agreement was reached between the parties themselves after the mediation (RTA 2004, s.96(2)(b) and 3(a)). That said s.121 is not stated to be an exhaustive list and s.96(3) specifically requires the s.121 procedure to be followed in either case, that is where an agreement was reached at mediation or subsequent to it.

[193] RTA 2004, s.96(3)(b) and s.96(5).

[194] RTA 2004, s.96(5).

[195] RTA 2004, s.96(4).

[196] RTA 2004, s.96(5).

[197] RTA 2004, s.123(1). The RTA 2004 does not specifically deal with the binding nature of a determination order that embodies an agreement that was not reached at mediation but

(iv) Procedure where no agreement reached

9–68 In circumstances where no agreement is reached through the mediation process or where the PRTB is informed (within the 21-day period required) that an agreement that had been reached no longer exists, the next step in the dispute resolution process is for the matter to be referred to a tenancy tribunal for determination.[198] The PRTB shall, however, only convene a tenancy tribunal where it is requested to do so by one or more of the parties to the dispute.[199] If none of the parties request a tenancy tribunal hearing, the PRTB will not process the dispute further.

12. ADJUDICATION

A. When is an Adjudication Convened?

9–69 An application made to the PRTB for dispute resolution services shall be referred directly to an adjudicator for determination if:

    (a) either or both of the parties do not agree to the matter being the subject of mediation or fail to respond to the PRTB's request asking them whether they wish to engage in mediation[200]; or

    (b) an application for interim or interlocutory relief in aid of the dispute resolution process has been made to the Circuit Court pursuant to s.189 of the RTA 2004 and the PRTB considers it appropriate that the full hearing of the application should be dealt with at adjudication.[201]

B. Adjudication

(i) Hearing

9–70 Where a dispute is referred to adjudication, an adjudicator will be appointed by the PRTB from its panel of adjudicators.[202] The parties will be

---

subsequent to mediation as envisaged by s.96(2)(b). It would appear to be the intention (although not explicitly provided for) that such a determination order is to be dealt with in the same way as an agreement reached during a mediation. The RTA 2004 contains no provision for it being treated in any other way.

[198] There is no mechanism under the RTA 2004 for allowing the dispute to be the subject of an adjudication.

[199] RTA 2004, s.96(6). In practice, when the PRTB serves a notice on the parties in accordance with s.96(1) and (2) (see para.9–65), it also informs the parties that they may request a tenancy tribunal hearing where no agreement has been reached through the mediation process. The s.96 notice is usually accompanied with a form which a party must complete, if they wish the matter to proceed to a tenancy tribunal hearing. A fee is payable where a party requests a tribunal hearing (Procedural Rules 2009, para.14). See the PRTB's website (*www.prtb.ie*) for up-to-date information on the fees payable.

[200] RTA 2004, s.93(3) and s.97(1).

[201] RTA 2004, s.94(a)(i) and s.97(1).

[202] RTA 2004, s.93(3) and 94(a)(i). See also s.164 of the RTA 2004 which deals with the appointment of adjudicators and their terms and conditions of appointment.

informed by the PRTB of the time and date of the adjudication hearing. The PRTB will only grant an adjournment in very limited circumstances.[203] The parties may attend at the adjudication themselves or with the adjudicator's permission, another person may appear on a party's behalf at the hearing.[204] If a party fails to attend at the adjudication hearing, the hearing may continue at the discretion of the adjudicator.[205] If the party who made the application for dispute resolution services to the PRTB fails to attend, the adjudicator may deem the application to be abandoned or withdrawn at his or her discretion.[206]

Generally, the conduct of an adjudication is at the discretion of the adjudicator, subject to any procedural rules made by the PRTB under s.109 of the RTA 2004. Adjudicators are, however, obliged to conduct the adjudication hearings without undue formality.[207] Like mediation, the adjudication process is confidential and only the parties to the dispute and certain other persons permitted by the adjudicator may attend at the hearing.[208] Witnesses often attend at adjudication hearings to give evidence on behalf of a party. It is the practice of the PRTB to request the parties to inform it within a certain period prior to the adjudication hearing, whether any witnesses will be attending at the adjudication to give evidence on their behalf. The parties are also asked to confirm whether they will be represented at the hearing.[209]

At an adjudication hearing, the adjudicator is required to inquire fully into each relevant aspect of the dispute.[210] Typically, the adjudicator will hear the evidence of the parties in turn, including that of any witnesses who attend on their behalf. To assist with the determination of the dispute, the adjudicator may provide to and receive from each party, such information as is appropriate.[211] The adjudicator is also empowered to require either party to the dispute to furnish him or her with documentation or other information.[212] An adjudication hearing usually takes place in one sitting. However, on occasion, if necessary, the hearing may be convened on additional days.

---

[203] See para.9–57.

[204] RTA 2004, s.97(7). See also para.7 of the Procedural Rules 2009.

[205] Procedural Rules 2009, para.12. Paragraph 12 also provides that the exercise of the adjudicator's discretion to continue with the hearing, is based on the possibility of reaching a determination with the papers submitted in advance of the hearing.

[206] Procedural Rules 2009, para.12.

[207] RTA 2004, s.101(4).

[208] See also RTA 2004, s.101(1)(c) and s.112. These provisions impose obligations of confidentiality on adjudicators with respect to the adjudication, statements or information received by the adjudicator during this process and the report prepared by the adjudicator. These provisions also deal with the limited circumstances where disclosure of such confidential information can be made.

[209] See para.9–110 that considers legal representation in the context of dispute resolution process before the PRTB.

[210] RTA 2004, s.97(2).

[211] RTA 2004, s.97(2).

[212] RTA 2004, s.97(3).

(ii) Paper based

9–71 The Procedural Rules 2009 provide that the PRTB may delegate authority to management to arrange for certain categories of cases to be addressed by means of a paper based adjudication instead of an oral hearing.[213] Where a dispute is deemed suitable for a paper based adjudication, the steps in that process are as follows[214]:

(a) The respondent is copied with the applicant's form for dispute resolution services and any accompanying documents. The respondent is notified that they may submit to the PRTB replying submissions within the period stated in the notice. The applicant is also afforded the opportunity to submit further submissions within the same period;

(b) The submissions received (if any) are forwarded by the PRTB to the other party and then each party is invited to respond, within a certain period, with counter-submissions; and

(c) At the end of this period, any submissions received by the PRTB, together with the application form and any other documents submitted by the parties, are provided to the adjudicator. The adjudicator will then make a determination based on these papers.

C. Determining the Dispute

(i) Overview

9–72 An adjudicator may determine a dispute by reaching a decision in his or her own right or by adopting as a determination, an agreement reached by the parties during the adjudication process.[215] Where the adjudicator determines the dispute, he or she shall immediately proceed to prepare a report and this is considered at para.9–75. There is an additional process that must be followed by an adjudicator where an agreement is reached between the parties, which is dealt with at paras 9–73 to 9–74 below.

---

[213] Procedural Rules 2009, para.9. See also para.9–56 that deals with the circulation by the PRTB of documents submitted by the parties to a dispute in advance of an adjudication hearing.

[214] In 2009 paper based adjudications were introduced by the PRTB to deal with certain disputes considered appropriate for that process. As paper based adjudications are not explicitly provided for under the RTA 2004 (while at the same time it appears not excluded by its provisions), there is no procedure specified by the RTA 2004 for the conduct of an adjudication on the papers. The summary of the procedure provided in this paragraph reflects the practice of the PRTB at the time of publication. Reference should be made to any new procedural rules adopted by the PRTB for paper based adjudications under s.109 of the RTA 2004, the PRTB's website (*www.prtb.ie*) and (if a party to such proceedings) all correspondence received from the PRTB.

[215] RTA 2004, s.97(4)(a) and (b).

(ii) Parties reaching an agreement

9–73 An adjudicator may adopt as the determination of the dispute, an agreement reached between the parties during the adjudication.[216] The RTA 2004 permits adjudicators to provide assistance to the parties in agreeing a resolution to the dispute, where the adjudicator considers that this would be of practical benefit. In providing assistance, the adjudicator may even inform the parties of any provisional conclusion that he or she has reached in relation to the matters in dispute between them.[217] There are conditions imposed in relation to the provisional conclusions that may be conveyed to the parties and when this can be done. In particular, an adjudicator may not provide the parties with an indication of his or her provisional conclusions until every document submitted by the parties and any initial oral submissions made by them, have been considered by the adjudicator. In addition, an adjudicator is not permitted to make any provisional conclusions in relation to any issue of fact in dispute between the parties, unless this is specifically requested by them.[218]

9–74 Where an agreement is reached at adjudication, this will be followed by a 21-day "cooling off" period. That 21-day period runs from the date on which the parties first inform the adjudicator that they have reached an agreement in relation to the matters in dispute between them.[219] In circumstances where the adjudicator is informed during this cooling off period that a party no longer accepts the agreement that had been reached, the adjudicator will proceed to determine the matter and the procedure considered at para.9–75 below shall then apply.[220]

On the other hand, if during the 21-day cooling off period the adjudicator is *not* notified by one or more of the parties that he or she no longer accepts the agreement that was reached, that agreement will be adopted by the adjudicator as his or her determination.[221] The adjudicator shall prepare a report setting out the terms of the agreement and shall then furnish a copy of the report to the PRTB, who in turn then serves it on the parties.[222] Importantly, there is no right of appeal in relation to an adjudicator's determination that constitutes the terms of an agreement reached between the parties themselves. This means that an adjudicator's report incorporating the parties' agreement, cannot be appealed to a tenancy tribunal or to any other forum.[223]

---

[216] RTA 2004, s.97(4)(b).
[217] RTA 2004, s.97(5). Any such conclusion made by an adjudicator is of a provisional nature only, made with a view to assisting the parties resolving the dispute between themselves. It will not absolve the adjudicator from his or her duty of determining the dispute impartially and in accordance with the requirements of procedural fairness, should the parties not reach an agreement themselves (RTA 2004, s.97(6)(c)).
[218] RTA 2004, s.97(6).
[219] RTA 2004, s.98(1)(a).
[220] RTA 2004, s.98(2).
[221] RTA 2004, ss.97(4)(b) and 98(1)(b).
[222] RTA 2004, s.99(1)–(3).
[223] RTA 2004, ss.98(4) and 123(1). Section 98(4) provides that when an adjudicator is first

(iii) Adjudicator determining the dispute

9–75 Where no agreement has been reached during the adjudication process or where any agreement that was reached breaks down, the adjudicator must proceed to determine the dispute. The adjudicator must prepare a report setting out the terms of his or her determination and a summary of reasons for that determination.[224] The RTA 2004 imposes no specific time limit within which an adjudicator must prepare a report and only requires that this is done "as soon as practicable" after the adjudicator has made a decision.[225]

9–76 Once an adjudicator has prepared his or her report, the adjudicator must provide it to the PRTB, who shall then serve a copy of it on each of the parties to the dispute.[226] One or more parties may appeal an adjudicator's determination to a tenancy tribunal within 21 days from the date the PRTB serves the adjudicator's report on the parties.[227] Where a party appeals an adjudicator's determination, a fee is payable for that appeal.[228]

D. Determination Order

9–77 After the PRTB has served the adjudicator's report on the parties, which either incorporates the adjudicator's own decision (and that has not been appealed) or an agreement of the parties, the PRTB shall then proceed to prepare a determination order.[229] The determination order will incorporate the terms of the determination recorded in the adjudicator's report. The determination order will become binding on the parties once issued to them.[230] If they fail to comply

---

informed by the parties that they have reached an agreement, the adjudicator is obliged to inform them at that stage that a decision made by him or her incorporating their agreement cannot be appealed to a tenancy tribunal and that it shall become binding on them once a determination order issues.

[224] RTA 2004, s.99(1), which also lists some additional particulars that must be contained in an adjudicator's report.

[225] RTA 2004, s.99(1). The PRTB has a discretion to adopt procedural rules prescribing the period within which an adjudicator must furnish his or her report (RTA 2004, s.109(2)(d)(ii)).

[226] RTA 2004, s.99(2) and (3).

[227] RTA 2004, s.100. When an adjudicator's report is served on the parties, it shall be accompanied with a statement (usually set out in the cover letter provided with the report) informing them that the adjudicator's determination will be adopted as a determination order under s.121 of the RTA 2004, unless the adjudicator's determination is appealed to a tenancy tribunal within 21 days and that appeal is not subsequently abandoned (RTA 2004, s.99(3) and (4)). As noted at para.9–74 above, this right of appeal exists only where an adjudicator has reached a determination in his or her own right. No right of appeal exists from a determination of an adjudicator that incorporates an agreement reached between the parties themselves.

[228] Procedural Rules 2009, para.15. See also the PRTB's website (*www.prtb.ie*) for up to date information on the fee payable.

[229] RTA 2004, s.99(4) and s.121(1).

[230] RTA 2004, s.123(1).

with its terms it is enforceable against them. The binding nature of a determination order and the consequences of not complying with its terms, are
considered at paras 9–101 to 9–103.

13. TENANCY TRIBUNAL

A. When is a Tenancy Tribunal Convened?

9–78 A tenancy tribunal is the final and most formal forum for dispute
resolution before the PRTB. The PRTB shall convene a tenancy tribunal to deal
with a dispute where:

(a) it is of the opinion that mediation or adjudication would not be an
appropriate forum for the resolution of the dispute[231];

(b) mediation has not been successful and one or more of the parties has
requested that the matter be referred to a tenancy tribunal[232];

(c) an adjudicator's determination has been appealed.[233]

B. Composition of Tenancy Tribunal

9–79 In a mediation or an adjudication before the PRTB, one person is
appointed to facilitate the dispute resolution process. In contrast, a tenancy
tribunal comprises of three individuals.[234] Each of these individuals must be a
member of the dispute resolution committee.[235] The members of the tenancy
tribunal are appointed by the PRTB and one of the members will be appointed
as the chairperson.[236] Where a member of the PRTB (through its membership of

---

[231] RTA 2004, ss.94 and 104(1)(a). The more serious type of cases are generally referred directly
to a tenancy tribunal. These cases frequently involve evictions from a dwelling or serious
allegations of antisocial behaviour. In addition to referring a matter directly to the tenancy
tribunal, the PRTB also has the option of seeking interim or interlocutory relief in aid of the
dispute resolution process. This involves the making of an application to the Circuit Court
pursuant to s.189 of the RTA 2004. The section 189 process is considered in further detail at
paras 9–111 and 9–117.

[232] RTA 2004, ss.96(6) and 104(1)(b).

[233] RTA 2004, s.104(1)(c). In the case of an appeal from a decision of an adjudicator, the tenancy
tribunal may have regard to the report of the adjudicator (RTA 2004, s.104(7)). Note, however,
para.17 of the Procedural Rules 2009 which provides that a tenancy tribunal hearing shall be
a full hearing on all of the facts (constituting a hearing de novo), although the parties may by
mutual consent, agree to limit the hearing to specific matters or issues arising from the
adjudication or to include matters that have arisen since the hearing.

[234] RTA 2004, s.103(1).

[235] RTA 2004, s.103(2). The dispute resolution committee is the committee appointed by the
PRTB, to assist it with the performance of its functions under Pt 6 of the RTA 2004, relating
to dispute resolution (RTA 2004, s.157(2) and (3) and s.159. See also para.11–08).

[236] RTA 2004, s.103(3) and (4).

the dispute resolution committee) has been appointed to a tenancy tribunal, that PRTB member shall always be the chairperson. If two or more members of the tenancy tribunal are also members of the PRTB, the PRTB shall determine who shall be the chairperson.[237] Tenancy tribunals operate by a decision of the majority, which is sufficient for any purpose.[238] The RTA 2004 specifically prescribes that a tenancy tribunal must be independent in the performance of its functions.[239]

C. Notification of Hearing

9–80 Where the PRTB convenes a tenancy tribunal, a notice shall issue to the parties to the dispute, informing them of the hearing date for the matter.[240] The notice must contain the date, time and venue of the hearing and an outline of the substance of the matters that will be dealt with. The parties are specifically informed through the notice that the hearing shall proceed and the tenancy tribunal will determine the dispute, unless it considers that there are substantial grounds for not conducting the hearing in the absence of a party. On being notified of the hearing date, the parties are also provided with a copy of the tenancy tribunal's procedures. These procedures provide an outline of how the hearing will be conducted.[241]

When being notified of the tenancy tribunal hearing, the parties are asked to submit to the PRTB within a certain period prior to the hearing date, any documentation they intend to rely on in support of their case.[242] In *Redmond v Cooke*,[243] the tenancy tribunal refused to allow into evidence, documentation concerning an alleged payment of rent that had not been furnished to the PRTB in advance of the hearing date.

9–81 The parties must be given at least 21 days notice of the date of the tenancy tribunal hearing.[244] There are two exceptions to this, when a shorter period of notice may be given. These exceptions arise in the following circumstances:

---

[237] RTA 2004, s.103(5).

[238] RTA 2004, s.103(7).

[239] RTA 2004, s.103(6). The preliminary results of the review of the RTA 2004 that was announced by the Minister for Housing and Local Services, identified that one of main issues to be addressed in proposed amending legislation, was the separation of the governance and quasi-judicial functions of the PRTB. See Press Release, "Minster Michael Finneran announces significant changes to the Private Residential Tenancies Board (PRTB) legislation", November 4, 2009, *www.environ.ie*.

[240] RTA 2004, s.104(3).

[241] RTA 2004, s.104(4). This section provides a full list of the matters that must be stated in the tribunal hearing notice. See also para.18 of the Procedural Rules 2009, which provides that the parties to the dispute are to be issued with tribunal procedures in advance of the hearing date.

[242] See also para.9–56.

[243] TR13/DR1256/2008, September 12, 2008.

[244] RTA 2004, s.104(5)(a). The 21-day period begins on the date of the giving of the notice.

(a) one or more of the parties requests that the tenancy tribunal hearing takes place with less than 21 days notice and the other party consents to this[245]; or

(b) the dispute concerns alleged behaviour by a landlord or tenant that poses an imminent danger of death or serious injury or imminent danger to the fabric of the dwelling concerned or the property containing the dwelling.[246]

Accordingly, if a party requests an early hearing date but the other party does not consent, the circumstances in which a tenancy tribunal may be convened with less than 21 days notice, are limited to the most serious of matters. In *O'Shea v Plunkett*[247] the landlord who submitted an application for dispute resolution services to the PRTB, maintained that by reason of the acts and threats of the tenant, there was a serious danger to the welfare and safety of himself, his family and the other tenants in the property in which the flat occupied by the tenant was situated. In evidence given by and on behalf of the landlord during the tenancy tribunal hearing, it was alleged that the threats made by the tenant included a threat by telephone to burn the property down and threatening text messages, including an apparent threat to kill one of the other tenants in the property. In that case the PRTB gave less than 21 days notice of the tenancy tribunal hearing. The landlord had made the application for dispute resolution services to the PRTB on August 27, 2007 and on that day the PRTB convened a tenancy tribunal. The parties were notified of a hearing date of September 3, 2007.[248]

9–82 Cases may also arise where a party to a dispute will not consent to an early hearing date but the matter does not involve a threat of death or serious injury or imminent danger to the fabric of the dwelling concerned. For instance, this may occur in cases of actual or threatened illegal evictions. In these circumstances, at the request of one of the parties, the PRTB may instead consider it appropriate to avail of the procedure under s.189 of the RTA 2004, without having to wait 21 days for a tenancy tribunal hearing to take place.[249] This procedure allows the PRTB to make an application for interim or interlocutory relief to the Circuit Court in aid of the dispute resolution process. The section 189 procedure is considered in further detail at paras 9–111 to 9–117.

---

[245] RTA 2004, s.104(5)(b)(i).

[246.] RTA 2004, s.104(5)(b)(ii).

[247] TR101/DR963/2007, September 3, 2007.

[248] The tenancy tribunal was adjourned for one day from September 3, 2007 to September 4, 2007. See para.9–58.

[249] For example in *Private Residential Tenancies Board v Sancta Maria Properties Limited t/a Citi Properties,* unreported, Circuit Court, ex tempore, Linnane J., October 27, 2006. In that case as the landlord/his agents did not consent to a hearing date with less than 21 days notice, the PRTB made an application to the Circuit Court pursuant to s.189 of the RTA 2004. See para.9–112.

D. Tenancy Tribunal Hearings and Witnesses

9–83 In contrast to the mediation and adjudication process before the PRTB, tenancy tribunal hearings are conducted in public.[250] A tenancy tribunal will not grant an adjournment of a matter except in exceptional circumstances.[251] Where a party fails to attend at a tenancy tribunal hearing and is the applicant or the appellant[252] that party may be liable to pay a contribution towards the costs of convening the tenancy tribunal. An applicant's/appellant's potential liability for such costs is considered in further detail at paras 9–96 to 9–100.

9–84 Depending on the complexity and number of issues in dispute, a tenancy tribunal hearing may last more than one sitting.[253] It is the general practice of the PRTB to have a transcript of the tenancy tribunal hearing taken, although this is not required by the RTA 2004. Tenancy tribunal hearings are conducted with more formality than mediation and adjudication, which is reflected in the provisions of the RTA 2004 dealing with the conduct of tenancy tribunal hearings, in particular those provisions dealing with the giving of evidence.[254] A tenancy tribunal may summons a witness, administer an oath[255] and require a person to produce to the tenancy tribunal, any document in his or her power or control.[256] A party to the dispute may ask the PRTB to summons a witness on its behalf. Where a tenancy tribunal does summons a witness to attend at a hearing, it may (but is not obliged to) direct that the witness is reimbursed their reasonable expenses. The monies for reimbursing witnesses who are summonsed by a tenancy tribunal are paid by the PRTB.[257]

At a tenancy tribunal hearing each of the parties to a dispute are entitled to be heard, to be represented and to present evidence and witnesses.[258] Generally tenancy tribunals will hear the evidence of the applicant or appellant party first, followed by the evidence of the respondent party. If a witness gives evidence on behalf of a party that witness may be cross-examined by or on behalf of the

---

[250] RTA 2004, s.106(1). Mediation and adjudication both involve a confidential process and are to be conducted in private. Although tenancy tribunals hearings are to be conducted in public, tenancy tribunals are however empowered to direct that the identity of one or more of the parties to the dispute is not to be disclosed (RTA 2004, s.106(2)).

[251] See para.9–57. Also, see s.104(4)(e) of the RTA 2004.

[252] The applicant will be the party who has referred a dispute to the PRTB for resolution and it becomes the subject of a direct reference to a tenancy tribunal for determination. The appellant will be the party who is appealing a decision of an adjudicator.

[253] RTA 2004, ss.104(2) and 107.

[254] Further, the application of s.101(4) of the RTA 2004, which provides that mediations and adjudications are to be conducted "without undue formality", does not extend to tenancy tribunal hearings.

[255] It is the general practice of tenancy tribunals to require witnesses to take an oath or affirmation prior to giving evidence.

[256] RTA 2004, s.105(3).

[257] RTA 2004, s.105(6).

[258] RTA 2004, s.104(6).

other party to the dispute.[259] Witnesses who give evidence at a tenancy tribunal hearing, are entitled to the same immunities and privileges as if he or she were a witness before the High Court.[260] A witness, however, shall be guilty of an offence, if having been summonsed by a tenancy tribunal, he or she fails to attend at the hearing,[261] refuse to take an oath, produce any document, answer any question or do any other thing, which would constitute contempt of court.[262]

E. Tribunal Determination

9–85 Once a tenancy tribunal hearing has concluded and the tenancy tribunal has considered all of the evidence, it will proceed to make its determination in relation to the dispute. The tenancy tribunal's determination is incorporated into a report prepared by it. The tenancy tribunal will notify the PRTB of its determination.[263] The PRTB shall then proceed to make a determination order, which will incorporate the decision of the tenancy tribunal.[264] The determination order, together with the tenancy tribunal's report is then served on the parties. The determination order becomes binding on the parties following the expiry of 21 days from the issue of the determination order,[265] unless before the expiry of that period, an appeal of the determination order is made to the High Court on a point of law pursuant to s.123(3) of the RTA 2004.

F. Appeal of Tenancy Tribunal Determination

9–86 An appeal to the High Court of a determination order may be made on a point of law only.[266] This was the subject of consideration in the matter of *Canty v Private Residential Tenancies Board*.[267] The tenant appealed a determination order made by the PRTB under s.123(3) of the RTA 2004 and sought orders to vary or cancel the determination order on the basis of "manifest error(s) of law committed in the purported adjudication thereof".[268] In the proceedings the

---

[259] RTA 2004, s.105(2).

[260] RTA 2004, s.105(4).

[261] Provided they have been tendered any monies that the tenancy tribunal has directed that they be paid to cover their expenses in accordance with s.105(6) of the RTA 2004.

[262] RTA 2004, s.105(5). Section 9 of the RTA 2004 sets out the liabilities that may be imposed on a party found guilty of an offence under the RTA 2004.

[263] RTA 2004, s.108(1).

[264] RTA 2004, s.121(1).

[265] RTA 2004, s.123(2) and (8). This section provides that the 21-day period begins on the date that the determination order concerned is issued to the parties.

[266] The right to appeal a determination order on a point of law to the High Court, exists only in cases where a tenancy tribunal has determined the dispute. At the time of publication there were no specific Rules of the Superior Courts which prescribed the procedure for making an application under s.123(3) of the RTA 2004. To date a number of these applications have been brought by special summons.

[267] [2007] IEHC 243; unreported, High Court, Laffoy J., August 8, 2007.

[268] [2007] IEHC 243; unreported, High Court, Laffoy J., August 8, 2007, at p.1.

applicant particularised 22 items on which he based his appeal. Laffoy J. held that only some of these items constituted points of law, which were justiciable under s.123(3). Amongst the matters that Laffoy J. held did not constitute points of law, was the applicant's contention that the PRTB manifestly erroneously misapplied and/or misconstrued the bona fides requirement of s.56(6)(b) of the RTA 2004, in relation to two notices of termination that had been served on him dated March 13, 2006. Section 56(6)(b) provides as follows:

> For the avoidance of doubt –
> (a) ...
> (b) this section is without prejudice to the tenant's right to put in issue, in a dispute in relation to the validity of the notice of termination referred to the Board under Part 6, the bona fides of the intention of the landlord to do or, as appropriate, permit to be done the thing or things mentioned in the notice.

Before the tenancy tribunal the applicant had challenged the landlord's bona fides in serving the second notice of termination of March 13, 2006. In his submissions to the High Court the applicant had contended the "twinning" of the ground 4 notice of termination with the ground 1 notice of termination[269] gave rise to a presumption of *mala fides* on the part of the landlord.[270] Laffoy J. held that this was not correct. She said that a landlord was entitled to invoke one or more of the grounds for termination provided for in the Table to s.34 of the RTA 2004. She held that in effect what the applicant was asking the court to do, was to review the decision of the tenancy tribunal on the merits, which was not permissible on an appeal under s.123(3). She further held that in an appeal under s.123(3), it was not open to the court to set aside a finding of fact made by the tenancy tribunal unless there was no evidence to support it.[271]

G. Cancel or Vary Determination Order

9–87 Having heard an appeal under s.123(3) of the RTA 2004, the High Court may direct the PRTB to cancel the determination order concerned or to vary it in the manner the High Court considers appropriate.[272] This is the extent of the

---

[269] The table to s.34 of the RTA 2004 lists six grounds on which a landlord may terminate a Part 4 tenancy. The termination of Part 4 tenancies is considered in detail in Ch.8.

[270] [2007] IEHC 243; unreported, High Court, Laffoy J., August 8, 2007, at p.38.

[271] Laffoy J. endorsed the dicta of Finlay C.J. in *O'Keefe v An Bord Pleanála* [1993] 1 I.R. 39 (at p.72), that, "I am satisfied that in order for an applicant for judicial review to satisfy a Court that the decision-making authority has acted irrationally in the sense which I have outlined above so that the Court can intervene and quash its decision, it is necessary that the applicant should establish to the satisfaction of the Court that the decision-making authority had before it no relevant material which would support its decision". Laffoy J. said in her view that this passage certainly outlined the appropriate principle in the judicial review context ([2007] IEHC 243; unreported, High Court, Laffoy J., August 8, 2007, at p.38).

[272] RTA 2004, s.123(5).

jurisdiction that is afforded to the High Court under s.123. In *Canty v Private Residential Tenancies Board*[273] the applicant had raised particular objections in relation to one of the notices of termination that had been served on him dated March 13, 2006. Laffoy J. held that notwithstanding the egregious breach by the applicant of the terms of his tenancy and of an interim determination order made by the PRTB and notwithstanding that the applicant did not pinpoint the precise infirmity in the landlord's reliance on ground 1 of the Table to s.34 to terminate the tenancy, it was not possible for her to hold the notice of termination of March 13, 2006 was valid. Laffoy J. held:

> "it is not possible to hold that the first notice of termination of 13th March, 2006 was validly given. The only courses open to the court under s. 123(5) are to let the determination order of 6th October, 2006 stand or to vary it. Despite having considerable sympathy for the landlord, I have come to the conclusion that the determination as to the validity of the first notice of 13th March, 2006 cannot stand".[274]

H. Appeal Final and Conclusive

9–88 The determination of the High Court on an appeal in relation to a point of law under s.123(3) of the RTA 2004 is "final and conclusive".[275] In *Canty v Private Residential Tenancies Board*[276] the appellant sought to appeal the judgment of Laffoy J. of the High Court[277] in relation to the application that the appellant had made pursuant to s.123(3). The Supreme Court held that it had no jurisdiction to hear an appeal by reason of the provisions of s.123(4) of the RTA 2004, which provides that, "[t]he determination of the High Court on such appeal in relation to the point of law concerned shall be final and conclusive".[278] The Supreme Court, however, reserved judgment on whether or not the appellant was nonetheless entitled to appeal the order for costs made against him by the High Court, following his unsuccessful application under s.123(3).[279]

The Supreme Court later dealt with the issue of whether s.123(4) of the RTA 2004 prohibited an appeal of an order for costs made by the High Court when determining an appeal under s.123(3).[280] Kearns J.[281] held that the question could only be resolved by considering the precise wording of any statute which

---

273 [2007] IEHC 243; unreported, High Court, Laffoy J., August 8, 2007.

274 [2007] IEHC 243; unreported, High Court, Laffoy J., August 8, 2007, at p.24.

275 RTA 2004, s.123(4).

276 Unreported, Supreme Court, ex tempore, Kearns, Macken and Finnegan, JJ.,, April 4, 2008.

277 *Canty v Private Residential Tenancies Board* [2007] IEHC 243; unreported, High Court, Laffoy J., August 8, 2007.

278 Unreported, Supreme Court, ex tempore, Kearns, Macken and Finnegan JJ., April 4, 2008.

279 The appellant argued that the wording of s.123(4) was not sufficiently clear or specific to exclude the jurisdiction of the Supreme Court to entertain an appeal confined to the issue of costs.

280 *Canty v Private Residential Tenancies Board* [2008] 4 I.R. 592.

281 With whom Macken and Finnegan JJ. concurred.

purports to limit the right of appeal to the Supreme Court. Kearns J. considered the limitations imposed on the right of appeal in other legislation, such as s.50(4)(f)(i) of the Planning and Development Act 2000, which provides that, "[t]he determination of the High Court of an application for leave to apply for judicial review, or of an application for judicial review, shall be final and no appeal shall lie from the decision of the High Court to the Supreme Court in either case ...". Kearns J. said that the word "decision" of the High Court in s.50 could be taken as including any determination of the issue of costs which forms part of its decision in the case. Kearns J. drew similar analogies in the context of s.42(8) of the Freedom of Information Act 1997 and s.39 of the Courts of Justice Act 1936. With respect to each of these sections, Kearns J. said that he had no difficultly in construing them as altogether precluding any further appeal, even one confined to costs. In contrast, however, Kearns J. said that s.123(4) of the RTA 2004 was unsatisfactorily drafted in a number of respects and was much less clear. He said that if s.123(4) simply referred to "the determination of the High Court on such an appeal", one could well argue that the decision of the High Court in relation to costs was incorporated in the determination. However, he said the wording actually used in s.123(4) contextualises the determination of the High Court by reference specifically "to the point of law concerned".[282] Kearns J. held that any statute which purports altogether to remove, even a limited right of appeal on an issue such as costs, should be phrased so as to make that intention clear.[283] In these circumstances, he allowed the appellant's appeal on the issue of costs.

9–89 Accordingly, where a determination made by a tenancy tribunal is appealed on a point of law pursuant to s.123(3) of the RTA 2004, the decision of the High Court will be final and conclusive. However, an award of costs made by the High Court, having considered the appeal under s.123(3), may be the subject of an appeal to the Supreme Court.

I. Consistency between Tribunal Determinations

9–90 The PRTB is empowered by s.122 of the RTA 2004 to ensure consistency in tenancy tribunal determinations. The PRTB has a discretion but is not obliged to act if it considers a tenancy tribunal determination is inconsistent with previous tenancy tribunal decisions.[284] It may only exercise this discretion where the issues are the same and the facts the same in all material respects between the dispute in question and the previous cases.[285]

---

[282] [2008] 4 I.R. 592, at 593.
[283] Kearns J. further held that this was not to say that express wording in a statute is a prerequisite for this purpose, but rather that the overall intention that no further appeal should lie from any aspect of the decision of the High Court judge should be obvious from a reading of the provision in question ([2008] 4 I.R. 592 at 596).
[284] RTA 2004, s.122(1).
[285] RTA 2004, s.122(1) and (4).

If the PRTB is of the opinion that a determination of a tenancy tribunal is inconsistent with previous determinations, it may notify the tenancy tribunal of that opinion and request each of its members' views. Having considered any observations made by the tenancy tribunal members, it must notify all parties to the dispute of its opinion in relation to the inconsistency, and ask whether the parties consent to a new determination being made or whether they wish to make representations to the PRTB in relation to the matter. If the parties give consent or the PRTB considers it appropriate having regard to any represen-tations made to it by the parties, the PRTB may direct the tenancy tribunal to make a new determination in relation to the dispute.[286] Before the tenancy tribunal does so, however, a re-hearing of the matter must first take place.[287]

14. WITHDRAWAL OF A DISPUTE

9–91 A party who has made an application for dispute resolution services to the PRTB may withdraw the matter at any stage.[288] The party must inform the PRTB in writing of this or if the matter is at mediation, adjudication or before a tenancy tribunal, the party may inform the mediator, adjudicator or tenancy tribunal orally that the party wishes to withdraw his or her application.[289]

Once a party has given notice that he or she wishes to withdraw an application, the matter will be considered withdrawn and the PRTB, mediator, adjudicator or tenancy tribunal is not permitted to deal with it any further.[290] However, as in proceedings before the courts there may be cost implications where an application is withdrawn. The PRTB, mediator, adjudicator or tenancy tribunal as appropriate, must ascertain whether the other party to the dispute objects to the withdrawal of the matter. If an objection is raised, the party withdrawing the dispute may be directed to pay some or all of the costs and expenses of the other party that have been incurred in dealing with the application made against him or her to the PRTB.[291]

9–92 In *John v Mohan*[292] the tenant had leased a number of apartments from the landlord. The landlord had served notices of termination on the tenant in respect of these apartments. The tenant disputed the notices and submitted applications for dispute resolution services to the PRTB. In these applications the tenant also raised issues in relation to the standard and maintenance of the

---

[286] RTA 2004, s.122(2).
[287] RTA 2004, s.122(3).
[288] RTA 2004, s.82(1).
[289] RTA 2004, ss.82(2) and (3).
[290] RTA 2004, s.82(4).
[291] RTA 2004, s.82(5). Where an adjudicator or tenancy tribunal make a direction under s.82(5), this shall be subject of a determination order made by the PRTB (RTA 2004, s.121(1)(d)).
[292] TR03/2008/DR968&DR975/2007, June 25, 2008.

apartments and other breaches of the landlord's tenancy obligations. The tenant later withdrew his applications for dispute resolution services. The landlord made an application under s.82(5) of the RTA 2004, for the costs and expenses he maintained he had incurred as a result of the tenant withdrawing the applications late in the dispute resolution process.

The reason given by the tenant for withdrawing his applications before the PRTB was that the notices of termination that had been served by the landlord had been withdrawn and new notices served. As the new notices of termination would then be the subject matter of the dispute between the parties, the tenant submitted that it would be more appropriate to have the matter dealt with afresh. The landlord on the other hand argued that although the landlord had withdrawn the notices of termination first served by him, matters in respect of the standard and maintenance of the rented apartments and other breaches of the landlord's obligations had not been withdrawn by the tenant until close to the date of the tenancy tribunal hearing.[293]

The tenancy tribunal refused the application made by the landlord under s.82(5) of the RTA 2004, for costs and expenses incurred as a result of the late withdrawal by the tenant of his applications for dispute resolution services. The tenancy tribunal was of the view that the applications submitted by the tenant were not vexatious or frivolous and that the tenant had been co-operative throughout the dispute resolution process. In its findings it also referred to the tenancy tribunal procedures that had issued to the parties, which stated that in most cases legal or other professional or expert costs would not be awarded.

15. Redress in Resolution of a Dispute

A. Reliefs

9–93 Section 115(1) of the RTA 2004 empowers adjudicators and tenancy tribunals to make directions which they deem appropriate for the purposes of determining a dispute. Without prejudice to this general power, s.115(2) lists a number of specific directions that may be made by an adjudicator or tenancy tribunal. These directions are as follows:

    (a) an amount of rent or other charge be paid by or from a particular date[294];

---

[293] The tenancy tribunal hearing was convened to deal only with the issue of the landlord's application of costs under s.82(5) of the RTA 2004.

[294] See also s.119 of the RTA 2004. This section provides that an amount of arrears of rent stipulated to be payable in a determination shall be the gross amount of rent and other charges considered to be in arrears, reduced by (i) any just debts due by the landlord to the tenant (see s.48 of the Landlord and Tenant Law Amendment Act Ireland 1860), (ii) any expenditure incurred by the tenant for carrying out repairs to the rented dwelling, where a landlord has refused or failed to do so in breach of his or her tenancy obligations (see s.87 of the Landlord and Tenant (Amendment) Act 1980 (the "1980 Act")), (iii) any compensation for improvements

(b) the rent set under a tenancy of a dwelling does or does not reflect the market rent[295];

(c) a deposit be returned to the tenant in whole or in part[296];

(d) an amount of damages or costs or both be paid[297];

(e) a dwelling be vacated by a particular date;

(f) a notice of termination is valid or invalid;

(g) a tenant may continue in occupation of or has the right to return to a dwelling[298];

(h) a term of a lease agreement is void by reason of the fact that the purpose of the term, is to facilitate a party being in a position at all times to terminate the tenancy, on the grounds that the other party has not complied with the term in question[299]; and

(i) the whole or part of the costs or expenses incurred by the adjudicator or tenancy tribunal in dealing with the dispute, be paid by one or more of the parties. A direction made in this regard will only be made where special circumstances arise which warrant the making of such a declaration.[300]

As noted above, s.115(2) of the RTA 2004 provides a non-exhaustive list of the directions that may be made by an adjudicator or tenancy tribunal in dealing with a dispute. One matter, however, that an adjudicator and tenancy tribunal is specifically prohibited from making a direction in relation to, is the title to any

---

owed by the landlord to the tenant under Pt IV of the 1980 Act (see s.61 of the 1980 Act), and (iv) any other amount that the adjudicator or tenancy tribunal considers warranted. The gross amount of rent arrears may also be increased by an amount considered appropriate in respect of (i) costs incurred by the landlord in pursuing arrears of rent, (ii) damages payable to the landlord or (iii) the cost of repairs to the rented dwelling caused by the tenant's breach of his or her tenancy obligations.

[295] Where the rent does not reflect the market rent the adjudicator or tenancy tribunal must give an indication as to what would in his, her or its opinion reflect the market rent (RTA 2004, s.115(2)(b)). In making a determination in relation to the amount of rent that ought to be set under a tenancy or when a review of rent ought to take place, the financial or other circumstances of the landlord or tenant may not be taken into consideration by the adjudicator or the tenancy tribunal (RTA 2004, s.120).

[296] One of the preliminary recommendations made as a result of the review of the RTA 2004 carried out by the Minister for Housing and Local Services, was the introduction of fixed fines where deposits are illegally retained by landlords. See, Press Release, "Minister Michael Finneran announces significant changes to Private Residential Tenancies Board (PRTB) legislation", November 4, 2009, *www.environ.ie*.

[297] "Costs" are to be interpreted by reference to s.5(3) and (4) of the RTA 2004.

[298] An adjudicator's or tenancy tribunal's direction may include a declaration to the effect that any interruption in the tenant's possession of the dwelling, is to be disregarded for one or more purposes (RTA 2004, s.115(2)(g)). This may be an important declaration for a tenant to seek, where the tenant's possession of the dwelling was interrupted for a period during the first six months of the tenancy and but for this interruption, the tenant would have a right to a Part 4 tenancy. Of additional note is s.118 of the RTA 2004. Section 118 gives an adjudicator or tenancy tribunal a discretion to make an award of damages in favour of a tenant wrongfully deprived of possession of a dwelling, where an order permitting the tenant to re-occupy the dwelling, would cause hardship or injustice to a party who had taken up occupation.

[299] See s.184 of the RTA 2004.

[300] See paras 9–96 to 9–100 below.

lands or property. Title to lands or property cannot be drawn into question in any proceedings before the PRTB (including at mediation).[301]

B. Interim Relief

9–94 In addition to making orders which incorporate a final determination, adjudicators and tenancy tribunals may also make interim directions to have effect during the course of the dispute resolution process. The interim relief granted does not necessarily have to be or reflect the relief granted in the final determination of the matter.[302] In *Canty v Connolly*[303] the tenancy tribunal made an interim determination order directing the tenant to pay arrears of rent to the landlord.

C. Directions in Respect of Damages and Rent

9–95 The amount of damages[304] and arrears of rent or other charges that an adjudicator or tenancy tribunal may award to a party is limited by s.115(3) of the RTA 2004.[305] Section 115(3) provides that the amount (other than costs and expenses of whatsoever kind) that an adjudicator or tenancy tribunal may direct one party to a dispute to pay to the other, shall not exceed the following:

> (a) if the amount consists of *damages* only – €20,000[306];
> (b) if the amount consists of *rent or other charges* only[307] – €20,000 or an amount equal to twice the annual rent of the dwelling concerned, whichever is higher but subject to a maximum award of €60,000[308];

---

[301] RTA 2004, s.110.

[302] RTA 2004, s.117.

[303] TR33/DR201&294/2006, January 27, 2006.

[304] The RTA 2004 does not distinguish between special damages (by way of example compensation for the actual monies paid by a landlord in carrying out repairs to a dwelling) and general damages (for example compensation paid in respect of the distress caused to a tenant when his or her tenancy was unlawfully terminated).

[305] Where a party's claim for damages or rent or other charges exceeds the limits in s.115(3) of the RTA 2004, the party may institute proceedings before the courts (RTA 2004, s.182). See also Seanad Éireann, Vol.177, Col.727, July 2, 2004, second stage, when Minister Ahern in discussing Pt 6 referred to the "overall limitations applying to the board's functions will be €20,000 in damages and, in the case of arrears of rent or other charges, twice the annual rent or €20,000, whichever is greater, but subject to an overall maximum of €60,000. Cases involving monetary amounts greater than those will still have to be taken through the courts".

[306] RTA 2004, s.115(3)(a).

[307] The RTA 2004 does not define the term "charges". In the absence of a specific definition, the term would seem to cover the charges lawfully agreed by the landlord and tenant to be paid under the terms of the tenancy. For further consideration of charges in the context of landlord and tenant law, see Wylie, *Landlord and Tenant Law*, 2nd edn (Dublin: Butterworths, 1998), Ch.13 on "Outgoings, Taxes and Charges".

[308] RTA 2004, s.115(3)(b).

(c) if the amount consists of *both* damages and arrears of rent or other charges, the limits set out in (a) and (b) apply but a determination is made combining both. In other words, a determination of an adjudicator or tribunal may not exceed €80,000 in total, being an amount of up to €20,000 in damages plus up to €60,000 in arrears of rent and other charges.[309]

As noted above, the amounts referred to at (a)–(c) are exclusive of "costs and expenses of whatsoever kind". This phrase is not defined specifically for the purposes of s.115(3) of the RTA 2004. The term "costs", however, is defined in the interpretation provisions of the RTA 2004. Section 5(3) defines "costs" in relation to a matter being dealt with by the PRTB, a mediator, adjudicator or tenancy tribunal as *not* including:

(a) legal costs or expenses; or
(b) costs or expenses of any other professional kind or of employing any person with technical expertise for the purposes of giving evidence in any proceedings before the PRTB.

Section 5(3) of the RTA 2004 is subject to s.5(4), which provides that the PRTB or with the consent of the PRTB, a mediator, an adjudicator or a tenancy tribunal, may make a direction awarding legal costs or expenses or other professional costs, if in their opinion the "exceptional circumstances" of the case warrant such an award. Accordingly, a determination of an adjudicator or tenancy tribunal may include (in addition to an award of damages or a direction for the reimbursement of rent or other charges), a direction that one party is to pay some or all of the legal or professional costs and expenses incurred by the other party to the dispute.

D. Costs of an Adjudicator or Tenancy Tribunal

9–96 An adjudicator or tenancy tribunal may direct a party to pay all or part of the costs incurred by the adjudicator or tenancy tribunal in dealing with a dispute, where the "special circumstances" of the case warrant such an award.[310] The approach generally of tenancy tribunals is that it will direct a party to pay its costs, where the party has acted in contempt of the tenancy tribunal, has abused the dispute resolution process of the PRTB or is the applicant or appellant and has failed to attend at a hearing without good excuse.

---

[309] RTA 2004, s.115(3)(c).
[310] RTA 2004, s.115(2)(i). Paragraph 20 of the Procedural Rules 2009 gives an example of such "special circumstances" as being where a party to the dispute does not co-operate or where the applicant or appellant is not present without good cause.

9–97 In the matter of *O'Mahony v Drapata*[311] the tenant submitted an application for dispute resolution services to the PRTB seeking the return of the security deposit that the landlord had retained at the end of the tenancy. At adjudication it was determined that the landlord was to return the deposit in full to the tenant. The landlord appealed the adjudicator's determination, however, failed to attend at the tenancy tribunal hearing convened by the PRTB. The tenancy tribunal determined that as the landlord did not attend at the hearing to present his appeal, nor did he provide good reason for his failure to attend, the landlord was directed to pay the sum of €3,000 to the PRTB as a contribution towards the costs of the tenancy tribunal, within five days of the date of the issue of its determination.

9–98 In *Dunne v Farrell*[312] the landlord appealed the determination of the adjudicator who heard the matter at first instance. The landlord had failed to attend at the adjudication and at the tenancy tribunal hearing explained that he had forgotten to attend, as he was under considerable pressure of work at that time. In its report the tenancy tribunal stated that it did not find the landlord's reasons for his non-attendance at the adjudication to be acceptable. It further stated that had the landlord made himself available to the adjudicator, the need for a further tribunal hearing, which had involved additional cost to the PRTB and the other party, might have been avoided. Accordingly, the tenancy tribunal determined that the landlord was to pay to the PRTB within 21 days of the issue of its determination, the sum of €1,000 towards the costs incurred by the tenancy tribunal in dealing with the matter.

In the matter of *Horan and Anor v Hubrich*[313] the landlords also failed to attend at the adjudication hearing and appealed the determination that was made by the adjudicator. When one of the landlords was asked by the tenancy tribunal to explain his failure to attend the adjudication, the landlord referred to the tenant's application for dispute resolution services, which stated that the landlord had refused to deal with the tenant because of nationality and age. The landlord said that he took this to be an allegation of racism on his part and for this reason chose not to take part in the adjudication hearing. No other reason was proffered by the landlord for his failure to make himself available to the adjudication process. The tenancy tribunal in its report stated that it did not find the landlord's reason for his non-attendance at the adjudication acceptable. It also had regard to the fact that during the tenancy tribunal hearing, the landlord had by his own admission accepted the adjudicator's findings were correct. The tenancy tribunal determined that the landlords were to pay the sum of €2,000 to the PRTB, as a contribution to the costs of the tenancy tribunal, within 21 days from the date of issue of its determination.

---

[311]   TR07/DR72/2009, March 20, 2009.
[312]   TR91/DR736/2008, March 11, 2009.
[313]   TR02/DR831/2009, March 9, 2009.

9–99 In *Kelly v Flood*[314] a tenancy tribunal was convened with less than 21 days notice,[315] as the result of an alleged illegal eviction of the tenant by the landlord. In making an award of costs against the landlord pursuant to s.115(2)(i) of the RTA 2004, the tenancy tribunal stated that:

> "Tribunals are established on an emergency basis by the [PRTB] only in the gravest of circumstances. The Tribunal are of the view that the exchequer should not bear the full cost of the establishment of an emergency tribunal when the actions of one party resulted in the initial application for a Tribunal".[316]

In *John v Mohan*[317] the tenancy tribunal made no order of costs against the tenant pursuant to s.115(2)(i), as it had found that the application for dispute resolution services made by the tenant was not vexatious or frivolous and that the tenant was co-operative and engaged fully with the PRTB at all times.

9–100 In the matter of the *Private Residential Tenancies Board v Burgess*[318] a determination order came before the Circuit Court for enforcement under s.124 of the RTA 2004. The determination order contained a direction in relation to the costs of a tenancy tribunal made in accordance with s.115(2)(i). Although the Circuit Court was not ultimately required to deal with the enforcement of that term of the determination order, O'Donnabháin J. stated that he was troubled by the PRTB's award to itself.

16. DETERMINATION ORDERS

A. Nature of and Binding Effect of Determination Orders

9–101 Determination orders are prepared by the PRTB in accordance with s.121 of the RTA 2004. Determination orders record the terms of an agreement reached at mediation or the decision of an adjudicator or tenancy tribunal (where there has been no appeal).[319] The PRTB also issues a determination order where a party has withdrawn an application for dispute resolution and a direction is made that the withdrawing party pay the costs and expenses of the other party. Interim determinations made by an adjudicator or a tenancy tribunal, are also the subject of a determination order made by the PRTB.[320] All determination

---

[314] TR07/DR521/2008, May 29, 2008.
[315] See para.9–81.
[316] Tenancy tribunal report, p.3.
[317] TR03/2008/DR968&DR975/2007, June 25, 2008.
[318] Unreported, Circuit Court, ex tempore, December 3, 2008.
[319] RTA 2004, s.121(1)(a)–(c).
[320] RTA 2004, s.121(1)(d).

orders prepared by the PRTB are issued by it to both the applicant and respondent parties to the dispute.[321]

When preparing a determination order, the PRTB is not permitted to change the terms of the mediation agreement, any decision made by an adjudicator or tenancy tribunal or any other decision that is to be made the subject of a determination order as described above. It may, however, express the terms in a different manner to remove any ambiguity or to clarify the terms where it considers this will be of benefit to the parties or will facilitate compliance.[322]

9–102 Determination orders are similar to court orders in the sense that they are binding on the parties concerned and enforceable against them.[323] A party who fails to comply with a determination order is guilty of an offence.[324] Determination orders must be sealed with the seal of the PRTB.[325] Where the seal is authenticated by the signature of the Chairperson and the Director of the PRTB (or such other persons authorised by the PRTB to authenticate the seal), judicial notice must be taken of the determination order. It shall be admitted into evidence and deemed an instrument of the PRTB without further proof, unless the contrary is shown.[326] This is of relevance in the context of facilitating proceedings for the enforcement of a determination order pursuant to s.124 or a prosecution of the offence of failing to comply with a determination order contrary to s.126(1).[327]

9–103 The PRTB may publish its determination orders.[328] The PRTB exercises this discretion and publishes determination orders on its website (*www.prtb.ie*).

---

[321] The preliminary results of the review of the RTA 2004 that were announced by the Minister for Housing and Local Services, made clear that the focus of proposed amending legislation was on streamlining and expediting service delivery before the PRTB. One of the main issues it was announced would be addressed in amending legislation, was the introduction of a statutory objective of six months for the issuing of determination orders arising out of dispute resolution applications. In other words the statutory objective would be that the dispute resolution process before the PRTB would take no longer than six months from start to finish. See Press Release, "Minister Michael Finneran announces significant changes to Private Residential Tenancies Board (PRTB) legislation", November 4, 2009, *www.environ.ie*.

[322] RTA 2004, s.121(2) and (3). If the PRTB is uncertain as to whether to express the terms of a determination order in a different manner to a mediation agreement or an adjudicator's or tenancy tribunal's report, s.121(5) of the RTA 2004 provides the PRTB may consult with the mediator, adjudicator or tenancy tribunal as appropriate and even with the parties themselves. Section 121(4) of the RTA 2004 requires the PRTB to have regard to the summary agreement or statement provided to it by the Director following a mediation or an adjudicator's report in the case of an adjudication, when considering whether it is appropriate to exercise its power under s.121(2).

[323] RTA 2004, s.124. Section 124 provides for the enforcement of determination orders before the Circuit Court.

[324] RTA 2004, s.126(1).

[325] RTA 2004, s.121(6).

[326] RTA 2004, s.173(2) and (3).

[327] See paras 9–118 to 9–126 on s.124 of the RTA 2004 and paras 9–127 to 9–129 on s.126 of the RTA 2004.

[328] RTA 2004, s.123(7).

B. Cancellation of Determination Orders in Cases of Non-Appearance

9–104 In circumstances where a person has established to the satisfaction of the PRTB that there were good and substantial reasons for his or her failure to appear at the relevant adjudication or tenancy tribunal hearing that resulted in the making of a determination order, the PRTB may cancel the determination order and direct a re-hearing.[329] Before exercising these powers, the PRTB must afford the other party to the dispute an opportunity to make representations to the PRTB in relation to the matter.[330] If notwithstanding any representations made, the PRTB proceeds to cancel the determination order and directs a re-hearing, it may impose conditions on the person seeking the cancellation of the determination order. The RTA 2004 provides guidance in relation to the type of conditions that may be imposed, namely they are conditions analogous to those the High Court may impose when setting aside a judgment made in the absence of a relevant party.[331] In this regard, Ord.36 r.33 of the Rules of the Superior Courts 1986 provides as follows:

> Any verdict of judgment obtained where one party does not appear at the trial may be set aside by the Court upon such terms as may seem fit, upon an application made within six days after trial.[332]

There is a dearth of judicial consideration relating to the operation of Ord.36 r.33, which provides for the setting aside of judgment where a party fails to appear at trial. Order 13 r.11 of the Rules of the Superior Courts 1986 applies where judgment is entered for failure to enter an appearance. Although invoked in a somewhat different situation to Ord.36 r.33 or the circumstances where the PRTB may cancel a determination order in cases of non-appearance at an adjudication or a tenancy tribunal hearing, the judicial consideration of this rule is helpful in assessing what type of conditions may be imposed when setting aside judgment or a determination order. Order 13 r.11 provides:

> Where final judgment is entered pursuant to any of the preceding rules of this Order, it shall be lawful for the Court to set aside or vary such judgment upon such terms as may be just.

In *Petronelli v Collins*[333] judgment was set aside pursuant to Ord.13 r.11 on condition that the amount of the judgment debt be lodged in court. In *AIB v*

---

[329] RTA 2004, s.125(1)(a) and (2). The Circuit Court also has similar powers in the context of an application made under s.124 of the RTA 2004 (see para.9–122).

[330] RTA 2004, s.125(5).

[331] RTA 2004, s.125(3) and (6).

[332] Rules of the Superior Courts 1986 (S.I. No. 15 of 1986). Although, Ord.36 r.33 states that such an application can only be made six days after trial, it is clear from s.125(3) of the RTA 2004 that it does not look to the Rules of the Superior Courts in respect of the time limit which should be imposed for the making of an application to the PRTB for the cancellation of a determination order. Order 36 r.33 is relevant only in respect of the conditions that may be imposed on a party seeking the cancellation of the determination order.

[333] [1996] WJSC HC; unreported, High Court, Costello J., July 19, 1996.

Lyons[334] the High Court also set aside a default judgment on the basis of Ord.13 r.11. In considering what conditions would be appropriate to impose on the defendant, the High Court noted that since obtaining judgment in the matter, the plaintiff had entered a judgment mortgage in respect of the defendant's property. Peart J. was of the view that this was significant in assessing what conditions if any should be imposed, as the plaintiff had lost a significant measure of comfort. In addition the defendant did not have the means to lodge money into court. Peart J. accordingly imposed the following conditions—that the defendant would give an undertaking she would not dispose of, or even contract to dispose of her property pending the determination of the case and further in the event of judgment being granted against her, she would not attempt to dispose of her property for a period of six weeks. In *Fox v Taher*[335] the High Court set aside judgment and required the defendant to pay the costs of the judgment and the motion to the plaintiff.

Other types of conditions that have been imposed in making an order pursuant to Ord.13 r.11, are temporal in nature to expedite the subsequent proceedings, after judgment having being set aside. For instance in *Maher v Dixon*[336] the High Court directed that the defendant had two weeks to deliver a defence and three weeks to swear an affidavit of discovery to expedite matters. The plaintiff in addition was entitled to the costs of the defendant's motion to have judgment set aside.

17. STATUS QUO PENDING THE DETERMINATION OF THE DISPUTE

A. Where Status Quo must be Maintained

9–105 Section 86 of the RTA 2004 prescribes the status quo that must be maintained between the parties to a tenancy pending the determination of a dispute by the PRTB.[337] The interpretation of s.86 the RTA 2004 was the subject of consideration in the judgment of Laffoy J. in *Canty v Private Residential Tenancies Board*.[338]

(i) Payment of rent

9–106 A tenant must continue to pay rent under a tenancy or a sub-tenancy, pending the determination of a dispute referred to the PRTB, even in circumstances where the dispute relates to the rent payable under the tenancy.[339]

---

[334] [2004] IEHC 129; unreported, High Court, Peart J., July 21, 2004.

[335] Unreported, High Court, Costello J., January 24, 1996.

[336] [1995] I.L.R.M. 218.

[337] If a dispute is not dealt with or ceases to be dealt by the PRTB in accordance with ss.82, 83, 84 or 85 of the RTA 2004, s.86 of the RTA 2004 does not apply (RTA 2004, s.86(2)(d)).

[338] [2007] IEHC 243; unreported, High Court, Laffoy J., August 8, 2007.

[339] RTA 2004, s.86(1)(a). The RTA 2004 gives no guidance as to the amount of rent payable,

The only exception to this is where the landlord and tenant agree to the payment of rent being suspended pending the PRTB's determination.[340] In *Canty*, Laffoy J. held that s.86(1)(a) required the rent under a tenancy to continue to actually be "payable" and it was not the case that rental payments merely accrued.[341]

(ii) Rent increase

9–107 If the dispute relates to the amount of rent payable, there can be no increase in rent, pending the determination of the dispute by the PRTB.[342] The only exception to this is where the landlord and tenant both agree to a rent increase.[343]

(iii) Termination of tenancy

9–108 The termination of a tenancy may not be effected pending the determination of a dispute referred to the PRTB.[344] This is subject to one exception which arises in circumstances where (i) the dispute does *not* relate to the validity of a notice of termination or the right of a landlord to serve it,[345] _and_ (ii) a notice of termination is served either;

    (a) before the dispute was referred to the PRTB; or
    (b) after the dispute was referred to the PRTB and the required period of notice given was 28 days or less.[346]

Unless the circumstances described above exist, the termination of a tenancy may not be effected pending the determination of a dispute by the PRTB. Importantly, however, while the termination of the tenancy may not be *effected*, this does not prevent the service of a notice of termination. In *Canty*, Laffoy J.

---

where the rent under the tenancy is in dispute between the landlord and tenant, who each maintain a different amount is payable. Any under or over payment in rent ultimately found to have been made however, is a matter that can be dealt in the determination of the dispute.

[340] RTA 2004, s.86(2)(a).
[341] [2007] IEHC 243; unreported, High Court, Laffoy J., August 8, 2007, at p.32. Notwithstanding, that s.86(1)(a) of the RTA 2004 makes express provision for the payment of rent pending the determination of a dispute by the PRTB, in the preliminary results of the review of the RTA 2004 announced by the Minister for Housing and Local Services, it was recommended that there be the introduction of measures that would address the non-payment of rent by tenants during the dispute process. One of the measures suggested was that where there was non-payment of rent, it would be lawful for the landlord to terminate the tenancy. See Press Release, "Minister Michael Finneran announces significant changes to Private Residential Tenancies Board (PRTB) legislation", November 4, 2009, *www.environ.ie*.
[342] RTA 2004, s.86(1)(b). Also see comments at fn.339 at para.9–106 above.
[343] RTA 2004, s.86(2)(b).
[344] RTA 2004, s.86(1)(c).
[345] RTA 2004, s.86(3).
[346] RTA 2004, s.86(2)(c).

held that the service of a notice of termination does not effect termination of a tenancy, the expiry of the required notice period does[347]:

> "... the effect of s.86(1)(c) is to prevent the tenancy being treated as terminated notwithstanding the expiration of the relevant notice period. That means that termination which, apart from that provision, would have been effected is effectively suspended until the determination is made."[348]

B. Pending the Determination of a Dispute

9–109 As discussed in the preceding paragraphs, s.86 of the RTA 2004 prescribes the status quo that must be maintained "pending the determination of a dispute"[349] before the PRTB. The meaning of "pending the determination of a dispute" was considered in *Canty*. The applicant argued that a dispute was "pending" until a determination order made by the PRTB became binding on the parties. He maintained that in the case of a determination of a tenancy tribunal, that determination became binding on the parties on the expiry of 21 days from the date it is issued to them, unless an appeal was made to the High Court on a point of law under s.123(3) of the RTA 2004. In her judgment, Laffoy J. considered that an alternative interpretation of "pending the determination of a dispute", could be that it meant pending the making of a determination order. However, as that argument was not advanced by any party to the proceedings, Laffoy J. proceeded on the assumption that the applicant's interpretation was correct.[350] The meaning of "pending the determination of a dispute" therefore remains open to further judicial consideration.

18. Legal Representation

9–110 One of the main purposes for the establishment of the PRTB was "to replace a court system that is frequently confrontational, expensive and difficult to access with a non-confrontational, affordable, user-friendly and accessible mechanism."[351] In establishing the PRTB it was the intention therefore that legal representation would not be necessary and disputes could be resolved "cheaply and speedily".[352] Nevertheless, there is no prohibition in the RTA 2004, on a party being legally represented before any of its forums of dispute resolution. In particular in relation to tenancy tribunal hearings, s.104(6) of the RTA 2004 specifically provides that each of the parties shall be entitled to be represented

---

[347] [2007] IEHC 243; unreported, High Court, Laffoy J., August 8, 2007, at p.29.
[348] [2007] IEHC 243; unreported, High Court, Laffoy J., August 8, 2007, at pp.30–31.
[349] RTA 2004, s.86(1).
[350] [2007] IEHC 243; unreported, High Court, Laffoy J., August 8, 2007, at p.28.
[351] Minister Ahern TD., Seanad Éireann, Vol.177, Col.727, July 2, 2004, second stage.
[352] See the Long Title to the RTA 2004.

before the tenancy tribunal. However, legal costs or expenses will only be awarded to a party in exceptional circumstances, even if the party has been successful in their application or successful in defending a complaint made against him or her.[353] This limitation on the award of legal costs and expenses arises because of the definition given to "costs" in s.5 of the RTA 2004, which is considered in further detail at para.9–95 above. In summary "costs" is defined as not including legal costs or expenses.[354] However, if the PRTB, a mediator, an adjudicator or tenancy tribunal is of the opinion that the exceptional circumstances of the matter warrant an award of legal costs, they may make a direction in this regard.

19. PROCEDURES IN AID OF DISPUTE RESOLUTION

A. Interim/Interlocutory Relief before the Circuit Court

9–111 On *the request of a person* who has referred or is referring a dispute to the PRTB, the PRTB may apply to the Circuit Court on that person's behalf for interim or interlocutory relief in aid of the dispute resolution process.[355] This procedure is facilitated by s.189 of the RTA 2004. In deciding whether to make an application to the Circuit Court for interim or interlocutory relief, the PRTB may have regard to the merits of the referring party's contentions and the amount of damages the PRTB is likely to have to pay to the respondent, in the event that the application made by it is unsuccessful or proves unnecessary.[356] The PRTB must not have regard to its potential liability to damages, if the referring party undertakes to be liable for any amount of damages that may be awarded against the PRTB and the PRTB is satisfied that the party has the means to fulfil this undertaking.[357]

9–112 A case of serious antisocial behaviour, is an example of where it may be appropriate to make an application for relief under s.189 of the RTA 2004. Another example is where there has been a threatened or an actual unlawful eviction of a tenant from a dwelling. For instance, if it has not been possible for the PRTB to set up a tribunal hearing with less than 21 days notice and the tenant has requested the PRTB to make a s.189 application, the PRTB may consider it an appropriate case to seek an interim or interlocutory order against the landlord, that he or she refrains from interfering with the tenant's occupation

---

[353] This is in contrast to proceedings before the courts where, as a general rule, costs follow the event. In other words, the party who has been successful in bringing or defending proceedings before the courts, will be awarded costs.

[354] RTA 2004, s.5(3).

[355] RTA 2004, s.189(3).

[356] RTA 2004, s.189(4). This section also provides that none of these factors shall be conclusive for the purposes of the PRTB making its decision, as to whether to proceed with an application under s.189(3) or not.

[357] RTA 2004, s.189(5).

of the rented dwelling pending the determination of the dispute by the PRTB.[358]
In *Private Residential Tenancies Board v Sancta Maria Properties Limited t/a
Citi Properties*[359] Linnane J. made an Order pursuant to s.189 directing that the
respondent refrain from interfering with the tenant's peaceful and exclusive
occupation of the rented dwelling and from terminating the tenancy, pending
further order and/or resolution of the dispute by the PRTB.

B. Nature of Relief Granted

9–113 When an application is made to the Circuit Court pursuant to s.189 of
the RTA 2004, it may grant such interim or interlocutory relief as it considers
appropriate[360] and may order that any interlocutory relief granted, is to have
effect pending the final determination of the dispute by the PRTB.[361] It may also
make an order authorising an adjudicator or tenancy tribunal dealing with the
dispute or to whom the dispute is to be referred, to include in any determination
made, an award for the costs incurred in bringing an application under s.189.[362]
As it is only the PRTB that is authorised to make such an application, these shall
always be the costs of the PRTB. If an award of costs is made by an adjudicator
or tenancy tribunal, they may however be taxed in the same manner as an award
of costs made by the Circuit Court.[363] In *Private Residential Tenancies Board v
Goodman*,[364] O'Shea J. made an order pursuant to s.190(2)(b) of the RTA 2004
that the PRTB was to determine the question of costs. The tenancy tribunal that
ultimately dealt with the matter directed that on being furnished with an invoice,
the landlord was to promptly pay the costs of the application by the PRTB to the
Circuit Court, such costs to be taxed in default of agreement.[365]

C. Procedure

9–114 All applications for interim or interlocutory relief under s.189 of the RTA
2004, must be made in accordance with Ord.51A of the Circuit Court Rules
2001.[366] The application must be brought in the Circuit in which the tenancy or
dwelling concerned is or was situate.[367] The application must be made by way

---

[358] See para.9–82.
[359] Unreported, Circuit Court, ex tempore, Linnane J., October 27, 2006.
[360] RTA 2004, ss.189(6) and 190(1).
[361] RTA 2004, s.190(2)(a).
[362] RTA 2004, s.190(2)(b).
[363] RTA 2004, s.190(3).
[364] Unreported, Circuit Court, ex tempore, O'Shea J., October 19, 2006.
[365] *Obube v Goodman* (TR68/DR980/2006, November 6, 2006).
[366] The Circuit Court Rules (Residential Tenancies Act 2004) 2005 (S.I. No. 388 of 2005)
provided for rules dealing with the procedure to be followed in applications made to the Circuit
Court pursuant to ss.124 and 189 of the RTA 2004.
[367] Circuit Court Rules 2001, Ord.51A r.3(2).

of notice of motion (or in cases of urgency ex parte docket), which must set out the grounds on which the PRTB relies for the relief sought. The notice of motion or ex parte docket must also be supported by a grounding affidavit setting out the facts relied upon in seeking relief.[368] Where the application is made by way of notice of motion, no less than four days notice of the application must be given to the respondent. Service of the notice of motion and grounding affidavit must be effected by way of personal service or by leaving a copy of the proceedings at or by posting by pre-paid registered post to, the respondent's residence or place of business.[369] All applications under s.189 are heard on affidavit evidence or as may be determined by the Circuit Court.[370]

D. Cases

9–115 In the matter of *Obube v Goodman*[371] a tenant had made an application for dispute resolution services to the PRTB. He claimed that he had been illegally evicted from the dwelling rented by him, having returned one evening to find that the locks had been changed and that someone else was residing there. Attempts were made to re-house the tenant but these were unsuccessful. The PRTB made an application to the Circuit Court for relief pursuant to s.189 of the RTA 2004.[372] The Circuit Court ordered the landlord to allow the tenant to re-occupy the dwelling pending the resolution of the dispute by the PRTB or in the alternative to provide or fund alternative accommodation for the tenant.

When the matter came before the tenancy tribunal, it determined that the tenant had been illegally evicted and directed the landlord to pay the tenant damages in the sum of €8,000. The tenancy tribunal also determined that the landlord's agent had acted in a manner calculated to delay and undermine the workings of the PRTB, by failing to comply with the order of the Circuit Court made pursuant to s.189. In accordance with s.115(2)(i) of the RTA 2004, the tenancy tribunal directed that the landlord was to pay the sum of €1,000 towards part of the costs of the PRTB in convening the tenancy tribunal.[373]

9–116 In *Neary v Meagher*[374] the tenant submitted an application to the PRTB on October 10, 2006, complaining that the arrears of rent which had been claimed by the landlord were incorrect. On October 20, 2006 the electricity supply to the rented dwelling was cut. At the request of the tenant, the PRTB made an application to the Circuit Court pursuant to s.189. Before the Circuit

---

[368] Circuit Court Rules 2001, Ord.51A r.3(1).
[369] Circuit Court Rules 2001, Ord.51A r.3(3).
[370] Circuit Court Rules 2001, Ord.51A r.3(4).
[371] TR68/DR980/2006, November 6, 2006.
[372] Unreported, Circuit Court, ex tempore, O'Shea J., October 18, 2006.
[373] TR68/DR980/2006, November 6, 2006.
[374] TR69/DR972/2006, November 9, 2006.

Court Linnane J. made an order for interim relief that the respondent (the landlord's agent) and any other party having notice of the order, refrain from interfering with the tenant's peaceful and exclusive occupation of the dwelling. The respondent was also ordered to refrain from terminating the tenancy. These orders were to have effect pending further order and or resolution of the dispute by the PRTB. Linnane J. also directed the respondent to furnish the PRTB's solicitors with the name and address of the landlord of the premises.[375]

9–117 In *Danilrva v Deighan*[376] the landlord became concerned as to the tenant's ability to pay the rent as it fell due and attempted to retake possession of the dwelling. The tenant made an application for dispute resolution services to the PRTB. An application was subsequently made by the PRTB to the Circuit Court pursuant to s.189, for orders preventing the tenant being evicted from the dwelling. Before the Circuit Court, Hunt J. made an order for interim relief directing the landlord and any other party having notice of the order, to refrain from interfering with the tenant's peaceful and exclusive occupation of the dwelling and also to refrain from enforcing any notice of termination served. The landlord was also ordered to provide the tenant with a set of keys for the dwelling and to return all her personal belongings to her.[377]

20. ENFORCEMENT

A. Application to the Circuit Court

9–118 Where there has been non-compliance by a party with the term(s) of a determination order, an application for enforcement may be made to the Circuit Court. Section 124 of the RTA 2004 provides for the making of such an application. The application may be made by either the PRTB or the person seeking to enforce the term(s) of the determination order made in his or her favour.

B. Procedure

9–119 All applications pursuant to s.124 must be made in accordance with Ord.51A of the Circuit Court Rules 2001.[378] The application must be brought in the Circuit in which the tenancy or dwelling concerned is or was situate.[379] An application for enforcement under s.124 must be made as follows:

---

[375] *Private Residential Tenancies Board v Sancta Maria Properties Limited t/a Citi Properties*, unreported, Circuit Court, ex tempore, Linnane J., October 27, 2006.

[376] TR06/DR424/2008, May 15, 2008.

[377] *Private Residential Tenancies Board v Deighan*, unreported, Circuit Court, ex tempore, Hunt J., May 2, 2008.

[378] Order 51A also applies with respect to applications made pursuant to s.189 of the RTA 2004. See para.9–114.

[379] Circuit Court Rules 2001, Ord.51A r.2(2).

(a) by way of notice of motion and grounding affidavit;
(b) the notice of motion must be in accordance with Form 44C of the schedule of forms to the Circuit Court Rules 2001;
(c) the original determination order or a certified copy of it must be annexed to the notice of motion.[380]

The RTA 2004 provides that judicial notice shall be taken of every document purporting to be an instrument of the PRTB that is sealed with the PRTB's seal and authenticated in accordance with s.173(2). Such a document shall be received into evidence and deemed to be an instrument of the PRTB without proof unless the contrary is shown.[381] Accordingly, to lessen the evidential burden of a party making a s.124 application, it is advisable that the party ensures the determination order attached to the notice of motion is sealed[382] and that the seal has been authenticated.

9–120 The respondent party to the s.124 application must be served with the grounding affidavit and notice of motion no later than 10 days prior to the return date assigned by the Circuit Court.[383] Service of the notice of motion and grounding affidavit must be effected by way of personal service or by leaving a true copy at or by posting by pre-paid registered post to the respondent's residence or place of business.[384] All applications under s.124 of the RTA 2004 shall be heard by way of affidavit evidence or as may be determined by the court.[385] If the respondent intends to oppose the application and the applicant is not the PRTB, the respondent must notify the PRTB of his or her intention to object, no later than five days prior to the return date specified in the notice of motion.[386] The PRTB shall be entitled to appear and be heard at the hearing of the application.[387]

C. Defences and Security for Costs

9–121 Where an application is made to the Circuit Court under s.124 of the RTA 2004, the Circuit Court must make an order directing the respondent party to comply with the determination order of the PRTB. An exception to this arises

---

[380] Circuit Court Rules 2001, Ord.51A r.2(1), copy of Form 44C is attached at Appendix 19.
[381] RTA 2004, s.173(3). See para.9–102.
[382] Original determination orders are required to be sealed in accordance with s.121(6) of the RTA 2004.
[383] In certain cases it may be appropriate to make an application for short service in accordance with the Circuit Court Rules 2001.
[384] Circuit Court Rules 2001, Ord.51A r.2(3).
[385] Circuit Court Rules 2001, Ord.51A r.2(4).
[386] Circuit Court Rules 2001, Ord.51A r.2(3). A notice of intention to oppose shall be served by leaving a true copy at, or by sending by pre-paid registered post to, the registered offices of the PRTB.
[387] RTA 2004, s.124(6).

where the Circuit Court considers there are substantial reasons relating to or the respondent party shows to the satisfaction of the court, that in the proceedings before the PRTB:

(a) the process was not procedurally fair;
(b) a material consideration was not taken into account;
(c) a manifestly erroneous decision in relation to a legal issue was made; or
(d) the determination of the adjudicator or tenancy tribunal was manifestly erroneous.[388]

Where a respondent opposes the making of an order for enforcement by the Circuit Court on any of those four grounds, the applicant can seek security for costs. The Circuit Court may require the respondent to provide security for costs, where there is reason to believe the respondent will be unable to pay the costs of the applicant in so far as they relate to the respondent's opposing application.[389] Section 124(5) specifically provides for the making of orders in favour of the applicant where the determination order, the subject of the proceedings, is one requiring the dwelling to be vacated and a valid notice of termination was served because of the tenant's failure to pay rent. In these circumstances, before hearing any evidence from the respondent who seeks to oppose the enforcement of a determination order on the grounds set out at (a)–(d) above, the Circuit Court may order the respondent to lodge in court or pay to the applicant the amount of rent said to be due, in addition to such other rent in respect of the tenant's continued occupation of the dwelling.[390]

D. Cancellation of Determination Orders in Cases of Non-Appearance

9–122 Section 125 of the RTA 2004 provides a further ground on which the applicant can oppose the enforcement of a determination order under s.124. In circumstances where a person has established to the satisfaction of the Circuit Court that there were good and substantial reasons for his or her failure to appear at the relevant adjudication or tenancy tribunal hearing, which resulted in the making of the determination order, the Circuit Court may cancel the determination order and direct a re-hearing before the PRTB. The Circuit Court may require the respondent to comply with certain conditions before it cancels the determination order. These conditions are considered at para.9–104 above.[391]

---

[388] RTA 2004, s.124(2) and (3) RTA 2004. It is necessary only that one of these grounds exists, although in certain cases more than one may apply.
[389] RTA 2004, s.124(4).
[390] RTA 2004, s.124(5).
[391] Section 125 of the RTA 2004 also applies to the PRTB and empowers it in the same way as the Circuit Court, to make orders cancelling a determination order and directing a re-hearing. The exercise by the PRTB of its power under s.125 is considered at para.9–104.

E. Enforcement of Determination Order and Further Compliance

9–123 The Circuit Court must make an order directing the respondent party to comply with a determination order of the PRTB, unless the Circuit Court is satisfied that any of the circumstances considered at para.9–121 exist or there is a basis for the cancellation of the determination order under s.125 of the RTA 2004. When making an order enforcing the determination order, the Circuit Court may also make such ancillary or other orders as it considers just.[392] This may include an order for costs against the respondent party.

Where the Circuit Court enforces a determination order under s.124 of the RTA 2004 a situation may also arise where the amount of arrears of rent, charges or other amounts awarded in a determination order, exceed the Circuit Court's jurisdiction.[393] In *Private Residential Tenancies Board v Whelan and Anor*[394] the Circuit Court made an order enforcing a determination order where the arrears of rent the tenants were directed to pay the landlord was €48,929, being an amount in excess of the Circuit Court's jurisdiction. Notwithstanding this, the Circuit Court made an order enforcing the determination order of the PRTB. In *Whelan* no objection was raised by the tenants to the making of the order on the grounds that it exceeded the Circuit Court's jurisdiction. However, as the Circuit Court is given sole jurisdiction to enforce the terms of a determination order under the RTA 2004 (and must enforce a determination order subject to limited exceptions), the Circuit Court's approach in *Whelan* appears to have been that its jurisdiction was not compromised by reason of the fact that an award made in a determination order exceeded its monetary jurisdiction.

9–124 Where the Circuit Court makes an order pursuant to s.124 enforcing a determination order and the respondent party then fails to comply with that Circuit Court order, execution of the order may be pursued by any of the means permitted by the Circuit Court Rules.[395] For instance where a tenant is overholding, the Circuit Court Order directing the tenant to vacate the property may be directed to the Sheriff. In the more serious of cases where a tenant has failed to vacate a dwelling, it may be appropriate to seek an order for attachment and committal.[396]

---

[392] RTA 2004, s.124(7).
[393] See para.9–43 which considers the monetary jurisdiction of the PRTB being a maximum of €20,000 in damages and €60,000 in respect of arrears of rent and other charges.
[394] Unreported, Circuit Court, ex tempore, Linnane J., July 29, 2009.
[395] Circuit Court Rules 2001, Ord.36.
[396] Circuit Court Rules 2001, Ord.37.

F. Cases[397]

9–125 In the *Private Residential Tenancies Board v Batt*[398] the Circuit Court enforced the determination order requiring the tenant to vacate the dwelling forthwith and to pay the landlord arrears of rent of €18,000 within 21 days. The costs of the application were also awarded against the tenant. In *Private Residential Tenancies Board v Taghavi*[399] the Circuit Court made an order enforcing the terms of a determination order requiring the tenant to vacate the dwelling within seven days and to pay the sum of €462.45 in ESB charges to the landlord. The tenant was also ordered to pay the costs of the application.

9–126 In *Private Residential Tenancies Board v Tawfig Mohamed*[400] the Circuit Court made an order enforcing a determination order and directed that the tenant pay the landlord the sum of €10,978.24. This amount was calculated from the sum of €17,517.64 in arrears of rent, less a security deposit and one month's rent paid by the tenant, with a deduction also allowed for the costs incurred by the tenant in repairing and re-decorating the dwelling. The tenant and all persons residing in the dwelling were directed to vacate the dwelling by August 17, 2009 and to pay rent at the rate of €1,100 per month, until such time as they gave up possession. The costs of the application were awarded to the PRTB.

21. PROSECUTION

A. Offence to Fail to Comply with a Determination Order

9–127 Section 126(1) of the RTA 2004 makes it an offence to fail to comply with one or more terms of a determination order. Where a person has failed to comply with a determination order, they may be prosecuted by the PRTB.[401] A prosecution for an offence under s.126 is not a means of enforcement of a determination order (although the possibility of criminal sanction may often have the effect of compelling compliance). Where the PRTB prosecutes a party who has failed to comply with a determination order, the PRTB may

---

[397] The cases considered below deal with applications made by the PRTB pursuant to s.124 of the RTA 2004. It should be noted that any party in whose favour a determination order has been made, may also make an application for enforcement pursuant to s.124 (see para.9–118). The consent of the PRTB for the making of such an application is not required, although it may be necessary for the party who seeks to enforce the determination order to obtain correspondence or other form of communication from the PRTB, for the purpose of adducing evidence on affidavit that there has been a failure to comply with the determination order.
[398] Unreported, Circuit Court, ex tempore, Deery J., November 26, 2009.
[399] Unreported, Circuit Court, ex tempore, Griffin J., February 5, 2009.
[400] Unreported, Circuit Court, ex tempore, Mahon J., June 17, 2009.
[401] RTA 2004, s.9(3).

nevertheless, seek a compensation order for the benefit of the party in whose favour the term of the determination order has been made.[402] Furthermore, an application for enforcement may still be made under s.124 of the RTA 2004, notwithstanding a party is guilty of an offence under s.126 and is/or has been prosecuted for such an offence.[403]

9–128 Where a party is found guilty of an offence for failing to comply with a determination order, they will be liable on summary conviction to a fine not exceeding €3,000 and/or a term of imprisonment not exceeding six months.[404] A person convicted of an offence pursuant to s.126, shall not be sentenced to any term of imprisonment if he or she shows that the failure to comply with the terms of a determination order, was due to his or her limited financial means.[405]

B. Prosecutions

9–129 The PRTB actively prosecutes those parties who fail to comply with determination orders.[406] In *Private Residential Tenancies Board v Mullery*[407] the tenant had failed to comply with a determination order directing her to pay the sum of €13,800 in arrears of rent up to September 30, 2008 and €42.74 per day thereafter until such time as she vacated the dwelling. The District Court convicted the tenant of an offence of failing to comply with a determination order and imposed the maximum fine on summary conviction of €3,000. The tenant was also ordered to pay costs incurred by the PRTB for its investigation, prosecution and detection of the offence. The tenant was given 30 days to pay these amounts, in default of which the tenant was to be imprisoned for 45 days, unless the sum she was ordered to pay was discharged sooner.

In *Private Residential Tenancies Board v Ryan*[408] the tenant failed to comply with a determination order directing him to pay the sum €14,800 to the landlord of a dwelling that the tenant had rented. The tenant was convicted of the offence of failing to comply with a determination order and fined €100. He was also ordered to pay costs incurred by the PRTB in the investigation, prosecution and detection of the offence. In addition, a compensation order of €6,348, being the maximum monetary jurisdiction of the District Court, was made in favour of the

---

[402] Criminal Justice Act 1993, s.6.

[403] RTA 2004, s.126(2).

[404] RTA 2004, s.9(1). See also paras 9–130 to 9–131 below, which considers the prosecution of offences under the RTA 2004 in further detail.

[405] RTA 2004, s.126(3).

[406] In the PRTB's annual report for 2008, the PRTB reported that in the majority of cases it is the policy of the PRTB to pursue a criminal conviction against parties who do not comply with its determination orders. ("Private Residential Tenancies Board, Annual Report & Accounts 2008", p.37.)

[407] District Court, Connellan J., September 4, 2009.

[408] District Court, Dempsey J., September 7, 2009.

landlord. The tenant was given 90 days to pay these amounts, in default of which he was to be imprisoned for the period of two days, unless the total sum he was ordered to pay was discharged sooner.

In *Private Residential Tenancies Board v Coilog*[409] the landlord had failed to comply with a determination order directing him to return a tenant's property, in the absence of which he was directed to pay the tenant €6,158. Before the District Court the landlord was convicted of an offence of failing to comply with a determination order. A fine of €2,000 was imposed on the landlord and he was ordered to pay a compensation order for the sum of €6,158 to the tenant. A costs order was also made payable to the PRTB. The landlord appealed his conviction to the Circuit Court, which affirmed the District Court's Order.

22. OFFENCES

9–130 There are 15 offences under the RTA 2004 and these have been considered throughout this text. All offences under the RTA 2004 are summary offences. Proceedings in relation to an offence under the RTA 2004 may be brought and prosecuted by the PRTB.[410] Any proceedings for an offence under the RTA 2004 must be instituted within one year after the date of the offence.[411]

9–131 A person who is found guilty of an offence under the RTA 2004, is liable to a fine not exceeding €3,000 and/or imprisonment for up to six months.[412] If a person has been convicted of an offence but continues to commit it, that person is guilty of a further offence on every day on which the contravention continues. For each such continuing offence, the person shall be liable on summary conviction to a fine not exceeding €250.[413] Where a person is convicted of an offence under the RTA 2004, the court shall order the person to pay the costs and expenses incurred by the PRTB in the investigation, detection and prosecution of the offence. However, the court is not required to make such an order, if it satisfied that there are special and substantial reasons for not doing so.[414]

23. SERVICE

A. Service of Notices

9–132 Service of notices under Pt 6 (and all other Parts of the RTA 2004)[415] is dealt with at s.6 of the RTA 2004. However, where an application is made to the

---

[409] Circuit Court, ex tempore, Matthews J., July 16, 2008.
[410] RTA 2004, s.9(3).
[411] RTA 2004, s.9(4).
[412] RTA 2004, s. 9(1).
[413] RTA 2004, s.9(2).
[414] RTA 2004, s.9(5).
[415] See para.8–69 that considers s.6 of the RTA 2004, in the context of the service of notices of termination.

Circuit Court pursuant to s.84(5),[416] s.88(4),[417] s.189[418] or s.124[419] of the RTA 2004, any proceedings, orders or other documents required to be served for the purposes of those applications, must be served in accordance with the Circuit Court Rules 2001.[420]

Section 6(1) provides that a notice required or authorised to be served or given under the RTA 2004, must be addressed to the person concerned by name.[421] The notice may be served or given to the person in one of the following ways:

(a) By delivering it to the person;

(b) By leaving it at the address at which the person ordinarily resides or in the case in which an address for service has been furnished, at that address;

(c) Be sending it by post in a prepaid letter to the address at which the person ordinarily resides or, in a case in which an address for service has been furnished, to that address;

(d) Where the notice relates to a dwelling and it appears that no person is in actual occupation of the dwelling, by affixing it in a conspicuous position on the outside of the dwelling or the property containing the dwelling.[422]

For the purposes of service, a company shall be deemed to be ordinarily resident at its registered office and every other body corporate and every unincorporated body shall be deemed to be ordinarily resident at its principal office or place of business. Where a notice is served on behalf of a person it shall be deemed to have been served by that person.[423]

B. Notice not Received on Time

9–133 In proceedings before the PRTB under Pt 6 of the RTA 2004, if a notice was served or given in accordance with the provisions of s.6, the onus shall be on the recipient to establish to the PRTB, the adjudicator or tribunal tenancy that the notice was not received in sufficient time to enable compliance with the relevant time limit specified under the RTA 2004.[424] This may arise for example,

---

[416] See para.9–35.

[417] See para.9–52.

[418] See para.9–114.

[419] See paras 9–119 to 9–120.

[420] Circuit Court Rules 2001, Ord.51A.

[421] Section 6(2) of the RTA 2004 provides however that where the name of the person cannot be ascertained by reasonable inquiry and that person is the owner, landlord, tenant or occupier of the dwelling, it is sufficient that the notice is addressed to the person using those descriptions.

[422] RTA 2004, s.6(1). In circumstances where a notice is affixed to the outside of a dwelling, a person who removes, damages or defaces the notice during the three-month period after it has been affixed, shall be guilty of an offence (RTA 2004, s.6(4) and (5)).

[423] RTA 2004, s.7.

[424] RTA 2004, s.6(6).

where after a mediation the PRTB serves a notice on the landlord and tenant asking them to confirm within 21 days whether the parties still agree to the terms of a settlement or agreement reached at mediation.[425] The tenant for instance may claim that that notice was not received in sufficient time to enable him or her to notify the PRTB within the 21-day period that he or she no longer accepts the agreement reached at mediation. In these circumstances, the onus will be on the tenant to establish the notice was not received in sufficient time.

---

[425] RTA 2004, s.96. See para.9–65.

CHAPTER 10

REGISTRATION OF TENANCIES

1. BACKGROUND

10–01 Section 20[1] of the Housing (Miscellaneous Provisions) Act 1992 (the "1992 Act") empowers the Minister[2] to make regulations requiring the landlord of a house, let for rent or other valuable consideration, to register any residential tenancy of that house. Under s.20 the tenancy is to be registered with the housing authority in whose functional area it is situated. The Housing (Registration of Rented Houses) Regulations 1996 (the "Registration Regulations 1996") were enacted under s.20, with the result that since May 1, 1996 landlords have been obliged to register residential tenancies of houses rented by them.[3]

Under the Registration Regulations 1996, landlords were obliged to pay an application fee for registration and an annual fee thereafter.[4] Housing authorities with whom the tenancies were registered were in turn required to maintain a register of all tenancies of houses within their functional area and were charged with enforcing the Registration Regulations 1996.[5]

10–02 The Commission on the Private Rented Sector (the "Commission") gave consideration to the registration system that was introduced by the Registration Regulations 1996.[6] The Report of the Commission records that the purpose of the tenancy registers maintained by local authorities was to assist the local authorities, amongst other matters, in the effective enforcement of the Housing (Standards for Rented Houses) Regulations 1993 (the "Housing Standards Regulations") and the Housing (Rent Books) Regulations 1993 (the "Rent Book Regulations"). The purpose of the registration fee payable by landlords was to provide resources to assist local authorities in maintaining registers, carrying out inspections and ensuring compliance with the provisions of all the aforementioned regulations. The Commission noted that an added benefit that

---

[1]   As amended by Sch.2 of the Local Government Act 1994 and s.200 of the Residential Tenancies Act 2004.

[2]   Minister is defined at s.1(1) of the 1992 Act, as the Minister for the Environment (now the Minister for the Environment, Heritage and Local Government).

[3]   S.I. No. 30 of 1996. Registration Regulations 1996, art.5(1) *(revoked)*. See para.10–03 below.

[4]   Registration Regulations 1996, arts 5(4) and 8 *(revoked)*. See para.10–03 below.

[5]   1992 Act, s.20(4). Section 116(1) of the Housing Act 1966 gives a housing authority the power to prosecute.

[6]   Report of the Commission on the Private Rented Residential Sector, July 2000 (the "Report of the Commission"), paras 4.9 to 4.10.

had been envisaged from the registration system, was the provision of valuable data on the rented sector.[7]

The Registration Regulations 1996 faced opposition from landlords and various provisions of the registration scheme became the subject of litigation.[8] Compliance with the Registration Regulations 1996 was low and the Commission's report records that information received from local authorities showed that the number of registered houses at the end of March 2000 was only 26,199. This low level of compliance by landlords went hand in hand with a very low level of enforcement of the Registration Regulations 1996 by local authorities. As of the date of the Commission's report, there had been no conviction of a landlord for non-compliance with the obligation to register under the Registration Regulations 1996.[9]

The Commission concluded that the operation of the registration system should be a function of the proposed Private Residential Tenancies Board (the "PRTB"). It recommended that the mechanism for registering tenancy details should not be unduly bureaucratic and might simply involve a detachable insert from the rent book, to be completed and signed by both the landlord and tenant at the commencement of the tenancy. It also recommended that failure to comply with the new registration requirements would be an offence on the part of landlords and that the new registration system would have tax incentive and exemption implications.[10]

10–03 The Residential Tenancies Act 2004 (the "RTA 2004") revoked the Registration Regulations 1996. In line with the Commission's recommendations, the PRTB was given responsibility for a new registration system that was established under Pt 7 of the RTA 2004.[11] Henceforth, all landlords must register any tenancy of a dwelling rented by them with the PRTB.[12]

10–04 The registration obligations imposed under Pt 7 appear to have been met with less resistance than the Registration Regulations 1996, as evidenced by the number of tenancies now being registered. By the end of 2005, 83,983 tenancies had been registered with the PRTB. At the end of 2006 this figure had increased to 137,961 and to 202,078 by the end of 2007, with in excess of 206,000 tenancies registered by the end of 2008.[13] This stands in sharp contrast to the

---

[7]   Report of the Commission, para.4.9.1.

[8]   Report of the Commission, para.4.9.4.

[9]   Report of the Commission, paras 4.9.5. and 4.10.2.

[10] Report of the Commission, para.8.4.6.

[11] Part 7 came into force on September 1, 2004, pursuant to the Residential Tenancies Act 2004 (Commencement) Order 2004 (S.I. No. 505 of 2004). Section 10(2) of the RTA 2004 revoked the Registration Regulations 1996.

[12] RTA 2004, s.134(1). The dwelling concerned must come within the jurisdiction of the PRTB, for the registration obligations under the RTA 2004 to apply. See Ch.3 the Application of the Residential Tenancies Act 2004.

[13] See, "Private Residential Tenancies Board, Annual Report 1/9/2004–31/12/2005", p.11; "Private Residential Tenancies Board, Annual Report 2006", p.14; "Private Residential

number of tenancies that were registered pursuant to the Registration Regulations 1996.

10–05 The PRTB has actively pursued landlords who have failed to register tenancies in accordance with Pt 7 of the RTA 2004.[14] It has also used the registration fee paid by landlords as an incentive to local authorities to enforce the Housing Standards Regulations and the Rent Book Regulations. In this regard, part of the funding generated from registration fees paid to the PRTB, is passed on to local authorities to take account of the fact that since the introduction of Pt 7, they no longer receive the tenancy registration fee paid by landlords. However, the PRTB has distributed this funding to local authorities not only on the basis of the number of tenancies registered in each local authority's functional area, but also on the basis of the number of inspections carried out by the local authority for the purposes of enforcing the Housing Standards Regulations and the Rent Book Regulations.[15]

In its annual reports, the PRTB has considered the necessity of the obligation imposed on landlords to register details of their tenancies. It has highlighted that registration is relevant to the PRTB's function in providing a dispute resolution service, especially in dealing with disputes relating to rents, rent reviews, tenancy terminations, security of tenure, as well as other matters. Furthermore, the PRTB has identified a need to systematically capture relevant information required to understand more fully the operation of the market for rented residential property and to assist that market in operating more efficiently.[16]

2. REGISTRATION UNDER THE RTA 2004

10–06 Under the RTA 2004 landlords are required to make an application to register a tenancy of a dwelling let by them *within one month* from the commencement of the tenancy.[17] It should be noted that it is the tenancy of the dwelling that must be registered as opposed to the dwelling itself.

Tenancies Board, Annual Report & Accounts 2007", p.14; and "Private Residential Tenancies Board, Annual Report & Accounts 2008", p.22.

[14] See para.10–23.

[15] See, "Private Residential Tenancies Board, Annual Report 1/9/2004–31/12/2005", pp.13 and 14; "Private Residential Tenancies Board, Annual Report 2006", p.15; "Private Residential Tenancies Board, Annual Report & Accounts 2007", p.16; and "Private Residential Tenancies Board, Annual Report & Accounts 2008", p.25. Section 146 of the RTA 2004 permits an exchange of data between the PRTB and local authorities to assist in the performance of their respective functions relating to rented dwellings and housing.

[16] See, "Private Residential Tenancies Board, Annual Report 1/9/2004–31/12/2005", p.10; "Private Residential Tenancies Board, Annual Report 2006", p.13; and "Private Residential Tenancies Board, Annual Report & Accounts 2007", p.13.

[17] RTA 2004, s.134(2). Where a tenancy was in being before September 1, 2004 (the date Pt 7 came into force), a landlord was obliged to register the tenancy within three months of September 1, 2004. Where a tenancy commenced within three months after the coming into

Each new tenancy created in respect of a dwelling must be registered.[18] If a landlord owns two or more separate dwellings which he or she rents, the landlord is obliged to register the tenancy of each of those dwellings.[19] If a dwelling is available for rent for residential use but has not yet been let, no requirement to register arises.

Where a tenancy becomes a Part 4 tenancy (that is on the expiry of six months from its commencement) there is no requirement to register the Part 4 tenancy.[20] However, the coming into being of a further Part 4 tenancy, that is a tenancy which has run into its fifth year, does give rise to an obligation to register.[21]

3. How to Register a Tenancy

10–07 To register a tenancy a landlord must complete a form known as the "Form PRTB1".[22] This can be downloaded from the PRTB's website.[23] Prior to the enactment of the Housing (Miscellaneous Provisions) Act 2009 (the "Housing Act 2009"), s.135(2) of the RTA 2004 required the Form PRTB1 to be signed by the landlord of the dwelling (or his or her authorised agent) and each of the tenants. The requirement for a tenant's signature often caused difficulties for landlords, who were prohibited from registering a tenancy where the tenant refused to sign the registration form. Of more significant consequence, however, was the fact that any dispute arising with the tenant could not be dealt with through the dispute resolution services provided by the PRTB. This was because the RTA 2004 requires that a tenancy must be registered before any dispute submitted by a landlord can be processed by the PRTB.[24] Section 100(4) of the Housing Act 2009 deleted s.135(2) of the RTA 2004 and

---

force of Pt 7, the landlord was obliged to register the tenancy by December 1, 2004 or within one month from the commencement of the tenancy, whichever date occurred later. See s.134(2)(b)(i) and (ii) of the RTA 2004.

[18] RTA 2004, s.135(1)(a).

[19] See Ch.3 that considers the categories of dwellings which fall outside the jurisdiction of the RTA 2004.

[20] RTA 2004, s.135(1)(b). A Part 4 tenancy arises after a tenant has resided in a dwelling for six months. The effect of a Part 4 tenancy is to give a tenant security of tenure for a further period of three and a half years, after the tenancy has been in existence for that initial six-month period. Part 4 tenancies, their meaning and effect, are considered in detail in Ch.7.

[21] RTA 2004, s.135(1)(c). See para.10–15 which considers the registration of further Part 4 tenancies.

[22] Section 134(3) provides that an application for registration must be in the prescribed form. The Form PRTB1 was adopted by the PRTB to facilitate registration. The Form PRTB1 requires landlords to provide the particulars required by s.136 of the RTA 2004. Its format has been revised from time to time by the PRTB (see, "Private Residential Tenancies Board, Annual Report 2006", p.15 and "Private Residential Tenancies Board, Annual Report & Accounts 2007", p.16).

[23] *www.prtb.ie*.

[24] Section 83(2) of the RTA 2004 provides that the PRTB shall not deal with a dispute referred to it by a landlord if the tenancy concerned is not registered under Pt 7. See also paras 9–38 to 9–39.

accordingly there is no longer a requirement for the Form PRTB1 to be signed by the tenant.

10–08 Once completed, the Form PRTB1 must be submitted by the landlord to the PRTB, together with the relevant fee.[25] Separate applications are required for separate tenancies and therefore the information provided in a Form PRTB1 can relate to one tenancy only.[26] Accordingly, if a person is a landlord of more than one tenancy, he or she must complete a separate Form PRTB1 in respect of each tenancy.

10–09 In order to register a tenancy with the PRTB, a landlord must provide the following information, all of which is requested in the Form PRTB1:

(a)   the address of the dwelling;

(b)   the name and address (for correspondence) and the personal public service number ("PPSN") of the landlord and if the application is made by landlord's authorised agent, these details in respect of the agent also;

(c)   if the landlord is a company, the registered office and company registration number of the company and if the application is made by the landlord's authorised agent being a company, these details in respect of the agent also;

(d)   the number of occupants of the dwelling;

(e)   the name and the PPSN of each of the tenants (unless the PPSN cannot be ascertained by reasonable inquiry);

(f)   the name of the housing authority in whose functional area the dwelling is situated;

(g)   if the dwelling is in an apartment complex, the name of the management company, details of its registered office and company registration number;

(h)   a description of the dwelling indicating the estimated floor area, the number of bed spaces, the number of bedrooms and whether the dwelling is the whole or part of a house, a maisonette, an apartment, a flat or a bedsitter and, in the case of a house or a maisonette, an indication as to whether the house or maisonette is detached, semi-detached or terraced;

(i)   the date on which the tenancy of the dwelling commenced[27];

(j)   the amount of rent payable, when this is payable and any taxes or other charges required to be paid by the tenant;

(k)   the length of the tenancy if it is for a fixed term;

(l)   if the tenancy consists of a sub-letting, an indication of this;

(m)   the registration number (RT number) of a previous tenancy of the dwelling the subject of the application but only where the name and PPSN of the tenant(s) are the same, and;

(n)   such other matters as may be prescribed.[28]

---

[25]   See paras 10–12 to 10–14 that deal with fees for registration.

[26]   RTA 2004, s.134(6).

[27]   Section 142 of the RTA 2004, states that in any proceedings under Pt 6, it shall be presumed unless the contrary is shown that the date stated in the PRTB's register is the date on which that tenancy commenced.

[28]   RTA 2004, s.136(a)–(o).

10–10 If a person in completing the Form PRTB1, knowingly or recklessly furnishes to the PRTB information which is false or misleading in a material respect, that person is guilty of an offence.[29] The PRTB is empowered to authorise a person to enter and inspect a dwelling for the purposes of determining whether any particular specified in the application for registration is correct.[30] However, the PRTB is not permitted to authorise a person to inspect a dwelling unless it has reasonable grounds for believing that a particular specified in the Form PRTB1 is false or misleading in a material respect. Any person who impedes an inspection authorised by the PRTB is guilty of an offence.[31]

10–11 If a Form PRTB1 received by the PRTB is incomplete or is not accompanied by the correct registration fee, the PRTB is obliged to notify the applicant that the application is incomplete and invalid. The Form PRTB1, together with the registration fee and any other information submitted with the application, shall be returned to the applicant.[32] Each tenancy that is registered with the PRTB is assigned a unique number, which is referred to by the PRTB as a tenancy's "RT number".[33] The PRTB issues a confirmation letter to the landlord or his or her agent as appropriate, confirming registration of the tenancy and providing details of the RT number.[34]

4. REGISTRATION FEES

A. Fees Payable

10–12 A landlord must pay a fee for the registration of a tenancy. The fee is payable to the PRTB and must be submitted with the Form PRTB1.[35] The fees which are payable on the registration of a tenancy are set out below. The PRTB has a discretion to vary these fees, in so far as it approximates to the percentage increase or decrease in the value of money generally in the State.[36] Accordingly,

---

[29] RTA 2004, s.143.
[30] RTA 2004, s.145(1).
[31] RTA 2004, s.145(2) and (3).
[32] RTA 2004, s.135(5), as amended by s.100(4)(b) of the Housing Act 2009. Prior to the enactment of the Housing Act 2009, if a Form PRTB1 received by the PRTB was incomplete or not accompanied by the relevant fee for registration, the landlord was given a reasonable opportunity to rectify the incomplete application or the non-payment of the registration fee. Now landlords are not afforded such an opportunity and the application is simply returned to them.
[33] RTA 2004, s.135(3).
[34] See www.prtb.ie. Section 135(4) of the RTA 2004 provides that the PRTB is to acknowledge in such form as it considers appropriate, receipt by it of an application for registration and the relevant registration fee.
[35] RTA 2004, s.134(3).
[36] RTA 2004, s.138.

when registering a tenancy regard should be had to the PRTB's website for up to date details of the registration fees payable.[37]

Currently a €70 registration fee is payable when a tenancy is registered on time, that is within one month from the commencement of the tenancy.[38] Where a person is a landlord of multiple tenancies of dwellings in the same property, he or she may opt to pay a single composite fee of €300.[39] Regardless of the fact that a composite fee may be payable, a separate Form PRTB1 must still be completed by the landlord in respect of the tenancy of each dwelling. The option of paying the composite fee is also only available to landlords who register all the relevant tenancies within the property at the same time and where the tenancies are registered within one month of their commencement.[40] By way of example, if a landlord is seeking to register six tenancies of dwellings within the same property, he or she will not be able to avail of the composite fee for all six, if one of the tenancies commenced six weeks after the other five tenancies. If the landlord pays the composite fee to register the five dwellings, no fee however is payable on the registration of the sixth tenancy, as the landlord may avail of the exemption considered at para.10–13 below.

B. Exemption from Fees

10–13 Provided an application to register a tenancy has been made within one month of its commencement, no fee is payable where in the preceding 12 months:

    (a) two payments for the registration of tenancies of the same dwelling have been made to the PRTB[41];

    (b) the applicant has paid the single composite fee to register several tenancies of dwellings within the same property and the dwelling, the subject of the application for registration, is also in that property[42];

    (c) an application under the Registration Regulations 1996 has been made with payment of the relevant fee under those regulations.[43]

10–14 As considered in further detail at para.10–20, a landlord is required to update details of a tenancy registered with the PRTB where there has been a change in the rent payable under the tenancy. No fee is payable to update the details of a tenancy currently registered.[44]

---

[37] *www.prtb.ie.*

[38] RTA 2004, s.137(1)(b).

[39] RTA 2004, s.137(2)–(4). As the registration fee for one tenancy is €70, the composite fee will only be advantageous to a landlord where his or her property consists of five or more dwellings.

[40] RTA 2004, s.137(3) and (5).

[41] RTA 2004, s.134(4) and (5)(a).

[42] RTA 2004, s.134(4) and (5)(b).

[43] RTA 2004, s.134(4) and (5)(c). As s.10(2) of the RTA 2004 revoked the Registration Regulations 1996, the circumstances where this exception will apply are now limited.

[44] RTA 2004, s.139(3).

5. Registration of a Further Part 4 Tenancy

10–15 Landlords are obliged to re-register a tenancy that has lasted four years. A tenancy that enters its fourth year, is known for the purposes of the RTA 2004, as a "further Part 4 tenancy".[45] A further Part 4 tenancy is treated in the same way for the purposes of registration, as if the tenancy had just commenced.[46] Accordingly, a landlord is required to complete a Form PRTB1, pay the appropriate registration fee in respect of that further Part 4 tenancy[47] and register it within one month of its commencement. On receipt of an application for the registration of a further Part 4 tenancy, the PRTB shall assign it a new RT number and shall issue a letter to the landlord confirming its registration and setting out the details of the new RT number. If a landlord fails to register a further Part 4 tenancy, he or she will also be prohibited from availing of the dispute resolution services of the PRTB.[48]

10–16 As noted above, a further Part 4 tenancy comes into being four years after the date that the tenancy commenced. The obligation to register a further Part 4 tenancy arises from the date it comes into being, as opposed to four years from when the first tenancy was originally registered. By way of example, where a tenancy commenced on October 5, 2004, a landlord would have been obliged to register the further Part 4 tenancy (in effect re-register the tenancy), within one month of October 5, 2008. In that instance, if the landlord had in fact only registered the tenancy for the first time in say August 2008, he would still be required to register the further Part 4 tenancy within one month of October 5, 2008, as opposed to four years from August 2008.[49]

10–17 In circumstances where a person has purchased a dwelling without an existing tenancy being terminated, the new owner/landlord will be required to

---

[45] See para.7–13 that considers further Part 4 tenancies in greater detail.

[46] Section 135(1)(c) of the RTA 2004, states that for the avoidance of doubt, the coming into being of a further Part 4 tenancy in respect of a dwelling does give rise to a requirement under s.134 to apply to register that further Part 4 tenancy.

[47] The same fees are payable for the registration of a further Part 4 tenancy, as when a tenancy is registered for the first time. See para.10–12 that sets out the fees payable for the registration of a tenancy. The late fee (being double the fee for a tenancy registered on time) is also payable in circumstances where a landlord does not register the further Part 4 tenancy within one month of its commencement.

[48] Section 83(2) provides that the PRTB shall not deal with a dispute submitted to it by a landlord if the tenancy of the dwelling concerned is not registered. Section 83(2) applies by reason of s.135(1)(c) of the RTA 2004, which requires landlords to register further Part 4 tenancies.

[49] In the case of multiple tenants, a Part 4 tenancy will subsist so long as one of the original tenants of the tenancy remains in occupation of the dwelling. Accordingly, where three of the original four tenants of a dwelling have left and been replaced, the Part 4 tenancy of that dwelling will continue so long as that one remaining original tenant stays in occupation. If a further Part 4 tenancy comes into being, the landlord will be required to register that further Part 4 tenancy within one month of its commencement, regardless of the fact that only one of

register a further Part 4 tenancy of that dwelling, if and when one comes into being.

10–18 The existence of a fixed term tenancy does not affect the operation of Pt 4 of the RTA 2004.[50] Accordingly, where the term of a fixed term tenancy is for example of four and a half years, the landlord is still obliged to register the further Part 4 tenancy within one month of its commencement, regardless of the fact that the terms of the fixed term tenancy may provide that it is to terminate within six months.

6. SUB-TENANCIES

10–19 The RTA 2004 does not contain a provision specifically stating that where a sub-tenancy has been created, it must be registered in addition to the head-tenancy arrangement. The obligation under the RTA 2004 is that a landlord is obliged to register the *tenancy* of a dwelling to which the RTA 2004 applies.[51] The grant of a sub-tenancy creates a new tenancy or a new relationship of landlord and tenant.[52] A "tenancy" is defined for the purposes of the RTA 2004 as including "a sub-tenancy ... and a sub-tenancy that has been terminated".[53] The particulars that a landlord must provide in an application for registration under Pt 7 include, "if the tenancy consists of a sub-letting, an indication to that effect".[54] Therefore, notwithstanding that there is no express provision in the RTA 2004, providing that sub-tenancies are to be registered, it seems that Pt 7 does apply to sub-tenancy arrangements and they must also be registered. This is consistent with the approach of the PRTB which requires sub-tenancies to be registered.

In practice therefore, if a dwelling is let by a landlord to a tenant and the tenant sub-lets it to another individual,[55] both the head-tenancy and the sub-tenancy must be registered. The head-landlord will have been obliged to have registered the head-tenancy within one month of its commencement. Similarly, the head-tenant will also have been obliged to register the sub-tenancy within one month of its commencement. Accordingly, there may be more than one tenancy of a dwelling registered at the same time. Both the head-tenancy and the sub-tenancy will be assigned their own unique RT number by the PRTB.

---

the tenants has been in occupation for four years. See paras 7–22 to 7–28 that deal with Part 4 tenancies and multiple tenants.

[50] This is considered in further detail at paras 7–37 to 7–40.

[51] RTA 2004, s.134(1).

[52] On the grant of a sub-tenancy, the tenant retains his or her interest in the demised premises and remains liable to the landlord in respect of the terms of the head-tenancy. See Wylie, *Landlord and Tenant Law*, 2nd edn (Dublin: Butterworths, 1998), para.22.01.

[53] RTA 2004, s.5(1).

[54] RTA 2004, s.136(m).

[55] Section 16(k) of the RTA 2004 provides that a tenant must obtain a landlord's consent to sub-let a

7. UPDATING OF THE REGISTER BY THE LANDLORD

10–20 A landlord is obliged to provide the PRTB with updated details of a tenancy already registered, where a new rent becomes payable under the tenancy.[56] An alteration in the rent is the only change in the details of a tenancy that triggers an obligation to update the register. However, when notifying the PRTB of a change in the rent, a landlord is also obliged to provide the PRTB with updated details of any other particulars relating to the tenancy that have changed since the tenancy was first registered or since the registration details were last updated.[57] Where there is an alteration in the other particulars of the tenancy but no change in the rent, no obligation to update the register arises.

A landlord is obliged to inform the PRTB of a change in the details of a tenancy registered with it, within one month from the date of an alteration of the rent payable under the tenancy.[58] Upon notification of a change in rent under a tenancy and of any other changes in the particulars of a tenancy recorded in its register, the PRTB shall amend the register to reflect these changes.[59] The PRTB is also obliged to amend the register if it becomes aware that any of the details of a tenancy recorded in it are incorrect. The PRTB may consult with the landlord or tenant for this purpose.[60] If a landlord knowingly or recklessly furnishes to the PRTB information to update the register, which is false or misleading in a material respect, he or she is guilty of an offence.[61]

8. DELETION OF A TENANCY ON THE REGISTER

10–21 A landlord is obliged to notify the PRTB in writing if he or she is of the opinion that the dwelling, in respect of which a tenancy has been registered, has ceased to be a dwelling which comes within the jurisdiction of the RTA 2004. This notification must be made within one month from the date which, in the opinion of the landlord, the dwelling has ceased to fall within the jurisdiction of the PRTB.[62] By way of example, the RTA 2004 will no longer apply to a dwelling where there is a change of use of the dwelling that brings it outside the ambit of the RTA 2004. Accordingly, if the tenant agrees with the landlord to use a dwelling (initially rented for residential use) solely for business purposes,

---

dwelling. Section 186(2) of the RTA 2004 provides that if a landlord refuses his consent to a sub-letting of a tenancy, the tenant may serve a notice of termination on the landlord and terminate the tenancy. See para.8–107.

[56]   RTA 2004, s.139(1).
[57]   RTA 2004, s.139(2).
[58]   RTA 2004, s.139(1).
[59]   RTA 2004, s.139(4).
[60]   RTA 2004, s.140.
[61]   RTA 2004, s.143.
[62]   RTA 2004, s.141(1) and (2).

it will fall outside the jurisdiction of the RTA 2004.[63] If the PRTB is satisfied that the dwelling is no longer a dwelling to which the RTA 2004 applies, it shall delete the entry for the tenancy from the register.[64] No refund of the registration fee is payable to the landlord if this occurs.[65]

9. CONSEQUENCES OF A FAILURE TO REGISTER

A. Dispute Resolution

10–22 It is a landlord's obligation to register the tenancy of a dwelling let by him or her. The PRTB has no jurisdiction to deal with a dispute referred to it by a landlord for resolution, where the tenancy the subject of the dispute has not been registered.[66]

There is no specific sanction under the RTA 2004 for a tenant who obstructs the registration process. A tenant may, however, face consequences if a dispute concerning the tenancy comes before the PRTB. In *Hemat v Donnolly*,[67] when considering the amount of damages awarded to the tenant for his illegal eviction by the landlord, the tenancy tribunal stated that it had borne in mind that the tenant had been obstructive towards the landlord in his attempts to register the tenancy with the PRTB. In *S&L Management Limited v Mallon and Private Residential Tenancies Board*,[68] Linnane J. in the Circuit Court stated that the PRTB did not have jurisdiction to deal with a dispute if the tenancy is not registered but furthermore that a non-compliant landlord could not avail of the courts to determine a dispute due to his or her failure to register a tenancy.

Since the introduction of the Housing Act 2009 and the deletion of the previous requirement that the tenant sign the application form for registration (the Form PRTB1), it is now more difficult for a tenant to interfere with the registration process.[69]

B. Prosecution

10–23 If the PRTB is of the opinion that a tenancy to which the RTA 2004 applies has not been registered, it shall serve a notice on the person whom it believes to be the landlord of the particular tenancy.[70] The notice served shall

---

[63] RTA 2004, s.3(2)(a).

[64] RTA 2004, s.141(3).

[65] RTA 2004, s.141(4).

[66] RTA 2004, s.83(2).

[67] TR32/DR981/2007, March 16, 2007.

[68] Unreported, Circuit Court, Linnane J., April 3, 2009. This decision was judicially reviewed and judgment of the High Court was delivered on April 23, 2010 by Budd J. However, the point considered at this paragraph was not subject to the judicial review proceedings.

[69] See paras 9–39 and 10–07.

[70] RTA 2004, s.144(1).

give the landlord a specified period of time within which to furnish reasons as to why the tenancy should not be registered, if that is the case.[71] If no such reasons exist or unsatisfactory reasons are furnished to the PRTB, in circumstances where the tenancy continues to remain unregistered, the PRTB shall serve a further notice on the landlord in question. The notice shall state that the landlord is required to apply to the PRTB for registration of the tenancy and if the landlord fails to do so within 14 days of receipt of that notice, he or she is guilty of an offence.[72] If the tenancy is not ultimately registered within that period, the landlord may be liable to prosecution by the PRTB and summary conviction in accordance with s.9 of the RTA 2004.[73]

Where the PRTB considers that a tenancy to which the RTA 2004 applies is not registered but does not know the identity of the landlord of the dwelling, it is empowered to serve a notice on the tenant for the purposes of ascertaining the landlord's identity. This notice may request that the tenant provide the PRTB with the landlord's contact details or any particulars that could reasonably lead to it ascertaining the identity of the landlord or his or her address.[74] If a tenant fails to do so or provides information which is false or misleading, or is reckless as to whether the information is false or misleading, he or she is guilty of an offence and may also be liable to prosecution and summary conviction in accordance with s.9 of the RTA 2004.[75]

10–24 The PRTB actively issues notices to landlords who have failed or it suspects have failed to register a tenancy of a dwelling let by him or her.[76] The PRTB is assisted in identifying potentially unregistered tenancies by information provided to it by local authorities,[77] members of the public, residents' associations and from tenants referring disputes to the PRTB or contacting the PRTB in relation to the registration of the tenancy.[78]

10. Data Exchange

10–25 As discussed at para.10–23 above, the PRTB is assisted in identifying potentially unregistered tenancies from information it receives from third parties. Sections 146–148 of the RTA 2004 provide for the exchange of data

---

[71] RTA 2004, s.144(2).
[72] RTA 2004, s.144(3).
[73] RTA 2004, s.144(4).
[74] RTA 2004, s.145(4).
[75] RTA 2004, s.145(5). See para.9–131 that considers the penalties applicable on a conviction under s.9 of the RTA 2004.
[76] In the PRTB's "Private Residential Tenancies Board, Annual Report & Accounts 2008", p.22, it is recorded that the PRTB had served over 7,800 enforcement notices on landlords.
[77] Section 146 of the RTA 2004, permits the exchange of data between the PRTB and local authorities to assist in the performance of their functions.
[78] See, "Private Residential Tenancies Board, Annual Report 1/9/2004–31/12/2005", p.11 and

between the PRTB and local authorities, the Department of Social and Family Affairs and the Revenue Commissioners.[79] As a result, local authorities, the Department of Social and Family Affairs and the Revenue Commissioners can request the PRTB for information contained on its tenancy register, which will include the particulars discussed at para.10–09. Notably, however, while the PRTB can request a local authority or the Department of Social and Family Affairs for information necessary for the performance of its functions, there is no provision under the RTA 2004 for the PRTB to request information from the Revenue Commissioners.

11. REGISTRATION AND RENTAL INCOME INTEREST DEDUCTION

A. Requirement for Registration

10–26 Section 97(2)(e) of the Taxes Consolidation Act 1997 (as amended) (the "TCA") allows a deduction on rental income chargeable to tax, where interest is paid on borrowed money employed in the purchase, improvement or repair of a rented residential property. Section 11 of the Finance Act 2006 amended s.97 of the TCA to provide that the entitlement to such a deduction is conditional on compliance with the registration requirements of Pt 7 of the RTA 2004.[80] The person claiming a deduction on the rental income chargeable to tax must be in a position to show that the registration requirements of Pt 7 of the RTA 2004 have been complied with in the relevant chargeable period.[81] In this regard, a written communication from the PRTB to the chargeable person confirming the registration of a tenancy, shall be accepted as evidence that the registration requirement has been complied with.[82] Landlords should therefore retain written confirmation received from the PRTB confirming registration and providing details of the RT number for the tenancy concerned. If the Revenue Commissioners become aware that a landlord has failed to comply with the registration requirements for a chargeable period, any interest relief that has been claimed

---

p.34; "Private Residential Tenancies Board, Annual Report 2006", pp.14 and 33; "Private Residential Tenancies Board, Annual Report & Accounts 2007", pp.14–15; and "Private Residential Tenancies Board, Annual Report & Accounts 2008", p.22.

[79] Section 147A of the RTA 2004, was inserted by the Housing Act 2009, to provide that the PRTB shall disclose to the Revenue Commissioners information in the PRTB's tenancy register which is reasonably necessary for the Revenue Commissioners in the performance of their functions. See "Private Residential Tenancies Board, Annual Report & Accounts 2008" at p.25.

[80] Section 97(2I)(a) of the TCA, as inserted by s.11(1) of the Finance Act 2006.

[81] Section 97(2I)(a) of the TCA, as inserted by s.11(1) of the Finance Act 2006. Chargeable periods for the purposes of s.97(2I)(a) are (i) where the chargeable period is a year of assessment, the year of assessment 2006 and subsequent years, and (ii) where the chargeable period is an accounting period of a company, for accounting periods beginning on or after January 1, 2006 (Finance Act 2006, s.11(2)).

[82] Section 97(2I)(b) of the TCA, as inserted by s.11(1) of the Finance Act 2006.

will be withdrawn. Such a withdrawal of interest relief may result in an underpayment of tax and expose the landlord to interest and penalties.[83]

B. Late Registration

10–27 Failure by a landlord to register the tenancy within one month as required,[84] will not however preclude the landlord from claiming interest relief. An acknowledgement from the PRTB confirming (late) registration will be accepted by the Revenue Commissioners as evidence that a chargeable person has complied with Pt 7 of the RTA 2004. A person must be in a position to indicate compliance with Pt 7 when making an annual tax return. Interest relief that has been denied for a particular chargeable period because a tenancy was not registered by the return filing date for that period, can subsequently be restored if the landlord avails of the PRTB's late registration procedure, subject to the usual four-year time limit on claims for the repayment of tax.[85]

C. Property with Several Dwellings

10–28 Where a property comprises of more than one or contains several dwellings, being self-contained residential units for the purposes of the RTA 2004, the Finance Act 2006 makes no provision for apportionment of interest relief on monies borrowed where, only some of the tenancies of the dwellings in the property are registered. Accordingly, if all tenancies are not registered for a particular year, all interest relief in respect of that property will be lost.[86]

12. CONTROLLED DWELLINGS AND REGISTRATION

10–29 Dwellings that were formerly controlled under the Rent Restrictions Act 1960 and 1967,[87] are commonly known as "controlled dwellings". The nature of and conditions that must be satisfied for a dwelling to be a controlled dwelling, are considered at paras 3–29 to 3–34. The Minister[88] is empowered by s.24 of the Housing (Private Rented Dwellings) Act 1982 (the "1982 Act"),[89] to

---

83 See Tax Briefing 63 and Revenue eBrief No. 54/2007.
84 See para.10–06.
85 See Revenue Instruction [4.8.10], "Letting of Residential Property – Interest Deduction", at p.3.
86 See Revenue Instruction [4.8.10], "Letting of Residential Property – Interest Deduction", at p.2. Also, see *www.revenue.ie*.
87 Housing (Private Rented Dwellings) Act 1982 applies to these dwellings.
88 Minister is defined at s.2(1) of the the Housing (Private Rented Dwellings) Act 1982, as the Minister for the Environment (now the Minister for the Environment, Heritage and Local Government).
89 As amended by the Housing (Private Rented Dwellings) (Amendment) Act 1983, which established the Rent Tribunal.

make regulations requiring landlords of any class of dwelling let for rent to register the tenancy of each dwelling with the housing authority in whose functional area the dwelling is situated. The Housing (Private Rented Dwellings) Regulations 1982 (the "1982 Regulations"), were enacted under s.24.[90] The 1982 Regulations require landlords of controlled dwellings,[91] to register the tenancy of the controlled dwelling with the housing authority in whose functional area the dwelling is situated. Application forms for registration are obtainable from housing authorities. The particulars that must be provided by the landlord in its application include:

(a) the name and address of the landlord;
(b) the address of the dwelling;
(c) the name of the tenant;
(d) the rent at which the dwelling was let immediately before the commencement of the 1982 Regulations;
(e) a description of the nature of the dwelling (e.g. whether it is a house, a flat (self-contained or otherwise) or a single room).[92]

A fee must also be paid by the landlord and provided with his or her application for registration.[93] If a change takes place in any of these particulars, the landlord must within one month from the date they change, apply in writing to the housing authority to enter up-to-date particulars in the register. The updating of the register in these circumstances is free of charge.[94]

Where a new rent for a dwelling has been agreed between the landlord and the tenant or has been fixed by the courts, the landlord must apply in writing to the housing authority to enter particulars of the new rent in the register. Again this updating of the register is free of charge.[95] This registration requirement does not apply where the rent agreed or fixed by the court is less than the existing rent.[96]

---

[90] S.I. No. 217 of 1982, as amended by the Housing (Private Rented Dwellings) (Amendment) Regulations 1983 (S.I. No. 286 of 1983).
[91] 1982 Regulations, art.4(1). The 1982 Regulations only apply to controlled dwellings, that is a dwelling which Pt 2 of the 1982 Act applies.
[92] 1982 Regulations, art.5.
[93] 1982 Regulations, art.9.
[94] 1982 Regulations, art.6.
[95] 1982 Regulations, art.7, as substituted by art.4 of the Housing (Private Rented Dwellings) (Amendment) Regulations 1983.
[96] 1982 Regulations, art.7(2).

CHAPTER 11

THE PRIVATE RESIDENTIAL
TENANCIES BOARD

1. INTRODUCTION

A. The Commission on the Private Rented Residential Sector

11–01 The Commission on the Private Rented Residential Sector (the "Commission") recommended the establishment of a statutory Board to deal with disputes between residential tenants and landlords. It considered other functions of the Board could include research, monitoring and providing policy advice on the operation of the sector for the Government and the public generally, developing model leases and good practice guidelines for periodic tenancies, providing information for landlords, tenants, citizen advice centres and voluntary agencies operating in the private rented sector. These functions would be of benefit to the sector as the Board would be an objective and independent body, while in the performance of its functions it would take into account the opinions and obligations of both landlords and tenants.[1]

B. The Residential Tenancies Act 2004

11–02 The long title of the Residential Tenancies Act 2004 (the "RTA 2004") states that it was enacted:

> with the aim of allowing disputes between [landlords and tenants] to be resolved cheaply and speedily, for the establishment of a body to be known as an Bord Um Thionóntachtaí Cónaithe Príobháideacha, or in the English language, the Private Residential Tenancies Board and the conferral on it of powers and functions of a limited nature in relation to the resolution of such disputes.

Part 8 of the RTA 2004 provides for the establishment of the Private Residential Tenancies Board (the "PRTB"). The establishment day for the purposes of Pt 8 was September 1, 2004.[2]

---

[1] Report of the Commission on the Private Rented Residential Sector, July 2000 (the "Report of the Commission"), paras 8.4.1 and 8.4.2.

[2] See the Residential Tenancies Act 2004 (Establishment Day) Order 2004 (S.I. No. 525 of 2004).

2. The Functions of the PRTB

A. Functions

11–03 The principal functions of the PRTB are set out in s.151(1) of the RTA 2004. They are as follows:

(a) The resolution of disputes between tenants and landlords in accordance with the provisions of Part 6 of the RTA 2004;

(b) The registration of tenancies in accordance with the provisions of Part 7 of the RTA 2004;

(c) The provision to the Minister[3] of advice concerning policy in relation to the private rented sector[4];

(d) The development and publication of guidelines for good practice by those involved in the private rented sector[5];

(e) The collection and provision of information relating to the private rented sector, including information concerning prevailing rent levels;

(f) The conducting of research into the private rented sector and monitoring the operation of various aspects of the sector or arranging for such research and monitoring to be done[6];

(g) The review of the operation of the RTA 2004 (and in particular Part 3 on rent and rent reviews) and any related enactments;

(h) The making of recommendations to the Minister for the amendment of the RTA 2004 and any related enactments.

The Minister may confer additional functions on the PRTB.[7] The Minister may also issue guidelines to the PRTB in relation to the performance of its functions under the RTA 2004, with the exception of its dispute resolution functions under Pt 6.[8] If requested, the PRTB must give information to the Minister relating to its functions and the private rented sector.[9]

---

[3] The Minister for the purposes of the RTA 2004 is the Minister for the Environment Heritage and Local Government (RTA 2004, s.4(1)).

[4] For the purposes of s.151(1)(d), "private rented sector" means the sector of commercial activity in the State consisting of the letting of dwellings (RTA 2004, s.151(4)).

[5] Guidelines published under s.151(1)(d) of the RTA 2004 may include a precedent for a model lease of a dwelling (RTA 2004, s.152(1)).

[6] Research initiatives of the PRTB have included "Third Party Complaints of Anti-Social Behaviour in the private residential tenancy sector", Candy Murphy and Associates, February 2007; "Dispute Resolution Mechanisms in relation to deposit retention", Candy Murphy and Associates, February 2007; "Analysis of Determination Orders and Disputes referred to the Private Residential Tenancies Board (PRTB) 2005 & 2006", Naomi Feely, Centre for Housing Research, November 2008.

[7] RTA 2004, s.151(3). The Minister in conferring additional functions on the PRTB may consult with the PRTB, another Minister of Government (if that Minister has requested that additional functions be given to the PRTB) and the Minister for Finance.

[8] RTA 2004, s.183.

[9] RTA 2004, s.151(2).

B. Reports

11–04 The PRTB is required to furnish a report to the Minister not later than June 30 each year on the performance of its functions and activities during the preceding year. The Minister must present the annual report to each House of the Oireachtas.[10] The PRTB may request a Minister for Government or a local authority to furnish it with reports on any matter, which in the PRTB's opinion concerns the private rented sector.[11]

3. COMPOSITION AND MANAGEMENT OF THE PRTB

A. PRTB

11–05 The PRTB must consist of at least nine members but cannot exceed 15 members.[12] The members are appointed by the Minister and are persons who in the Minister's opinion have experience in a field of expertise relevant to the PRTB's functions.[13] The term of the members' appointment is fixed by the Minister but cannot exceed five years.[14] The Minister must also appoint a chairperson from amongst the PRTB's members.[15] Meetings of the PRTB are held as necessary for the performance of its functions.[16]

B. Body Corporate and Official Seal

11–06 The PRTB is a body corporate with perpetual succession. It has the power to sue and be sued in its corporate name. It has powers necessary, expedient for or incidental to the performance of its functions under the RTA 2004.[17]

The PRTB also has an official seal. The PRTB's seal is authenticated by the signature of the Chairperson of the PRTB and the signature of the Director of the PRTB. The PRTB may authorise another member of the PRTB to authenticate the seal on behalf of the Chairperson and another member of staff

---

[10] RTA 2004, s.180(1).

[11] RTA 2004, s.181.

[12] RTA 2004, s.153(1). On November 4, 2009, Michael Finneran TD, Minister for Housing and Local Services, announced the preliminary results of a review of the RTA 2004. One of the recommendations made was a reduction in the number of members of the PRTB. See Press Release, "Minister Michael Finneran announces significant changes to Private Residential Tenancies Board (PRTB) legislation", November 4, 2009, *www.environ.ie*.

[13] RTA 2004, s.153(2). A person who accepts nomination as a member of Seanad Éireann, is elected to either House of the Oireachtas or to the European Parliament or becomes a member of a local authority, cannot be a member of the PRTB (RTA 2004, s.169(1)).

[14] RTA 2004, s.153(5).

[15] RTA 2004, s.155.

[16] RTA 2004, s.156(1). A quorum for a meeting of the PRTB is five (RTA 2004, s.156(3)).

[17] RTA 2004, s.150.

to authenticate the seal on behalf of the Director.[18] Judicial notice is to be taken of the seal of the PRTB. Every document purporting to be an instrument made by the PRTB and sealed with the PRTB's seal (which is authenticated) must be received in evidence and be deemed such an instrument without proof unless the contrary is shown.[19] Applications made to the Circuit Court under s.124 of the RTA 2004 for the enforcement of a determination order made by the PRTB, must have a copy of the determination order attached to the notice of motion.[20] As discussed at para.9–119, if the determination order is sealed and the seal authenticated, this will lessen the evidential burden on the applicant party.

C. The Director and Staff

11–07 The chief officer of the PRTB is the Director. The Director is appointed by the PRTB. The Director manages and controls generally the administration and business of the PRTB. The Director may also be given other functions by the PRTB.[21] The Director may make proposals to the PRTB on any matter relating to its activities. The Director may not be a member of the PRTB or any committee of the PRTB but he or she may attend meetings of the PRTB and its committees.[22]

In addition to the Director, the PRTB may also appoint staff. The staff of the PRTB perform functions given to them by the Director. The PRTB must obtain the consent of the Minister and the Minister for Finance before it appoints any member of staff.[23]

4. Committees

11–08 The PRTB may establish committees to assist and advise it on matters relating to any of its functions. The Committees may consist in whole or in part of persons who are members of the PRTB.[24] One committee that the PRTB was required to establish was a "Dispute Resolution Committee".[25] The Dispute Resolution Committee cannot exceed 40 members of which at least four must be members of the PRTB.[26] Each member of the PRTB's tenancy tribunals that

---

[18] RTA 2004, s.173(2).
[19] RTA 2004, s.173(3).
[20] Circuit Court Rules 2001, Ord.51A r.2(1). See para.9–119.
[21] RTA 2004, s.160.
[22] RTA 2004, s.161.
[23] RTA 2004, s.162.
[24] RTA 2004, s.157(1).
[25] RTA 2004, s.157(2).
[26] RTA 2004, s.159(2). A PRTB member shall not be eligible for appointment as a member of the Dispute Resolution Committee unless the unexpired period of his or her term of office as a PRTB member is three years or more (RTA 2004, s.159(3)). A person who accepts nomination as a member of Seanad Éireann, is elected to either House of the Oireachtas or to the European

deal with disputes under Pt 6 of the RTA 2004 must be members of the dispute resolution committee.[27] Other committees that have been established by the PRTB include a Research Committee, Audit Committee, Finance Committee, Legislative Committee and a section 189 Committee.[28]

5. Appointment of Mediators and Adjudicators

11–09 The PRTB appoints mediators and adjudicators to carry out functions for the purposes of the dispute resolution process under Pt 6 of the RTA 2004.[29] The PRTB has two panels, one comprising the names of the persons who are appointed as mediators and those appointed as adjudicators, although it is possible to appoint a person as both a mediator and an adjudicator.[30]

An adjudicator can be removed from the adjudicator's panel if it appears to the PRTB that an adjudicator has been guilty of misconduct in his or her capacity as adjudicator.[31] However, the PRTB must apply to the District Court for the removal of an adjudicator. If the District Court is satisfied that the adjudicator has been guilty of misconduct in the capacity of an adjudicator, it can make an order authorising the PRTB to remove the adjudicator from the panel.[32] Misconduct in this context is defined as including the following:

(a) any demonstration by an adjudicator of bias towards the interests of a party whose dispute the adjudicator is dealing with;

(b) gross discourtesy by an adjudicator to one or more of those parties; and

(c) wilful failure by an adjudicator to attend to his or her duties as an adjudicator.[33]

Parliament or becomes a member of a local authority, cannot be member of the Dispute Resolution Committee (RTA 2004, s.169(1)). See also in relation to the validity of appointments to the Dispute Resolution Committee, s.2 of the Residential Tenancies (Amendment) Act 2009.

[27] RTA 2004, s.103(2).

[28] "Private Residential Tenancies Board, Annual Report & Accounts 2008", pp.16–19. By way of background to the section 189 Committee, s.189 of the RTA 2004 empowers the PRTB to make applications to the Circuit Court for interim or interlocutory relief in aid of the dispute resolution process provided under Pt 6. The PRTB may only exercise this power if requested by a party to a dispute to make such an application (see para.9–111). The section 189 Committee meets whenever called upon by the Director of the PRTB as a result of a request received by the PRTB to make an application under s.189 of the RTA 2004. The function of the section 189 Committee is to decide whether or not the PRTB should make an application to the Circuit Court under s.189 ("Private Residential Tenancies Board, Annual Report & Accounts 2008", p.18).

[29] RTA 2004, s.164(1) and (2).

[30] RTA 2004, s.164(3) and (4).

[31] RTA 2004, s.165(1) and (2).

[32] RTA 2004, s.165(2) and (3). The adjudicator can appeal such a finding to the Circuit Court (RTA 2004, s.165(4)).

[33] RTA 2004, s.165(6).

It is noteworthy that there is no similar provision for the removal of a mediator under the RTA 2004.

6. DISCLOSURE OF INTERESTS AND INFORMATION

11–10 Where a member of the PRTB, a member of one of its committees, a member of its staff or a consultant or adviser[34] has a pecuniary interest or other beneficial interest in a matter being considered by the PRTB or a committee, he or she must do the following:

(a) disclose their interest and the nature of the interest to the PRTB in advance of any consideration of the matter;
(b) neither influence nor seek to influence a decision in relation to the matter;
(c) take no part in any consideration of the matter;
(d) withdraw from any meeting considering the matter for so long as it is being considered and shall not vote in relation to the matter.[35]

A person who contravenes these requirements is guilty of an offence.[36]

11–11 A person may not without the consent of the PRTB disclose confidential information obtained by him or her while performing functions as a member of the PRTB, a member of one of its committees, a member of its staff or as an adviser or consultant to the PRTB.[37] A person who contravenes this provision is guilty of an offence.[38] Confidential information includes information which is expressed by the PRTB or a committee of the PRTB to be confidential, information that concerns proposals of a commercial nature or tenders submitted to the PRTB by contractors, consultants or any other person.[39] Confidential information also includes information that is received by the PRTB on the registration of a tenancy but is not contained on the published register of tenancies because it discloses the identity of the landlord or tenant or the amount of rent payable under the tenancy.[40]

---

[34] A consultant or adviser may be engaged by the PRTB, as it considers necessary for the performance of its functions (RTA 2004, s.166).
[35] RTA 2004, s.170(1). See also s.170(2) and (3), which considers some of the circumstances where a person shall and shall not be regarded as having a "beneficial interest" in a matter.
[36] RTA 2004, s.171(3).
[37] RTA 2004, s.172(1).
[38] RTA 2004, s.172(2).
[39] RTA 2004, s.172(4)(a) and (b).
[40] RTA 2004, s.172(4)(c).

APPENDICES

Please note that the following appendices contain sample documents only. It will be necessary in all cases to adapt the sample documents to each particular tenancy situation.

RESIDENTIAL TENANCY AGREEMENT[1]

Date: **[Insert date of the agreement]**

Premises: **[Insert address of Premises]**

Landlord: **[Insert name of Landlord(s)]**

Tenant: **[Insert name of Tenant(s)]**

---

[1] This Residential Tenancy Agreement is relevant only to tenancies to which the RTA 2004 applies. It is intended as an outline sample agreement only and does not purport to serve as a comprehensive precedent for every tenancy situation.

Index

1. INTERPRETATION

In this Agreement unless the context otherwise requires:

1.1 Words importing the masculine gender where the context so admits include the feminine gender and vice versa.

1.2 Words importing the singular where the context so admits include the plural and vice versa.

1.3 If there is more than one landlord and / or tenant to this Agreement, the terms and covenants contained in this Agreement:

(a) apply to each landlord and / or tenant equally;

(b) may be enforced against the landlords jointly and severally;

(c) may be enforced against the tenants jointly and severally.

2. TERMS OF THE TENANCY

This Agreement is made between the Landlord and the Tenant for the lease of the Premises on the terms set out in clause 2 and subject to the covenants of the Landlord and Tenant set out in clauses 3 and 4.

2.1 Date of Agreement: **[Insert date]**

2.2 Landlord: **[Insert Landlord's name]**
[Insert Landlord's address]

2.3 Landlord's Agent: **[Insert Agent's name and/or company name]**
[Insert Agent's address]

2.4 Contact Details of Landlord/Landlord's Agent:
[The Landlord] [The Landlord's Agent] may be contacted in respect of all matters arising in relation to the tenancy at:

Address: **[Insert address]**

Contact Telephone Number: **[Insert telephone number]**

[If necessary insert additional or other details by which the Tenant may, at all reasonable times, contact the Landlord/the Landlord's Agent]

2.5 Tenant: **[Insert Tenant's name]**
                                     [Insert Tenant's address]

2.6 Premises: **[Insert address of rented Premises]**

2.7 Contents: The Landlord agrees to let the Premises together with the Contents, which are listed in Schedule 1 to this Agreement.

2.8 Rent: The Rent is € **[*]** per **[week][calendar month]** and is payable **[*] [week(s)][one calendar month]** in advance.

                                     The Rent is payable by the Tenant to the Landlord on **[insert date][insert day] [every week][every month]**.

                                     The Rent shall be paid by the Landlord to the Tenant in the manner set out in the Schedule 2 to this Agreement.

                                     The first payment of Rent is to be made on **[insert date]**.

2.9 Security Deposit: € **[*]**.

                                     The Security Deposit shall be paid by the Tenant to the Landlord by **[insert date]**.

                                     The Security Deposit shall be paid by the Tenant to the Landlord in the manner set out in Schedule 3 to this Agreement.

2.10 Term of Tenancy: **[*] [week(s)][month(s)][year(s)]**.

                                     [The Landlord and the Tenant agree that the tenancy is for a fixed term. If the Tenant wishes to remain in occupation on the expiry of the fixed term, the tenant shall notify the landlord of this no earlier than three months and no later than one month before the expiry of the fixed term].

2.11 Commencement   **[Insert date]**.
Date of tenancy:

2.12 Residential   The Residential Tenancies Act 2004 (as amended)
Tenancies Act 2004   (the "RTA 2004") applies to this Agreement. Both
(as amended):   the Landlord and Tenant must comply with their
obligations under the RTA 2004. Reference should
be made to the RTA 2004 for the rights and duties
of the Landlord and the Tenant that apply in
addition to the terms of this Agreement.

2.13 Special Conditions: The Landlord and the Tenant agree that the
Premises is let subject to the Special Conditions
set out in Schedule 4 to this Agreement.

3. TENANT'S COVENANTS

3.1   The Tenant shall pay to the Landlord the Rent specified in clause 2.8 of
this Agreement or as validly varied, on the **[date][day]** and in the manner
set out in Schedule 2.

3.2   The Tenant shall pay to the Landlord the Security Deposit specified in
clause 2.9 of this Agreement, on the **[date][day]** and in the manner set out
in Schedule 3. The Tenant acknowledges that the Landlord is entitled to
retain part or all of the Security Deposit in accordance with s.12(4) of the
RTA 2004, for the Tenant's failure to pay rent or other taxes and charges
payable in accordance with this Agreement, or for causing a deterioration
in the condition of the dwelling beyond normal wear and tear.

3.3   The Tenant shall pay all charges and outgoings in respect of the Premises
including water, refuse, electricity, gas, oil and telephone. Any re-
connection costs arising as a result of the Tenant's failure to pay for the
charges and outgoings in respect of the Premises shall be the responsibility
of the Tenant.

3.4   The Tenant shall not alter or improve the Premises without the prior
written consent of the Landlord.

3.5   The Tenant shall keep the Premises in a good and clean condition.

3.6   The Tenant shall not damage the structure, interior or any of the Contents
of the Premises. The Tenant shall also not do anything that would cause a

deterioration in the condition that the Premises was in at the commencement of the tenancy, normal wear and tear excepted.

3.7 The Tenant shall repair any damage caused to the Premises (beyond that of normal wear and tear) or as necessary, replace any item damaged on the Premises. In the alternative, the tenant shall pay the Landlord the costs of repairing or replacing the item.

3.8 **[The Tenant shall keep the gardens, patios, driveway and exterior area of the Premises neat and tidy and shall cut the grass at regular intervals].**

3.9 **[The Tenant shall not do or allow anything to be done that would cause the shared services or common areas in the [specify apartment complex/building] to become obstructed, untidy, damaged or used for any purpose other than for which they are intended].**

3.10 Immediately before giving up possession of the Premises on the termination of the tenancy, the Tenant shall at his or her own expense clean the Premises thoroughly, including all sanitary facilities, cookers, fridges, carpets and all other items or compliances provided with the Premises.

3.11 The Tenant shall not do or allow anything to be done which would invalidate any insurance policy for the Premises or increase the premium payable for such insurance.

3.12 The Tenant shall not behave within the Premises or in the vicinity of it in a way that is anti-social. The Tenant shall not allow other occupiers of or visitors to the Premises to behave within it or in the vicinity of it in a way that is anti-social. To "behave in a way that is anti-social" for the purposes of this Agreement has the same meaning as provided by s.17 of the RTA 2004.

3.13 The Tenant shall notify the Landlord in writing of the identity of each person (other than a multiple tenant) that ordinarily resides in the Premises.

3.14 The Tenant shall not assign or sublet the tenancy of the Premises without the prior written consent of the Landlord.

3.15 The Tenant shall not use the Premises other than for residential purposes, unless the written consent of the Landlord is obtained to change its use.

3.16 The Tenant shall not keep any animals, birds or other living creatures on the Premises without the prior written consent of the Landlord.

3.17 The Tenant shall allow the Landlord or the Landlord's Agent access to the Premises at reasonable intervals (but on a time and date agreed in advance between the parties) for the purposes of inspecting the Premises.

3.18 The Tenant shall notify the Landlord or the Landlord's Agent of any defect that arises in the Premises that needs to be repaired so that the Landlord can comply with his or her obligations set out at clause 4.2.

3.19 The Tenant shall allow the Landlord and any person acting on the Landlord's behalf reasonable access to the Premises for the purposes of allowing any works to be carried out, which are the responsibility of the Landlord.

3.20 The Tenant shall not alter or change the locks or have additional locks installed on the Premises without the prior written consent of the Landlord. The Tenant is responsible for the replacement of any lost keys, access cards or fobs for the Premises.

3.21 The Tenant shall be responsible for insuring his / her own possessions in the Premises.

3.22 The Tenant shall not terminate the tenancy save in accordance with the provisions of the RTA 2004 and must give the Landlord the required notice period as prescribed by Part 5 of the RTA 2004.

3.23 The Tenant acknowledges that he / she has obligations pursuant to the RTA 2004 and agrees to comply with these obligations.

4. LANDLORD'S COVENANTS

4.1 The Landlord shall allow the Tenant to enjoy peaceful and exclusive occupation of the Premises.

4.2 The Landlord shall carry out to the structure and interior of the Premises all such repairs as are necessary and must ensure the structure and interior of the Premises are in compliance with any standards prescribed by statute. This obligation is subject to the Tenant's obligations contained at clause 3.6.

4.3 On the termination of the tenancy the Landlord must return promptly the Security Deposit to the Tenant in accordance with section 12(1)(d) of the RTA 2004.

4.4 The Landlord shall not at any time set the rent for the Premises at a rate that is greater than the market rent for the tenancy within the meaning of section 24 of the RTA 2004.

4.5   The Landlord shall insure the Premises against damage to and loss and destruction of the Premises. **[The Landlord shall insure the Contents as set out in Schedule 1 to this Agreement].** The Landlord's obligation to insure does not include an obligation to insure the Tenant's possessions.

4.6   The Landlord shall provide the tenant with a rent book and complete and update the rent book as required by the Housing (Rent Books) Regulations 1993, as amended by the Housing (Rent Books) Regulations 1993 (Amendment) Regulations 2004.

4.7   The Landlord must notify and keep the Tenant updated with the name and contact details of his or her agent or any person who is authorised by the Landlord to act on his or her behalf in respect of the Premises.

4.8   The Landlord shall not terminate the tenancy save in accordance with the provisions of the RTA 2004 and must give the Tenant the required notice period as prescribed by Part 5 of the RTA 2004.

4.9   The Landlord acknowledges that he / she has obligations pursuant to the RTA 2004 and agrees to comply with these obligations.

5. General Provisions

5.1   Any notice that a Landlord serves on a Tenant in relation to the tenancy shall be served by sending it by registered or pre-paid post to the Premises or by leaving the notice addressed to the Tenant at the Premises.

5.2   Any notice that a Tenant serves on the Landlord in relation to the tenancy shall be served by sending it by registered or pre-paid post to or by leaving it at the Landlord's address as set out in clause 2.2 of this Agreement. Where an agent acts on behalf of a Landlord in respect of the tenancy, the notice may also be served on the Landlord by sending it by registered or pre-paid post to or by leaving it at the address of the Landlord's Agent as set out in clause 2.3 of this Agreement.

SCHEDULE 1

Inventory of Contents

1. Kitchen
   [List contents]

2. Sitting Room
   [List contents]

3. Living Room
   [List contents]

4. Hallways / Stairs
   [List contents]

5. Bedroom 1
   [List contents]

6. Bedroom 2
   [List contents]

7. (Downstairs) Toilet
   [List contents]

8. Bathroom
   [List contents]

9. Garden
   [List contents]

10. Garden Shed
    [List contents]

SCHEDULE 2

Rental Payments

The Rent is payable by the Tenant to the Landlord in accordance with clause 2.8 of this Agreement and in the following manner:

Payee: **[Insert Name of Landlord / Landlord's Agent]**

Payment Method: **[Insert Name of Bank]**
[Insert Account Name]
[Insert Account Number]
[Insert Sort Code]

OR

[Specify cheque or other method of payment]

SCHEDULE 3

Payment of Deposit

The Security Deposit is payable by the Tenant to the Landlord in accordance with clause 2.9 of this Agreement and in the following manner:

Payee: **[Insert Name of Landlord / Landlord's Agent]**

Payment Method: **[Insert Name of Bank]**
[Insert Account Name]
[Insert Account Number]
[Insert Sort Code]

OR

[Specify cheque or other method of payment]

SCHEDULE 4

Special Conditions

1. **[Insert any special conditions which may apply to the tenancy. For example it may be appropriate to insert special conditions where the Premises is contained within an apartment complex].**

2. **[Insert special condition].**

3. **[Insert special condition].**

4. The Landlord and the Tenant acknowledge that it is not possible to contract out of the RTA 2004.

5. The Landlord and Tenant further acknowledge that both or either of them has no obligation to comply with any Special Condition contained in this Schedule that is inconsistent with the provisions of the RTA 2004.

SIGNED BY THE LANDLORD:

_____   _____
Name of Landlord   **Date**

In the presence of:

_____   _____
Name   **Date**

SIGNED BY THE TENANT:

_____   _____
Name of Tenant   **Date**

In the presence of:

_____   _____
Name   **Date**

RENT BOOK

REQUIRED STATEMENT OF INFORMATION

Rent books must set out the following statement of information[1]:

1. This statement of information is included in the rent book in accordance with the Housing (Rent Books) Regulations 1993. It does not purport to be a legal interpretation.

2. The tenant of a house is entitled to enjoy peaceful and exclusive occupation of the house.

3. Notice of termination of a tenancy must be in writing and must be made in accordance with the provisions of the Residential Tenancies Act 2004.

4. The landlord is prohibited from impounding the goods of a tenant to secure recovery of rent unpaid.

5. The landlord is obliged to provide a tenant with a rent book for use throughout the term of the tenancy. The landlord must enter the particulars relating to the tenancy in the rent book, and, in the case of a new tenancy, complete the inventory of furnishings and appliances supplied with the house for the tenant's exclusive use.

6. The landlord is obliged to keep the particulars in the rent book up to date. Where the rent or any other amount due to the landlord under the tenancy is handed in person by the tenant, or by any person acting for the tenant, to the landlord, the landlord must, on receipt, record the payment in the rent book or acknowledge it by way of receipt. Payments not handed over directly, for example those made by bankers order or direct debit, must, not more than 3 months after receipt, either be recorded by the landlord in the rent book or acknowledged by way of statement by the landlord to the tenant.

7. The tenant is obliged to make the rent book available to the landlord to enable the landlord to keep the particulars in it up to date.

---

[1] Schedule to the Housing (Rent Books) Regulations 1993, as amended by s.2 of the Housing (Rent Books) Regulations 1993 (Amendment) Regulations 2004. See also para.5–57 that sets out the other information that must be contained in a rent book.

8.   The landlord of a private rented house is obliged to ensure that the house compiles with the minimum standards of accommodation laid down in the Housing (Standards for Rented Houses) Regulations 2008. However, in the case of an "existing tenancy" articles 6 to 8 of the Housing (Standards for Rented Houses) Regulations 2008 will not apply until 1 February 2013 and articles 6 and 7 of the Housing (Standards for Rented Houses) Regulations 1993 will continue to have application in respect of private rented houses up to that date. An "existing tenancy" means a house let for rent or other valuable consideration solely as a dwelling at any time from 1 September 2004 to 31 January 2009.[2] The Housing (Standards for Rented Houses) Regulations 1993 and the Housing (Standards for Rented Houses) Regulations 2008 do not apply to houses let on a temporary or holiday basis, local authority demountable dwellings and communal type accommodation provided by health boards and certain approved non-profit or voluntary bodies. The standards relate to structural condition, provision of sinks, waterclosets, baths/showers, cooking and food storage facilities, safety of electricity and gas installations, availability of adequate heating, lighting and ventilation and maintenance of common areas, etc.[3]

9.   The duties of a landlord referred to in paragraphs 5 to 8 above may be carried out on the landlord's behalf by a duly appointed agent. Any reference in this statement to 'house' includes a flat or maisonette.

10.   Copies of the Housing (Rent Books) Regulations 1993, the Housing (Standards for Rented Houses) Regulations 1993 and the Housing (Standards for Rented Houses) Regulations 2008, may be purchased from the Government Publications Sale Office, Sun Alliance House, Molesworth Street, Dublin 2, or from the housing authority.

11.   Responsibility for the enforcement of the law relating to rent books and standards rests with the housing authority for the area in which the house is located. The name, address and telephone number of the relevant housing authority are as follows:

Name: _____

Address: _____

              _____

              _____

Telephone: _____

---

[2]   See para.5–14.
[3]   Note that the Schedule to the Housing (Rent Books) Regulations 1993, has not been amended to incorporate reference to the Housing (Standards for Rented Houses) Regulations 2008. The updated references cited have been inserted by the authors.

EXAMPLE NOTICE OF RENT REVIEW

Notice served pursuant to section 22 of the
Residential Tenancies Act 2004

To: [INSERT NAME(S) OF TENANT(S)].

Dwelling: [INSERT ADDRESS OF RENTED DWELLING].

This notice is to inform you that a new rent is to be set for your tenancy of the dwelling.

The new rent is to be € **[state amount and when payable, e.g. weekly/ monthly]**.

The new rent is to have effect and shall be payable by you from **[insert date which is at least 28 days after the notice is served]**.

This notice is served on _____ **[INSERT DATE OF SERVICE]**.

Signed: _____
      Landlord

WARNING NOTICE

BREACH OF OBLIGATION OF A PART 4 TENANCY

Notice served pursuant to paragraph 1 of the Table to s.34 of the Residential Tenancies Act 2004

TO: [INSERT NAME(S) OF TENANT(S)].

This notice relates to your tenancy of the dwelling at **[INSERT ADDRESS OF RENTED DWELLING]**.

You are in breach of the terms of your tenancy as you have **[set out breach of obligation e.g. failed to pay rent in accordance with the terms of the tenancy agreement / refused the Landlord access to the dwelling for the purpose of carrying out repairs / sub-let the dwelling without the Landlord's consent.]**

By this notice, the Landlord gives you a period of **[specify the period of time[1]]** to remedy the breach of your tenancy obligation(s). Should you fail to do so within this period, the Landlord is entitled to terminate your tenancy pursuant to Part 5 of the Residential Tenancies Act 2004.

This notice is served on _____ **[INSERT DATE OF SERVICE]**.

Signed: _____
        Landlord / Landlord's Agent

---

[1] The Landlord must specify a period of time which is reasonable in the circumstances. See paras 8–32 to 8–33.

14 DAY WARNING NOTICE

FAILURE TO PAY RENT

Notice served pursuant to section 67(3) of the
Residential Tenancies Act 2004

TO: [INSERT NAME(S) OF TENANT(S)].

This notice relates to your tenancy of the dwelling at **[INSERT ADDRESS OF RENTED DWELLING].**

You have failed to pay rent in accordance with the terms of the tenancy agreement and your obligations under the Residential Tenancies Act 2004.

Your rent arrears are now in the sum of € _____ as of **[INSERT DATE].**

If you fail to pay the rent arrears due within 14 days, the landlord is permitted to terminate your tenancy giving you 28 days notice and by serving a notice of termination on you.

This notice is served on _____ **[INSERT DATE OF SERVICE].**

Signed: _____
        Landlord/Landlord's Agent

EXAMPLE NOTICE OF TERMINATION

Termination of a Tenancy which is less than 6 months

To: [INSERT NAME(S) OF TENANT(S)].

Your tenancy of the dwelling at **[INSERT ADDRESS OF RENTED DWELLING]** will terminate[1] on **[INSERT TERMINATION DATE (DAY, MONTH and YEAR)]** (the "Termination Date").[2]

You have the whole of the 24 hours of the Termination Date to vacate possession of the dwelling.

Any issue as to the validity of this notice or the right of the Landlord to serve it, must be referred to the Private Residential Tenancies Board under Part 6 of the Residential Tenancies Act 2004 within 28 days from the date of receipt of it.

This notice is served on _____ **[INSERT DATE OF SERVICE].**

Signed: _____
       Landlord/Landlord's Agent

---

[1] If the tenancy has been sub-let and the head-landlord is terminating the tenancy, the head-landlord must also state whether or not he or she wishes the head-tenant to terminate the sub-tenancy – "You are [not required] [also required] to terminate the sub-tenancy". See, s.70(2) of the Residential Tenancies Act 2004.

[2] Ensure the recipient of the notice of termination receives the correct number of days notice as prescribed by Pt 5 of the Residential Tenancies Act 2004. See paras 8–72 to 8–83. 28 days is the standard period of notice (if there has been no breach of obligation) where the tenancy has been in existence for a period of less than six months, unless a longer period is prescribed by the tenancy agreement. The longer notice period, however, cannot be greater than 70 days. See para.8–72.

EXAMPLE NOTICE OF TERMINATION

Termination by Landlord pursuant to paragraph 1 of the Table to s.34 of the Residential Tenancies Act 2004

To: [INSERT NAME(S) OF TENANT(S)].

Your tenancy of the dwelling at **[INSERT ADDRESS OF RENTED DWELLING]** will terminate[1] on **[INSERT TERMINATION DATE (DAY, MONTH and YEAR)]** (the "Termination Date").[2]

The reason for termination of the tenancy is due to the breach of your tenancy obligation(s). **[Specify the breach of obligation(s)]**.

You have the whole of the 24 hours of the Termination Date to vacate possession of the dwelling.

Any issue as to the validity of this notice or the right of the Landlord to serve it, must be referred to the Private Residential Tenancies Board under Part 6 of the Residential Tenancies Act 2004 within 28 days from the date of receipt of it.

This notice is served on _____ **[INSERT DATE OF SERVICE]**.

Signed: _____

       Landlord / Landlord's Agent

---

[1] If the tenancy has been sub-let and the head-landlord is terminating the tenancy, the head-landlord must also state whether or not he or she wishes the head-tenant to terminate the sub-tenancy – "You are [not required] [also required] to terminate the sub-tenancy". See, s.70(2) of the Residential Tenancies Act 2004.

[2] Ensure the recipient of the notice of termination receives the correct number of days notice as prescribed by Pt 5 of the Residential Tenancies Act 2004. See paras 8–72 to 8–83.

EXAMPLE NOTICE OF TERMINATION

**Termination by Landlord pursuant to paragraph 2 of the
Table to s.34 of the Residential Tenancies Act 2004**

To: **[INSERT NAME(S) OF TENANT(S)]**.

Your tenancy of the dwelling at **[INSERT ADDRESS OF RENTED
DWELLING]** will terminate[1] on **[INSERT TERMINATION DATE (DAY,
MONTH and YEAR)]** (the "Termination Date").[2]

The reason for termination of the tenancy is because the dwelling is no longer
suitable to your accommodation needs [and those of the person(s) residing with
you] having regard to the number of bed spaces in the dwelling and the size and
composition of the occupying household.

You have the whole of the 24 hours of the Termination Date to vacate possession
of the dwelling.

Any issue as to the validity of this notice or the right of the Landlord to serve
it, must be referred to the Private Residential Tenancies Board under Part 6 of
the Residential Tenancies Act 2004 within 28 days from the date of receipt of it.

This notice is served on _____ **[INSERT DATE OF SERVICE]**.

Signed: _____
        Landlord/Landlord's Agent

---

[1] If the tenancy has been sub-let and the head-landlord is terminating the tenancy, the head-
landlord must also state whether or not he or she wishes the head-tenant to terminate the sub-
tenancy – "You are [not required] [also required] to terminate the sub-tenancy". See, s.70(2) of
the Residential Tenancies Act 2004.
[2] Ensure the recipient of the notice of termination receives the correct number of days notice as
prescribed by Pt 5 of the Residential Tenancies Act 2004. See paras 8–72 to 8–83.

EXAMPLE NOTICE OF TERMINATION

Termination by Landlord pursuant to paragraph 3 of the Table to s.34 of the Residential Tenancies Act 2004

To: [INSERT NAME(S) OF TENANT(S)]

Your tenancy of the dwelling at **[INSERT ADDRESS OF RENTED DWELLING]** will terminate[1] on **[INSERT TERMINATION DATE (DAY, MONTH and YEAR)]** (the "Termination Date").[2]

The reason for termination of the tenancy is because the landlord intends to sell the dwelling within three months after the termination of the tenancy.

You have the whole of the 24 hours of the Termination Date to vacate possession of the dwelling.

Any issue as to the validity of this notice or the right of the Landlord to serve it, must be referred to the Private Residential Tenancies Board under Part 6 of the Residential Tenancies Act 2004 within 28 days from the date of receipt of it.

This notice is served on _____ **[INSERT DATE OF SERVICE]**.

Signed: _____
                    Landlord/Landlord's Agent

---

[1] If the tenancy has been sub-let and the head-landlord is terminating the tenancy, the head-landlord must also state whether or not he or she wishes the head-tenant to terminate the sub-tenancy – "You are [not required] [also required] to terminate the sub-tenancy". See, s.70(2) of the Residential Tenancies Act 2004.

[2] Ensure the recipient of the notice of termination receives the correct number of days notice as prescribed by Pt 5 of the Residential Tenancies Act 2004. See paras 8–72 to 8–83.

EXAMPLE NOTICE OF TERMINATION

Termination by Landlord pursuant to paragraph 4 of the Table to s.34 of the Residential Tenancies Act 2004

To: [INSERT NAME(S) OF TENANT(S)].

Your tenancy of the dwelling at **[INSERT ADDRESS OF RENTED DWELLING]** will terminate[1] on **[INSERT TERMINATION DATE (DAY, MONTH and YEAR)]** (the "Termination Date").[2]

The reason for termination of the tenancy is because the Landlord requires the dwelling or the property containing the dwelling for **[his or her own occupation]** / **[occupation by a member of his or her family]**.

[Insert either]:

The landlord, **[insert name]**, expects to occupy the dwelling for/until **[specify intended duration of occupation]**.

[or, alternatively, if the intended occupant(s) is not the Landlord]:

[Insert name of intended occupant(s) and relationship to the Landlord]. [Insert name of intended occupant(s)], expects to occupy the dwelling for/until **[specify intended duration of occupation]**.

The Landlord will offer you the opportunity to re-occupy the dwelling if:

(a) the dwelling is vacated by **[name of intended occupant(s)]** within the period of 6 months from expiry of the period of notice given by this notice of termination or, if a dispute in relation to the validity of the notice is referred to the Private Residential Tenancies Board under Part 6 for resolution, the final determination of the dispute;

---

[1] If the tenancy has been sub-let and the head-landlord is terminating the tenancy, the head-landlord must also state whether or not he or she wishes the head-tenant to terminate the sub-tenancy – "You are [not required] [also required] to terminate the sub-tenancy". See, s.70(2) of the Residential Tenancies Act 2004.

[2] Ensure the recipient of the notice of termination receives the correct number of days notice as prescribed by Pt 5 of the Residential Tenancies Act 2004. See paras 8–72 to 8–83.

(b) the tenancy to which this notice relates has not otherwise been validly terminated by reason of a ground specified in paragraph 1, 2, 3 or 6 of the Table to s.34 of the Residential Tenancies Act 2004;

(c) you give your contact details to the Landlord within 28 days from the service of this notice or the final determination of a dispute referred to the Private Residential Tenancies Board relating to the validity of this notice;

(d) you notify the Landlord as soon as possible of any change in your contact details.

You have the whole of the 24 hours of the Termination Date to vacate possession of the dwelling.

Any issue as to the validity of this notice or the right of the Landlord to serve it, must be referred to the Private Residential Tenancies Board under Part 6 of the Residential Tenancies Act 2004 within 28 days from the date of receipt of it.

This notice is served on _____ **[INSERT DATE OF SERVICE].**

Signed: _____

          Landlord/Landlord's Agent

EXAMPLE NOTICE OF TERMINATION

Termination by Landlord pursuant to paragraph 5 of the Table to s.34 of the Residential Tenancies Act 2004

To: [INSERT NAME(S) OF TENANT(S)].

Your tenancy of the dwelling at **[INSERT ADDRESS OF RENTED DWELLING]** will terminate[1] on **[INSERT TERMINATION DATE (DAY, MONTH and YEAR)]** (the "Termination Date").[2]

The reason for termination of the tenancy is because the Landlord intends to substantially refurbish or renovate the dwelling or the property containing the dwelling in a way which requires the dwelling to be vacated for that purpose.

The following works will be carried out:

[Specify nature of works to be carried out].

The Landlord will offer you the opportunity to re-occupy the dwelling if:

    (a) the dwelling becomes available for re-let;

    (b) the tenancy to which this notice relates has not otherwise been validly terminated by reason of a ground specified in paragraph 1, 2, 3 or 6 of the Table to s.34 of the RTA 2004;

    (c) you give your contact details to the Landlord within 28 days from the service of this notice or the final determination of a dispute referred to the Private Residential Tenancies Board relating to the validity of this notice; and

    (d) you notify the Landlord as soon as possible of any change in your contact details.

You have the whole of the 24 hours of the Termination Date to vacate possession of the dwelling.

---

[1] If the tenancy has been sub-let and the head-landlord is terminating the tenancy, the head-landlord must also state whether or not he or she wishes the head-tenant to terminate the sub-tenancy – "You are [not required] [also required] to terminate the sub-tenancy". See, s.70(2) of the Residential Tenancies Act 2004.

[2] Ensure the recipient of the notice of termination receives the correct number of days notice as prescribed by Pt 5 of the Residential Tenancies Act 2004. See paras 8–72 to 8–83.

Any issue as to the validity of this notice or the right of the Landlord to serve it, must be referred to the Private Residential Tenancies Board under Part 6 of the Residential Tenancies Act 2004 within 28 days from the date of receipt of it.

This notice is served on _____ **[INSERT DATE OF SERVICE]**.

Signed: _____
　　　　Landlord/Landlord's Agent

EXAMPLE NOTICE OF TERMINATION

Termination by Landlord pursuant to paragraph 6 of the Table to s.34 of the Residential Tenancies Act 2004

To: [INSERT NAME(S) OF TENANT(S)].

Your tenancy of the dwelling at **[INSERT ADDRESS OF RENTED DWELLING]** will terminate[1] on **[INSERT TERMINATION DATE (DAY, MONTH and YEAR)]** (the "Termination Date").[2]

The reason for termination of the tenancy is because the Landlord intends to change the use of the dwelling or the property containing the dwelling.

It is intended that the dwelling shall be used:

[Specify nature of intended use].

The Landlord will offer you the opportunity to re-occupy the dwelling if:

(a) the dwelling becomes available for re-let within the period of 6 months from expiry of the period of notice given by this notice of termination or, if a dispute in relation to the validity of the notice is referred to the Private Residential Tenancies Board under Part 6 for resolution, the final determination of the dispute;

(b) the tenancy to which this notice relates has not otherwise been validly terminated by reason of a ground specified in paragraph 1, 2, or 3 of the Table to s.34 of the Residential Tenancies Act 2004;

(c) you give your contact details to the Landlord within 28 days from the service of this notice or the final determination of a dispute referred to the Private Residential Tenancies Board relating to the validity of this notice; and

---

[1] If the tenancy has been sub-let and the head-landlord is terminating the tenancy, the head-landlord must also state whether or not he or she wishes the head-tenant to terminate the sub-tenancy – "You are [not required] [also required] to terminate the sub-tenancy". See, s.70(2) of the Residential Tenancies Act 2004.

[2] Ensure the recipient of the notice of termination receives the correct number of days notice as prescribed by Pt 5 of the Residential Tenancies Act 2004. See paras 8–72 to 8–83.

(d) you notify the Landlord as soon as possible of any change in your contact details.

You have the whole of the 24 hours of the Termination Date to vacate possession of the dwelling.

Any issue as to the validity of this notice or the right of the Landlord to serve it, must be referred to the Private Residential Tenancies Board under Part 6 of the Residential Tenancies Act 2004 within 28 days from the date of receipt of it.

This notice is served on _____ **[INSERT DATE OF SERVICE]**.

Signed: _____
      Landlord/Landlord's Agent

EXAMPLE NOTICE OF TERMINATION

Termination by a Tenant

To: [INSERT NAME(S) and ADDRESS OF LANDLORD(S)]

The tenancy of the dwelling at **[INSERT ADDRESS OF RENTED DWELLING]** will terminate on **[INSERT TERMINATION DATE (DAY, MONTH and YEAR)]** (the "Termination Date").[1]

Any issue as to the validity of this notice or the right of the Tenant to serve it, must be referred to the Private Residential Tenancies Board under Part 6 of the Residential Tenancies Act 2004 within 28 days from the date of receipt of it.

This notice is served on _____ **[INSERT DATE OF SERVICE]**.

Signed: _____
      Tenant

[OR]

I **[insert name of signing tenant]** sign this notice on my own behalf and I am also authorised to do so by and on behalf of the other tenants named below[2]:

1.   **[Name of Tenant]**

---

[1] Ensure the recipient of the notice of termination receives the correct number of days notice as prescribed by Pt 5 of the Residential Tenancies Act 2004. See paras 8–72 to 8–74 and 8–84 to 8–86.

[2] If the tenancy is being terminated by multiple tenants, it is sufficient if the notice of termination is signed by one of the tenants on behalf of all of the tenants, provided: (a) all the tenants are named in the notice and (b) the signing tenant states he/she is signing on behalf of all of the tenants. See, s.73 of the Residential Tenancies Act 2004.

2.   **[Name of Tenant]**

3.   **[Name of Tenant]**

Signed: _____
          Tenant

NOTICE TO QUIT[1]

To: [NAME OF THE TENANT(S)].

TAKE NOTICE that you are hereby required to quit and deliver up to me or my agent possession of ALL THAT AND THOSE the dwelling **[describe / insert address of dwelling]** which you hold as a **[weekly/monthly/yearly]** tenant for €_____ **[insert amount of rent and when payable e.g €_____ a week / month].**

You are required to quit and deliver up possession of the dwelling on the **[insert the gale day[2] or if the gale day is not certain, state a date after the expiration of the relevant notice period].**[3]

Dated:

Signed: _____

      Landlord/Landlord's Agent

---

[1] This Notice should be served if a person proposes to terminate a residential tenancy which falls outside the remit of the Residential Tenancies Act 2004.

[2] In the case of a periodic tenancy, the notice period must expire on a gale day, which day coincides with the commencement date of the tenancy. A gale day is the day on which a periodic payment of rent is due. If the notice expires after the gale day, then another period of the periodic tenancy begins and this will have to expire before the notice becomes effective to terminate the tenancy (see para.8–123).

[3] The minimum statutory notice period is four weeks when terminating a tenancy but the parties are permitted to agree to a longer period of notice. Subject to these rules, the notice that must be given of the termination of a tenancy will depend on the tenancy itself. If a tenancy is weekly, four weeks' notice must be given (the statutory minimum). If a tenancy is a monthly tenancy, one month's notice is required, three months notice is required to terminate a quarterly tenancy and if a yearly tenancy is being terminated, 183 days' notice is required (see para.8–123).

FORFEITURE NOTICE

To: [INSERT NAME(S) OF TENANT(S)]

Dwelling: [INSERT ADDRESS OF RENTED DWELLING]

You are currently in occupation of the above named dwelling under a tenancy agreement for **[state duration of the tenancy agreement]** dated the **[give date of the tenancy agreement]**.

Under the provisions of this agreement, you entered into an express/implied covenant **[state condition e.g. to keep the property in good and substantial repair]**. You are currently in breach of this covenant insofar as you have **[describe the breach of covenant]**.

I am writing to require you to comply with your obligations under the tenancy agreement and remedy[1] your breach of covenant and/or provide compensation for the breach.

If you fail to do so within **[state time period which should be reasonable]**, the Landlord shall proceed to effect a forfeiture of the tenancy.

Signed: _____
                Landlord/Landlord's Agent

Date:

---

[1] This is only necessary if the breach is capable of remedy. See para.8–127.

NOTICE OF INTENTION TO CLAIM RELIEF[1]

Landlord and Tenant (Amendment) Act 1980

(Section 20)

Date[2]:

To[3]: **[the landlord(s) and any other person who should be served with the notice, e.g. any superior landlord]**

1. **[Description of tenement to which the notice refers.]**

2. **[Particulars of relevant lease or tenancy e.g. state the amount of rent, date of the lease or tenancy agreement, parties to the agreement, length of the tenancy]**

TAKE NOTICE THAT I _____

[Insert 1., 2. or 3. as appropriate]

1. Intend to claim a new tenancy under Part II of the Landlord and Tenant (Amendment) Act 1980, in the above tenement;

2. Intend to claim €_____ compensation for disturbance.

3. Intend to claim €_____ compensation in respect of the improvements of which particulars are set out in the Schedule to this Notice (or as already furnished to the landlord)

Signed by the Tenant _____

Address _____

_____

_____

---

[1] This Notice should be served if a person proposes to claim a new tenancy under Pt II of the Landlord and Tenant (Amendment) Act 1980 (the "1980 Act"), compensation for Improvements and compensation for disturbance.

[2] A claim made in this notice may be made at any time up to three months after valid notification made by the landlord to the claimant of the termination of the claimant's tenancy (subject to any extension that may be granted under s.83 of the 1980 Act).

[3] Insert name(s) of landlords and each person against whom the claim is intended to be made. When claiming a new tenancy insert the name(s) of any superior landlord.

Schedule

[Item]

[Insert full description of the work comprising the improvement].

[Insert probable life of the improvement].

[Insert addition to letting value of the tenement at termination of the tenancy due to the improvement and probable further duration of such addition].

[Insert capitalised value of addition to the letting value at termination of the tenancy].

[Insert particulars of benefits (if any) received by the tenant or his predecessors in title from the landlord in consideration of the improvement].

FORM 44A
CIRCUIT COURT RULES 2001

CIRCUIT   **COUNTY OF**

IN THE MATTER OF THE RESIDENTIAL TENANCIES ACT 2004

**NOTICE OF APPEAL PURSUANT TO SECTION 84(5) OF THE
RESIDENTIAL TENANCIES ACT 2004**

BETWEEN

Plaintiff

AND

Defendant

TAKE NOTICE that an appeal will be made to the Court on the _____
day of _____ or the next opportunity thereafter against the decision
of the Private Residential Tenancies Board to deal/not to deal **[delete as
appropriate]** with a dispute between _____ and
_____ .

AND the Plaintiff will apply for the following reliefs:

[Here insert details of the relief sought by way of appeal]

The said application will be grounded on the affidavit of _____
filed on the _____ day of _____ a copy
of which is served herewith.

Any affidavit intended to be used in reply thereto should be filed and delivered
before the hearing of the application.

Dated the _____ day of _____

Signed: _____
        Plaintiff/Solicitor for the Plaintiff

To: _____
    Defendant/Solicitor for the Defendant

And

To: The County Registrar

FORM 44B
CIRCUIT COURT RULES 2001

CIRCUIT   **COUNTY OF**

IN THE MATTER OF THE RESIDENTIAL TENANCIES ACT 2004

NOTICE OF APPEAL PURSUANT TO SECTION 88(4) OF THE RESIDENTIAL TENANCIES ACT 2004

BETWEEN

Plaintiff

AND

Defendant

TAKE NOTICE that an appeal will be made to the Court on the _____ day of _____ or the next opportunity thereafter against the decision of the Private Residential Tenancies Board to extend the time limited/not to extend the time **[delete as appropriate]** for the referral to it for resolution of a dispute between

AND the Plaintiff will apply for the following reliefs:

[Here insert details of the relief sought by way of appeal]

The said application will be grounded on the affidavit of _____ filed on the _____ day of _____ a copy of which is served herewith.

Any affidavit intended to be used in reply thereto should be filed and delivered before the hearing of the application.

Dated the _____ day of _____

Signed: _____
          Plaintiff/Solicitor for the Plaintiff

To: _____
          Defendant/Solicitor for the Defendant

And

To: The County Registrar

FORM 44C
CIRCUIT COURT RULES 2001

CIRCUIT   **COUNTY OF**

IN THE MATTER OF THE RESIDENTIAL TENANCIES ACT 2004

NOTICE OF MOTION FOR RELIEF UNDER SECTION 124 OF THE RESIDENTIAL TENANCIES ACT 2004

BETWEEN

Applicant

AND

Respondent

TAKE NOTICE that an application will be made to the Court on _____ at _____ or at the next opportunity thereafter for the following reliefs:

[Here insert details of the relief sought by way of enforcement]

AND FURTHER TAKE NOTICE that the said application will be grounded upon:

1. **[Here insert grounds upon which the Applicant is relying for the reliefs sought to include all facts relevant to the alleged failure to carry out the determination order]**

2. **[Here insert basis of jurisdiction]**

3. **[Here insert name, address and description of the Applicant]**

4. **[The following documents must be annexed to this Notice of Motion namely the original determination order or a certified copy of same,**

certified by the Applicant as being a true copy of the determination received from Board and sought to be enforced]

Dated this day of _____ 20 .

Signed: _____
          Applicant/Solicitor for the Applicant

To: _____
        Respondent/Solicitor for the Respondent

And

To: The County Registrar

INDEX